UNOFFICIAL RELEASE

SELF-RELEASED AND HANDMADE AUDIO IN POST-INDUSTRIAL SOCIETY

THOMAS BEY WILLIAM BAILEY

A Belsona Books publication, MMXII

First printing 2012. Published by Belsona Books, Ltd.

Futher information available at www.tbwb.net

Cover design by Thomas Bey William Bailey
Cover photography by Scott Konzelmann (front- "Hammerhead" speaker construction, back- detail from Chop Shop "Smolder" CD sleeve)

ISBN-10: 0615611273
ISBN-13: 978-0615611273

For Liz & Joe

CONTENTS

Part 1: *Play:* Developments and Perspectives

Part 2: *Pause:* New Challenges

Acknowledgements

The period of time over which I composed this book (roughly 2009-2011) was one defined, sadly, by personal losses rather than personal gains- this time was a turbulent rollercoaster ride of near-fatal car crashes, employment-related anxiety and increasing isolation from valued friends. Among the many intrepid spirits lost during this time, at least two - Conrad Schnitzler and Peter Christopherson - were instrumental in providing much of the sonic material that it is the task of this book to investigate.

Another unpleasant drama involving my previous book - *Micro Bionic*, as released on the fraudulent publisher Creation Books - added significantly to the challenges noted above. Their inability to provide royalties, or to spend any noticable effort on any aspect of this book's printing and distribution, was merely the tip of the iceberg in a larger scandal involving a not insignificant number of other aggrieved authors. So, in a way, an acknowledgement should be given to the staff at Creation Books, since their poor handling of that project lessened my anxieties about how my next book would be perceived if it appeared through an "on-demand" publisher or other non-traditional channel. It's only fitting, in the end, that a book examining such subject matter would end up in this format: this will not be the last time that this book will mention the compromises involved in any kind of "officially" marketed creative endeavor, and the freedoms that can be had by embracing smaller-scale forms of releasing.

All this aside, there are many individuals who deserve a friendlier acknowledgement for helping to shape this book's contents into a personally satisfying final draft. All of the interviewees in the book provided assistance not only by contributing to the text, but by arranging connections with other helpful parties and by sending me reference materials (often rare and out-of-print) at their own expense. That distinguished group includes Joseph Nechvatal, Al Margolis, Ken Montgomery, Rod Summers, Vittore Baroni, Don Campau and GX Jupitter-Larsen. Other individuals from the self-released audio community, despite not being represented by a full interview here, also took time out of otherwise busy days to accommodate me in their homes or business places, and, again, to share research materials which were not even accessible in the digital wilderness of the World Wide Web. Daniel Plunkett of *ND* magazine deserves special credit here.

The staff at the SONM sound lab in Murcia, Spain are also worthy of the highest praises for all their assistance in the summer of 2011. Though my residency there was not associated with this book, the SONM audio library was stocked with hundreds of artifacts from the self-released audio world, and being granted access to this archive helped me to definitively confirm or deny statements I had made in the rough drafts of this book. My hat is off to curator Francisco López and director Susana López (no relation) for all their assistance in this endeavor, and also for providing me with an enchanting time in the Andalusian region during the hours spent not doing research work.

Thanks as always to the friends and strangers who have sent thought-provoking, encouraging, or just entertainingly spiteful correspondence to me in the wake of my first book. Lastly, gratitude goes out to my parents for their enduring support of me, and to my brother Tim for showing me not only how to cheat death, but how to then return to exuding creative energy like never before.

Introduction:
Portrait Of The Author As An Unofficial Artist

In a way, I've been concerned with self-determined art, and the ways in which it differs from mass-produced media, since I was still in elementary school. To set the scene: I was around 9 years old, and freshly transplanted to a new school (the fifth one in as many years), where I was desperately leaping through whatever hoops I could in order to win over new friends. Being that I was acutely asthmatic, though, this ruled out the vast majority of the roughhousing activities that normally served as rites of passage en route to friendship. Couple this with the fact that I wasn't really clued in to the ultraviolent modes of pop culture that my schoolmates craved, and I was more or less doomed to sadly toe the margins of that social milieu. Out of desperation, I decided to invent a role for myself that didn't really exist in that environment yet: I became a "dealer" of bizarre homemade tchotchkes and inexpensive novelties cobbled together in my basement.

These objects were the result of my pondering what I could do to pique the curiosity of kids whose lives were already saturated with explosive hyper-real entertainment. What could I offer to these young people, whose parents had already bought them every techno-diversion on the market to keep them busy? The answer was, of course, to return a bit of the primitive to their lives by way of my handmade fetish objects, all endowed by me with some laughably bogus "magic power"- often they were no more than a pair of plastic "googly eyes" pasted onto a fuzzy ball and rudely stuck onto the end of a pipe cleaner or a pencil. Or maybe you'd get lucky, and I'd sell you a googly-eyed fuzz ball with a flimsy felt pair of "feet" and a felt baseball cap as well. I charged from 25 cents to a dollar for these (let's face it) useless artifacts, depending on the amount of menial labor invested in them. And, I'll be damned if these didn't actually *sell* at a prodigious rate, becoming a hit with both girls and boys (even Nintendo's coveted 8-bit home gaming system, introduced around this time, couldn't claim such broad cross-gender appeal among my peers!) More importantly, though, these artifacts provided me with that much-needed sense of purpose I was seeking out, and connected me with those couple "real" friends who stuck with me after the mob of novelty-seekers had predictably thinned out. Some of them are still with me today (hello, Jeff.)

The only problem was that apparently business was *too* good, because I distinctly remember some agitated school staff telephoning my house and complaining to my parents that I was "exploiting" my fellow students. I was ordered, in no uncertain terms, to stop immediately, even though my hawking hadn't caused any major ruptures in the fabric of day-to-day school life: studies proceeded pretty much as usual, and I generally made a point to respect school decorum by limiting my sales to recess periods and lunch breaks. The curtailing of my activities raised a whole host of anxious questions within me. For one, was I not just engaging in a small-scale version of the kind of hype game played out endlessly by major manufacturers of collectible toys, right down to the mischievously dishonest advertising? Why was *my* activity "exploitation," when other kids could peddle pre-packaged candy for their 'Cub Scout' or 'Brownie' fund-raisers and not meet with the same kind of reprimands? And wasn't this the kind of entrepreneurship I was supposed to be learning as a pint-sized American citizen of the high-pressure, competitive 1980s? I'm still not sure I have the answer for these questions, although my first guess was that my creation of an "underground economy", however feeble, was taking money away from the school coffers: kids were using their money on my dubious handicrafts instead of on school lunches and participation in those school activities where a little cash contribution was required. I can also remember at least one other student at this school who started making a "knock-off" product comparable to my own, once the popularity of my rough-hewn junk had crested- I think the authorities saw a chain reaction in the making, and consequently the opening up of a whole anarchic mini-marketplace proliferating beyond their ability to easily regulate it. "That Nintendo crap was bad enough, and now *this...*", I could imagine them groaning!

At any rate, the formal "sanctions" (after-school detention periods, etc.) only emboldened me, and I started branching out into pursuits that required some skill in more commonly recognized categories of art- I had acquired a nascent skill for drawing cartoon-style portraits, and thought that might be a better way to preserve my unique social status as an oddball creator. It certainly appealed to others' vanity, and soon came the *pièce de résistance* of my kiddie production line: kids began paying to have themselves drawn into the storylines of full-length comic books, which I cobbled together using little more than computer printer paper, colored pencil, India ink, staples, and a straight-edge of some kind for drawing the individual panels. Unsurprisingly, given the enthusiastic reception of these pieces by my peers (which I never made copies of, since I was afraid to take them to adults with access to photocopying equipment), I was found out by the authorities again. However, by this time the punishment was meted out to me for the content of my work rather than for the mere act of making it available. The second round of "sanctions" was inexplicably less harsh than the first; maybe my minders had cultivated some kind of grudging respect for the zeal of a boy who could waste hours and hours drawing and scripting his own comics, as opposed to just reading them. I even caught one of my more reasonable minders chuckling as he saw himself caricatured in one of the puerile sci-fi comic epics that had been confiscated from me.

In the end, it wasn't the intervention of authority figures that killed off my work's value as an idiosyncratic piece of 'local culture', but the ineluctable rise of the suburban skate-punk aesthetic: if you didn't have demonstrable proficiency with a skateboard, along with looks and lingo swiped from the pages of *Thrasher* magazine, you could pretty much forget about any social status points that had been accumulated previously. To be honest, I succumbed to the allure of this aesthetic: I liked the asymmetrical sheaves of hair, the fluorescent-and-black 'hazard' color scheme of the clothing and skate deck designs, the breakneck musical soundtrack and even the piercing sarcastic laughter of the much older girls (derisively referred to as 'Skate Bettys' at the time) who saw me continually falling on my face while trying to look impressive. So, I voluntarily went on hiatus before it could be said I was supplanted outright: when I did draw or make something by hand, it now served the purpose of hailing the new breed of Tony Hawk-worshipping skateboard miscreants.

More trends would come and go, and times would become considerably more frightening as I aged, but I've never forgotten the odd hysteria that surrounded my first few attempts at trading in handmade goods. I couldn't comprehend the sheer astonishment of my adult authority figures and my schoolmates; the shock arising from someone trying to do something like this "all on their own." Something that seemed perfectly natural for me, as an individual forced to improvise in order to gain some sense of self in a hostile environment, seemed to others like a direct affront. These otherwise trivial incidents from my childhood provided me with my first lessons in independent creativity and its relation to a larger power structure. If the adults were shocked that I could create something of my own volition without any help from them at all (ok, save for maybe providing transportation to the arts-and-crafts store), I was equally shocked to learn that I could operate within the rules of my given environment (don't be obscene, don't bully others, don't disrupt classes) and *still* be overstepping my boundaries.

Moving from negative reinforcement to positive reinforcement, optimistic tropes like "be yourself!" and "let your spirit shine!" really were the order of the day in the public school system; I guess I was just naïve enough to take these statements at face value and to not see the considerable fine print accompanying these statements. The moment I learned that something as simple as "be yourself!" could encompass a statement as contradictory as *"be yourself, but stay within a set of boundaries that will continue shifting according to our personal whims"*- that was the moment I knew I was going to be doing things independently, and by hand, for a long time to come. It wouldn't take long to realize that, despite all the contemporary homilies about "doing your own thing", "doing" was supposed to be a stand-in for "consuming" rather *making* or *producing* your own thing. To make things in accordance with your own desires, rather than to accept a one-size-fits-all culture of planned obsolescence, was to make things "difficult" on bureaucratic authorities whose very existence relied upon the propagation of false needs.

Flash forward to the present, and the world of recorded audio has become an indispensable part of my life, sticking to me much more tenaciously than any of the aforementioned creative activities did. Records, tapes, CDs, minidiscs and digital downloads from all creative genres have provided me with a comprehensive worldview more than compensating for my lack of fluency in other dominant media, mainly television programming and video games. Audio fanatics are probably already familiar with the liturgical inventory of life-affirming effects that audio artifacts have provided me with: they have served as the "icebreakers" leading to lasting relationships (and as aids in overcoming broken relationships), they have been trans-media reference points leading to interest in great works of literature and visual art, they have helped to ease the anxiety of travel and residence in foreign lands, and they have had so many curious psychic and physiological side effects that I should stop myself now before devoting the rest of this book to their variety and efficacy. Let's just conclude this particular reverie by saying that, as far as modern media are concerned, audio recordings have been the "it" thing for me- stoking the blazes of my imagination and serving as practical communicative tools in a way so far unparalleled by even the most phantasmagoric films.

Curiously, it was probably the aforementioned "skate-punk" phase, and, yes, the pages of *Thrasher,* which made me aware that there even was a world of recorded music beyond the stuff being played on the 3 most popular Chicago-area radio stations (venerable 'indie' record labels like SST advertised heavily within the skater bible.) There was no cable television in my family home - and hence no Music Television - and so any sound output had to be extremely compelling; capable of conjuring mental images that could hold the attention of a spaced-out pre-teen like myself. I was still too young to be infected by the music genre jargon that I catch myself babbling today, but eventually I discovered that all the music I enjoyed the most was considered "alternative" or "independent" (hey, Independent was the name of a respected manufacturer of skateboard components, too, so this *had* to be good!) Consequently, I made sure to ask for it by name, and collected what little I could from library borrowings, from hip older kids, from taping it off the radio (wasn't that supposed to have 'killed' the record industry? Oops...), and from occasionally even buying some real cassettes from a real shop. Doing some more junior detective work, I came to understand that "independent" in music terminology meant recording for a label that was owned by you or by people sympathetic to you, rather than working for a company which would lose interest in you as soon as you stopped generating sales. Being independent also seemed to mean you could play whatever type of sounds you wanted, so long as you were willing to take upon yourself the risk of not being liked by as many people as the 'stars.'

Now, in my eternal naiveté, I couldn't understand why *anyone*

wouldn't like this stuff. The college radio show I taped from, "The Third Rail," would play music from artists like Big Black or Sonic Youth, and I'd delight in hearing their guitar sounds approximate swarms of metallic laser-guided insects or enraged elephants. From the middle of the maelstrom, the vocalists would howl and shout vaguely worded yet strangely potent statements that pricked up the skin even with no real knowledge of their meaning: it reminded me of the cryptic graffiti scrawls I'd see in the city, although more animated and intense. Meanwhile, the rhythm sections would grind and lunge to life like huge anthropomorphic trains- I could see that, with concentrated listening, this aesthetic was going to become a way of life, or at least a considerable part of a larger communicative approach. Not having acquired any musical skills on my own yet, I started using my doodling and cartooning talents to design my own "j card" inlays for cassette albums of imaginary bands (again, often ones involving my friends as the players, producers, even label bosses.) It was with great satisfaction that I learned, only a few years ago, that the reclusive Washington D.C. artist Mingering Mike (profiled in a later chapter) took this practice to whole new levels of prolificness.

The more I began to proselytize independent music (through handing out mix tapes, designing crude artwork for imaginary albums, or just running at the mouth endlessly), the more I learned about the reasons why most of my peers were repelled by it: interestingly enough, it was again for reasons that had little to do with the *content* of the recordings. One memorable complaint came from a boy who hated my newfound sounds because "I've never even heard of these people in my life!"- something very akin to the tautology "people like pop music because it's popular." Indeed, the more I dwelled on it, the more the objections to any sort of self-determined creative act failed to move beyond these simple tautologies. If it wasn't that, there was a feeling that an improvisational attitude towards recording technology was tantamount to blasphemy. Our technocratic society was seen as the best of all possible worlds, and this best of a possible epochs had been brought about by the best of all possible technological means. Therefore, the highest-priced tech often came imbued with a high moral value. Anyone who could afford the best equipment must have done something exceptional to deserve it, and must have had a grasp on higher moral qualities, as the logic went, but this ethos was widely misapplied when it came to the audio field. The music video

had brought us an interchangeable sequence of cyborg entertainers who employed high technology not because of some Social Darwinist rise to the top of their musical game, but because lack of studio technology would reveal their true form: fairly unremarkable mannequins assembled one piece at a time by an entourage of analysts and consultants. Like it or not, people saw in these hastily assembled lab creations something to celebrate, and I would submit that their artificial nature was not a 'turn-off,' but the very core of their appeal in an age seduced by unquestioning techno-lust. In such an atmosphere, following an improvisational 'make do with what you have' strategy was a perverse failure to respect all 'we' had accomplished; it was a party-crashing temper tantrum from some freaky-looking sore losers. Everything from changing the tunings on one's guitar to 'bending' the circuitry within a cheap keyboard was, for too many, seen as some kind of sick abnegation of positivist values, as a cynical attempt to drag down the rest of society into a grubby pit of chaos.

The Decline And Fall Of Indie America

As this attitude persisted into the late 1980s and well beyond, it was probably inevitable that a good swath of "alternative" or "indie" culture would be subject to it as well, championing formalism over expressive value. The indie world would cultivate its own parallel cast of players - superstar producers, etc. - who needed to have more than an ancillary role in the music-making process, and seemed to be claiming authorship of individual artists' musical works when their producer credits were loudly trumpeted on the albums' packaging (to his credit, the "producer" Steve Albini has always rejected this title and chosen to be credited as a "recorder".) A sort of "professionalism envy" eventually crept into parts of the scene, a sense that *if only we had better "x" [production, equipment, packaging, representation etc.], people would come to realize the strength of our ideas*. In hindsight, we can see the results of this wishful thinking- since there was a good deal of agreement upon exactly which advanced means of production and promotion would lead to the promised breakthrough, a greater number of identical records began appearing (not only in the U.S. market) and the much-vaunted ideas began to take a back seat to formalistic flourishes. Let's be frank about this situation: when a higher

standard of professionalism did present itself, few independent musicians would have continued as before. Few would continue to grind out their meager existence in broken-down vans when comfortable tour buses finally became an option, nor would they have refused to book time in a nice 24-track studio when those were also made available. A happy lack of squalor and hardship, in and of themselves, did not go hand-in-hand with a surge of mediocre creativity. But, on the other hand, a more streamlined technological approach and more collaboration with inessential bureaucratic personnel did not exactly make for a Renaissance era of independent music, let alone a widespread comprehension of alternative ethics.

On The Shores Of DIY: Unofficial Media Takes Up The Slack

Luckily, the advent of affordable home recording and duplication did make it possible to opt out of *both* the mainstream and those sectors of so-called DIY ['do-it-yourself'] culture which, by the 1990s, were rapidly allowing themselves to be authored by third parties. Besides, what were your options if you wanted to use recording media for recording things other than *music*? The consumer populace, mainstream or 'indie,' seemed trained to view recording media solely as vessels for music entertainment, as could be noted by a visit to just about any music retailer. This attitude made it considerably difficult for someone to make a commercial release of field recording, spoken narrative, poetic reading, *hörspiel* or any attempt at presenting sounds in and of themselves. It should come as no coincidence that people trafficking in these sounds were among the first to up the ante of do-it-yourself audio culture, and to not just stop at having one's own record label: *everything* was now to be done by hand. Recordings would be made and edited on home equipment, then dubbed onto cassettes, with hand-designed artwork, and made available by mail order catalogs or direct contact (with a small number of sympathetic retail shops also getting in on the game.) The revolution in handmade audio was perhaps one of the keys to the survival of radical sonic eclecticism into the 21st century, for reasons that will be fleshed out in the main body of this text. This still largely unsung practice, by virtue of its similarities with other participatory networks like mail art, allowed for some crucial innovations:

you didn't have to live in one of the central hubs of commerce to experience unorthodox recorded sounds, you were allowed to approach recording from the standpoint of something other than a trained musician, and you could make works available in venues that took a more holistic (i.e. 'multi-media') approach to new art. With this schematic in place, other deviations from mass media presentation would follow: you could even present your audio recording as being one component in a portable *gesamtkunstwerk*, housing a cassette in an elaborate piece of sculpture that reflected or enhanced the messages contained on the magnetic tape.

It really can't be stressed enough that "do-it-yourself" audio was never wholly synonymous with "handmade" or "unofficial" audio. While much of DIY music is still recorded and produced using makeshift means, and does not involve the presence of any mediating personae during these same processes, it can still take full advantage of other forces of mass production. It's not uncommon these days to find music recorded in one's bedroom with the most humble of tools, and yet released in 10,000-unit runs on deluxe formats (heavyweight vinyl records with gatefold covers, digipak compact discs with lavish booklets, etc.) Perhaps no better example of DIY audio can be provided than the tortured, reclusive, "free folk" music of the Texas musician Jandek, and yet the mystery man has made every one of his impenetrable works available on professionally duplicated LP or CD. The same goes for Chicago's late schizophrenic troubador Wesley Willis, who somehow managed to obtain funding to release dozens of pro-duplicated CD titles even while being terminally unemployed and occasionally without shelter. So, our focus here is on audio in which every phase of the creative process, with the possible exception of creating the recording medium itself, is handled by the creators proper: with no reliance on disc duplicators, printing presses, mastering and post-production facilities, professional graphic design services and so on. Now, this is not to belittle those independent artists who do rely on these services, and it has to be admitted that there's a certain sexiness involved in beating major-league media conglomerates at their own game: it's always a thrill to find an audio work that is alluringly packaged, yet makes no compromises when it comes to the actual audio content. However, the story of such DIY audio has been more than adequately documented elsewhere, and our focus here is on those who have struggled to make as authentic an expressive *corpus* as possible without seeking out (or *wanting* to seek out) any form of assistance from third parties.

As stated above, releasing one's work through an independent record label does not spell the end of outside interference full stop. For one, the history of 'indie' recording is rife with incidents in which particular albums had their original cover artwork rejected by every printing press in their country of origin. Another common setback in the early days of 'indie' music was experienced by artists who saw their records' release delayed indefinitely by record pressing plants, who attributed the unorthodox quality of certain audio works to faulty equipment rather than to the creators' intentions (as the logic went, there was *no way* the artists could have *really* "wanted it to sound like that!") Make no mistake, such incidents are taken into consideration by artists who must weigh the cost-benefit analysis of dealing with such services: should one break the bank to make the cosmetic features of an audio work better reflect its 'soul'? Is it really worth it in the long run?

This question of whether or not to break the piggy bank also takes on an added importance in the light of recent studies on the "Long Tail" theory (popularized by Chris Anderson of *Wired* magazine.) According to this theory, markets with a high degree of consumer choice, like today's oversaturated market for audio recordings, have been shown to buy 20% of all available product (the "head") in large quantities, while the remaining 80% (the "tail") is bought in comparatively meager quantities. This holds especially true for the online / digital download market, in which some 10 billion songs out of a total 13 billion failed to register a *single* download in 2008. It is highly likely that, for most independent artists who sign up for the bare minimum order of 500 professionally-duplicated discs (and having such discs is a prerequisite to having them also made available on popular digital download sites like iTunes and eMusic), few of those will ever actually sell in numbers that will recoup the artists' original monetary investment in the discs. Getting them into physical record shops, where such can be found, is not a given either (considering the limited amount of rack space available in the shops), nor is the process of having them taken by an independent record distributor.

With all these grim near-inevitabilities in play, any concerned artist will probably reevaluate their commitment to professional duplication. Of course, some are still quite willing to shoulder the tremendous cash losses, because a lasting artistic legacy is at stake: as the story goes, many audio artists want to have the most attractive artifact possible to proudly show their progeny some day, regardless of whether or not it sold more than a dozen units or garnered more than a capsule review in a little-known 'Net fanzine. In other words, the risky expenditure of resources in the present is a kind of "down payment" on a better posthumous appraisal of one's life work. A good deal of wildly unpopular sonic art from the recent past has become the subject of critical reappraisals, anthologizing, and *ex post facto* romanticism bordering on outright apology ("why were we so stupid to miss it the first time around", etc.), and so nowadays it is not uncommon to release recordings with the intention of their *eventually* being re-considered by the same public that is currently relegating them to the thinnest segment of the Long Tail.

For myriad reasons that will, again, be discussed soon enough, plenty of artists tire of cosmetically enhancing their product while waiting for the charming prince of critical praise and financial reward to rescue them, and they choose to go the unofficial route, artistic legacy be damned. Disillusionment is just one possible factor in choosing this route, though: this book will attempt to distinguish, on a case-by-case basis, incidences in which artists did so out of financial necessity, or did so because they felt handmade works brought them closer to some kind of pure artistic intent. To be sure, many have never even attempted to release something approximating a professionally duplicated product- the idea never crossed their minds, and so they never had the chance to be fatigued by dealing with said practice. This rich culture is one in which pragmatism and utilitarianism are engaged in a constant dance with the passionate flaring of spirit typically associated with artists of any stripe, and as such it's foolhardy to claim one set of guiding principles behind the creation and distribution of handmade audio wares. Plain disgust with the "industry", the desire to intentionally limit one's fan base to those who will remain in intimate contact with the artist, the possibility of releasing "time-sensitive" artistic statements without waiting one's turn in a record label's release schedule, the will to subvert the cash-based economy and make items available for trade/ barter or as gifts to those who deserve them…all these, and more, are catalysts for the creation of handmade audio art in the late

20th and early 21st centuries. We will see which of these motivations apply to which artists, but we will also see how the unofficial ethos has differed from normal DIY practices when it comes to succeeding in these aims.

On Pluralism and Authenticity

Much will be said in this book about the 'democratizing', 'decentralizing,' and 'non-hierarchical' potential of this media, and the role it plays in the grand battle for some sort of global awareness or reconciliation between rival cultural factions. This is an important vein of knowledge to be tapped, but as we go along we should be careful not to read 'democratizing' here as being equivalent to 'cultural leveling' or homogenizing: if anything, the existence of this media has provided us with a dizzying amount of heterogeneity, eclecticism...whatever one chooses to call it. Some could argue that the major media institutions have also been paragons of a peaceful and fun-filled pluralism where everyone gets their say - they've certainly marketed themselves as such - but who really believes that these institutions do so purely for altruistic reasons? Maybe my age is showing, but I find it hard to extract a unifying message from this kind of presentation beyond - to quote Deng Xiaoping - "to get rich is glorious." Can an MTV-dictated world, in which everyone essentially marches in lockstep to the same hyper-materialistic cultural imperatives (despite the video stars' differences in ethnicity, gender etc.), really be called a "pluralistic" culture? Calling it a corporate monoculture would, in my humble opinion, cleave closer to the truth.

In contrast to the incongruous culture projected by MTV and its siblings, the unofficial music cultures manage to project a real pluralism *not* by using inherited differences as a 'front' for a common materialistic ideal, but by making the ideals of the sound works themselves as diverse as possible: the unofficial networks, so far, have refused to take a censorious attitude towards even the most extreme of information, and have even allowed releases with intentions apparently contrary to this democratizing / non-hierarchical impulse to flow freely through the underground streams. For all the 'strength through diversity' cheerleading of the major media, how many such outlets would be willing to include the works of, say, a rightist 'neo-classical' musician in their programming, as an ultimate display of their openness and their commitment to free expression? How many major publications would be able to print reviews of releases from both the aforementioned musician, as well as some adversarial figure (e.g., a Marxist sampling artist) without attempting to promote either as "correct"? Such things have happened, and still do happen, in the world of unofficial audio- and therein resides another reason why people have chosen to work in this milieu. This ecumenical approach is not just a lazy type of resignation, but a means towards the continued survival of the network: to use a loose analogy from encryption theory, protection schemes that have used "concealed" algorithms have been less secure in design than schemes which are completely open to the public. So, the refusal to isolate and conceal any one particular unsavory element is not contradictory to the unofficial networking ethic, but is its very lifeblood: the network quietly remains a repository for authenticity, in all its variations, while the most pervasive mainstream media channels claim the adoption of consensus falsehoods is "keepin' it real."

It's not impossible for individual nodes on the network fall out of favor or be seen as inferior to others, but value judgments of this kind are most often made by parties acting independently of each other- as stressed before, there is no single Unofficial Media Central Planning Committee to steer opinion. If one underground cassette label or handmade audio artist is eventually decided by consensus to be 'better' than others, they are often chosen on a meritocratic basis (namely, for having worked as hard as possible to maintain the superstructure of unofficial audio) rather than for their consistent adherence to a particular set of ideals. With this in mind, one wonders if this whole project can be called a utopian one. Past (unrealized) utopias have always been heavy on "plans" and on "inevitabilities" that will arise once those plans are enacted- the makers of unofficial audio seem to be making no such grand statements. On the whole, they are content to let any collective work grow organically; to create in spite of historical deterrents as well as 'scientific' projections of what should happen if a given creative activity is sustained for a certain period of time.

As the writer Bart Plantenga has astutely pointed out, there was a time when virtually every human artifact was a result of DIY practice: it took the Industrial Revolution to reverse this trend, and to eventually make the handmade aesthetic an anomaly rather than an everyday occurrence. Only now, in our era of unprecedented ecological panic and economic catastrophe, is the handmade ethic being reassessed. The cool cachet associated with being an "ethical consumer" is arguably greater than at any time in the last 40 years, and, to some extent, that also translates into a greater respect for the minimally wasteful production methods of small-scale artisans. As you wade into this book, though, I encourage you not to be put off by the occasional lack of real sincerity and commitment that can come about when a well-meaning phenomenon gets tagged as a trend. Hucksters and fakers manage to find their way into every possible area of human endeavor, so their sporadic appearances in this scene should come as no surprise. While some of their missteps are cataloged here and do warrant examination, I mainly hope you will benefit from the copious examples of real innovation and pure creative intent on hand. I also hope this text will bury the myth that "unofficial" audio is merely a shorthand for "audio made by those who can't afford anything else." This is not just a method of economic last resort, but one that offers its own distinct set of psycho-spiritual rewards to those who willfully engage in it.

A Caution Against Completion

A final introductory word is necessary before we start our journey in earnest: when it comes to documenting art movements in general and the audio arts in particular, I am not a completist: I feel that a "complete" work on this particular subject, while it would boost my own credentials as an authority somewhat, would also do much to extinguish the exploratory drive of the reader. At this point in the game, I have no pretensions to authority, but I am highly interested in generating a polyphony of reactions and prompting further explorations in turn. This interest in audience reactions, and specifically how they are generative of new mutations to creativity, played no small role in making the world of unofficial audio what it was, and making it a subject demanding of concentrated study. So, in the age of online hyper-convenience, it would not be impossible to construct a complete encyclopedic work featuring every artist to have ever recorded "unofficially," yet I feel such a staggering monument would actually be counter-productive, especially if the writer's aim is both elucidation *and* encouragement to continue along the paths outlined by the writing. As such, readers will also notice that much of this book proceeds in a non-sequential fashion (for example, an artist who is only briefly mentioned in an early chapter will be given a full introduction much later on, rather than the more typical reversal of this scenario.) Given the actual non-sequential way in which "unofficial audio" discoveries are made, with no mandatory set of progressive steps that must be followed towards enlightenment, I felt this compositional quirk was appropriate to the subject at hand.

Because of my opposition to the "completist" project, it is my hope that readers will also forgive my occasional use of personally familiar phenomena, artifacts, and experiences to illustrate broader and more universal ones. For the most part, I offer only possible, and not ultimate, manifestations of anything. My recurring mentions of Japanese culture, for example, are not really intended to steer the historical narrative closer to Japan and to give them more than a fair share of credit for their contributions to unofficial audio. By the same reckoning, my discussion of Soviet-era State censorship is not an attempt to paint Soviet censors' techniques as being the 'last word' on that practice. The biographical "close-ups" I've included were merely the ones I felt that I could write with conviction, due to my peer relationship with the biographical subjects. The ones that went unwritten (for now) should *not* be seen as a kind of implicit "criticism by exclusion". It is, after all, the special conviction of the releasing artists, and not the completion of the unofficial audio project, that allows research on this subject to enrich everyday life.

PART ONE

Play: Developments and Perspectives

Telescopic Creativity:
The Dawn Of Networked Art

A popular trope of vintage science fiction was the alien invader who, speaking in a chilly monotone voice, made the demand *"take me to your leader!"* to the person making first contact with the invasion force (typically this was some clueless, tongue-tied "everyman" farmer or citizen.) If such an invasion force suddenly materialized, and threatened my life if I couldn't produce such a "leader" in connection with this book's subject matter, I'm afraid I'd be vaporized on the spot. The culture of self-released audio is one of individuals reaching similar conclusions in different locales, over roughly the same time period, in which any singular great act of origination has long since been forgotten by the adherents to this culture. From the outset, we'd be wise not to think that everyone in this culture has an equal ability to express and to impress- yet, even when taking these differing potentialities into account, and imagining this culture as a meritocracy in which those who give the most receive the most in return, there is seemingly no one handing down orders and directives. Sure, helpful "suggestions" are regularly made in the secondary communications (e.g. printed and online forums) that arise in the wake of the primary creative acts. However, these suggestions are made by such a broad cross-section of individuals in the self-releasing networks, and met with such varying degrees of acceptance and rejection, that we are quickly back to "square one," looking for a single magnetizing nexus of influence.

A certain lack of iconic images within this culture, of retinal equivalents of the shot-heard-round-the-world phenomena, is also crucial to mention here: mass culture has long since been inundated with the idea that the image, especially a tele-visual one, is necessary to concretize and universalize moments of seismic change. From the exaggerated gyrating of Elvis Presley's hips to the enthusiastic dismantling of the Berlin Wall, the televised image still functions like the opening of curtains on the world stage, the heralding of completely novel and irreversible phases in historical development. Well, this is one revolution that - speaking of tropes - has never been televised (let alone broadcast over high-powered radio transmitters or given plenty of column inches in major newspapers.) The most telegenic images are ones of rupture, explosion, orgasm, giving the more naïve among us the impression that history is just an interlinked series of such ruptures, with yawning intervals of pondering and thumb twiddling in between. In reality, though, every literal or figurative explosion results from a steady accretion of imperceptible micro-events, from somewhat more banal sequences of processes and transactions. These processes, where self-released audio is concerned, are often more important than the final product, and - making things yet more difficult for any would-be television documentary crews - the explosive "Eureka!" moment is largely internalized in one's own mind and spirit. By contrast, the passion of emperors, kings and other leaders for "defining moments" of violent coming-into-being is considerable, and, as they often see it, is much more effective in winning popular attention than focusing on those micro-events that build towards the pinnacle moment. As media theorist Friedrich Kittler suggests, though, no one is ever immune to the imperceptible and gradually emerging, even when it ironically involves the buildup of climactic images themselves: Kittler recalls how "the Wall fell as a result of a constant 25-year bombardment of television broadcasts."[1]

Now, there may very well be a single intrepid spirit within this culture who beat everyone else to the punch, and can back such a claim with a variety of forensic evidence from dated envelopes to recorded conversations. The fact is, though, that as of this writing, seemingly no one has stepped forward to personally make this claim. A survey of this culture shows that there are more individuals being *nominated* as the "king" of this particular domain than there are individuals personally daring to ascend that throne. In a modern world where the ego gratification of the 'anyone can be a star' entertainment economy reigns supreme, being faced with such a vacancy is unusual, to say the least. A closer look reveals, though, that any act of throne-taking would be seen as detrimental to the activities of the culture, and would bring it that much closer to those things in mainstream / commercial audio production which make documenting that world such a chore: the endless, emotionally

---

[1] Friedrich Kittler, *Optical Media*, trans. Anthony Enns, p. 43. Polity Press, Cambridge MA, 2010.

heated discussions over who-did-what-when trivia and the pervasive need to develop a universally recognized taxonomy of creativity. Moreover, in a culture that generally chooses to propagate itself through collaboration rather than competition, what would a claim to the throne really mean? Being 'the first' in this milieu does not automatically confer a title of 'the best' upon anyone: to believe so would be to fall prey to the 'genetic fallacy' whereby artists' origins are seen as more important than their current activities.

Spontaneity, And The Rejection Of "Avant-Antagonism"

This kind of culture is not only anomalous for the world of recorded music, but for the arts as a whole. Critic Donald Kuspit has gone so far as to propose a "....Hobbesian influence on creativity and innovation...the war of all artists against all other artists, even when they temporarily cooperate for social purposes."[2] The stakes are high in this internecine conflict among artists, since there is an incredibly limited number of financially rewarding positions in the culture to be claimed (through government and philanthropic grants, prize money from contests, etc.) The same can be said for the limited number of arts-related posts conferring public recognition, whether that comes with a corresponding set of financial rewards or not. Kuspit suggests that the competitive nature of contemporary art making has, by and large, not been limited to those artists who toe the line when it comes to current tastes. Rather, it has only been inflamed by the presence of a radical avant-garde:

> Such attacks, which are commonplace of the avant-garde artists' attitude, demonstrate what [Renato] Poggioli calls the antagonism...basic to the avant-garde approach to art. Anyone who doesn't conform to one's position is

---

[2] Donald Kuspit, lecture given at the School of Visual Arts (MFA Art Criticism & Writing), September 6 2007. Available online at http://deimos3.apple.com/WebObjects/Core.woa/Browse/sva.edu.1363555220.0136355522 2. Retrieved July 17, 2010.

automatically decadent, retarded, and wrong-headed. Anyone who does is automatically advanced, progressive, and right thinking. The myth of progress in art is basic to avant-garde self-belief.[3]

Given, much of what constitutes the "unofficial" network of self-determined audio artists would be considered avant-garde stylistically, and the networked visual art culture that preceded them often made clear acknowledgements of influence from earlier modes of the avant-garde (e.g. the Russian mail artist Rea Nikonova, a modern-day practicioner of the 'zaum' poetry movement begun in 1913.) However, these artists do not exhibit the same do-or-die competitive drive that Kuspit notes here. Why is this? The simplest answer, albeit a generalization on my part, is that the degree of purposiveness in this culture is much lower than it is in the "official" art world: for the latter, bodies of artwork are usually the means leading towards the aforementioned goals of public acknowledgement and financial remuneration. In the "unofficial" art world, the process of creation and the stimulation of further creation, via a network of similarly inclined contacts, is an end in itself. This is not to say the activities of these networks are free from any kind of purposive character, but it can be said that the results have little to do with material need or utility. As such, we could say that the social networks that arose from self-released audio were a prime example of the spontaneous social order posited by thinkers from Chuang Tzu to Johan Huizinga to F.A. Hayek. This order has arisen from human *action* but not by human *design*, it generally favors practical knowledge over theoretical knowledge (given that some aspects of this practical knowledge remain difficult to articulate), and the success or failure of certain elements in this culture owes itself more to a kind of 'natural selection' than by official decree. This kind of a system does away with the Hobbesian "Prisoner's Dilemma" characteristic of the competitive culture that Kuspit describes: according to John Gray, this type of social order "...generalizes the insight contained in the theory of peaceful trading, that voluntary exchanges are not typically zero-sum exchanges (in which one side gains but the other loses) or negative-sum exchanges in

---

[3] Donald Kuspit, lecture given at the School of Visual Arts (MFA Art Criticism & Writing), September 6 2007. Available online at http://deimos3.apple.com/WebObjects/Core.woa/Browse/sva.edu.1363555220.0136355522 2. Retrieved July 17, 2010.

which both parties lose."[4] For all of this to be possible, participants in this spontaneous culture cannot expect any kind of liberation to arise as a result of social organization: organization must follow as a result of a 'creative space' being carved out by individual cells within the larger order.

As can be expected with characteristics like these, the spontaneous social order of self-released audio rarely ends up turning a profit (something hinted at by the artist Ken Montgomery's delightful slogan "Art Is Throwing Money Out The Window".)[5] The best that can usually be hoped for is that the unorthodox methods of exchange agreed upon by the network will prevent it from operating at a (financial) loss. If one is prepared for that eventuality, though, the social and immaterial rewards of participating in the culture can be great. The lack of need to maintain 'avant garde' status purely as a selling point means less anxiety and inhibition with regards to the actual creative process, which in turn leads, ironically, to works more critically recognizable as 'progressive' than much of the art advertising itself as such. It cannot be emphasized enough, though, that any form of critical recognition is unimportant for the propagation of networked art, as is the support of the other two components of the modern art market 'trinity' (the circuits of galleries and museums.) This cavalier attitude towards official criticism results from a simple re-envisioning of publicly transmitted artwork as - in Italian mail artist Vittore Baroni's reckoning - a palpable and personal *gift*, rather than as a neutered, impersonal artifact meant to be kept at arm's length from its admirers. He expands on this concept as follows:

> Mail art placed itself from the beginning in an *art beyond art* perspective, breaking all sorts of taboos concerning the preciousness and sacredness of the work of art as masterpiece (in the mail art practice the materials are often recycled, dismembered, passed from hand to hand like *cadavres exquis*), beyond the myth of the artist as a demiurge of genius isolated on his / her pedestal.[6]

---

[4] John Gray, *Hayek On Liberty*, p. 124. Routledge, New York, 1998.

[5] One issue of the network art-themed *Arte Postale* magazine, printed by Vittore Baroni, demonstrated this very literally by including a coin attached to the magazine cover (with instructions on how to use it.) It was, in effect, paying readers to read it.

Baroni also insists that these activities are most often "carried out mostly by *non-artists* in their *spare time.*" Two separate points of interest are contained in this brief declaration. Firstly, work done by *non-artists* would mean that the works resulting from this activity are those of amateurs. However, "amateur" has too often connoted someone who "has no idea what they're doing" and who will give up their petty dalliances on a moment's notice, usually once a more colourful distraction comes along. Many networked artists are assuredly amateurs, but few who make the effort to participate in this practice are ever this half-hearted about their creations. Rather, their amateurism cleaves closer to the original Latin definition of the word, stemming from *amare* [to love]: prior to the modern distinction between the professional public artist and the self-amused dilettante (which in itself would mean, in Latin, someone who is "delighted by" something), there was an understanding that creative works carried out for the furtherance of pleasure - as opposed to a career - were not ignoble, nor did they unanimously convey a sense of disrespect towards the historical grand masters. Furthermore, the amateur attitude was not one of selfishness and seclusion, since it was, by its very definition, the propagation of love and enthusiasm.

So, it is regrettable that "amateur" and "diletannte" have been "turned into terms of contempt to denote bunglers and triflers."[7] Worse still, though, is the contempt that is reserved for anyone who finds the aforementioned spare time to "waste" on amateurish acts. The evolutionary value of leisure has been inexplicably downplayed since the industrial age, or has at the very least been viewed as an "empty" period of stasis, devoid of any real evolutionary potential. Johan Huizinga notes that, in the Greece of antiquity, knowledge and science were not the result of a formal and career-oriented educational system, but "the treasures of the mind were the fruit of [man's] leisure."[8] Additionally, the word "school" originally *meant* leisure, and only more recently "acquired precisely the opposite sense of

---

[6] Vittore Baroni, "Art As Gift (It's A Net, Net, Net World)," *Sentieri Interrotti / Bassano 2000: Crisi della rappresentazione e iconoclastia nelle arti.* Derive Approdi, Rome, 1999.

[7] Jacques Barzun, *The Culture We Deserve,* p.21.Wesleyan University Press, Middletown CT, 1989.

[8] Johan Huizinga, *Homo Ludens: A Study Of The Play Element In Culture,* p. 147. Beacon Press, Boston, 1955.

systematic work and training, as civilization restricted the free disposal of the young man's time more and more, and herded larger and larger classes of the young to a daily life of severe application from childhood onwards."[9]

Special Deliveries: The Making Of Mail Art

The mail art movement, while not entirely laying the groundwork for networked audio, shares a good deal of DNA with it. Both have suggested, implicitly and explicitly, that the use of "inauthentic" creative materials (Xeroxed sheets, rubber stamps, cassette tapes) does not mean isolation within a virtual state that excludes "authentic" contact with other people: these practices can actually maximize the possibility of greater personal contact. Both cultures have largely understood that, by working with these mechanically reproduced materials, the starting point for authenticity and originality merely shifted location, i.e. originality became re-imagined as the clever discovery and assembly of visual or audial materials ("appropriation," "found sound," etc.), rather than as an act of *ex nihilo* creation from blank canvas or *tabula rasa*. Lastly, both movements have exploited the objectively recognized "flaws" in these media in order to create aura rather than to annihilate it. Pioneering 'xerographer' Louise Odes Nederland, who taught the first course in copy art, illustrates this when claiming "an art of unique grays and saturated blacks...of tantalizing distortions from a shallow depth of field" was her "true art form."[10]

Of course, it took the introduction of the cassette tape, and the associated home recording practices, to bring audio materials into the mix, and so the chronology of networked art circulating through the postal system begins with printed materials: the Haloid / Xerox 914 photocopier, introduced in 1960, had quite a head start on cassettes, whose playback quality would not reach a universally acceptable standard until the 1970s. And even then, technology for creating acceptable visual facsimiles of originals was not a prerequisite for using postal networks as an expressive

---

[9] Johan Huizinga, *Homo Ludens: A Study Of The Play Element In Culture*, p. 148. Beacon Press, Boston, 1955.

[10] Hillel Schwartz, *The Culture Of The Copy*, p. 238. Zone Books, New York, 1996.

tool, nor was allegiance to any established avant-garde: for example, the seminal fantasy author J.R.R. Tolkien regularly sent lavishly designed envelopes to his children over the holidays, which were labeled as being sent via "elf post" or from the "North Pole." Others who were representative of or synonymous with the European avant-garde, like the Italian Futurists, sent out postcards made of metal, while Yves Klein painted a "postage stamp" of his characteristic International Klein Blue color onto a postcard. Marcel Duchamp, who was circulating ideas via postcard as early as 1916, shouldn't be left out of this 'roll call' either. His regular reminder about the etymology of the word "art" (from the Sanskrit "to make"), and the creative freedom that followed from this realization, have made him a familiar guide for new networkers working in any medium.

Ray-O-Graph

However, Detroit-born artist Ray Johnson, who initiated his 'Correspondance School'[11] in 1962, remains one of the most commonly cited names when trying to determine the origins of mail art as a practice (the Fluxus "fluxkits", yearbooks, and "yearboxes" were another significant contemporaneous development that shaped the discourse of networked art to come.) Although it's likely that his activities are not unprecedented, they remain a touchstone that is used to illustrate all that this culture is supposed to be "about." An alumnus of the Black Mountain College along with John Cage, Robert Rauschenberg, and Merce Cunningham, Johnson began using the postal service as an artistic medium as early as 1943, yet did not transform this into a collective endeavor until 1955, when he first assembled a mailing list from the names of a couple hundred individuals active within the cultural scene of the day. Johnson has been praised by Vittore Baroni as "the Brian Wilson, the eccentric genius behind the growth of the wide mail art tree... such a fine-tuned mind, such an exquisite collagist, never a small detail out of place!"[12] Another fellow networker,

---

[11] Note the intentional misspelling of "correspondence," which implies a performance behind each act of communication undertaken in this style.

[12] Vittore Baroni, "Psychopathia Postalis." Previously unpublished (2004.)

the Crackerjack Kid, can confidently say that Johnson birthed "the largest international art community and movement in the history of art."[13] Perhaps most importantly for our upcoming discussions of networked audio, though, Ray Johnson sparked a state of affairs in which, according to John Held, Jr., "'networkers' were using Mail Art not as a collateral activity (as previous avant-gardes had done), but as an intrinsic part of their creative expression."[14]

Johnson was also knowingly returning certain words to meanings they had before their bastardized versions arose in post-industrial society: his "school" was truly a school in the sense of 'edifying leisure' mentioned above. Meanwhile, his acknowledgement of differences between the "art *world*" and the "art *community*" allowed him to re-frame the ""the art community" as the one that was really representative of global realities: the former term had taken on a mid-20th century gloss of willful exclusion that was seemingly the opposite of interacting with the "world."

This is not to say Ray Johnson had never participated in that lofty enterprise that we have come to know as the "official art world": while living in Manhattan, he moved in Abstract Art circles and exhibited alongside the monochromatic master Ad Reinhardt. Modern art historian Steven Watson mentions him as a "prominent figure in the [New York art] community" alongside "composer / musician LaMonte Young, choreographers Merce Cunningham and James Waring, and poet Diane di Prima."[15] His place in the lineage of Pop art is often overlooked, considering he was making photo collages of Elvis Presley some seven years before Andy Warhol. This is to say nothing of his participating in Fluxus circles before that movement had decided upon its name (he was never an "official" member of Fluxus, despite maintaining friendly relations with them throughout the 1950s and 1960s.)

---

[13] Crackerjack Kid quoted at "Artistamp Gallery: Ray Johnson." Available online at http://www.actlab.utexas.edu/emma/Gallery/galleryjohnson.html#TRIBUTE. Retrieved October 13, 2010.

[14] John Held Jr., ""The Mail Art Exhibition: Personal Worlds To Cultural Strategies." *At A Distance: Precursors To Art And Activism On The Internet,* ed. Annmarie Chandler and Norie Neumark, p. 94. MIT Press, Cambridge MA, 2005.

[15] Steven Watson, *Factory Made: Warhol And The Sixties,* p. 61-62. Pantheon Books, New York, 2003.

Some of Johnson's most recognizable icons were strangely amorphous and wavering black figures, something like a cross between the characters in an early *Felix The Cat* cartoon and Rorschach blots. One of these, Johnson's famous "bunny head" with perfectly spherical and entranced-looking eyes, underwent numerous permutations throughout his career-this was especially true when it was sent out to numerous other artists with instructions to be modified and then sent back to Johnson. It was a gesture that set the tone for much of what has followed, in both the visual and audio fields of networked art: artworks were supposed to communicate the distinct genius or mania of their creators in a final form, not in one that left itself open to the mercies of others, like a pie left to cool on a windowsill. It seemed like Johnson was just begging for incredible mischief to be done to his originals. The thing was, though, that the originals were quite mischievous in the first place: their wobbling visual contents were anchored by speech bubbles and cryptic text messages that were either riddles to be unlocked, ridiculous *non sequiturs*, or harmless in-jokes played on fellow cultural icons. By way of example, one of his "bunnies" came with an accompanying speech bubble saying "Bianca Jagger is my favorite Fluxus artist"- a wry play on Yoko Ono's marriage to pop royalty and participation in Fluxus. His overall aesthetic, grounded in Taoist thought and an apparent disregard for utility, led to ideas like his *Locust Valleyer* magazine (a take-off on the *New Yorker*, which was to be a one-page affair), and at least one absurd impromptu performance situation worth recounting in full:

> Ray would say "Dorothy [Podber], do the shoe thing." She'd go into the other room and bring out a large box filled with shoes of different sizes, and she would put it in the middle of the room. He would play records he and Dorothy had found - stuttering records – that's part of the grotesque humor. She would circle the box, put on a shoe, circle the box again and put on a shoe over the first, then circle the box and put on a third shoe, until she had on so many shoes she couldn't walk and she'd fall down. Ray would say, "thank you, Dorothy."[16]

---

[16] Dale Joe quoted in *Factory Made: Warhol And The Sixties* by Steven Watson, p. 60.

Johnson, noted by many as a loner in spite of his love for collaboration over great distances, would eventually commit suicide by drowning in 1995. It was an act which friend Mark Bloch believed was carried out because "it was the most artistic, perfect alternative for a life peppered with references to water and death from the very beginning....it coincided with his Taoist sensibility which holds emptiness and the doing of 'nothing' as its highest aspiration."[17]   Indeed, Johnson's work was consonant with the "anti-conceptualist" Tao- with its distrust of the need to govern and with its principle of *hsian sheng* [mutual arising], whereby the universe forms our consciousness at the same time as our consciousness forms the universe. Johnson's correspondence work, in providing no instructions other than to modify and return to him, or pass it along to others, also seemed to imply a Taoist principle of "non-deviation": there was no compulsory action to be followed or disobeyed, nor a "right" and "wrong" interpretation of Johnson's humorous cryptograms. So, unsurprisingly, it is Chuang Tzu whose thoughts on 'mastery,' 'accomplishment' and other ideas bound up in the art world provide a perfect synopsis of Johnson's approach to creative life:

> Chao Wen's lute, music master Kuang and his baton, Hui Tzu leaning on the Wu tree...how much these three learned! All so mastered their respective arts that we still remember them today. What they cared for they differentiated, they made a "that" of it. What they care for they desired to illuminate, but that was not the illumination of enlightenment. [...] blazing chaos is the light that guides the sage. Rather than merely using things, the sage dwells in the ordinary. This may be called illumination.[18]

Not all of the networkers who appeared in the wake of Johnson's efforts would adhere to these precepts: many of the artistamps, rubber

---

Pantheon Books, New York, 2003.

[17] Mark Bloch quoted at http://www.panmodern.com/cornering_rayjohnson.html. Retrieved October 14, 2010.

[18] *The Essential Chung Tzu,* trans. and ed. Sam Hamill and J.P. Seaton, p.13. Shambala, Boston / London, 1999.

stamps, stickers etc. "illuminated" the desirability of maintaining positive international communications, and appeared to advertise the network itself. Personalized rubber stamps bore legends such as "cultural diffusion," "art-virus contagion," or the Ghanaian Ayah Okwabi's "global better life." Numerous other slogans cheered on further actions, some with more specific political ends than the ones mentioned here. This was not necessarily incompatible with Johnson's ethos- it was just the case that Johnson's work largely advocated these democratic exchanges without the aid of further commentary. And, at any rate, it is misleading to say that these stamps had no function other than a "missionary" one: when placed in the vicinity of official postage stamps, which suggested their own beacons of national greatness and local color, these designs took on the role of comic foils or drew attention back to qualities that were meant to transcend the "local," without necessarily being hostile or antagonistic.

Regardless of the degree of intentionality in the network after Johnson, the spirit of inspiring absurdity managed to survive him. Materials for sending and receiving mail artworks became steadily more experimental, moving beyond the realm of paper products while still finding ways to squeeze into a standard post office box. Ruud Jansen's successful delivery of a partially inflated hot air balloon to Belgian Guy Bleus, with proper postage affixed to it, was one breakthrough in this sense. Methods of interactivity also became more complex as more individuals, from the 1970s onward, made their way to the network. *Faux*-"official" questionnaires circulated in which "answers" could be supplied with attached photos or drawings as well as traditional text, while imaginary currencies such as Julie Paquette's "Fluxus Bucks" became means of "buying" equally imaginary commodities. Elsewhere, the growing "net" population also made some networkers take up cataloging as their main contribution: small magazines were given over, in their entirety, to single practices within the network (e.g. the rubber stamp compilations *National Stampagraphic* or *Rubberstampmadness*.)

New Materials, New Artists, New Dilemmas

Meanwhile, as the raw materials became more fascinating and

involving than the usual monochrome Xerox sheet or hand-painted envelope, it was only a matter of time before the more "time-based" arts came to circulate through the network of the 1980s and beyond: radio programs like those of Willem de Ridder and Peter R. Meyer (in the Netherlands and Sweden, respectively) even took the non-exclusionary philosophy of mail art to their radio programs, each of them soliciting tapes of everything from street sounds to telephone conversations and weaving them together into unpredictable - but not totally inchoate - narratives. Gradually, involvement with networked art meant not just involvement with artwork of the "suitable for framing" variety, but with any portable material that could be molded, manipulated or animated. Yet the utopian potential of this medium, within a few decades of Ray Johnson's famous forays into it, was already running into a predictable thicket of problems: "the more the merrier," indeed, but individual networkers' archives were starting to expand beyond their ability to store them, while the quantity-vs.-quality debate surrounding other areas of post-industrial production intensified with each wave of new recruits, and with the medium's expansion into realms where its practicioners had to wonder if it was being taken seriously or not. While some networkers saw nothing wrong with, say, mail art being a graded project worked on by children in public elementary schools, others frowned upon this introduction of the medium into institutional culture, and saw this as inconsistent with the aforementioned ideals of spontaneity and self-determination.

That said, it is difficult to pinpoint any one particular "crisis moment" for the culture- even Ray Johnson's passing did not discourage the surge of activity that he had helped to initiate. From the evidence we have available, mail art never reached a state where the networks became a means for predatory or harassing individuals to issue cheap come-ons and statements of unalloyed hate. The spectrum of possible moods, from sassy to sinister, was indeed greater than what might have been achieved in a more public forum: on one end there were Anna Banana's sweetly funny invocations of her favored yellow fruit (often imaginatively combined with her interest in psychoanalysis), and on the other were COUM Transmissions' "Gary Gilmore Memorial Society" postcards (in which members of COUM were photographed sitting in electric chairs- an homage to the murderer sentenced to death in Utah in 1977.)[19] Only with the next waves of participatory art, based on 'zines and audio recordings, did specialized misanthropic sub-networks form. It would appear that this had more to do with the progress / regress of Western societies as a whole rather than with any sudden "sea change" in networkers' attitudes. The 1990s embittered quite a few people of creative temperament, what with their failure to resolve any of the great problems of the 20th century (e.g. the return of genocide in Africa and the Balkans), a sad ending that could not be entirely countered with the dramatic changes in the velocity and omnipresence of communications media. This is to say nothing of those who saw the irreversible forward thrust of hi-tech as part of the problem: though he had been busy with his mail bomb insurgency since the late 1970s, the 1995 publication of Ted Kaczynski's "Unabomber Manifesto" (a.k.a. *Industrial Society And Its Future*) even managed to cast a shadow upon the use of the postal service for self-expression.

Vittore Baroni also mentions "a mysterious saboteur" who appeared around this time, "circulat[ing] for months a large number of invites to fake mail art projects, with the intention of generating chaos."[20] Baroni recalls how "the network peacefully withstood the attacks, until the agent provocateur got tired of causing troubles and desisted."[21] We can only guess at the intentions of the "mysterious saboteur": like the pranks of the malicious "griefers" that make life hell for subscribers to virtual online worlds like Second Life, the motivations for disruptive counter-network activity can range from crushing boredom to the negative adolescent puritanism that causes them to hate and fear anyone apparently having a good time. Whatever the case, the network's self-regulatory nature usually makes quick work of isolated gatecrashers. Those who assail it often do so because of what they see as a sanctimonious streak or a smug morality: but, as outlined by 'distance art' scholars Annemarie Chandler and Norie Neumark, "commitment to a more 'democratic' practice was not a moral(istic) position, but an invigorating stimulus to playful inventiveness, even for the least 'political' artists."[22] If Baroni's account above is true, the

---

[19] "One card was sent, on the day of the execution, to the Governor of the prison in Utah with 'WISH YOU WERE HERE, love Gary' written on it. See *Wreckers Of Civilisation* by Simon Ford, p. 7.6. Black Dog Press, London, 1999.

[20] Vittore Baroni, "Psychopathia Postalis." Previously unpublished (2004.)

[21] *Ibid.*

[22] Annmarie Chandler and Norie Neumark, *At A Distance: Precursors To Art And Activism*

network's universal dismissal of would-be nuisances is also amusingly ironic, since the attackers who wanted to make a point about the fragility of the network's supposed "harmony" actually brought that harmony about by being unanimously rejected.

Another problematic feature of mail art was the double-edged nature of its intimacy. While it provided the opportunity to form true friendships with other artists - instead of merely using said artists as "contacts" to provide an "in" to the official institutions - this intimacy also made it possible to receive a deluge of unrequested and unwanted correspondence. Once "art tourism" became a going concern in the late 1980s, networkers were also introduced to the phenomenon of unannounced visits from mail art contacts in possession of their home addresses (sometimes happily inebriated upon arrival.) Andrej Tisma, one of the most consistently supportive proponents of mail art from the former Yugoslavia, uses a fishing analogy to illustrate this dilemma, noting how one could not just "get rid of" a network contact once some kind of reciprocal communication had been made:

> The best comparison is with fishing: you throw the fishhook, or even a fishnet, and you wait for what is going to happen. If you are lucky, and if your "bait" is good enough you will catch plenty of "fishes." But in that plenty, they will not be all of good quality, and in mail-art there is no throwing back "fishes" into the water. They all must be kept and "eaten." And that sometimes causes little problems. In other words, doing your own project you can't choose your correspondents, except if your invitations are strictly personal.[23]

Regular users of present-day online social networks should be familiar with this Catch-22 situation: once User A receives an unwanted "add request" from User B hoping to join User A's network, a refusal will result in a bruised ego (and possibly User B telling everyone in his own network that User A is a contemptible snob, or worse.) Meanwhile, *accepting* User

---

On The Internet, p. 442. MIT Press, Cambridge MA, 2005.

[23] Andrej Tisma quoted at http://jas.faximum.com//library/tam/tam_45a.htm. Retrieved October 13, 2010.

B's request will potentially open up the floodgates to dozens more requests (and more chances to replicate this awkward situation), coming from people who have progressively less in common with User A and who seek contact for increasingly more banal reasons. Resorting to the second option, while more diplomatic in the short run, can lead either to a state of overload-induced exhaustion or to forgetting one's original intent for participating in the network, situations which Tisma also describes:

> Another problem with the [sic] one's own project is that you suddenly begin to receive a huge amount of mail, without a physical possibility to reply to it (a printed catalog after [a mail art exhibit] is not a real mail-art reply to an artwork). It can also give you the (wrong) impression that you are such an important personality in the net, because you get ten to fifteen pieces daily from all over the world. That feeling is very pleasant, but when the project is over your mailbox becomes sadly empty. That's the reason, I suppose, why some people in the network are running new projects one after the other. But it is not real creativity.[24]

The sudden feeling of importance that Tisma mentions, and its attendant emotional high, could also lead to periods of intense deflation when the mail stopped rolling in from certain individuals. What did it mean when the mail ceased to arrive from a fellow networker- was it a "silent treatment" meant to telegraph that a previously sent work was not up to snuff, or maybe offensive? Or did something tragic happen? In some cases, it was triumph rather than tragedy that led to a cessation of contacts - as when the post-Soviet territories of Eastern Europe once again experienced communicative freedoms that had been previously denied - and no longer needed to rely on mail art as the window onto the West (of course, the raising of postal prices to Western standards was also a deterrent to further mail networking activity.)

The mail art exhibit has also proven to be a point of contention for

---

[24] Andrej Tisma quoted at http://jas.faximum.com//library/tam/tam_45a.htm. Retrieved October 13, 2010.

critics and networkers alike. With veteran networkers like Lon Spiegelman proclaiming that "money and mail art don't mix," and having this sentiment supported by numerous compatriots (see Ken Montgomery's slogan above), there was bound to be resistance to any event in which patrons had to pay for the privilege of viewing works. While many networkers have, as Tisma outlines above, poured their resources into organizing shows of mailed artifacts, others feel that it is counter-productive to take these items out of network circulation and place them in the museum / gallery circuit. Ray Johnson's exhibit of mail art at the Whitney Museum in 1970, which became a kind of personal Waterloo, earned the condemnation of *Artforum* critic Kasha Linville, who likened it to "pinning down a living thing in flight."[25] Since networked art, including Johnson's own pieces, featured a high degree of material that was sent out with the intent of being further modified by its recipients, this criticism was not entirely groundless. Furthermore, entrusting mail art to galleries also meant allowing for curators to be more selective about what did and did not appear in these showcases, even though one of the few mail art "rules" was that *everything* sent in to a proposed exhibition would be hung or shown. Predictably, one major "official" exhibit of mail art - the 1996 "Project Paper Road" curated by Anne Vilsbøll and sponsored by Post Denmark - had more selective criteria. Equally predictable was the fact that it would not "just" be a homage to the untapped potential of postal communications, but a means of drumming up support for a postal service already feeling embattled by the "rival" Internet.

Exhibition catalogs also invited occasional complaints from those who had spent long periods of time developing their pool of trusted contacts: like the common complaints now heard about free music blogs that make the discovery of outré music "too easy," some saw it as unfair that a complete newcomer could just waltz into a gallery, take note of the names listed in the exhibition catalog, and get down to business in a fraction of the time required of his or her forebears. However, it is still debatable whether taking such shortcuts automatically results in the production of a less sincere and more slapdash body of work. Nor did the amount of time logged in the network automatically confer "status": one could be involved

---

[25] Sharla Sava, "Ray Johnson's New York Correspondence School: The Fine Art Of Communication." Ray Johnson: Correspondences, ed. Donna DeSalvo and Catherine Gudis, p. 126. Flammarion, Paris, 1999.

with it for years, yet mainly confined to producing items like the eternally disappointing "chain letter" or other materials that revealed nothing about the sender's unique disposition (if she or he had one.)

Although a considerable number of avid networkers found exhibitions to be problematic, for these and other reasons, there was still a desire to close the gap between the 'virtual space' of the networks and the objective reality in which all of the senses were engaged. As such, different initiatives came about that would, by mobilizing its creators to the far ends of the earth, allow for mail art to make good on its promise of being "communication art." 1986 was remembered as a year of 'tourism' (in which mail artists were encouraged to make a communicative work out of their travels and meetings with their fellows), while 1992 saw some of the most successful networkers' congresses on record (the "World-Wide Decentralized Networkers' Congress," organized by Swiss artist H.R. Fricker.) While probably not essential to the survival of the network, these moments of repudiating its "virtuality" did much to keep enthusiasm alive, and to further blur the categories of supposedly purposeless fun and purposeful self-proclamation.

Media(ted) Mail?

For many outside observers, the concept of thriving yet 'headless' culture is odd enough, yet there is still more peculiarity lodged within the concept. If nothing else, it often seems as if the audio networks are a vast playground for the apparently paradoxical: for example, many of their individual nodes are people who would prefer to be left alone by society at large, yet still feel a strong need to communicate their innermost desires, fears and speculative visions. Still others, in the process of releasing work that is clandestine or of limited availability, manage to court a larger base of followers than if their work was easily available on the open market (this holds especially true in the age of 'ripping' and downloading audio from non-digital formats, allowing a recording with an original pressing of 250 copies to be traded amongst tens of thousands of fans.)

Certainly, the critics of mail art have been nearly as diverse in their backgrounds as the individuals who actually created and distributed it. Cultural conservatives have, predictably, lambasted it for lacking seriousness, for encouraging ephemerality, and for inferring "'x' *must* be done" from the fact that "'x' *can* be done." They are not alone, though: some critics on the Left, including the anarchist portion of that orientation, have bones to pick with the "pretensions" of networked art. "Ontological anarchist" Hakim Bey throws in his lot with these critics when he states the following:

> The mail art of the 70s and the 'zine scene of the 80s were attempts to go beyond the mediation of art-as-commodity [...] However, they preserved the mediated structures of postal communication and xerography, and thus failed to overcome the isolation of the players, who remained quite literally out of touch. We wish to take the motives and discoveries of these earlier movements to their logical conclusion in an art which banishes all mediation and alienation, at least to the extent that the human condition allows.[26]

This is one of the central dilemmas we have to deal with as this story of unofficial audio unfolds: can art-at-a-distance really use the technological apparatus, so criticized for compartmentalizing and isolating individual units of humanity, to melt away these very distinctions? Does the usage of this reproduction technology still favor those forces antithetical to "art," even as an increasing number of artists incorporate these technological extensions into their work? Bey himself would seem to think so: "the problem is that any possibility of action remains atomized. There's no chance of molecularity…that's what capitalism is so good at - separation!"[27] Bey's views on this subject extend, naturally, to the hypermodern networking of the Internet, and here his critique converges with those who consider the 'Net to be the ultimate generator of "symbolic action," or an emulator of a schizophrenic state in which nomadic life and imprisonment exist simultaneously (with this, he also finds unlikely companions on the

---

[26] Hakim Bey, Immediatism, p. 11-12. AK Press, Edinburgh / San Francisco, 1994.

[27] Hakim Bey quoted at http://sasha.miltsov.org/krasoty/bey2/. Retrieved June 17, 2010.

opposite end of the political spectrum.)[28]

Of course, this makes the bold assumption that people involved in art-at-a-distance make it for purposes of explicit cultural critique- as was already mentioned in the above overview of mail art, many of its creators are perfectly content with using it to form friendships and to disrupt life's more quotidian habits, rather than to foment political revolution. More than that, though, it makes an implicit statement that people, in all cases, *have* the choice of local vs. global communication. What are communication-minded artists to do if, for all their best efforts, their efforts are met in their local area with total indifference? And is their subsequent desire to reach out to other more accepting target locales not just a replication of American celebrities' "telescopic philanthropy" (e.g. adopting poverty-stricken "3rd-world" children while ignoring the poverty in their own backyards?) John Held Jr. disagrees, suggesting that knowledge of the distant provides for that much more understanding of one's immediate neighbors:

> If one can overcome language problems, cultural differences, governmental obstacles, and technical difficulties when contacting correspondents from different countries, then you get a better understanding and appreciation of those closer at hand.[29]

So, in other words, knowledge of the peripheries informs knowledge of the center.

Various strains of anarcho-primitivism look upon mechanical development, and its resultant anthropocentrism, as an absolute evil with which no compromises are to be made. As far as the more established

---

[28] Take for example, the complaint of 'New Right' philosopher Alain de Benoist: "In addition to nomadism there is cocooning. Internet is a communication tool, but its form of communication abolishes the dimensions of space and time, that are (were) the context in which, until yesterday, human freedom was expressed. In this way, the net imprisons the individual in a private sphere that is more and more limited to the abuse of a remote control or of a keyboard." (trans. A. Boraschi.)
http://home.alphalink.com.au/~radnat/debenoist/alain5.html. Retrieved September 20, 2010.
[29] John Held, Jr. quoted at http://jas.faximum.com//library/tam/tam_02a.htm. Retrieved October 13, 2010.

anarcho-primitivists like John Zerzan are concerned, the patent distrust of technology should extend as far as man's original 'extensions', the written and spoken word. Interestingly, though, great amounts of deforestation and resource depletion had been set into motion long before the Fordist / Taylorist principles of the 20th century could really come to fruition. As Hakim Bey's nemesis Murray Bookchin notes in his acerbic *Social Anarchism or Lifestyle Anarchism,* much of the erosive damage to North American soil had already been carried out with pre-industrial hand tools and plows, while "...apart from the textile villages and towns of Britain, where mass manufacture made its historic breakthrough, the machines that meet with the greatest opprobrium these days were created long after capitalism gained ascendancy in many parts of Europe and North America."[30] Upping the ante in his criticism of techno-phobic revolutionaries, Bookchin continues:

> Ironically, even the collective that produces *Fifth Estate* found it could not do without a computer and was 'forced' to purchase one - issuing the disingenuous disclaimer, 'we hate it!' Denouncing an advanced technology while using it to generate anti-technological literature is not only disingenuous, but has sanctimonious dimensions: such 'hatred' of computers seems more like the belch of the privileged, who, having overstuffed themselves with delicacies, extol the virtues of poverty during Sunday prayers.[31]

Although this unresolved Bookchin / Bey donnybrook makes for high drama, we will have to stop this particular debate here: the issue at hand is not the proper anarchist orientation, but the relationship with technological mediation that most benefits an ethos of "communication art." Besides, demanding that creative people restrict their technological enhancement to a certain level is, indeed, a form of "mediation" or an intervening measure where "pure" communication is involved. Artificial

---

[30] Murray Bookchin quoted at http://libcom.org/library/socanlifean6. Retrieved October 15, 2010.

[31] Murray Bookchin quoted at http://libcom.org/library/socanlifean7. Retrieved October 15, 2010.

social restraints can rise up independently of technological advancement, as Lewis Mumford notes: "the decade that saw the triumph of air transportation likewise saw the universal restoration of national passport restrictions."[32]

Of course, we could debate all day, and deep into the night, about whether art-at-a-distance is a tremendous liberator of creative and activist potential, or just another step downwards into tech-mediated oblivion. The personal take of this author is that the former is closer to the truth: there are now quite a few documented examples of the would-be 'alienating' technologies providing the spark for more traditional, face-to-face encounters and consummations of friendship (there are more to come in this book alone.) Framing the argument solely in terms of technology, however, forces this entire story to become the story of creative means rather than one of the drives which led to their eventual adoption: that is to say, the story of inspiration as furthered *with* tools but not *because* of them. This story is, after all, just one in the chronicle of self-determined creativity and its challenges to unyielding systemic thought. As Vaclav Havel once noted, "a better system will not automatically ensure a better life. In fact, the opposite is true: only by creating a better life can a better system be developed."[33] By accepting the inherent flaws and moral conundrums of technology, yet refusing to frame its project in technological terms (e.g. making technological perpetuation or destruction the "goal" of this collective work), networked art has done what it can to give its participants a taste of that better life.

---

[32] Lewis Mumford, *The Myth Of The Machine: The Pentagon Of Power*, p. 208. Harcourt / Brace / Jovanovich, New York, 1970.

[33] Vaclav Havel, "The Power Of The Powerless." Trans. Paul Wilson. Vaclav Havel Et. Al., *The Power Of The Powerless*, p. 52. M.E. Sharpe Inc., New York, 1985.

Social Sculpting: Interview With Andrej Tisma

When Robert Filliou's notion of "The Eternal Network" was used to describe mail art, this utopian proclamation must have raised the eyebrows of the more skeptically minded, within and without that network. After all, any creative practice that relies on international postal service can be nullified once international relations deteriorate, in spite of networkers' best efforts to maintain the peace. Could networked art, let alone any kind of art, persist in territories where warfare and its attendant privation was the order of the day? This question was raised, in a most unequivocal way, as ethno-nationalist battles shredded the social fabric of the Balkans shortly before the dawn of the 21st century.

The former Yugoslavia had hardly existed in artistic isolation prior to the merciless conflicts of the 1990s, with each of the separate republics containing its own unique artistic orientation: the Serbian intellegentsia favored a more Parisian-style culture, while Slovenian artists looked towards German or Austrian points of reference. The 20th century continental avant-garde hardly passed Yugoslavia by; in fact archetypal characters like the Italian Futurist poet F.T. Marinetti lent support to the Zagreb-based Zenitist movement, at one point even helping to release the officially censored Zenitist artist Ljubomir Micić from prison. The homegrown avant-culture was hardly a 2nd rate imitation or "guesstimate" of activities happening further west, though. The aforementioned Zenitism of the 1920s set the stage for much of what was to come, with its concept of the "barbarogenius" (a sort of Balkan parallel to the Nietzschean *Übermensch*) straddling stereotypical conceptions of East and West while delighting in the deployment of paradoxical concepts (admonitions like "don't be ashamed of being confused, dear reader!" were common in the influential *Zenit* journal.) It is particularly poignant, in light of the Balkan events of the 1990s, that one of Micić' boldest pronouncements from the old Zenitist house organ declares "we, who remained as the last guard, we endure a common ache in our hearts, a common soul of despair, a common protest: no more war! Never! Never!"[34] Written in the mid-1920s, his words could have easily been written in the aftermath of the second World War, or after the Yugoslav wars of the 1990s. While Micić' protests did not resonate in the ears of the political opportunists and megalomaniacs who fueled the furnaces of those respective wars, the "last guard" did at least take on new manifestations as each new challenge arose.

Between the seminal period of Zenitism and the pre-millenial plunge into warfare, there was a fairly rich harvest of Balkan avant-gardism and otherwise challenging art: this culture manifested itself in Tito's Yugoslavia, from roughly 1951 to 1973, as the "happening"-based Belgrade group Mediala, the New Tendencies movement, the Slovenian OHO collective (which adopted the philosophy of "reism" or "a return to things themselves"), and a catalog's worth of other notable entries. On the cusp of the 1990s, more typically 'Eastern' innovations (such as the Russian sotsart' / 'apt-art' tradition of exhibiting art within private apartments) could be found in Ljubljana's burgeoning arts scene alongside myriad forms of 'Western' video art, with the intensely local creative content obscuring these respective forms' points of origin. With the soil of creativity thus fertilized, it seemed unlikely that the 1970s-1980s surge in networked art would pass the Balkans by. Some of the best local representatives of that culture, such as Dobrica Kamperelic and Andrej Tisma, had had formal or "official" artistic training, yet held a very non-institutional practice of integrating art into the 'everyday,' and vice versa, until the distinction between these two categories was as irrelevant as the 'East / West' divide alluded to above.

Several years before the outbreak of full-scale war in the Balkans, Tisma was commemorating the 1984 Sarajevo Olympic Games with his inaugural project, "Mail-Art Olympic Games:" the project gained enough international attention to be done in conjunction with the official television station in Novi Sad (the works collected from other networkers were displayed in the TV studio.) With his local reputation growing from this and subsequent projects (including an ambitious full-color book with contributions from nearly 400 participants), a cosmetics manufacturer in

---

34 Ljubomir Micić quoted in "Avant-Garde, Neo-Avant-Garde, and Post-Avant-Garde Magazines And Books" by Darko Šimičić. *Impossible Histories: Historical Avant-Gardes, Neo Avant-Gardes, and Post Avant-Gardes in Yugoslavia, 1918-1991*, p. 298-299. Ed. Dubravka Duric and Misko Sukakovic. MIT Press, Cambridge, 2003.

the Croatian town of Ojisek tapped Tisma to assemble a project linking the concepts of "nature" and "beauty". The project was to have featured a foreword from the screenwriter of Michaelagelo Antonioni's *Blow-Up*, thoughts on the state of the ecology, and much more besides. However, the project conceived in 1988 was not realized by 1991, at which point

> ...the situation in the former Yugoslavia was slowly changing. Croatia prepared its secession and soon my sponsor informed me about "financial problems". They suggested that I wait, but things were going worse and worse. Soon, in 1991, military clashes in Croatia began, so it became clear to me that I will have to realize the book myself (I had promised it to participants), and find another exhibition space.[35]

Reports of such dashed expectations are common throughout the Balkan arts scene of the time, and soon the allocation of arts funding to more pressing emergencies would be accompanied by a full spate of prohibitive actions. The Croatian mail artist Svjetlana Mimica (active as such since around 1989) recalls that, at the outset of the Serb-controlled JNA [Yugoslav National Army] offensive against Croatia in late 1991, international mail was being intercepted by Serbian forces at the Croatian borders. As of 1995, she was still reporting that "it is not easy to be a mail-artist here, [or] even a hobbyist of correspondence...you are promptly under suspicion!"[36] While Mimica's statements will not be unfamiliar to anyone who has experienced life in a war zone, or even studied the metrics of desperation that can be experienced there, they are worthy enough of being brought into our discussion about the possibility of art in such an environment:

> I think mail art can be understandable only to people who lived abroad and know "how Europeans live wonderful". Maybe the most clear *[sic]* answer I received from one young artist last week: "What can you expect here? People

---

[35] Andrej Tisma quoted at http://jas.faximum.com//library/tam/tam_45a.htm. Retrieved October 13, 2010.

[36] Svjetlana Mimica quoted at http://jas.faximum.com//library/tam/tam_07.htm. Retrieved October 14, 2010.

live bad, very bad, they haven't even the everyday food. While lots of them commit suicide, you can't expect enthusiasm & creativity of young artists, unemployed and with so many existential problems....! When you haven't got the food + life, you can't think about some other "luxury" things.... or maybe you can.... The sense of man is to combat the bad situations and to win them. I think so... and try to live so![37]

The situation Mimica mentions was made more desperate by the UN embargo placed upon all forms of trade in the rapidly fragmenting Yugoslavia, including 'official' cultural exchange, in 1992. Andrej Tisma's *Networking Statement 4: Networking Under Embargo* aimed to bring outside observers up to speed on the effect that this blockade was having; paying particular attention to its unfairness towards "...we, the intellectuals who have protested and fought against the war in Yugoslavia from its beginning...we feel innocent in this situation, which is totally unpredictable."[38] Tisma, realizing that the postal system might break down under these conditions, only half-joked that he might have to rely on "telepathic communication" to continue with artistic interchanges. In a characteristic act of defiance, he called for an "Anti-Embargo Net Congress" in Kamperelic's mail art journal *Open World*, an 'art tourism' event in the style of H.R. Fricker that would symbolize the solidarity of networkers - on Yugoslav soil - against both the wars and the unnecessarily sweeping international reaction to them. However, despite a hotel being reserved in the town of Sr. Karlovci for an expected number of foreign guests, along with other offers that were quite generous for a time of hyperinflation, no one showed- Tisma was clearly devastated by the non-response, while his colleague Kamperelic went on Belgrade television to discuss its exacerbation of an already tense socio-political situation. Having long made personal rubber stamps as a mode of expression in the network, Tisma sardonically fashioned a "Embargo On Tourism" stamp with the subtitle ("sorry, H.R.F.") to "commemorate" the occasion.

---

[37] Svjetlana Mimica quoted at http://jas.faximum.com//library/tam/tam_07.htm. Retrieved October 14, 2010.

[38] Andrej Tisma quoted at http://www.mailartist.com/johnheldjr/OpenWorldofDobricaKamperelicPart2.html. Retrieved March 31, 2011.

It would have been easy, at this point, for the Yugoslav members of the mail art networks to fold their cards and adopt a bunker mentality. However, Tisma and his fellow Yugoslav networks instead chose to make the cultural embargo the raw material of future works- as other networkers learned of the sad fate of the "Anti-Embargo Net Congress" and the still sadder fate of the Yugoslav nation as a whole, they began to produce anti-embargo works within the less hostile confines of their own countries. The full range of materials, from "artistamps" to simple printed essays, leaked into the "net" from other nodes in Europe and America, and generated an equally varied number of reactions. The resulting dialogue about the Yugoslav wars, as chronicled in the issues of *Open World* that continued to appear in their midst, provided an invaluable look into the 'micro' events that accreted to form the 'macro' structure of daily life under duress. As such, they are often more substantial than the documentaries done for official media.

Andrej Tisma, in our dialogue below, confirms that artists like Svjetlana Mimica were not alone in their determination. While any number of mail networkers could have been called upon to illustrate how this practice fed into networked and self-released audio, Tisma's special brand of resilience makes him an excellent spokesman for the culture as a whole, either in peacetime or under siege.

++++++++

Despite the global nature of the mail art network, I imagine that, in many networkers' home countries, there were certain obstacles to participating in the network. For example, the expenses of sending material in the post, or the possibility of having one's mail inspected by police authorities. Did you encounter such obstacles throughout the 1980s-1990s, and if so, how did you manage to overcome them?

I had the luck to live in a pretty open country from the socialist group - in Yugoslavia, which was actually nonaligned and out of the Soviet bloc, so I always argued that Yugoslavia is not an Eastern European country but rather Western. The influence of Western culture was evident since the 50s, and was growing with time. I traveled a lot, mostly in the 80s, visiting my mail art friends worldwide: in New York, Paris, Stockholm, Amsterdam etc. So our communication with the world went without problems in the 80s. The problems came later in the 90s, in the time of conflicts within Yugoslavia, and of the international economic and cultural embargo imposed by the United Nations. But already in the mid '80s we encountered some economic problems, inflation, high prices, poverty, as Yugoslavia - once engineered by Tito, who passed away in 1980 - began to fall apart by will of separatist republics. So communication with the world became an economical problem, especially for us mail artists who sent out works daily and in big quantities. That is why, in 1986, I made a rubber stamp saying "one stamp for US = one kilo of bread". In order to keep in touch with friends overseas I had to choose each time whether to pay for a stamp or to buy my family a kilo of bread. Our salaries were so miserable that we had money almost only for bread and rent. In the 90s, the situation worsened, so in 1993 inflation was 300% daily! So it was really an ethical question, whether to spend money on mailing or on food. But I always chose mailing because it made me closer to friends abroad, and eliminated the effects of isolation of my country, which became tougher with time. For sending out some heavier publications like books or catalogs in bigger quantities, I usually managed to find sponsors (galleries, publishing houses, the post office) who sent them worldwide for me.

Concerning freedom of mailing and police inspection I could say it was free, and sometimes I deliberately provoked post office clerks or postmen by printing some strange content, textual messages or open erotic scenes on my postcards, which I then sent without an envelope. I also imprinted my rubber stamps and stuck on my own [self-designed] postal stamps to perplex them completely. Once I printed a big image of girl sucking a dick as a graphic work on a post-card and sent it away to artist friends, but without a return address, testing to see how many of them would receive it. Some received it only months later.

From your observations, were the "mail networkers" in the former Yugoslavia a completely separate group of people from the artists who exhibited in galleries and performance spaces? Or, was there some overlapping between the cultures of mail art and more "officially recognized" art?

The members of the Yugoslavian mail art community, which was not so big (ranging between 20-30 active participants in different periods) were mostly active in the official art scene simultaneously. They were not in conflict with the system, as I suppose most of the mail artists in the Eastern European countries under direct Soviet influence were (in the so called Warsaw Pact.) In our country, galleries and other institutions were open to mail art, and I can tell from my own experience: I have organized mail art shows in the biggest and most prestigious state art galleries and museums of contemporary art all over former Yugoslavia, while promoting mail art on the radio and TV. Also, those galleries printed nice catalogs (sometimes with all participants' works in color) and sent them worldwide to participants. I kept it as my mission to give the mail art phenomenon a place in culture it deserves: as the most avant-garde, open and dynamic art movement of that historical moment in the world.

But also, besides mail art, I also exhibited my own photographic works, which did not have anything in common with mail art. I did performances, in such prestigious galleries but also in some alternative places. Most of my mail artist colleagues had exhibitions of their works, collages, photos, performances, art actions, and installations in official galleries, but also exhibited mail art projects in official gallery spaces, so there was the first mail art show in Yugoslavia organized by the Novi Sad artist Bogdanka Poznanovic, which after the Novi Sad premiere in 1974 was shown in Zagreb's Contemporary Art Gallery in 1978, and Miroljub Todorovic, the founder of the Signalist art movement, has exhibited mail art postal stamps as early as in 1970 in Museum of Contemporary Art in Belgrade. Todorovic is also an outstanding poet and essayist and has published about 60 books of poetry and about 20 on Signalism, etc., mostly on the imprint of the official state publishing houses. Artist Katalin Ladik, who was concerned, alongside mail art, with visual and sound poetry, performance, gesture poetry etc., has performed in official state galleries, theatres, and cultural centers. She published several books and LPs. Slavko Matkovic, also an early and well- known mail artist, exhibited his collages and conceptual art in official galleries. And so it goes.

Here in the U.S., we have not been as much of a 'producing' nation as we were in, say, the post-WWII era, with much of our manufacturing capacity now moved overseas. Even before this, though, I think that the very 'homemade' work of artisans was quite a rare thing - and this affected the way average people viewed the very homemade, 'do-it-yourself' nature of mail art...it was either something very special because of its authenticity and directness, or it was seen as something cheap and insulting to the 'true' artists who painstakingly collected large amounts of raw material in a formal studio, and made their works from that. Was this attitude the same in your area- namely, were "big", expensive-to-produce, one-of-a-kind artworks more respected and valued than the "little," compact, duplicated artifacts of the mail network?

Mail-art was never considered as mainstream art in Yugoslavia, rather like an alternative. This was not because of the materials and production that were more "primitive" and "cheap", but because of its principles of openness; no selection of works, all can take part etc. Academic artists could not accept that everyone can be an artist in the mail art network. But I always stated that mail-art is not about the sent papers, collages, stamps, but about communication between people, living persons with their emotions and opinions, which makes the network live. I have seen the entire network as a pulsing spiritual sculpture encompassing the planet. And that is why mail-art movement was great for me. Every person, participant was just a small piece of the network, a "brain cell" of the entire brain in which the whole world was reflected. The *exchange itself* makes for the poetry of the mail art network, not the material artifacts or skills. From mail-art we consequently arrived at Internet art, web.art, or net.art.

OK- you mentioned previously that mail art is not about the artifacts but about the communication involved. All the same, did you create or initiate any specific works, actions or collaborative pieces that you consider to be exceptional or "standout" works? Can you recall any single piece that really manifested everything important about your creative practice?

For me, it is not easy to choose something "standout" from my 25 or so years of production in the frame of mail art activity, because most of my works I consider much involved in that sort of art and thinking. Hundreds of my rubber stamps, printed postcards, international mail art exhibition projects and publications had that effect of linking people, initiating exchange and collaboration worldwide, making all of us feel as if part of one huge creative network. Also it would take much time and space to elaborate here on the more specific themes and visual contents I realized during all those years. Therefore, I will mention one typical example, one rubber stamp I made in 1986, that had an interesting destiny, and in an obvious way became a part of the network: getting its independent life, illustrating what I was talking about when I stated that mail art is not so much about physical works but about communication poetics.

It was my *"No Ism!"* rubber stamp, which I carved out of an eraser in December 1986. It was a reaction to Hans Ruedi Fricker's well known rubber stamp *"After Dadaism, Fluxism, Mailism comes Tourism"*. I declared that *"after all isms comes No Ism!"* and made a stamp with the last two words. For me *"No Ism"* was the shortest definition of the mail art network, because in it you can find all kinds of "isms", and that means there are no dominating styles and ideologies. It is free of all rules and represents a total freedom of creation. I began imprinting it on all my correspondence, envelopes and postcards. One day I was surprised to receive a small package from Japanese mail artist Ryosuke Cohen, with about three hundred stickers with my *"No Ism!"* logo reproduced in many different colors, with my name under it. Soon I began receiving mailings from mail artists worldwide with the same stickers, but with *their* names under the slogan (obviously also made by Cohen and sent out as presents.) These artists were using them without knowing who was the real author of the slogan. Everybody accepted it as their own. In that moment, I realized that my slogan had become an integral part of the network, circulating independently, free from my control. And that acceptance made me very content. Later on Ryosuke Cohen stated in an article :

> "Andrej Tisma sent me the seal of 'No-Ism' from Yugoslavia. No-Ism means that there is not just one ideology in the Mail Art World. "No" means 'brain' in Japanese. So, I ambiguously use "No" as the meaning of non-existence and Brain. I sent No-ism seals all over the world, too, in return. Likewise, I receive in everyday life many kinds of stuff such as postcards, Xerox copies, collage pieces, drawings, computer graphics, show catalogs, photographs, and cassette tapes by mail, fax, e-mail, and Internet. This gives us an amazing view,

showing the overwhelmingly plural ways of expression and concepts. I, therefore, regard the huge world of Mail Art as full of every kind of '-ism', mixed up like chaos. No wonder not a single rigid ideology survives or dominates."

Since we're dealing a little with Japan at the moment: I was reading an archived interview with Tetsuo Kogawa a while ago, the Japanese proselytizer of "Mini FM" radio. He explains his interest in this medium by saying "...after the mid-90s, more people became interested in mini-FM as something different from ordinary radio. I argued that in the age of public access via satellite communication, global communication would become somewhat banal; artists should be concerned instead with the micro-unit of the medium." What do you think about this statement, as it relates to your own artistic practice? He seems to suggest that 'universal access' to creative processes will cause those processes to become less interesting (and probably less diverse as well.) Do you think this has really happened?

I think it did not happen. The diversity does not depend on processes, but on people, artists, creators, their ideas, their inventiveness. Concerning the "universal access" I think it is a good thing, and I think all the new media of communication (electronic, digital, radio, internet, satellite etc.) are leading toward the direct exchange of inspiration that will happen between artists and the audience, by the method of telepathy. But we need time to develop a vehicle for that.

I was thinking of you when I was reading another interview, this time with the composer Arsenije Jovanovic. He was speaking about his difficulty working with trained musicians: "Very few [musicians] are completely free, without any cargo of tradition. Those few musicians are completely curious to do something outside of their experience. The rest of them, 99% and more, will not understand what I am doing because they are trained like animals, like dogs, to follow the score...to follow the patterns and cliches. [...] I have been told so many times by leading people of the music world, 'you are so lucky that you didn't attend any music school. Otherwise it would be more difficult for you.'" I thought about Jovanovic' statement in relation to mail art- do you think it is much more difficult for a trained / professional artist to become a mail networker, than it is for a non-professional individual to enter this culture?

It is a good question to address to me, because I am one of very few professional / trained artists who participated in the mail art network constantly for more than a decade. Namely, I finished painting at the Art Academy, but even as a student in 1973 I started sending out postings with my artistic rubber-stamped messages. I was doing classical painting and simultaneously doing mail art as an alternative, but from 1984 to 1996 I dedicated almost all of my time just to mail art networking, and partly to photography, video and performance.

Since, at the beginning, I was doing mail art in the same time period as classical art, it was a gradual transition from one to another. So when I dedicated myself to mail art in the 80s, I already had many mail art contacts and I could do it on a wide scale. But I guess it was more difficult for me than for a non-trained artist to leave all that I have learned behind, and to go into mail art. I had to sacrifice something, but also I think that this transition gave more quality to my dealing with mail art. I think that my mail art missives were more articulated in the visual sense than the average mail art missives in the net. Also, my experience with the traditional art world and contacts with established galleries and art critics (which I also was professionally), made it possible for me to present mail art works in the best way, in good professional galleries and museums, with good display and lighting, good quality catalogs, so in a way my contribution to the network was more significant because of my experience in the professional art world. I left the traditional art in favor of mail art, or communication art as I called it in the beginning, because I was searching for an alternative way of communication and art exchange, and the mail art network was giving me that opportunity. I was able to get to the most remote people and places and offer them my ideas and works, which in classical art was not possible. My art transcended all barriers (geographical, political, national, ideological) and I felt so free and globally present, which gave me a very good feeling and inspired me for new works. The feedback from the network, from distant and unknown creative people always provided a challenge and inspired me to go on. The exchange itself was a new phenomenon in art that attracted me so much. With appearance of the Internet (I bought my first PC in 1996), I left mail art and dedicated all my time to net.art or web.art in the last 15 years. It is a much bigger network with much faster communication, and it gives me even more joy and excitement than mail art used to.

I think your description of mail art as being 'communication art' is intriguing; especially because it contradicts an elitist image that some people have of networkers (namely, that mail artists are weird "anti-social" recluses who don't want to appear in public and don't want to show their art in galleries!) To me, this assumption is false and it makes me wonder who the true "outsiders" are.

Yes, that assumption is false, because we saw networkers meeting, traveling and congressing a lot in huge numbers worldwide. They used to also do street actions and public performances. Just remember Shozo Shimamoto's "Peace Run" that took place all over the world, or Peter Kusterman's year-long project of traveling world-wide to meet other mail artists, delivering them personal mail from fellow artists. Of course there are introverted artists, but we can find them even more often among the 'classical' artists. Not showing in galleries is not necessary a sign of anti-social behavior, but as mail-artists used to say: "the mailbox is my gallery"; they were exhibiting in mailboxes worldwide and it simply satisfied their need for exposition.

For some people, I wonder if this kind of artistic production is a kind of communication therapy: a way for them to learn communication / socialization skills that they have previously struggled with. With the recent arrival of virtual online environments like Second Life, there have been sufferers of autism and other illnesses that have finally found an outlet of 'normal' communication. Have you had any experiences in the mail network like this, where physically or socially disabled people finally found a way in which they could communicate with others?

The mail art network In the Iron Curtain period was an important opportunity for Eastern European artists to exhibit and be recognized in the West, also it gave Westerners a great opportunity to follow creative efforts done in the East. In that time mail art was maybe the only way for artists from East and West to exchange their ideas and art. Afterwards, as the Cold War tension weakened, personal contacts took place. Also, mail art as based on smaller formats, cheaper materials, and simpler production techniques gave a chance to creative people who otherwise could not express themselves. In those senses mail-art activity could have been therapeutic. But also the overall sense of freedom, the possibility to send your art by mail, not having to go after gallerists or curators, but just drop your work into a nearest street post-box, gave that relaxed feeling, which should be inherent to art and creativity.

Vie Ici: Interview With Rod Summers

We will see, time and again, that the world of self-released audio described in these pages has as much to do with methods of social organization as it has to do with methods of making art. The concrete poet, mail art enthusiast and sound artist Rod Summers, who was one of the key individuals providing a bridge between mail art and 'networked audio,' would be one of the first to tell you this. Though based for some time in the Dutch town of Maastricht, Summers' muse has regularly alighted upon Iceland, where we come across an interesting discovery relating to the dynamic between creative organization and art objects: in the Iceland of the tenth to thirteenth centuries (which lacked a king or any centralized power similar to that of other European nations at the time), the *Althing* or "thing" was a general assembly where the Law Council addressed grievances and acted as a judicial institution in lieu of an official executive branch. More notable for our discussion, though, the *Althing* also featured a good deal of ceremony and was "the main festival and social gathering of the year, where people exchanged storied and news, renewed acquaintance with old friends and relatives, and the like."[39] Of course, despite the etymology of the word "thing" taking this meaning of "assembly" or "gathering" into account, the modern definition of "object" remains the dominant one (at least in the English language). It has taken enterprising spirits such as Summers to again unite the two definitions through projects that make art objects the result of assemblies, and that encourage or inspire further organized activities of the same kind.

Rod Summers formed the VEC project in the mid-1970s; a project whose initials could be interpreted as the homophonous French expression *vie ici* ["life here,"] or as an acronym for "Visual-Experimental-Concrete", "Various Eccentric Characters", and so on (further interpretations by people other than Summers were not discouraged.) With "cultural intercourse between consenting artists" as its equally open-to-interpretation "purpose," the audio products issued by VEC did represent more of an ongoing conversation than a conclusive statement, of which the

---

[39] Örnolfur Thorsson, ed., *Sagas Of The Icelanders*, p. 737. Viking / Penguin, New York / London, 1997.

VEC Audio Exchange cassette series was proof. The Exchange, inaugurated in Maastricht in 1978, was one of the first collaborative projects using the cassette medium to suggest a correspondence between the two "things," and consequently one of the first manifestations of what could later be called "Cassette Culture" (note, in the conversation below, Summers' aversion to using VEC for the release of purely musical projects, a fact which shows his sympathies lie closer to that of the non-specialist mail networker.) This was a fluid and unpredictable form of networked art that, like the old Iceland from which Summers' beloved skaldic poetry came, no 'rule-by-decree' was present, yet some form of social organization managed to function smoothly for a considerable amount of time (it's also worth noting that the "all-father" god Odin was also the master poet of this culture.) Summers began his Audio Exchange as a "non profit-making, non-subsidized, artist initiative" in which he solicited works from artists (20 would be featured on each Exchange edition) and then blended the results together on cassettes copied in real-time.

In a way, the Audio Exchange was an outgrowth of his personal usage of open-reel tape recorders to make spellbinding or deftly humorous audio collages, like *Sad News*: compiled from a number of BBC 4 broadcasts that Summers had taped over the years 1973-1978, the piece featured repeated intonations of *"sad, very sad"* spliced between the forced neutrality of BBC announcers' reportage, whose different accounts of daily events eventually become as monotonous as their voices themselves. The cumulative effect of hearing *Sad News* is one of gradual mood swings from amusement to depression (and possibly back again, depending on the listener's personal inclinations.) Whatever the effect of this piece, which has been lauded by sound art documentarian Douglas Kahn, Summers protested that he did not wish for it to reach a listening audience in the traditional sense, but did want it to reach people who would finish what he had started: "it wasn't my policy to send to radio stations, I had very limited funds and the project was directed at getting artists to use their cassette recorders in a creative manner, rather than let the general listening public hear what a cacophonic world artists were living in."[40]

---

[40] Rod Summers quoted in Douglas Kahn, "Where Does Sad News Come From?" Unpublished as of this writing.

Summers' work as a whole has, either unwittingly or intentionally, mirrored the Icelandic situation of the old sagas, where Iceland "was by no means imagined as the center of the world...an element of movement - travel, discovery, and exploration - was an aspect of the earliest narrative literature in Icelandic."[41] Skaldic poetry has also frowned upon a situation of too much comprehensibility, seeing this as poor form- the VEC Audio Exchange programs, because of their strange polyglot glory rather than in spite of it, have managed to survive the fixed stylistic conventions of their time in order to become not just compelling documents of that time, but also raw materials for future invention. In the conversation below, Summers elaborates upon the whys and wherefores of this project, and much else to do with self-released or handmade audio.

++++++++

What were the circumstances that led up to the foundation of the VEC Audio Exchange? Had you previously approached other outlets with the intention of releasing the kinds of sounds you've made available, or was it decided from the outset that a completely DIY medium was the only way to properly present this material?

In 1978, it occurred to me to check out what other artists were doing with sound. By that time cassettes and cassette recorders were readily available everywhere on the planet, and affordable for most people. I had been working with tape recorders and sound for more than 15 years and had several complete works, a few of my mail art contacts had sent me cassettes of their audio works and sound poetry so the next logical step was to make a compilation cassette and use that as trade for audio works from other artists working the mail art network. The basic concept was to exchange and promote audio as a medium amongst artists, so the concept of approaching other outlets never entered my mind. The Exchange cassettes were only available in exchange for audio works- they were never for sale as such.

---

[41] Örnolfur Thorsson, ed., *Sagas Of The Icelanders*, p. xlix. Viking / Penguin, New York / London, 1997.

What was the difference between the VEC audio 'Exchange' and 'Editions' series of releases?

The VEC AUDIO EXCHANGE cassettes contained a mix of the works of several different artists whereas, with a couple of exceptions, each of the EDITIONS contained the work of an individual artist.

You mentioned how some of the people to send you sound works were active in mail art circles as well. I think because today's pop media culture [in America, anyway] tends to privilege recorded music above other art forms, a lot of these people - we'll use Vittore Baroni as an example - are seen as being mainly 'sound artists who had mail art as a side hobby', rather than as being fully-integrated multi-media artists. So, my question would be- how closely related were the 'lineages' of mail art and cassette-based independent music / sound art? Did you find, in the late 70s and early 80s, that there was a very large percentage of mail artists working within the sound medium, or was it just a handful of individuals whose real number has been distorted over time?

First thing I want to do is separate music from sound art. I work in conceptual art, I attended an academy of fine art, I am not a musician and I don't play any musical instrument. When home-produced music became the dominant content of the works being received for the VEC audio exchange project, I stopped the activity. Back in the Seventies there were very few audio artists, that is, fine artists who were using sound as a medium for the creation of art works. The material I had in my possession when I decided to begin the Audio Exchange was; the product of my own activity, read poems by John M. Bennett, a recording I made of an 'eating bananas' performance with Anna Banana, Bill Gaglione, Liesbet Summers and myself, a sound work by Leonhard Frank Duch who was living in Brazil at that time, and a work by Paul Carter from the U.K. The concept of multi-media was still in its infancy, as was that of networking. Mail art was a very convenient method of making contact with artists and suggesting the possibility of developing ideas with the medium of sound. It may be sheer arrogance on my part, but I like to think that many of the mail artists who turned their hand to audio art did so in order to participate in the VEC Audio Exchange Project. As for the number of mail-artists working within the sound medium... a rough estimate of the number of mail artists when the movement was at peak activity was some thousands world wide, the VEC Audio Exchange featured work from just 180 artists from 21 countries.

I don't think... better said I don't *know* if, there was much cross-fertilisation between audio mail art and the Indi-music cassette movement. They were parallel dimensions. The fundamental reason why both flourished had more to do with the global compatibility of the compact audiocassette and the inexpensive cost of recorders, cassettes and postage. Were you aware that this year [2009] celebrates 100 years of audio art? The first documented use of sound by artists was by the Futurist Russolo and, as Futurism celebrates the centenary of the publication of its manifesto by Marinetti this year, it could be claimed that audio art is also 100 years old.

What was it that first led you to record the aforementioned readings and actions-was it a simple need to preserve them, or the possibility that having them available on tape would add some hitherto unnoticed dimension to the work?

Way back when a single transistor was exciting, a tranny was a radio, and chips were made of thin slices of fried potato, I bought my first tape recorder. Just a couple of years later, whilst working at a military base which test fired ground-to-air anti-aircraft missiles, a missile engineer told me that computers were going to be the future, and here I am now inputting this text with one of my three computers in a room full of silicon chip controlled creativity- 3 computers and 2 REVOX B77's. I don't use the tape recorders a great deal anymore, but they are here as I love the solid mechanical technology- which will retain its efficiency long after the computers are languishing, awaiting disassembly in a recycling centre. There *are* things that can be done with sound on a tape recorder that are not possible using a computer. So I had a tape recorder in the beginning of the 60s, 1961 in fact, and in my mind's eye I can still see the machine sitting in the shop window. But what was I going to do with it? The canteen of the base where I was stationed had both a radio and a jukebox, so copying music was not an important option, but I knew from listening to the radio that most of the programmes I was hearing were pre-recorded on magnetic tape and that that tape could be edited to remove errors in the original recording or - and this was what I found most intriguing - edited to create new meanings from that which was originally recorded. For example in the 1950s there was a Saturday morning programme on BBC radio where the disc-jockey Jack Jackson interspersed the records he played with montages of recordings made of comedy records and programmes. So, soon after the purchase of that original tape machine, I bought an editing block and tape and began to create my own realities.

In 1969, whilst still in the RAF, I was serving at a NATO base in the city of Maastricht, in the southernmost province of the Netherlands, and it was there I bought myself a Sony tape recorder and built a tone generator from a Philips kit, and with these two things and an editing block I began to create sound works. Shortly thereafter I met Raul Marroquin, a Colombian artist who was studying at the Jan van Eyck Academy of fine arts in Maastricht, and he informed me that what I was doing could be considered as an art form. I began working with Raul, who was busy with video at the advent of that medium. At the same time I met the Welsh rock musician Tom Winter who was working from Maastricht, and who was also busy with tape recorders and manipulating recorded sounds, and began to produce works with him- one of which is still in existence and appears on the VEC Audio CD *Tacky's Lithe Leaden Lazer Guided Dinghy*. In 1972 I returned to the UK to complete the last year of my contract with the RAF, and within that last year I took a course on tape editing run by the BBC at the University of Hull, only to find that I had self-taught all the techniques offered by the course. On leaving the RAF I returned to Maastricht and entered the Jan van Eyck Academy where I studied Experimental Art and made many audio works like 'Sad News,' 'Severely Spliced,' and 'Purely for Vittore'. I continue to work with Raul Marroquin on his publication, and on communication projects. Tom Winter and I made sound works together, and continue to do so.

So the answer to your question is; I have been recording and manipulating sound as a creative activity since the early 60s- so recording readings, actions, programmes from the radio and naturally occurring events was and is the fundament of my work. Sometimes the recording is a method of preserving an occurrence, for example I record occasional news broadcasts and have American President Ford's last speech on tape but more often it is the collection of material for later manipulation into something that had not previously existed.

Of course reading one's poems and enacting a performance are two totally different things, but I'm still curious what inspires you to record these respective processes.

The concept suggests the medium. When I am trawling my mind banks or even when merely drifting on a tide of thoughts, an idea comes and the appropriate medium to produce the work comes with it. When I write poetry the sound aspect is paramount, all my poems are written to be read aloud. Often the treatment of the sound poem is suggested with the original thought to the point where a text might be written specifically to employ a particular effect. For my performances, I usually do minimal visual activity to a pre-recorded sound track, it is often the idea for the sound work that comes first and the visual aspect that follows. Mostly I prefer to let the sound be the totality of the work, and feel there is no visual aspect necessary- or even that any visual aspect, video or performance would distract from the impact of the sound work. I am a reluctant performer, I prefer to work things out here in my studio and I'm not really comfortable within the pressured atmosphere of creating before an audience. Recording sound, manipulating it and burning it onto a CD so that others can hear it is a very different activity than producing sound 'live'.

Regarding your earlier statements about the separation of music and sound art (and please forgive me for bringing up this old debate again), where does 'music' end and 'sound art' begin for you personally? I do think it's tragic that the majority of people purchasing recordings of any medium expect 'songs' rather than some other form of recorded information, but on the other hand, I tend to find musicality and latent structure in recordings of 'noise' and even the most chaotically assembled recordings of human voice, naturally occurring phenomena etc.

I wonder how many times this question has been raised. I suppose that I consider myself a poet first and artist second and that has an influence on my attitude to sound and music. In the past I have stated that my visual work is textually based and my text is visually based but now that sounds pretentious, so I don't know how valid the expression is anymore. Music... well, I don't much like the current trend for the formless noise music, sometimes the sound thus produced is sublime but mostly it's just noisy buggers who have nothing to say making the air waves shudder. I wonder how your idea of finding musicality and latent structure would apply to my audio dramas.

As I write this text, I am listening to the CD *Greatest Hits* by Tom Petty- but I come from the generation that appreciated Bing, Bach and Brubeck, and was [also] impressed with the conceptual invention of Cage and Stockhausen... I am burdened by the misconception that music has inherent limitations whereas audio art has none... how am I going to explain that now? Music performers are compelled to repeat the same works, over and over again, audio artists... performing audio artists rarely repeat a work... no, that's certainly not it! In most instances music is made by instruments recognised as being created to produce the sounds that constitute music, anything that makes sound can be used to create audio art... no that's not at all satisfying either... I feel as though I just walked into a bog! I don't know where music ends and sound art begins, it's not something I have ever had to think about, all I know is that I make audio art and not music because I'm an artist and not a musician. I am not limited by formal structures like musical notes or rhythms, keys, harmonics or instruments.

My next question would be one related to the international nature of the VEC Exchange project- much of the material on these tapes is based on poetic readings, spoken monologues / dialogue etc., and much of that is recorded in the authors' original languages rather than in the (supposedly) universal English of international commerce. Did you feel that works presented in, say, the various Scandinavian tongues could still convey their messages to listeners of different linguistic backgrounds? Or, put another way, did you feel they had a unique sonic quality that transcended the language barrier?

It has never bothered me to be in the company of people speaking a language I don't understand, I find pleasure in listening to the sounds of speech. Participants in the VEC Audio Exchange project were encouraged to make works in their own language. I was interested in sound, not in comprehensibility. To me the sound of the voice is as important as what the voice is actually saying, and this applies particularly to the audio dramas I produce because, although I do my best to give the scripts content, my main interest with audio drama is to expose voice colour or, as you express it, sonic quality. In my ears the most interesting languages I have heard are those of the Scandinavian lands, especially Icelandic. The first few times I visited Iceland; this summer's visit will be my 17th. Or 18th. I have lost count, I was bowled over by the sound of the language, I found it impossible even to distinguish individual words, I recognised nothing even when I knew the context of the conversation, it sounded to me as though the speakers were inventing what they were saying as they spoke, and I found the sounds they made fabulous. Now I know it is a notoriously difficult language to learn, with some of the grammar and syntax practically impossible for a non-native to learn. My own grasp of the language extends only as far as being able to order a hot dog, French fries with cocktail sauce or a smoked lamb sandwich.

I'm also curious about the Scandinavian artists represented on the tapes, some of whose names I'm seeing for the first time. Other international cassette labels that I've surveyed have focused more heavily on entries from the U.S., U.K. and Western Europe, how did this contingent of artists from the Scandinavian countries come to be involved with VEC?

Whilst at academy, there were Norwegians and Icelanders amongst my fellow students, I am unable to explain my affinity with the Nordics, but I have had an interest in the Viking Empire all my life and when five or six years old I saw pictures of war-time Iceland. In 1981 I was invited to do a performance at the Living Art Museum in Reykjavik and in the week or 10 days I was there I fell in love with the land of Ice and Fire. Immediately after my performance I was invited to teach at the art school for a month and whilst doing that made friends with some of the students who are still close friends today, you can see the videos we now make together by visiting YouTube and entering 'vecdor' into the search window. It has been suggested I must have been an Icelander in a previous life, I think it more likely that I am attracted to the courageous nature of the islanders, the fascinating living landscape, the bird population and the cold clean environment. Besides all of that, there is something about Nordic art I find particularly inventive especially in performance art. Swedish national radio was one of the first to dedicate a series of programmes to sound art; I think the Germans were the first. Audio art was invented by the Italians (Russolo the futurist) 100 years ago, and recorded audio art was developed by the Germans who started by editing the sound track on film, and then developed sound recording on wire, which then led to recording tape.

How much influence has your living environment had on the VEC projects?
Would this whole undertaking be possible if it were done from a different base of
operations than Maastricht? Would, say, Iceland be more suitable, or is your place
of residence ultimately irrelevant to how you create?

I had to think about this. It is rather difficult to isolate how living in
Maastricht had an influence on my creative projects even though that
influence has been significant. I made the decision to remain in Maastricht
on finishing the academy whilst most of my contemporaries moved to
Amsterdam. I stayed here for two reasons, firstly because I love this city
with its rich history, which reaches back 150 million years; there is a genus
of dinosaurs named after this district, the mosasaurs. The Romans crossed
the river here and created settlements in the area, this was the borderline
between the Latin speaking peoples and the Germanic-speaking peoples.
Not 10 kilometres from here French is spoken, 20 kilometres and you find
the Dutch-German border. Napoleon was here, and established a large
garrison in the city. The last major battle of the Austro-Hungarian War of
Succession took place just beyond the city walls. Some of the decisive
battles of the Second World War occurred in this area. In short, this is a
city of major historic significance and yet it is a peaceful place, somewhere
where I could concentrate on the production of my work without
interference or distraction from a perceived requirement to be part of a
'scene'. The second reason to stay here was that the city was kind to me,
welcoming and comfortable, it's hard to explain exactly why but I have
always felt that this is where I belong and perhaps it is that feeling of
stability of residence that led me to venture forth into the world of
international connections.

My love for Iceland is quite different, I stumble around the country in
awe of what I see and, to be honest, I spend more time gawking than
working; Maastricht has history, Iceland has geology. In the past, in the
days when air travel was too expensive to contemplate, I saw Maastricht as
perfectly located to be a base from which I could travel around Europe.

Along these lines, have there been any challenges involved in having a network of
VEC collaborators from around the world, as opposed to mainly interacting with a

'scene' within your own local area? Or, inverting that, have there been any advantages to maintaining a project like this that rather than restricting yourself to that same local culture?

I've answered quite a lot of this with what is written above. I seem to remember that back in the 80s a networking artist from Tilburg suggested that a mail-art networking cell be created to operate within the Netherlands, and at the time I couldn't see any point in that- it seemed that from its very inception mail-art was a system that transcended borders, and its very internationalism was what made it so interesting.

Let me approach this from a different angle: Recently Raul and I were using the video networking system ooVoo to work a 4 way multi-video link between Raul in Amsterdam and me here in Maastricht, and two of Raul's friends, one in Bogota and the other in Medellin. It was about 11 at night here in the Netherlands and 5 o'clock in the afternoon in Colombia, in the darkness of night here, and yet in late afternoon light in Bogota; in a moment of enlightenment I became aware of the globe of planet Earth spinning on its axis beneath solar rays in the vastness of space. Such moments are precious.

The global aspect of the VEC was, in part, a means of achieving an understanding, awareness if you like, of creative humanity. Sometimes, of course, small problems have arisen through language misunderstandings- but over time, one develops a language where these misunderstandings can be, in the large part, avoided, and anyway misunderstandings regularly occur between people who supposedly speak the same language. Most of the VEC core members have an excellent grasp of the English language. I can't remember any occurrence where language has been a barrier to participation in a VEC project, but then, I wouldn't, would I? If the person didn't understand the project they wouldn't bother to participate. As for local culture, Maastricht has its own distinctive dialect and most certainly its own culture, which has undoubtedly evolved from its historical heritage. It is interesting to note that there are at least four artists living in Maastricht who devote themselves almost exclusively to the medium of sound.

Having talked a little about the influence of your environment, I'm wondering what some of the other artistic influences were on your personal work? You mentioned the Futurists earlier, were there any other individuals or movements that pushed you in the direction of creating sound poetry?

In 1961, whilst working on the island of Gan in the Maldives Archipelago I saw (and bought) an album of experimental jazz by Dave Brubeck. This album, *Time Further Out,* featured a painting by Miro on the cover, both the music and the painting were enlightenment. I attended academy at the tail end of the Fluxist movement, and their works were and still are a major influence on mine. I met Robert Filliou, Joseph Beuys, Takako Saito, Emmett Williams, Eric Anderson and many other members of that 60s explosion of conceptualism. The biggest influences upon the way I make my art come from things I saw as a student at the Jan van Eyck Academy, particularly the works of Sigurður Guðumundsson the Icelandic performance artist; Raul Marroquin the Colombian video and media artist and Servie Janssen the Dutch conceptual artist. My current poetry performance work has certainly been influenced by my contact with Enzo Minarelli.

And now for a confession! I have studied several books on art history (Herbert Read et al) and I read two daily Internet Art magazines - one Austrian, one Dutch - but only very rarely do I visit museums or art galleries. For example, I was in Venice earlier this year and, during the five weeks of my residence there, the only museum I visited was the as-of-yet unopened art glass museum of the Berengo Studio. This year saw my first visit to the Maastricht's city museum, the Bonnefanten, and then only because I am exhibiting there in June. I actively avoid visiting art museums and galleries so that I am (hopefully) minimally influenced by the art of others.

I freely admit to influence by Lewis Carroll, Dylan Thomas, Flann O'Brien, and a sway of scientists like Darwin and Dawkins. The Icelandic sagas have also had a major influence on my writing. Several of my friends love pointing out the considerable influence the late Spike Milligan has had upon me.

Did doing all the 'curatorial' work for VEC also lead to a transformation of your art (i.e., did you start incorporating new techniques or approaches into your work that came about as a result of hearing contributions by the other artists featured in the Exchange?)

Undoubtedly! Some of the works I received made me livid, because I hadn't thought of doing that piece myself when, because of my practice, I should have done so. But I am English and a lover of cricket, so I have been programmed from birth to be a gracious loser!

I would think the works that have had the biggest influence on my own sound work have been other poet's pieces of experimental poetry. The work… the live work of people like Kubota and Sutherland (Canada) and Dutch Jaap Blonk is often staggering in its complexity and range of sounds produced by the human voice, their influence, or rather hearing their work has encouraged me to avoid even attempting to go down that vocal path. I have certainly been influenced by John M. Bennett from Columbus, Ohio, hearing him read and reading his printed texts over the last thirty years of our contact has led me to developing my own form of abstract poetry, an example here:

Frane The Virtual
Frane the virtual mori gloss
And barm in glory midas tock
Notter fen inbyro pressed
When quinsly Durham bilag lock
Full ennil bhutol durm intact
And japock frocks were kileray
Best green was in a tirade sterm
And murmer played the rudge all day
Then pult oh fromot liport yearned
Was thus the burlap empty cup
Lorn in excess pressed doily mange
Whilst fedro billing looked her up
Bright jiring elements were brash
Pre Raphaelite and over brushed
Through endless graze born phananthrope
In bobbing excess weedy rushed
No more the intent grim and foil
No more bereft than pindle bake

No more the dorey gimble oil
No more the stilted ingress flake
And so to hermane fillet brought
By verbose insight truly lost
Are brackish kalick wishing wrought
For sixpence and a far thing crossed
All lava braut in basket taal
Sought diamonds in the chilling moss
But finding nothing water raal
Was frane the virtual mori gloss.

(Rod Summers/VEC, Isleworth, 29 January 2008)

A few years ago (2001) John and I did a trans-Atlantic telephonic joint reading of a (via email) joint written poem, live for an audience at a theatre here in Maastricht. I like to believe that was the first ever trans-Atlantic joint reading.

As for new techniques, it may sound arrogant to say, but I believe back in the days of the Exchange project I was way ahead of most artists and poets of my generation when it came to tape recording and computer manipulation techniques of producing, developing and even restoring art sounds. That said, I admit that I saw computer-generated poetry probably 5 or 6 years before beginning to use a computer myself (1983). I also should add at this juncture that even though I've heard a lot, there is such a vast volume of work within the field of audio art and sound poetry that I haven't heard. It is well likely that there are technical tour de forces that way outshine my efforts. Furthermore, the latest generation of sound artists has a superior knowledge of the latest techniques- the question is, do they have the knowledge of experiences and history to be able to use their techniques to produce innovative yet real art?

This is something I've tried to get to the bottom of in my previous writing: how to make technologically-based art without the novel technique and technology involved becoming the main focus or "star" of audiences' / critics' attention. In my humble opinion, even the most radically 'inhuman' pieces can't be totally separated from their human origins [check Yasunao Tone's "Wounded Man'yo" experiments for a prime example of something that uses generative computer

techniques, yet still retains a good deal of the artist's character and experience.]
Why do you think people focus on the technological aspects of sound works so
much- perhaps a utopian pinning of hope onto machines, or some other reason?

Several young people I know have a concept of Utopia and its non-
achievable status, but they still continue to strive to make it manifest and
to a man (or woman) they believe it is humanity that will be the catalyst,
not the computer or its peripherals. I had a conversation today with
someone who shares my belief that dissolution of all religion is the first
step toward a better world.

Related to sound works I think, once again, we have to hark back to
the punk era and the idea of 'keeping culture out of the hands (and ears) of
the over cultured' which, to a larger degree, I agree with... however just
because you can recognise a resistor's polarity and know which is the hot
end of a soldering iron doesn't make you a Robert Moog, and the noise
music instrument you built in your garage does not give you the right to
deafen your audience with a surfeit of decibels and frequency sweeps and
anyway, back in the very early 80s, M.B. (Maurizio Bianchi) covered all
that screaming transistor/feedback phenomenon so, though it may seem
new to you, it has all been done before and to my ears done better. In the
1960s, I built tone-generators from kits; I think my friend Jon Paton in
Nottingham still has some of my built-into-cigar box instruments, and
when I came to play and (sound on sound / sound with sound) record
compositions with these instruments I tried to have a story, an imagined
image or sequence of events in mind and then - hashish assisted - render
and relate that story and its emotional depths and peaks with the sounds
produced by tortured transistors.

Form and content became objects of scorn at just about the same time
as academic achievement became something to be scoffed at. No matter
how hard and with what I have battered my brain, I could never shake my
consciousness free of its desire to give things meaning. There is a picture
behind every story I tell and I tell stories, I don't just blather gibberish... it
might appear so superficially (especially here!) but if anyone asks me
nicely I am always willing to reveal the concept and background to any
work I have made. This, I realize, might not be the current trend, but I
have never been one to follow trends. Style without content is a cul-de-sac

and a shallow one at that. I also realise this statement is not one to make me popular amongst critics and others of the trend following set but personally, sunshine, I don't give a flying f#@k. For me to be satisfied with a work, it needs to have a beginning, middle and an end, and have some non-regurgitated meat on the bone.

People focus on the technological aspect of sound works because they either have nothing to say, or simply that it is the technology that interests, satisfies and absorbs them. If a microchip can be overheated enough to make it make a sound like a bumble-bee with a digestive gas problem, all well and good, but if I go into the field or hedge to record said dyspeptic winged insect, at least I'm getting some fresh air and exercise.

So what kind of advice could you give to young sound artists or sound poets today, who have an unprecedented amount of access to creative technology?

Read a book or two! Read *SOUND BY ARTISTS* edited by Dan Lander and Micah Lexier. Read the books on audio art by Douglas Kahn. Research what the Futurists were doing 100 years ago; study the works of John Cage. Listen to John Lennon's "#9." Read the sound blogs by people like Harold Schellinx. Listen to Scott Williams on WFMU New Jersey, get informed, go Google. For would-be sound poets read the poli-poetry manifesto by Enzo Minarelli; get hold of a copy of the anthology of sound poets by Dmitry Bulatov. Avoid reinventing the wheel and do try giving some expression to your own creativity, have something to say. Unless you are 100% sure that the sound you have devised is previously unknown (a very unlikely situation) be inventive; apply your imagination to what you have realized technology can offer you.

Why We Tape:
Cassette Culture As A Real Alternative

Where to begin? As far as the divergent practices in this book are concerned, deciding upon a single, resolute 'genesis' point for their existence is a task verging on the impossible. When considering an art form where distance and delay once played a major role, and in which public unveilings of works were much rarer than the more gradual, perhaps 'viral' accretion of artistic influence, we have little to work with when trying to identify a singular *"... they called it 'unofficial audio', and it was good"* moment. With no such images on hand to make these book's practices seem on par with the aforementioned events in terms of its heroic significance, we'd have to draft up an image from scratch: although this would take us into the sillier realms of Social Realist artwork (I'm envisioning a image of a square-jawed, broad-chested 'audio worker' gallantly striding towards his local postal drop box to deliver some home recordings, as squadrons of airplanes fly by approvingly against a crimson background.)

Now, we could merely settle for an image in which human artifacts are present, but no historical 'actors' themselves, The stock image of the cassette tape, that celebrated recording medium of yesteryear, seems to exude its own romance as well as its own characteristic poignancy (of 'audio messages' and 'demo recordings' undelivered or unheard, of home-spun 'mix tapes' designed as a last-ditch attempt to communicate deep feelings towards an object of affection via a succession of pop-rock Cyranos.) Its perfect vertical symmetry also lends it a kind of anthropomorphic quality, with the tape spools seemingly staring back at the user like a pair of inquisitive eyes, with their tiny plastic spokes for 'eyelashes'. Arguably, part of the cassette tape's lasting appeal comes precisely from such an ability to play on humans' attraction to pareidolia (that is, the perception of ambiguous visual or audio information as resonating with deeply personal communications- e.g. the visage of Christ being seen on the toasted bread of a grilled cheese sandwich.) Cassettes have managed to survive long enough to be circulated in alternative distribution networks even today, so maybe there is something to this theory. At the very least, cassettes' pareidolic design point is not lost among the advocates of so-called music piracy past and present, who have replaced the skull in the skull-and-crossbones 'Jolly Roger' flag with a bone-white cassette tape. Meanwhile, the sight of unspooled magnetic tape contains its own analogies for this particular kind of human endeavor: seeing so much glistening raw material stuffed into an unassuming, tiny plastic shell, it's easy to begin contemplating limitless possibilities and to ignore the grim realities of inhabiting the finite system that is our planet. The surprisingly lengthy amount of magnetic tape that can be wound onto a reel can seem, at times, like a metaphor for the complex mass of organs and nerves compacted inside of our mostly symmetrical exteriors- or even the billions upon billions of synaptic connections that exist within something so humble in appearance as the human brain.

The word 'cassette', as my colleague GX Jupitter-Larsen reminds me, is French in origin and can be translated as "little box"- so quaint and unassuming when contrasted with the romantic symbolism above. Several variants of the "little box" have existed, with the chief in popularity being the now-iconic "compact audio cassette" design (which almost all the references to "cassette" in this book allude to), known in industry or scene jargon by other acronymic titles as "MC" or "K7." The easily pocketable micro-cassette, developed by Olympus at the tail end of the 1960s, has also existed for dictation or speech applications (though this has not stopped enterprising artists like the Tampa-based Hal McGee from recording decidedly more unorthodox audio on it.) The blank compact audiocassette would eventually become popular enough to spawn several different variations in *bias* (meaning the choice of either an alternating or direct electrical current to boost the audio signal) and the numerous types of magnetic tape coating (e.g. the chromium dioxide of DuPont / BASF.) Like many other portable media of a "little" or compact nature, the cassette's diminutive quality was not a drawback- it is, in fact, the very reason for whatever widespread popularity and value (exchange value, sentimental value and so on) that it enjoyed. If we follow the hypotheses of media studies titans like Marshall McLuhan and his forerunner Harold Innis, small and portable media have been responsible for such seismic cultural shifts as the replacement of idol worship with monotheism: the papyrus scrolls used to transmit Biblical texts played a major role in this regard, solidified by the eventual transition to codices (an early manifestation of the 'random access' method of reading, as opposed to the sequential reading demanded by scrolls.) Later on, the arrival of paper in Europe (from China by way of Arabia) also dramatically accelerated the rate of scientific and mathematical achievements on that continent. Though we should avoid a pure "media determinism" that ascribes the great leaps in human activity solely to these objects intervening in human relations, there is no denying them their role as the revealers of latent communicative faculties, as culture accelerators that re-excite dormant modes of thinking and feeling by giving these attitudes a 'new look'. To use Bruno Latour's terminology, such objects are never less than "co-producers" of society precisely because of these abilities to "embody," "materialize" and so on.[42] Along these lines, media theorist Friedrich Kittler notes tape's value as a cultural catalyst, as well as its being the content of another medium. According to Kittler:

> With the audiotape and the cassette, sound acquired for the first time the same material format as film: as a roll that allowed variable time axis manipulation, unlike the phonograph and he gramophone. Not only are time reversals possible, as with Edison, but also stop tricks, cuts, and montages, as with Méliès. The simple manipulable acoustics of audiotape led to rock music, as you know, which could in turn be coupled with manipulable videotapes, and the video clip was born.[43]

However, despite his invoking rock 'n roll, Kittler is not so quick to proclaim the use of audiotape (or really any recording medium) as giving societies' insurgents and revolutionaries the upper hand in the ongoing info-war against standardizing and centralizing authority. For example, regarding the introduction of sound film to the public, he reminds us that film's new sound component caused "...Hollywood to become a branch of the newly electrified record companies like Western Electric or General Electric, which possessed both radio stations and record companies at the same time and which, in turn, were only branched of large banks like

---

[42] See Bruno Latour, *We Have Never Been Modern*, p. 54. Trans. Catherine Porter. Cambridge University Press, Cambridge MA., 1993.

[43] Friedrich Kittler, *Optical Media*, trans. Anthony Enns, p. 192. Polity Press, Cambridge MA, 2010.

Rockefeller or Morgan."[44] It is a statement typical of a thinker who tends to see the military-industrial complex as one of, if not the, driving engines of modernity (lest we also forget the aforementioned GE's status as one of the most defense contractors in the U.S.) It is admittedly difficult, even when dismissing military operations as the *single* cause of audio-visual technologies' development, to find accurate technological histories that deny the military sector had any role in overseeing and refining certain functions of these new tools. The German army's early use of the tape recorder, for example, is outlined in an anecdote given by Nikita Krushchev. [45] And, interestingly enough, Krushchev would later have his own place in the history of recording technology when his 1959 "kitchen debate" with Richard Nixon was filmed using Ampex videotape (in typical Cold War fashion, the then-rare use of this medium became a boasting point for American technological advancement over that of the Soviets.)

All this aside, though, such examples are easy to uncover with just a minimum of research, and where direct military intervention does not lead to the design and production of new consumer technology, experience within the military sphere often provides non-material qualities that lead to future developments: the Sony corporation - home of both the TR-55 transistor radio and, more importantly for cassette propagation, the Walkman portable stereo - was formed by Akio Morita and Masaru Ibuka, who originally worked together designing bombs during WWII (the technological shift from vacuum tubes to transistors enabled not only portable radio technology, but the eventual upgrade from open-reel tapes to compact cassettes.) We do not always have to look to a culture of destruction for innovations in creative technology, though. The genesis of modern technologies, including information-duplicating technologies like

---

[44] Friedrich Kittler, *Optical Media*, trans. Anthony Enns, p. 194. Polity Press, Cambridge MA, 2010.

[45] "I remember once when I was at Stalin's, Molotov told the following story: he had summoned Schulenberg to his office, where Schulenberg noticed stenographers making transcripts of radio broadcasts and remarked, 'why do you have to make stenographic copies...?' Then he cut himself short, but Molotov stored the incident away in his memory. He realized from what Schulenberg had let slip, that apparently the Germans had some mechanical means of recording radio broadcasts and therefore didn't need stenographers. [...] Secret radiograms are transmitted very rapidly, and it's impossible for a stenographer to copy them down. [...] Thus, Schulenberg's offhand comment to Molotov gave us our first hint that the Germans had invented tape recorders." Nikita Kruschchev, *Kruschchev Remembers*, trans. Strobe Talbott, p. 131. Little, Brown and Co., Boston, 1970.

the cassette, is as caught up in the history of philanthropy and dreams of social harmony as it is in wartime contingency. Joe Wilson of the Xerox Corporation, and co-developer of xerography alongside Chester Carlton, was noted for his strides in these areas, as well as for his then-radical ambition to make his company one of the most racially integrated in the state.[46] Xerox, of course, has its own esteemed place within DIY history: though the Haloid-Xerox company's print ad campaign for its famous 914 copier exclusively stressed its office applications, there can be no doubt that the affordable operation of it and its progeny (which required no sensitized paper, film negative or liquid chemicals) sparked a multitude of folk art styles as well. Xerography enabled homemade poster / flyer art, mail art and other manifestations of extra-institutional artwork, not the least of which were the thousands of "j-card" cover designs accompanying one home-dubbed cassette after the next.

The above discussion is important because, when we talk about recording media, there is virtually nothing available that can be entirely built from scratch: whether the medium is magnetic or optical, analog or digital, there is no feasible option for creating the *medium itself* in one's own home or studio (even "de-physicalized" sound or video files require the use of computers, a decisive minority of which are purely homemade devices.) At least in this aspect of their work, "home tapers" - that contingent of creators that otherwise act independently of professional recording studios, established record companies, and collusion with advertisers and sponsors - are still at the mercy of some external forces. Consequently, the myth of completely independent production is one that needs to be dispelled before going much further. However, it's possible that framing the debate solely in terms of control over production is to take the wrong tack. "Cassette culture", like mail art before it, solved a problem that the Fluxus artist Nam June Paik outlined as follows:

> [Marx] thought that if workers (produced) OWNED the production's medium, everything would be fine. He did not give creative room to the DISTRIBUTION system. The

---

[46] Joe Wilson's "Fight On" initiative, co-organized with Rochester activist minister Franklin Delano Roosevelt Florence, was "the first attempt by the U.S. government and private industry to start a business wholly operated by African-Americans." See *Joe Wilson And The Creation Of Xerox* by Charles D. Ellis, p. 298. John Wiley & Sons, Hoboken, 2006.

> problem of the art world in the 60s and 70s is that, although the artist owns the production's medium, such as paint or brush, even sometimes a printing press, they are excluded from the highly centralized DISTRIBUTION of the art world [capitalizations in the original.][47]

Yet it was more than just a means of seizing the forces of distribution for oneself: distribution in the post-industrial age has taken on the gloss of a very impersonal activity, where communication with the distributors will revolve solely around the strategic movement and placement of product, while the distribution involved in cassette networks could be much more of a interpersonal affair: this interpersonal cassette distribution provided opportunities not just for more "shop talk" about who in the scene was recording what, but for insights into all aspects of the various creators' lived experience. It is the control of the distribution process that really differentiated the new form of "Cassette Culture" from other independent initiatives: this caused its weirder and wilder exponents to come about, but, more importantly, ensured that this particular form would never make a complete transition from *art* to *industry.*

Was it just a distrust of the recording industry - and industry in general - that kickstarted the revolution, though? This is not quite the case: A good deal of historical data points towards Cassette Culture's being born out of other contingencies. This brings us back, temporarily, to our musing about warfare being the motor of much civilian ingenuity. The 1973 OPEC oil embargo, resulting from the Yom Kippur war and the United States' decision to supply the Israeli army in that conflict, affected the cost of producing vinyl records and made them less desirable in a period when consumer spending was curtailed (owing to government mandates for energy use and to more localized, private fears.) Naturally, the supply-side shortage also meant that record companies were decidedly more cautious about the release of "experimental" or non-proven recordings. While this did not lead to an immediate public appropriation of the cassette and to a concurrent boom in self-releasing, we can speculate that this period had at least some effect on "non-essential" artists' attitude to the record industry:

---

[47] Nam Jun Paik quoted in "Fluxus Practice" by Owen F. Smith. *At A Distance: Precursors To Art And Activism On The Internet,* ed. Annmarie Chandler and Norie Neumark, p. 131. MIT Press, Cambridge MA, 2005.

that is to say, even a brief spell of economic hardship would cause the industry to cut loose purveyors of "new" sound. It was therefore prudent to identify and embrace alternatives to working with them. It's also notable that, though the compact audiocassette tape had been in use for audio applications since the 1960s (with the portable Norelco "carry-corder" making life easier for journalists and beat reporters), the increase in fidelity necessary for quality storage of music came about a few years after the 1973 crisis.

In times of blanket economic hardship, sound-makers would not be exempt from challenges themselves: and so, the cassette offered distinct advantages over the "closed" format of the vinyl record. For one, the availability of custom-length cassette tapes in a wide variety of different running times (commonly from 'C15' to 'C180,' with the number designating the total minutes' worth of recording space on the tape reels) gave artists greater freedom to make individual releases as long or short in duration as they saw fit, bypassing needless anxieties about having to "fill" a side of a record album. Alain Neffe, who fronted the Belgian umbrella organization Insane Music (comprising the electronic groups Pseudo Code, Bene Gesserit, Human Flesh, and others) saw in tapes a positive use that shouldn't go forgotten: "…if, for example, you [press] 1,000 albums and sell 100, you have 900 pieces of vinyl left, and what to do with them? If you release a cassette and don't sell it, you can record it again. There is no loss."[48]

Of course, Neffe's suggestion applies just as easily to the *purchase* of a cassette that has proven to be sub-par: the money or goods exchanged for the cassette can't be recovered, but at the very least its contents can be wiped clean and replaced with something more palatable. This practical usage of the cassette has gone overlooked in contemporaneous debates dealing mainly with sound quality and design aesthetics. The reusability of cassettes gave them a slight head start on the "recycling" culture that crested in the 1990s (thanks in part to the *Mobro 4000* barge debacle), and only with digital downloading has the issue finally become irrelevant. Few people who found themselves with unwanted compact discs ever used them as coasters - as the all-too-common criticism suggested for disappointing listens - and the practical uses of both CDs and vinyl records

---

[48] Alain Neffe quoted in "Insane Music," *N D* #10, 1988. *N D*, Austin, Texas.

did not, except for the most imaginative and resourceful individuals, extend far beyond their intended use as audio storage software. So it is interesting to note how much the recyclability of cassettes was taken advantage of, long before the habit of recycling became coded into law with regards to municipal waste disposal. In one amusing case - RRRecords' "Recycled Music" series - used cassettes of commercially released pop / rock albums were taped over by ignoring the easily circumvented write protection mechanism on these cassettes, with cover artwork being merely a strip of adhesive tape with the "new" artist's name plastered over the original artwork (adding to the black humor is the fact that, in some cases, the original audio bleeds through and forms jarring contrasts with the work of the "recyclers.")

What Kind Of Person Enjoys Home Taping?

Maybe a little too much time has already been spent on justifying the existence of this particular medium, without considering specific cases of artists who benefited from it. Yes, the cassette tape and all of its supplemental equipment (the 4-track "portastudio" and the like) enabled a mind-boggling array of different personalities to make some inroads into public consciousness, but it is unfair to treat the personalities themselves as mere side effects of the medium. Rod Summers, already introduced here, is a fine example of the kind of friendly iconoclast who would come to embody all the various minutiae of this practice, but countless other points of entry exist outside Summers' (admittedly wide) circle of influence.

Take for example the long-haul truck driver Mike Johnson, who music writer Bart Plantenga reminds us "...was already in trouble the day he chose country music because, you see, he is black."[49] Further removing Johnson from conventionality is his skill with yodeling, a musical signature that makes no concessions to "coolness" in an era where "fat" bass pulses and synthetic mirages (e.g. the voice-altering "Auto Tune" software) are the meat-and-potatoes of young music' fans sonic diet.

---

[49] Bart Plantenga, "DIYY: Do It Yourself Yodelers," p. 11. Previously unpublished, 2008.

Johnson began his yodeling habit in the mid-1950s, when "Western movies ruled the silver screen" and "singing cowboys were favorites [...] I imitated them too"[50] (Johnson also gives special acknowledgement to the swimming star Johnny Weissmuller, better known for popularizing the vigorous "Tarzan" call in the movies of the same name.) When cassettes first became a viable means of distributing music, Johnson began to entertain serious thoughts of becoming a country music singer:

> I'd been seeing cassettes in a number of truck stops and I thought why not? The first place to accept my homemade cassettes was the Union 76 in Montgomery, Alabama. The second was a Union 76 in Slidell, Louisiana and then one in Chicago. That led to a gradual expansion and I began exploring a marketing approach. I always had plenty of flyers [2000 at a time!] which I displayed on barroom walls, shop windows, western clothing stores and motel walls.[51]

Johnson had previously experimented with DIY methods (such as using a self-timer on his camera to make a record cover for his first 7" single), although the cassette offered more than just a means of getting his yodels into sympathetic shops and truck stops: it was a companion during the many hours on the road, where Johnson suddenly realized he could record vocals while still in his rig, rather than waiting for the end of the day when he settled into his hotel room. Johnson gleefully recalls how "you should have seen the faces of passing cars looking up, seeing this wild-eyed, wide-mouthed trucker just singing away!"[52]

It's unclear, from Plantenga's biographical portrait of Johnson, whether he doubled as an active participant in the cassette "network," by means of trading and correspondence with other active nodes. It seems doubtful that he would have been unable to find a home there if so desired. The surviving magazines and other documents of the culture showed a

---

[50] Mike Johnson quoted in Bart Plantenga, "DIYY: Do It Yourself Yodelers," p. 11. Previously unpublished, 2008.

[51] *Ibid.*, p. 16.

[52] *Ibid.*, p. 15.

significant amount of respect for individuals whose personal commitment encouraged reassessment of those styles that were otherwise out of favor with the critical *zeitgeist*.

In a separate audio galaxy from Johnson, there exists the work of bioacoustic researcher, former entomologist and legitimate nomad Francisco López, whose sonic output - inspired in no small part by the "schizophonia" concept of *musique concrete* maestro Pierre Schaeffer - comes completely from natural sources (López has regularly claimed that the earth itself is the most intriguing "sound generator.") López' simple "schizophonic" technique of not identifying his sources, coupled with demanding concert experiences wherein the role of the sound stage is nonexistent, have helped to cement a reputation for him as heir apparent to the sonic legacy of Futurism (albeit with no stereotypically 'futurist' political agenda.) Confessionals about encounters with his sound output are themselves quite evocative, ranging from " I felt like on a trip from hell to heaven" or "[like] flying inside gigantic moving machines" to visions of "dinosaurs eating soup" and "shreds of laminar light going through my body."[53] Now one of the foremost exponents within the field of "experimental music," with hundreds of distinct releases available in every commercial format, it is easy to forget that López also began his career in cassette circles (perhaps as a belated tribute to this, López has recently released a collaborative cassette with Louisville audio addict Zan Hoffman, the contents of which are a live performance using cassettes as sound generators.)

Prior to the days in which his globe-trotting began in earnest, and the Amazonian rain forest was as much of a home to him as his native Madrid, López was a regular collaborator with other experimenters such as New York avant-gardist Amy Denio, tape manipulator Rafael Flores, the jazz trio of Jorge Valdemar, and Miguel Ruiz, with whom he collaborated on a children's movie soundtrack (this period also proceeded López' characteristic habit of releasing most of his sound works as numbered "untitled" pieces in unadorned packaging.) López' talent for cross-cultural communication (local gossip in present-day Madrid claims that his English-speaking skill surpasses that of his mother tongue) clearly

---

[53] Francisco López, Personal email correspondence with the author, August 2, 2011.

developed during this time, providing an ancillary skill that would help him to retain contacts as his work - in the 1990s and beyond - became more highly personal and more demanding of active participation on listeners' behalf.

The inclusion of López as an example here is not being done simply to "play him off" of a character like Johnson, or to construct some inaccurate spectrum of cassette-based creativity that has "down-home American authenticity" at one end and "post-human schizophonic experimentalism" at the other (although it is interesting to note the common nomadism that comes from their highly differing professions.) Rather, this is a further attempt at illustrating just how many points of entry were available into this culture: one could be a techno or hip-hop producer slowly gaining clout through the local distribution of collaged "mix tapes," or a sound poet interrogating both language and the mechanisms that record and modulate it, or a Mike Johnson yodeling into his handheld tape recorder while driving down lonely stretches of American interstate highway. Once the decision to "home tape" was made, one could remain within a genre-specific "neighborhood" of the total network, or seek out experimental connections and provisional alliances with contrasting styles, via creative hubs like the VEC Audio Exchange or the many other labels built on this model. The latter was far from impossible- as one example, the superlatively quirky singer-songwriter Jad Fair occasionally appeared on cassette compilations where he was the "odd man out" in a mix of insistent electronics and mechanical pummeling.[54]

Many other artists involved in Cassette Culture defy full discographical reviews, because the emotional tenor of their recording activities is as diverse as what they experience in their everyday lives: while an artist like Zan Hoffman can capably collaborate with López in the realm of haunting or austere soundscapes, he can also engage in more humorous flights of fancy- one long-running projects of Hoffman's was an all-acoustic revue in which live sets consisted of "cover versions" of works from the cassette underground. Naturally, Hoffman's incessant activity has necessitated the creation of a personal label ('ZH27') to catalog it all. Kindred spirits, like the Californian Don Campau, follow a similar pattern

---

[54] See the 1982 "Kalkulator" cassette compilation on the Dutch "Tear Apart Tapes."

of trying anything and everything to paint the most accurate picture of where they currently stand in the game of life: spontaneously alternating pop structures and free-form experimentation as it personally suits them, rather than opting for a long-term strategy of pre-meditated "phases" of creativity.

The quest to delineate a single "home-taping" type is, indeed, futile, although detractors of the practice like to employ, from time to time, the expected caricature of an unattractive and inward-gazing reject who turns to rudimentary music-making as some kind of "last resort" for social acceptance. This is not to say that people fitting this description are completely non-existent, but enough evidence exists to shatter the claim that this stereotype encompasses the vast majority of Cassette Culture enthusiasts. For one, veteran sound fetishists such as Francisco López, John Hudak, Ken Montgomery, and Scott Konzelmann (a.k.a. "Chop Shop") have leavened their domestic taping activities with demanding itineraries of global travel. Others, like the pop maestro R. Stevie Moore, have made it clear that their status as so-called "reclusive" at-home musicians has little to do with social timidity, but much to do with a distrust of manipulation by market forces. Still others, like self-described French "trash artist" Jean-Louis Costes give so much of themselves in public performance actions that it is the audience that wants to retreat into more private spaces (Costes, in addition putting on the dementia-tinged morality plays alluded to here, once designed each individual J-card on his early tapes by hand.) All in all, the "first division" of cassette artists has made serious challenges to the accusations of insularity.

Shaky Alliances? The Art World, The Music-Buying Public, And Others

The individuals comprising this sector of the independent arts world did not, by and large, define themselves by the taping practice alone: one's self-identification as a participant in Cassette Culture did not automatically preclude other creative commitments, or signal an exclusive commitment to so-called amateurism (the career of Francisco López, again, provides an object lesson in this.) The relationship of the cassette artist to professionalism could at times be one of indifference, and occasionally one of outright hostility- to the point where music labels specializing in commercially available cassettes could be seen as diluting or misrepresenting the energies of the tape-trading and home-dubbing networks. Like any new communications technology, cassettes were prone to consumption by a market that cared only about their transitory or fashionable novelty value, and not about their potential to act as the conduit for a much more venerable tradition of self-determined creativity. In a 1983 editorial entitled *Die Casettenszene* written for the German *Katastrophe* 'zine (the brainchild of tape label proprietor Graf Haufen, and one of the earliest German-language periodicals to tackle the subject with gusto), Gerd Neumann[55] lashes out against the then prevalent trend of cassette festivals that were "really, for the greatest part, only third and fourth class rock music with a hint of modern, commercial electronic music."[56] His unequivocal shout of "fuck Ding-Dong and R.O.I.R." from the same editorial - directed at the pre-eminent outlets for 'commercial Cassette Culture' in the Netherlands and U.S., respectively - is a bit harsh and ill-advised considering those labels' representation of genuinely adventurous or otherwise neglected material, although Neumann's primary complaint was not unjustified (to wit: " green hair and '*legalize it*' is not enough [to bring about] a new impulse.")[57] Neumann's brief contribution to the *Casettenszene* 'roundtable' discussion implied that the search for a "new Punk" had reached desperation levels, only a couple years after the original manifestation had been declared dead: predicated on finding a perfect reconciliation of marketability and radicalism, some scene-makers were using the "radically new" recording medium of the cassette as a convenient stand-in for "radically new" content (a tacit admission that they had given up on attempting to find the latter.) Neumann's protests demonstrated, if nothing else, the existence of parallel "Cassette Cultures" with very different attitudes towards the medium's social significance.

Yet was it truly impossible for medium and content to *both* be something sufficiently, or even challengingly, new? One fear of home-

---

[55] Also of the post-industrial combo "Non Toxique Lost."

[56] Gerd Neumann quoted in "Die Casettenszene" by Graf Haufen. *Die Katastrophe* #11, p. 12. Graf Haufen, Berlin, 1983. Translated from the German by the author.

[57] *Ibid.*

tapers in the 1980s, as touched upon by Neumann above, was that any sort of compromise with institutions larger than one's own cottage industry would commence an inevitable 'regression to the mean' of commercial culture: the cassette, whatever its origins may have been, was providing a rare opportunity for artists to set the parameters of both production and distribution, and this was something to be fiercely protected. This, naturally, could lead to its own kind of counter-productive dogmatism, and suspicions that professionally duplicated products circulating in the same networks as the legitimately "homemade" items were attempting to dictate acceptable codes of conduct to those networks.

For many who did produce cassettes of that nature in the 1980s, the attraction was not the ability to craft an authentically "homemade" product, but rather the medium's built-in adventurous listenership and the alternative distribution network set up by them. The symbolic status of the cassette tape may have been appropriated by more professional concerns, but it was not always to the detriment of the die-hard home-tapers. The Tellus "cassette magazine", inaugurated after a meeting at New York City's Rum Runner Bar in 1983, was formed by a curator / artist alliance consisting of Claudia Gould, Joseph Nechvatal, and Carol Parkinson, and was itself an extension of the non-profit Harvestworks Media Arts program. Of Tellus' approach, Nechvatal states that, "the magazine concept lent itself well to avoiding the standard mixtape syndrome of a label. Also we did not represent artists. We presented interesting work thematically."[58] In this sense, Tellus had a kinship of sorts with other early attempts at using tapes as a "digest" of currently intriguing styles and attitudes, like Rod Summers' VEC Audio Exchange: the Tellus series saw new artists being featured alongside established ones, while completely new works were also programmed in close proximity to historically relevant works. One Tellus cassette was completely given over to the work of the Fluxus movement (as represented by Georges Maciunas, Dick Higgins, Alison Knowles, Emmett Williams and others), while another - *Power Electronics* - was a showcase of overloaded and confrontational 'pure electronic' music, something which would become a regular staple of Cassette Culture. Still other tapes explored the possibilities of audio works done by artists more commonly known for their visual work, or compiled

---

[58] Personal email correspondence with the author, April 22 2009.

experiments with texts spoken by computerized voices (*False Phonemes.*) Each of the three founding individuals behind Tellus had their own guiding interests, which influenced the themed "magazine issues," although Nechvatal insists that the 'editorial collective' dynamic was not incommensurate with more individualistic aspirations: "it was a combination of the two approaches...no rules, but we always agreed on the themes and supported each other's passions."[59]

The Tellus project's "official" institutional connections included sponsorship by the National Endowment for the Arts, HBO [Home Box Office Entertainment], and Philip Morris, while simultaneously achieving distribution through Cassette Culture bulwarks like Ron Lessard's RRRecords. Corporate endorsements are far from unheard of in the culture of the international, post-WWII avant-garde, but are an issue that must be taken on a case-by-case basis. Often these actions are supremely ambivalent, if not outright baffling, gestures of goodwill (like several corporations' donation of equal sums of money to *both* finalists in recent U.S. presidential races): they have insufficent power to influence cultural events. The rationale behind arts funding can be equally hazy: often the only corporate directive that can be extracted from this practice is that corporate culture should be tempered with more "innovative thinking" of any stripe. For the more cynically minded, these acts of stewardship are an unorthodox means of the funding bodies proclaiming their financial robustness (i.e. they can afford to divert profits into ventures that will not benefit them in turn.) At any rate, for many who saw Cassette Culture as being heir apparent to Ray Johnson's non-institutional, network-as-artwork paradigm, the mere association with art museums and their financial backers must have been tantamount to blasphemy. Yet a closer look at the Tellus catalog shows that it had as many connections with the grassroots Cassette Culture as it did with big name sponsorship: Nechvatal himself has contributed soundworks to other trusted labels (e.g. Al Margolis' Sound of Pig), while numerous cassette networkers have themselves appeared on Tellus releases. The cross-pollination that was characteristic of the networks continued unabated, and the threat of institutional intervention was fairly short-lived. In the final reckoning, virtually no sonic material from the "Cassette Culture" period has been

---

[59] Personal email correspondence with the author, April 22 2009.

recycled for use in advertising or for promoting contradictory agendas, a fact of which many independent-minded artists working in "official" media cannot boast.

Network vs. network

It was the wont of nearly every under-represented cultural faction in the American 1980s, from urbane classicists to gruff hardcore kids, to decry the lack of taste among the mainstream consumers who were now consuming in such visible quantities. It was amazing, they thought, that this impressionable droning herd of people clad in 'shop-'til-you-drop' t-shirts could consume in such quantity and yet never chance upon any of the cultural artifacts that were the pride of these under-represented groups. Coming to these mega-consumers' defense for the moment, though, they were far from being the only agents of taste making: a considerable number of behind-the-scenes string-pullers and independent promoters also proved instrumental in that regard, and were equally instrumental in deciding what did *not* get played on the airwaves as they were in cherry-picking certain recording acts for super-stardom. It's somewhat ironic that, in the midst of this narrative on networked audio, this criminally-connected enterprise of chart-fixers was referred to by recording industry insiders as 'The Network'- yet it would also be naïve to imagine a world where competing networks with conflicting interests don't exist. In this case, the 'Network' of independent promotion agents had as much of a hand as anyone in shaping the activities of the cassette network: thanks to their efforts at squeezing indie labels out of the radio market (and the retail shops whose buyers based their purchasing decisions on positive responses to radio airplay), other options became necessary for those who merely wanted their recordings heard. Using the flawless hindsight that is characteristic of the fiber-optically connected 21st century, it's easy to condemn the 80s consumer base alone for its paucity of resourcefulness and adventurousness- but this is far from being the whole story.

Perhaps it's also a little disingenuous to insist on a bi-polar music world split evenly between pure-hearted indie producers and criminal-minded racketeers in the service of the record industry (which, again, is a mere outgrowth of electronics multinationals such as Philips and Sony.) On the other hand, criminal manipulation of the record industry (most often through the unique form of bribery known as 'payola,' a portmanteau of 'payoff' and 'Victrola') is not something that is poorly documented. When such manipulation is not outright illegal, it does raise serious questions about how tastes are formed: namely, has the music that we deemed to be the most popular become that way because of a real consensus among listeners, or has this music become popular simply by default? That is to say, because listeners' choices were limited to music selections that were chosen by people who could afford to run the most cutthroat and persistent promotional campaigns?

It's hard determining to what degree the war on small record labels was fought over purely ideological or aesthetic grounds. To be sure, many top record executives of the era showed open disdain for more novel forms of music, especially ones they perceived to be in open revolt against conventional mores.[60] One thing that we can be fairly certain about is that small labels were seen as competition for a piece of the overall market share, not as potential collaborators. For those operating in the indie music world today, it is not uncommon to have an "open relationship" with a label and to have several releases concurrently available on different imprints. However, collaboration was not in the cards then, nor was the compromise that became more common in the 1990s, whereby an indie label would receive a certain number of 'points' from the major label that had just made a recording deal with one of the indie's marquee acts- thus allowing that act to help keep its former employers' operations afloat and to partially deflect the inevitable cries of "sellout." Irving Azoff, then president of MCA Records, suspected an anti-competitive function as one motivating force for the independent promoter network of the 1980s

---

[60] At least one clear example of this was MCA Records' refusal to distribute *Damaged*, the 1981 LP by the influential hardcore punk group Black Flag. *Damaged* was originally released on the Unicorn label, which had a distribution deal with MCA, although MCA distribution boss Al Bergamo intervened on the grounds that he found "nothing of redeeming social value" on the album, adding that "as a father of two children, I found it an anti-parent record." Seeing how Bergamo's disapproval would more likely energize Black Flag's fan base rather than alienate it, the band eventually warped his statement into a kind of endorsement for the record, printing it onto a sticker that covered the MCA logo on the album's sleeve.

(although he himself was making whatever use of the 'network' he could). Azoff claimed that his archrival at the head of CBS Records, Walter Yetnikoff,

> ...'tried to 'corner the market' on indies by hiking fees to the point where smaller labels wouldn't be able to afford them.' In a pre-trial deposition, Azoff said that Walter 'once told me that one reason CBS supported the indie system was that he felt it made the cost of entry for, shall we say, new upstart labels [too] high to get into the record business.[61]

Payola, on the whole, has not been a crime that has generated that many column inches in the press, especially when the payola-spawned pop musicians themselves provide such a rich source of material for the various tabloid papers and indignant opinion columns. Their tragicomic penchant for drug-fueled mayhem, domestic violence, and public obscenity charges have, over the years, provided far more grist for the mill of public outrage (and titillation) than their corporate minders' unethical attempts at maintaining financial advantage. Indeed, Fredric Dannen's authoritative book on the 'Network's' development claimed that, "...to date [the book's publication in 1990], no one has ever served a day in jail on payola charges. The law is hardly a strong deterrent."[62] Some rock 'n roll historians have even given the practice a kind of heroic cachet, claiming that the bribing of disc jockeys in that genre's formative days helped it to get on air in the place of the kind of vocal music that is now relegated to 'easy listening' playlists. Having criminal entities involved in getting rock 'n roll records aired would, for many rebellious youth, just have given an added jolt of excitement to an already exciting game of chicken played against decency and authority. Archetypal rock DJ Alan Freed had already gotten into trouble for opining to his Boston fans that "the police don't want you to have fun," setting the defiant tone for the frenzied early days of the genre. Of course, it was Freed's acceptance of record label payoffs that first led to the practice's being made illegal in

---

[61] Fredric Dannen, *Hit Men: Power Brokers and Fast Money Inside The Music Business*, p. 265. Random House, New York, 1990.

[62] *Ibid., p. 45.*

1960.

Champions of rock 'n roll might, however, stop seeing payola as a necessary evil when they realize that it was the much-maligned disco craze that really put 'The Network' on the map. Fredric Dannen chalks this up to a couple of different factors: disco not only "...breathed life into the Top 40 format, after a decade of strength in album-oriented radio," but was, more insidiously, "fueled by hype- by the mistaken belief that hits are bought, not born."[63] In effect, it provided the ideal climate for 'record men' to moderate public tastes rather than letting those tastes develop organically.

So, what was an "organic" and spontaneous social order supposed to do when the game was rigged against it? The simple answer would seem to be for it to just stop playing that particular game: to withdraw and reassess what it really wanted from its involvement with the audio arts. It's easy to conceive of this withdrawal as a retreat, accompanied by defensive rationalizations - "*I didn't want it anyway!*" - meant to alleviate the bitter pain of a dream deferred. Yet Cassette Culture, which blossomed on the same point of the musical timeline as "The Network," was spread at a manic and prolific pace by its constituents- the febrile energy that was put into these self-determined productions was not the kind of energy expended by depressed defeatists, but by enthusiastic people who had finally found an outlet for free communication. International fame and grand payouts may not have figured into this culture, but many of the other attractive features of modern music culture did: collectability, the thrill of watching selected artists develop and mature (or just implode in an intriguing manner) over the long term, and of course the promise of hitherto unexplored sensations and ideas. What ultimately compensated for the lack of monetary and compensation, though, was the increased likelihood that participants could further influence and warp these ideas, and personalize these new sensations.

Eventually, certain record company executives would become highly critical of 'The Network,' and, if not criticizing it from an ethical

---

[63] Fredric Dannen, *Hit Men: Power Brokers and Fast Money Inside The Music Business*, p. 157. Random House, New York, 1990.

standpoint, would come to see it as a budget-draining undertaking: it was an expense that could no longer be sustained, since the music industry was (in the estimation of these record executives) facing serious competition from the nascent video game industry. Shortly before devices like the Sony Walkman reconfigured where and how audio recordings could be enjoyed, home video game consoles were seen as something that would battle with the home stereo for consumers' leisure hours. Yet 'payola' and related practices have continued to shape the face of popular music, while the "big six" major labels of the 1980s (EMI, MCA, CBS, PolyGram, WEA, BMG) have been whittled down to a more imposing "big four" (following Sony's acquisition of BMG, and the MCA/BMG merger that formed the Universal Music Group.)

An important point to remember, in the midst of all this, is that distrust of international corporate networks did not mean a concomitant rejection of international contact and a retreat into provincialism. Bruce Russell, who curated the New Zealand label Xpressway from roughly 1988-1991, offers his own reasons for disconnecting from the world of "official" formats, however temporarily:

> ...there's another way of looking at it, and that is that there's people that are at the same level you are, with the band and the independent label, everywhere in the world. Those people are the ones often doing the interesting stuff you want to be associated with, and you build bridges directly across to them. You don't go up through the rungs of the hierarchy, you just ignore everything that's happening further up that chain and go straight across to people in the same position overseas.[64]

Just a perfunctory look at the websites archiving Cassette Culture will show that Russell's approach has been widely adopted: the scene as such was brimful of international cassette compilations, label rosters built up from artists separated by oceanic distances, and collaborations conducted by mail. The latter innovation deserves special attention, since, in the spirit

---

[64] Bruce Russell quoted at http://www.furious.com/perfect/deadc.html. Retrieved October 18, 2010.

of Ray Johnson's mail art projects, it envisioned correspondence as being carried out by means other than purely verbal communication. In this context, the home portastudio became less of a tool for fashioning "demos" and more akin to the present-day computer with Internet connectivity. The effect of the various international collaborative practices was to create a culture that, unlike much of the jet-setting cosmopolitan intelligentsia, saw the crossing of national borders as something more than just a way of staving off local boredom or a means of outpacing one's peers in the realm of "exotic" experience. International contact via tape did not provide a kind of ornamentation to help with social advancement, but was a leap into a world that could actually be quite humbling for those who thought of themselves as cosmopolitan. The challenge was then to convert this ego deflation into positive experience.

We should not be too hasty to praise the collaborative aspect of Cassette Culture as its most radical or novel feature. Rather, it is important to see it as being a post-industrial extension of an artistic tradition that stretches back for centuries and cuts across a wide swath of geographic territory. The Japanese 'collaborative poetry' practice of *renga*, originating as *lián jù* in Chin-dynasty China, involved "'chain poems' sometimes scores of verses long…collective creations that changed the writing of poetry from an art with social functions to a genuinely social pastime."[65] Its grounding in 'high' culture, despite its comparatively 'low' function of social entertainment, undoubtedly led to *renga* being "full of wit and spirit…spiced with puns and double meanings" although with "elaborate rules decid[ing] just where in the chain certain seasonal images must appear, as well as the number of times words such as 'moon' or 'flower' may be used."[66] Like Cassette Culture, *renga* composition parties also made a point of disregarding the social status of individual participants, who arrived at these parties disguised with masks: in the highly stratified Japanese society of the time, anonymity was required in order to keep participants from having any inhibitions about their poetry skill (e.g. the fear that they might be seen as trying to upstage the local magistrate.) The real novelty of Cassette Culture was not its collaborative aspect, which

---

[65] Yoel Hoffman, *Japanese Death Poems*, p. 16. Tuttle Publishing, Tokyo / Rutland, Vermont / Singapore, 1986.
[66] *Ibid.*, p. 271.

manifested itself in everything from compilation albums to elaborate *cadavre exquis*-style remixing projects, but, again, the transmission of these collaborative tendencies over oceanic distances.

Regarding networks in general (and the newer online social networks in particular), cultural critic Peter Sloterdijk raises an interesting question when pondering "might it be the case that networking itself designates only a state of organized weakness?"[67] It is true that many such support groups, especially those presently being formed with the help of services like Facebook, do little more than "connect" people whose energies are too widely dispersed to have a cumulative effect. Recognition of other people in a similar state of dejection or stasis may be very helpful for the individual survival of people within these groups, but something other than this mere acknowledgement of others is necessary for clearing open new spaces (virtual or otherwise.) So, even at this early point in this volume, it is worth taking an accounting of Cassette Culture and asking if it was, itself, a state of "organized weakness" or a sturdy counterweight to the official audio culture. To do this, some attention should be paid to the inventory of complaints lodged against the cassette networkers and their sympathizers.

Taping And Its Discontents

"Cassette Culture" came to be applied to such a broad variety of personalities, opinions, and intentions, that criticisms of its efficacy were almost certain to arise in amounts proportional to the praise lavished upon it by its proselytizers. At the forefront of these contentious issues was the issue of "instant access" that the cassette networks provided. Would there really be enough self-imposed restraints to keep these circuits from being overloaded with self-indulgent and distasteful throwaways? Would those who entered the networks as a refuge from the sentimental inclinations of "the people" play nicely with those who saw *all* homemade works as having documentary merit? As with the online social networks of the present, there was always an "ignore option" where pieces of poor

---

[67] Peter Sloterdijk, *Rage And Time: A Psychopolitical Investigation*, p. 184. Trans. Mario Wenning. Columbia University Press, New York, 2010.

craftsmanship were concerned, but would that alone suffice to make this virtual space a mutually profitable one for everyone involved? Speaking in *Electronic Cottage* (and with the benefit of some early 1990s hindsight) musician Murray Reams - erstwhile owner of the Sound And Fury cassette label - shines a skeptical light onto the cassette networks' perceived inability to criticize their own; something readily available in other musically inclined social environments:

> The audience [for Cassette Culture] has already dwindled, and will probably decrease more. Much of the Cassette Culture has worked in a negative way. Many people have put forth an appearance of being subversive or counterculture- they do this through band names, titles and the imagery that's connected to their band or label. But a lot of the music is not worth the tape it's recorded on...it's fluff. A different kind of fluff than Whitney Houston, perhaps, but it's still fluff. [...] A lot of the network has been made up exclusively of people who produce cassettes and work exclusively within their homes. They never perform live, for whatever reason they rationalize, and thus they never experience the reaction and criticism of a live audience.[68]

While he does not affirm Reams' comments about live performance, which imply "playing out" as being a necessary function of any "real" musician, former home-taper Jim O'Rourke does see another traditional institution (the professional sound studio) as being an essential ingredient of that "real" musicianship:

> I no longer record at home. I only record in studios now. Some people will call me elitist or something, but they are missing the point. Music is not a hobby for me; it is what I am doing with my life. [...] I just think this home-taping thing is in danger of sucking a lot of people into a situation where they look like hobbyists, dilettantes. Some people

---

[68] "Murray Reams Interview" by David Niklas, *Electronic Cottage* #6 (July 1991), p. 27. Hal McGee, Apollo Beach, Florida.

> are damn serious about doing it full time. It is a great
> starting place, I think the best, but you can't expect people
> to stay there for their whole lives.[69]

O'Rourke pours more fuel onto the fire by stating "...a lot of the politics of home taping bothers me. I don't want to get a tape in the mail from somebody on a cheap tape, and then they expect something of mine back. What the hell! I don't even have a copy of my own!"[70] While O'Rourke's comments may be understandable from the perspective of someone who fancies himself a tradesman (no pun intended), there is a certain amount of troublesome vagueness to the statement *it is what I am doing with my life,* as well as the distrust of "hobbyists" as an adversarial type of audio artist. These statements seem to posit a culture where an additional layer of technological superiority makes an activity more alive, or one where a reverent attitude towards (studio) technology marks the threshold between first order and second order creation. By viewing the home-taping culture as a way station *en route* to the terminus of "serious music", O'Rourke himself is missing the point already suggested by the mail art networks: when immediate and unfiltered communication is the goal of an artistic production, rather than, say, reputation building and concern for posterity, it becomes ineffectual to brand someone as a dilettante. There can be no denying that the benefits normally associated with studio technology - more tracks on which to record, more finely-tuned sound reinforcement systems, more options for mic'ing and room recording - can help to sculpt a more nuanced piece of expressive work. Yet, as the obstinate popularity of 'lo-fi' recordings attests to (as well as the more recent trend of using 'high' studio technology to *emulate* low fidelity), each level of technological enhancement carries its own message. That message is not perfectly replicable with technological means higher or lower than what that particular level affords.

With all this in mind, a key problem of the home taping network has been one of conflicting attitudes towards its ultimate purpose or non-purpose. Like a public bicycle trail, anyone is free to ride, yet the serious

---

[69] "Interview With Jim O'Rourke," by Jeph Jerman. *Electronic Cottage* #6 (July 1991), p. 69. Hal McGee, Apollo Beach, Florida.

[70] *Ibid.*

racing cyclists who frequent the trail curse the less speedy travelers who wreak havoc on their training routines, just as those same slow-but-steady bikers detest the arrogance and misplaced ambition of the bike racers. Similar attitudes, from time to time, played out within the network. For would-be serious composers such as O'Rourke, the cassette network was a virtual recital hall in which "auditions" took place. If all went well with these preliminary recordings, they would help to secure the contacts and financing that would lead to residencies in professional studios and collaborations with already established artists.[71] Seen this way, cassettes circulating in the network were like the "demos" meant to grab the attention of major label A+R men, although with the added bonus that these "demos" could still be treated as a normal saleable commodity if they failed to attract attention. Though this was one possible use of the cassette network, many who entered into it had no ambitions for working outside of it, nor did they perceive this lack of ambition as a character defect. When Don Campau states "I am interested in home recorded productions especially...I have NO interest in the music business...I welcome the music people create for fun and art"[72] he speaks for that portion of the network that sees it neither as a springboard towards respectability, nor as a last resort for posthumous recognition.

The many criticisms leveled at Cassette Culture's lack of seriousness should be familiar to anyone who has studied self-determined art or DIY in the post-industrial age. One of the popular rallying cries of diy media has always been something along the lines of "anyone can do 'x'". Of course, the potentially radicalizing "anyone can do 'x' serves to discourage as well as encourage, this being the stock dismissive phrase used by people who view anything but pure representational art as rank charlatanism- invoking the concept of universal access remains a convenient way to

---

[71] Jim O'Rourke is nothing if not a prolific collaborator: The interview already quoted mentions his live or recorded work with Derek Bailey, KK Null, Illusion Of Safety, and Morphogenesis, while stints in Sonic Youth, Gastr del Sol, and Fenn O'Berg would follow. Although his nose for high-profile collaborations has led to some critical claim, his greatest detractors have also seen this as a careerist attempt at 'positioning.' One ex-colleague of O'Rourke's, the composer Zbigniew Karkowski, claims "it's all about the need to be accepted...one of biggest cowards around is Jim O'Rourke." (personal correspondence with the author, December 29, 2009.)

[72] Don Campau quoted at http://www.doncampau.com/NoPigeonholesSubmit.htm. Retrieved November 2, 2010.

point out that the 'emperor has no clothes'; to proclaim that the divergent forms of avant-garde or experimental media are all a disingenuous bit of legerdemain conferring an undeserved power on a societal class with no other demonstrable skills. Whether this simple phrase is used for the encouragement or discouragement of further artistic developments, though, one thing remains clear: when we take "anyone" to be a shorthand for a perfectly average or unremarkable type of person, not everyone *has* done 'x', nor are they likely to do an about-face and begin doing 'x' in the near future. From Fluxus to Punk and so on down the line, art movements open to those without formalist skill have never completely succeeded in courting a so-called "average" type (and, in most cases, the influx of such everyman types into the scene only came about when these movements were already on the wane.) The post-industrial "average man" is one defined by passivity and by the reservation of productivity for designated working hours, a type that would generally not have the courage to submit deeply personal expressions to an international body of peers. For all the talk of home-tapers' inferior production values and slipshod works, it has to be said that they still maintain an above-average level of conviction, determination and sacrifice. Banal personalities may engage in these types of activities for a time, but soon wilt under the unexpectedly pressuring demands of an unsupervised creative process.

Carl Howard, who once ran the Audiofile Tapes label, admits that the chaotic non-purposive character of the home-taping network was simultaneously positive and negative. For example, the same openness that led to a more vibrant spectrum of audible sound made any kind of cataloging efforts a Sisyphean task:

> Several years back, when I was publishing *Artitude / Audiofile,* I began to believe that if I toiled long enough and dug deep enough, I would eventually become on top of all the ingrowths and outgrowths of the cassette music community. In a way it's comforting to know that no matter how hard you try, you just can't do this; the scope of the community is too vast and volatile. And just when you think you've got it down to something as cold and clinical as dBase, someone up and moves, or some new kid passes you off their first masterpiece and the cards will be

thrown up all over again.[73]

Of course, Howard was not alone in his attempts to properly document the network before it expanded beyond any ability to do so. Contemporaneous radio programs like the UB Radio Network of Das (Big City Orchestra) or GX Jupitter-Larsen's "New Sounds Gallery" made an admirable attempt at capturing this continually fluctuating phenomenon, while magazines such as *Sound Choice* and *Factsheet Five* seemed to exist primarily as an aid with the navigation process (offering constructive criticism of individual works was secondary to this.) Nevertheless, Howard's statements here point at an answer to our question posed above about the "organized weakness" of networks. When he states that he is comfortable working in a culture of perpetual unknowns, he implicitly shows that Cassette Culture is not a network in the sense of, say, the support groups available for everything from fantasy role-playing enthusiasts to overeaters: the crucial distinction is that the goal of its spontaneous organization is not stated at the outset, and this - along with its ability to constantly elude authority-seeking "experts" - paradoxically contributed to its strength and resilience. It was not uncommon for people to enter into home-taping and tape-trading with no clear idea of who they would encounter in the network; confessions of the kind made by Banned Productions' AMK (Anthony M. King) are plentiful in the scene: "I did a lot of my early [cassette] recordings in a vacuum. In fact I read more about new music than heard it.... I would find books in the library about the avant-garde, and try to duplicate what they where doing."[74]

The attacks on Cassette Culture's perceived flaws - its cynical assumptions that fellow marginalized individuals will "buy anything", its desperate and meaningless self-assertion - continue unabated, but now target the cassette medium's successors. These days, with digital audio workstations making respectable facsimiles of the recordings that are done

---

[73] Carl Howard, "Da Muse Ain't Enough." *Electronic Cottage* #1 (April 1989), p. 16. Hal McGee, Apollo Beach, Florida.

[74] Anthony M. King, Personal email correspondence with the author, July 1 2010. Curiously for "extreme noise" enthusiasts, AMK's addenda to this quote point to an influence outside the realm of electronic experimentation: "listening to [John] Coltrane's *Om* or *Ascension* was and still is a startling revelation. Music like this was being made before I was even born. I still think this is the most extreme music I have ever heard, not only because of how it sounds, but how it got there and why."

in professional sound studios, it appears that the "home-taping" culture has had the last laugh on those who follow the O'Rourke line, although this appearance of victory over official audio does not mean that the denunciations will taper off anytime soon. But what good, really, are these denunciations? They may repel some potential members of a listening audience, but it's safe to assume that the creators themselves will just continue to shrug at these critiques. They do, after all, base themselves on the assumption that Cassette Culture was the side effect of the professionalism that couldn't be attained, rather than a sidestepping of the professionalism that few participants cared about to begin with.

Did 'Taping' Survive 'Tapes'?

Those who have participated in Cassette Culture in the past are rarely prone to grumbling about how they had to "settle for" releasing their works on a cheap "2nd-class" format; they shrewdly approached the medium as they would any creative tool. With so many people in the cassette underground possessing advanced knowledge of the whole of modern art, and not just limiting their scope to the audio sphere, certain anxieties about public acceptance and critique were less prevalent than in the milieu of serious musicians: if nothing else, anyone who has set foot in a major art gallery can testify that the cost of artists' source materials does not play as much of a role in getting their work sold as do the shifting caprices of the art market itself. Such tastes seem to be formed largely out of buyers' desire for an artwork to comment upon, reflect and embody their life experiences, or to instill a sense of otherness beyond those experiences. With such variable criteria for determining artistic worth, a modest pencil sketch on an A4 sheet of paper can feasibly command the same market value as a painstakingly intricate, glass-blown fantasy object crafted by Dale Chihuly. So, armed with such knowledge of commodity fetishism and the general transience of creative works, the more well-heeled "tapeheads" rarely attached a sense of shame or inadequacy to their practice- seen from the larger perspective of full-stop creative practice and not through the narrower lens of commercial music production, many tape networkers understood well E.M. Cioran's aphorism: "the inexactitude of its ends makes life superior to death."[75]

When the self-released cassette medium did become 'ghettoized', it was normally done on the behalf of 3rd parties (music magazines etc.) rather than those who were directly involved in creating sound works on cassette. This has happened even in organs sympathetic to all things DIY and non-commercial: the influential 1980s New York City broadsheet *Op*, despite being one of the most dependable sources of information on this subject, still preferred to review self-released cassettes in a separate column entitled "Castanets," saving the main review section for the more established vinyl LP format (more tape-centric 'zines such as Bryan Baker's *Gajoob* capably picked up the slack.) As such, even one of the more authoritative voices of "indie" America tacitly acknowledged that different motivations for sound making required different types of journalistic treatment, and perhaps undermined its otherwise egalitarian approach to reviewing the sonic arts. Sure, cassette labels such as the Belgian Red Neon Tapes merely updated mail artist Lon Spiegelman's "mail art and money don't mix" maxim by commanding *"make music, not money"* on their packaging- yet this alone shouldn't have qualified them a status as curios or novelty items. Doing so puts too much focus on the static concept of *tapes* when dynamic *taping* was the true attraction to all of this: the tape, as a conveyor of self-released audio, was ideally an informative resource generative of more information, and not a "pure product" signaling the end of the creator-listener relationship. As we'll see in the chapters to come, those who acknowledged this fact allowed for the ethos of self-releasing to take on whole other incarnations.

---

[75] E.M. Cioran, *A Short History Of Decay,* p. 11. Arcade Paperbacks, New York, 1998.

Laser Sharp:
Self-Released Audio Goes Digital

In accordance with the Geneva 2006 Agreement, June 17th of 2015 is the date in which all analogue television transmissions must be switched out for digital signals, while the European Union has decreed the end of 2012 to be its own analog "switch off" deadline. Numerous Western nations (e.g. Switzerland, Finland, Andorra and the Netherlands) have already completed this transition ahead of deadline, and many more complete switchovers are now underway. For a book centered primarily on audio technology, rather than televisual transmissions, this seems like a meaningless aside- yet it is a valuable indicator of the state of digital communications as a whole. After all, many of the same arguments revolving around the digital TV transition echo the animated debates over other digital media: whether we are speaking of the leap from analog TV to digital TV, or the attempt to make analog audio obsolete, we encounter a brace of optimistic and pragmatic souls that see the digital technologies in utilitarian terms, and a host of skeptics that see this increased utility as an enticement to abandon spiritual values and cede control to centralized authority. Proponents of the TV switchover note its usefulness in freeing up radio spectrum, while some of its detractors see it as another ploy for State monitoring and tracking of its citizens (and, as the line of argument goes, the eventual auctioning of that 'freed' 84Mhz of radio spectrum will mostly benefit the government, whose coffers will be filled in the process.) Digital skeptics will also proudly note that the "superior quality" of digital television is a highly subjective determination, and one that glosses over digital TV's own unique defects (e.g. choppy pixelation, rough gradients between colors, and the occasional complete loss of signal.)

The digital television switchover has been yet another episode highlighting the irreconcilable differences between what Luciano Floridi identifies as the culture of "here" (analogue, carbon-based, offline culture) and the culture of "there" (digital, silicon-based, online culture.) Although he notes that the distinctions are "fast becoming blurred" and are "as much to the advantage of the latter as it is of the former,"[76] plenty of purists from either camp choose to gleefully ignore this attempt at pacification. As the battle rages with respect to television, it also rages within the worlds of photography, printed material, and all other digitized communications, not the least of these being audio. Once the "digital" imprimatur was stamped on all these diverse media, and came to designate a fully-integrated lifestyle (as still exemplified by *Wired* magazine, the sturdiest redoubt of "digitalist" culture), the battle lines were drawn between itself and the previous analog culture, valiantly fighting for its life against a bombardment of hyper-velocity, miniaturization and eventual immaterilization: these were phenomena that analog culture perceived as being boons to business, but a kind of blight on the soul. As its primary defense, analog culture defined itself as the preserver of intensities and continuities that, albeit more inconvenient to mankind in general, were crucial to the maturation of more ineffable qualities: this was not the case for "discrete state" technologies that allowed one to jump from one clearly defined state to another without any experience of a transition. Although we'll see in a while why this criticism of digital technology is erroneous, let's focus for now on the 'battle lines' themselves and not the correctness of the respective sides in this battle.

For the more fervent keepers of analog faith, the introduction of a more high-resolution, noise-resistant storage medium did not mean (and, in fact, likely detracted from) the development of higher quality content. It would be inconsiderate to claim that all of these digital skeptics saw the new speed of information delivery as being the deathblow to heterogeneous culture, or that they believed 'bad' culture was exclusive to digital media. All the same, a belief has persisted in some corners that digital technologies invade 'organic' social rituals and cultural artifacts in a way that somehow attenuated their potency. Taking this a step further, there is the belief that the analog signal - which fluctuates in accordance with the information received - provides a metaphor for a healthier mode of social organization than the digital signal, which is coded as a discrete set of either-or values. The 'science studies' theorist Brian Massumi provides a colorful summation of the romantic attraction to analog living when he describes it as

---

[76] Luciano Floridi, *Information (A Very Short Introduction)*, p. 16. Oxford University Press, Oxford / New York, 2010.

...a continually variable impulse that can cross from one qualitatively different medium into another. Like electricity into sound waves. Or heat into pain. Or light waves into vision. Or vision into imagination. [...] Variable continuity across the qualitatively different: continuity of transformation.[77]

Of course, objections to digital living do not come about purely because digital life does not unfold in as sensual or natural a manner as what Massumi describes above. Many analog loyalists distrust what they perceive as the purely utilitarian thrust of the digital project: by making the performativity of digital tools the main concern, their makers and appropriators are supposedly ignoring moral values of good and evil. By contrast, others might suggest that this very performativity is what causes digital technology to have something approaching 'good,' ethical values (e.g. the empowerment of the financially disadvantaged, or of underrepresented segments of the larger population.) Nicholas Negroponte - who, among other attempts at 'digital age ethics', co-developed the $100 XO1 "children's laptop"[78] with former UN Secretary General Kofi Annan - was one of the most prominent public figures to take this view, which he expressed as follows:

Being digital will change the nature of mass media from a process of pushing bits at people to one of allowing people (or their computers) to pull at them. This is a radical change, because our entire concept of media is one of successive layers of filtering, which reduce information and entertainment to a collection of 'top stories' or 'best sellers' to be thrown at different 'audiences.'[79]

However well-intentioned he may have been when writing this, Negroponte's words will not offer that much succor to the analog purist:

[77] Brian Massumi, *Parables For The Virtual (Movement, Affect, Sensation)*, p. 135. Duke University Press, Durham / London, 2002.

[78] The $100 list price has never been an actuality, though it was the eventual goal of the XO1 project.

[79] Nicholas Negroponte, *Being Digital,* p. 84. Alfred A. Knopf, New York, 1995.

what he describes above is more of a net benefit for the consumer rather than for the producer, those "process-oriented" individuals who gain more joy from constructing and modifying reality than from selecting, collecting, and appraising slices of "frozen" reality. So long as the "pro-analog" wing of self-determined culture conflates 'being digital' with 'being virtual' (a fallacy that, again, will be dealt with soon enough), it sees itself as the preserver of vitality, resilience, and the ability to truly effect evolutionary change.

Being Optical

Prior to the revolution in laser-readable or optical storage media, magnetic storage had been in use since the 1940s- with the former offering information storage capacity several orders of magnitude greater than the latter, it was only a matter of time before optical media became considered for audio applications.[80] The writing seemed to be on the wall already in 1979, when Philips offered its first public demonstration of the new technology in Eindhoven- in 4 years' time, consumer CD players would be available in the dominant music market of the U.S., and by 1985 optical storage media would also be available for home video entertainment (laser disc players) and for use in computer peripherals (the CD-ROM drive.) The compact disc seemed as frighteningly different from collective experience as any novel technology, with its stored information being encoded onto regions called "pits" and "lands," and with its mirrored, prismatic playing surface trapping the bewildered gaze of the user. Truth be told, most record companies reacted coolly to the new format, too, though it would come to eventually generate windfall profits for them. The development and popularization of the compact disc remained a high-stakes operation for a number of intimately linked conglomerates, especially considering Philips home audio division, Polygram[81], was experiencing its share of difficulties at the time. While in the developmental stages, the actual recorded content on the discs was only

---

[80] Erasable compact discs, of course, combined both magnetic and optical technologies: lasers were used to change the polarity of magnetized areas on their light-sensitive surfaces.

[81] Polygram itself was an umbrella organization for a number of different record labels, including Verve, Pickwick, and Casablanca.

one important element among many. As Fredric Dannen describes it

> ...the CD was a priority for its inventor, Philips, which viewed the record business as the software supplier for its all-important stereo hardware. Had PolyGram not been a means to help introduce the CD, it is questionable whether Philips would have borne the financial losses for as long as it did. Siemens, the German industrial giant that owned the other 50 percent of PolyGram, did not make stereos, and its impatience with the money-losing unit had reached a breaking point.[82]

Meanwhile, the home computer industry, which was experiencing a sales slump around the same time that the compact disc was in its infancy, pinned its hopes on the compact disc's potential to make computers accessible again to the layperson. Early CD-compatible peripherals, like the CD drive accompanying Digital Equipment Corporation's Rainbow and MicroVAX microcomputers, were indeed the toast of mid-'80s electronics trade shows, where they wooed numerous other industries with a severely increased level of cost efficiency for information accrual and transference. Elsewhere, converts like Dr. Dave Davies (the manager of 3M's nascent optical recording department) spoke in the enraptured tones typical to those who believe they are on the cusp of a revolutionary and progressive change, stating things such as "it becomes almost no longer a question of...any limits possible...it becomes to the point where a single disc can approach the human brain." Ironically, given the compact disc's eventual role in re-shaping the popular music landscape, some commentators within the computer industry did not see the CD as something which would act as a stand-alone audio playback format; these same commentators also envisioned the re-writable disc as coming into common usage long before the 'fixed' disc. Because of this, much thought at the time was put into scarcely remembered formats like the WORM disc (an acronym for "write once, read many"), which would not experience a resurgence until the CD-Rewritable (CD-RW) was introduced years later.

---

[82] Fredric Dannen ,*Hit Men: Power Brokers And Fast Money Inside The Music Business*, p. 253. Random House, New York, 1990.

It's interesting to note, given the high-tech mystique that accompanied the compact disc upon its arrival, who counted as its greatest supporters. Rather than a battalion of electronica fanatics and latter-day Futurists, it was the classical music audience who initially snapped up the silvery circular medium in such large quantities. Dannen again recalls that

> ...the music-buying public had gone compact disc crazy. It did not hurt that PolyGram had the world's richest classical catalog, since devotees of classical music were among the most ardent music customers. The demand was amazing. A vinyl LP of, say, a Strauss tone poem that you could not sell for $3.99 retail flew off the racks as a CD costing four times that amount."[83]

As Dannen alludes to above, the first 'test' CD to have been published was, indeed, a Herbert von Karajan / Berlin Philharmonic recording of Strauss' *Alpensinfonie*. Meanwhile, it was the electronica fanatics and latter-day Futurists leading the charge to preserve the large-groove vinyl record: the format became almost mandatory for club singles spanning the whole spectrum of electronic dance styles. The analog format's staying power within that subculture owed itself in part to the oft-cited (but rarely quantified) properties of "warmth" and "punch," although we can also theorize about the larger and more visible format's greater appeal as a stage prop for DJs who wanted to remain large and visible themselves.

Having said all this, perhaps the most articulate *cri de couer* against the nascent CD came from Steve Albini, the mercurial fanzine writer and studio engineer who had little love for electronic dance music (or any musical genre that saw the vaguely defined tasks of the 'producer' as being superior to the efforts of musicians themselves.) A compilation CD of material from Albini's band Big Black, entitled *The Rich Man's Eight Track Tape*, bore all the marks of being released as a grudging favor to his label Touch & Go: the CD's cover art was a sort of still life composed from the titular playback device and a host of other 1970s relics, while the disc's

---

[83] Fredric Dannen ,*Hit Men: Power Brokers And Fast Money Inside The Music Business*, p. 262. Random House, New York, 1990.

surface printing derided the consumer for choosing it over a superior vinyl product (among other things, the erudite Chicago noise merchant recommended that the disc's owners use it to make sandwiches on, since the durable construction of the disc provided its only real advantage over extant storage media.) Albini castigated Philips for using the CD as "the next stage of its market-squeezing bonanza," but ultimately took the optimistic long view that the flame of the compact disc fad would burn out soon enough ("the future belongs to the analog loyalists," proclaimed the sleeve of Big Black's 1987 LP *Songs About Fucking.*)

As it turned out, though, the future was a much less cut-and-dry affair: the "analog loyalists" did indeed remain a vociferous minority, whose backing turned the vinyl LP from a mundane household object into something of profound importance. The music retail world, however, shrugged at their protests and - in the case of larger chain stores like Virgin or Tower - all but totally eliminated vinyl from their shelves by the mid-1990s. For them, the benefits of the compact disc, such as the greater amount of product that could be stocked owing to its smaller size, far outweighed its aesthetic shortcomings. The compact disc was easily sold on the casual consumer of music, but there was already one audiophile elite (the aforementioned classical music audience) who favored the CD, and so there was little need for the record industry to cater to the needs of a second, less moneyed audiophile elite, with their subjective opinions about "warmth" and the kinesthetic quality of placing records on turntables. Plus, for those who were still able to sustain a vinyl-only musical diet, a 100% analog listening experience still required an analog amplifier as well.

Burning Issues: The Introduction Of Recordable CDs

If we can say one thing about the culture of self-released music, it is generally not dogmatic. So, when an opportunity for cheaply recording onto CDs finally presented itself, the culture did not stand as one to reject it, and did not waste a great deal of time howling about how the compact disc was the province of patronizing 'classical snobs' or bloodless audiophiles. In retrospect, the relatively cheap and widespread use of CD burning technology is an easy thing to take for granted: in the mid-80s infancy of the compact disc, industry insiders like Digital Equipment Corporation's Ed Schmidt were scoffing at the idea of a $700 drive to read CDs with fixed contents, let alone one with disc-writing capabilities ("I'll believe it when I see it," he said in response to a rumor that Atari was developing a drive of that price for its 520ST computer.)[84] Now that high-speed CD and DVD burning 'super drives' have become a regular fixture of every Apple laptop, Schmidt's skepticism joins the ranks of other famously off-the-mark techno-prognostications like Bill Gates' immortal "640k out to be enough for anybody." If the designers of the technology took some time to come to grips with its full potential, though, the record industry was even more in the dark.

The introduction of the recordable CD, or CD-R, caused a major conundrum for that industry because, while it clearly allowed for unauthorized copying of their content, it also enabled vast amounts of visual and textual data to be ported from home to office. So, unlike the tape decks of previous generations, record industry lobby groups could not raise a hue and cry against this new technology so easily: while they certainly may have lost sleep over its ability to 'steal' vast libraries of their product by making perfect facsimiles of the original recordings, they could not justifiably claim that music piracy was the unique allure of CD burning technology, any more than the pornography industry could point to the digital scanner as a tool solely used for the illegal dispersal of their own visual content. Of course, such a realization retrospectively paints the lobby groups' manufactured home-taping "controversy" of the 1980s for the absurd theater that it truly was: were not cassettes also valuable vehicles for storing and transmitting the audio content of university lectures, sermons, intimate person-to-person 'audio letters' and other materials on which no intellectual property claims were made? By ignoring the medium's use as a storage tool for personal and often a-musical contents, and by beseeching the U.S. Congress to place a sort of 'sin tax' on blank cassette purchases, groups like the RIAA[85] betrayed their own industry-centric narcissism, while unfairly implicating the tapers of a

---

[84] Despite this lack of foresight, DEC remained ahead of the curve in another sense: the corporation was the fifth entity overall to register for an Internet domain name (dec.com).

[85] Recording Industry Association of America.

thousand other ephemera as abetting those who committed amoral acts of thievery. While they could have tried this again with the introduction of the CD-R, it would have been preposterously arrogant in a business climate where such digital means were being increasingly embraced as a means of saving time and lowering operating costs. By going after a technology with as many applications as the CD-R, they may as well have tried to lobby against computers themselves on similar grounds (although they were tools that even the RIAA presumably used to facilitate their communications.)

The option to produce a full edition of CD-Rs in advance of any potential orders, or to simply burn them on demand (i.e. one at a time, as individual orders came in), allowed for greater flexibility in some artists' day-to-day operations. The "disc on demand" option was not just a means of clearing that all-important hurdle of having material available, though: it was an especially useful releasing alternative for those whose living spaces were too crowded with other possessions, or merely too small to begin with. Osaka-based computer musician Ishigami Kazuya, who has used this method of releasing for his NEUS318 label,[86] claims that

> ...in the process of going from one pressing to the next, the inside of my house would probably become buried in cardboard from the CD boxes. For this, the living conditions in Japan are the worst of any country (namely because of the dog kennel-sized homes for people), so it's a difficult dilemma.[87]

One example of the disc-on-demand method was provided by Staalplaat, the Dutch post-industrial record label and arts space, who briefly hosted a CD-R release series entitled "Open Circuit." Prospective Open Circuit artists would send in a master CD-R to be copied, along with a number of duplicated covers, and would have them listed for sale alongside more "officially" duplicated items in the Staalplaat catalog. Several lesser-known operations would come to imitate this method (or to

---

[86] The label's name is an anagram for "noise, electronics, unknown sounds."

[87] Personal email correspondence with the author, July 14, 2009. Translated from the Japanese by the author.

merely seize upon this method with no knowledge of what Open Circuit was doing concurrently.)

The Open Circuit system's populist intentions eventually came under fire by a couple of artists formerly associated with the organization - Vicki Bennett of People Like Us and Mark Hosler of Negativland - for allegedly not delivering on their promises, specifically that anything sent in to the label would be given space in the catalog and would not merely be set aside without any notification to the sender, as a normal "demo" sent to a record company would. Hosler in particular had harsh words directed at Staalplaat boss Geert-Jan Prins, whose selection process he felt more or less mirrored the content already available through the Staalplaat parent label, and who he also accused of doctoring applicants' artworks without their consent and printing additional unauthorized album copies without giving any proceeds from sales to the artist.[88] Whether these allegations are true or not, the availability of CD burning equipment would become widespread enough that anyone with Internet access could offer a "disc on demand" service without third party assistance.

If one is worried about the format's greater accessibility adulterating the head-spinning weirdness of that underground's outer limits, there is plenty of evidence to contradict this as well. Apocalyptic noise-mongers like Wolf Eyes, and their extended family, have taken to the format like ducks to water, as have neo-surrealist obscurities like Mustafio (the latter, little known outside of his short-lived New York City cable access show, delivered comically bizarre and cruel narratives in an imperious Dali-esque voice over seasick backing tracks.) Web anomalies like the 'Weirdsville' site, which offers a regular Internet audio stream, demonstrate that copious other examples abound as well: of the "mystery discs" that continually arrive at Weirdsville's physical mailbox, the site's editors boast that they are typically "...some strange CDR with an inexplicable cover - or maybe naked - no note, no website, no [promotional] one-sheet. Just the tiniest hint of contact info, and the prospect of something wonderful hidden within. These are the sweetest of the forbidden fruit, some of the weirdest weird."[89] The audio stream

---

[88] Both the protests of Hosler and Bennett are archived at the Detritus Rumori discussion list: http://detritus.net/contact/rumori/200011/0106.html. Retrieved March 28, 2011.

associated with the website regularly confirms this to be the case, showcasing the innate incapability of the so-called 'outsider artist' to self-censor their work or set aside their spiritual convictions, however esoteric, for the sake of receiving official approval (see the chapter *We're All Outsiders Now* for a more in-depth examination of this phenomenon.) Weirdsville has also helped to provide a sense of historical linkage between the kind of 'weirdness' currently appearing on CD-R, and its antecedents from other eras.

There is more than enough reliance on cliché within the CD-R set, though. Starting with the presentation itself, an inordinate number of the self-released discs come either completely unadorned (save for the manufacturer's label), or with the disc surface spray-painted a solid color, rather than with a more inventive label design (although labels such as Quebec's Brise-Cul attempt to at least add some patterning and layering into their spray jobs.) Elsewhere, the possibility of releasing on "odd" shaped CD-Rs (primarily the mini 3" versions, and those shaped like business cards) often provides a novel cover for lack of gripping audio content. Artists' lack of inventiveness is not uniquely the fault of the format, though, and it is foolhardy to imagine easy access to recording media will instill a highly individuated and original artistic sensibility in everyone who utilizes it. The process of recording has never been more wide open for participation, but this does not mean that the general socio-cultural environment is proceeding at the same utopian pace: stressful periods of economic malaise, geo-political conflict and startlingly quick technological transition tend to flatten or eliminate the nuances in the majority of human communications, and this naturally extends to the prevailing modes of folk art. The CD-R landscape has, for over a decade now, been peppered with some unimpressive sound-alike products, yet these remain valid folk expressions of the climate that produced them: finding transcendent exceptions still requires a challenging process of inquiry, but the percentage of "standouts" within the whole recording population remains, arguably, the same as at any other point during the brief lifespan of DIY media. All this raises the question: how would

---

[89] Available online at http://www.weirdsville.com/featured13.html. Retrieved March 24, 2011.

standards of releasing quality be affected once the physical format itself became a much more unstable concept?

The Age Of Optimal Coding

As it turns out, it wouldn't take long for the industry to damn the computer for being the digital-age pirate's vessel of choice, after all. There was a very thin sliver of time in which CD-Rs and file sharing were not seen as being two heads of the same monster. This interregnum would come to a screeching halt with the popularization of the MP3 audio codec [compressor-decompressor], conceived in 1987 at the Fraunhofer Institut Integrierte Schaltungen [Fraunhofer Institute For Integrated Circuits] and code-named "EUREKA Project EU147". Named as such because the codec's standard was overseen by MPEG (Motion Picture Expert Group, itself incorporated into the International Standards Organization) the 'MPEG Layer III' or MP3 was an audio-only codec following on the heels of MPEG's two prior compression codecs for video. The brainchild of Fraunhofer developer and psycho-acoustic scholar Karlheinz Brandenburg, the MP3 algorithm was known by other names prior to MPEG's involvement (as of 1989, it was still 'OCF' [Optimal Coding in the Frequency Domain]): whatever name it went by, its ultimate purpose was to remove redundant audio information or imperceptible nuances in order to provide a highly compressed and thus quickly transmittable form of digital sound.

In its gestation phases, the format had to be exchanged on 3.5" floppy disks, and computer power was such that only 20 seconds of audio using the MP3 codec could be played back at one time: the more recent leaps in processor speed and available storage space would eventually reward its engineers' patience with exponentially longer playback times (another quaint anomaly from the MP3's "rollout" period was SaeHan's MP-Man portable audio player, whose flash memory stored a grand total of about 4 audio tracks.) The patent and licensing for the MP3 is now in the hands of Technicolor, and usage of MP3 files is now possible through virtually every form of audio playback software, from the Windows Media Player to the Ableton Live home recording suite. As with brand names like 'Xerox' or 'Kleenex', MP3 now stands as a metonym for the whole range of de-physicalized audio files. Considering the record industry's alternately frosty and enraged reception towards the MP3, it's amusing to note Fraunhofer engineer Ernst Eberlein claim that Atari computers were instrumental in designing the original MP3 algorithms (Atari was, after all, the same company that was giving the music industry nightmares during the period when home video gaming was seen as a direct competitor to the home enjoyment of audio products.)

The eventual inclusion of metadata in MP3 files - associated information such as track titles, lyrics, and authorship credits - helped to personalize the format somewhat and arguably made it seem like a legitimate successor to, or at least supplement to, existing physical media. The first playback software to gain popular acceptance (Justin Frankel and Dmitry Boldyrev's Winamp, a Windows port of Tomislav Uzelac' AMP Playback Engine) featured a small spectrum analyzer for individual songs, and a side-scrolling track title indicator, but lacked the personalized data (e.g. the 'album artwork' display pane) that would come to make iTunes and its synchronized iPod hardware the standard of the immaterial audio era. The more recent selection of "iTunes LP" releases, which supplement downloaded audio files with animated album covers, lyric sheets and other user-manipulable extras, make good on a promise of interactivity that has been neglected or just deemed unnecessary by the majority of MP3-releasing artists (of course, iTunes downloads are regularly encoded using the .mp4 or .m4a extension of the post-MP3 Advanced Audio Coding [AAC] format, but the freely distributed MP3 remains the precedent for these purchaseable files.)

Unsurprisingly, some of the first backers of MP3 were independent music labels: in February of 1999, the storied Seattle indie Sub Pop was either the first (or most visible) label to offer MP3 tracks as purchasable "releases,"[90] and by doing so they showed that the hand-assembled, spartan culture of indie "authenticity" was not incommensurate with technology's onward march towards etherialization. This was done in spite of the anti-digital dissent previously voiced by close allies (although Steve

---

[90] As claimed at http://inventors.about.com/od/mstartinventions/a/MPThree.htm (retrieved March 16, 2011) and elsewhere.

Albini, who acted as an engineer for some of the label's flagship acts, has been remarkably open-minded about the spread of audio files and their concomitant sharing.) Others, like the heavily computerized Fals.CH organization (a port of call for adventurous trans-institutional artists like Zbigniew Karkowski, Kim Cascone and Florian Hecker), lauded MP3's compression rate as revolutionary and devoted an entire project - a 3" compilation CD entitled *FB25* - to spreading the MP3 gospel. To that end, an explanatory chunk of text taken from the Fraunhofer Institute makes up a large portion of *FB25's* stylishly restrained fuschia cover art, and the tiny palm-sized disc (requiring a tray-loading CD drive) contains some 3 hours of music, web links and QuickTime videos. Just as unsurprising as the "indie" embrace of increased storage capacity was the larger industry's rejection of it. CD audio MP3s like *FB25*, by the year 2005, were playable not only on computers but on standalone CD players, leading Phillippe Pasquier and Marie-France Thérien (of Quebec City's "Avatar" audio center) to speculate as follows: "the idea of encapsulating the complete works of a popular singer on a CD-audio-MP3, which could not be sold at the cumulative price of the ten or twelve albums it contains, has no allure for an industry whose shareholders would consider it bad business."[91]

The follow-up salvo of Pasquier and Thérien cleanly illustrates how little the terms of the debate have changed from the introduction of one "democratic" recording medium (e.g. cassette) to the next: "obscurity and anonymity constitute much more important threats for artists than the pirating of their works...of the tens of thousands of musicians who produce their own works every year, only a few hundred will reach the public through the music industry in its established form."[92] As in the cassette days, the retail store infrastructure is not up to the task of handling this sheer volume, let alone organizing and categorizing this material in the maximally profitable manner. And, as with that earlier medium, the ease of duplication was seen as a boon to the marginalized audience rather than as a curse. However, at this point in the game, it is disingenuous to lay all the blame at the doorstep of "the industry" for neglecting the MP3 audio CD: as soon as the physical storage format became an *optional* means

---

[91] Phillippe Pasquier and Marie-France Thérien, "Avatar Audio And The 12-Hour-And-20-Minute-CD." *Music Works* #93 (fall 2005), p. 7. MusicWorks Society Of Ontario, Toronto.
[92] *Ibid.,* p. 8.

for distributing and broadcasting music, rather than a *mandatory* means, questions about the real role of the format intensified in their frequency: were these magneto-optical discs just needless fetish items, or was their presence intrinsic to the listening experience? In a useful analogy, the Peruvian writer Chiu Longina recalls Christian Marclay's famous *Broken Music* exhibit, in which tiles of the gallery floor were replaced by a carpet of naked vinyl record albums, which patrons had to step on if they wanted to navigate through the gallery to see the artist's other works. While Longina notes the original hesitancy of the audience to do this, connected to the perceived intimacy of these objects, he claims that eventually "...the work had the opposite effect and surprisingly, when stepped on by the public, this imaginary association was surpassed: [the audience] was released and was able to see the material of the disks, that is to say, they are nothing more than pieces of black plastic that can be used as material to build a functional floor."[93] So, as Longina does in his own writing, it is tempting to draw the same conclusions regarding the appearance of the immaterial format and its relation to independent music production.

The establishment of sites for distributing MP3s by self-releasing artists was as important an event as its adoption by indie institutions like Sub Pop, and this story has unfairly been neglected in favor of the inevitable RIAA / file-sharing showdown of the late 1990s. In fact, too much credit has already been given to the RIAA by the unconscious adoption of their deceptive terminology, namely the re-branding of non-profit *file sharing* as "piracy" (which traditionally refers to the illegal, profitable *resale* of goods.) At any rate, this showdown was nothing if not a great spectacle, made more entertaining by the presence of multi-millionaire recording artists brow-beating their own audiences for helping to promote their work. Seeing a formerly independent-minded group like Metallica fighting alongside the RIAA was just one episode from this period spiked with humorous irony, especially considering how that group's early popularity had expanded thanks to the heavy metal underground's tape-trading networks. As many lessons as there are to be learned from this period, though, it is not as essential to our discussion as

[93] Chiu Longina, "Netlabels: Paraísos Sonores". Reproduced in *La Mosca Tras La Oreja: de la música experimental al arte sonore en España,* ed. Llorenç Barber and Montserrat Palacois, p. 327. Translation from the Spanish by the author. Ediciones Autor, Madrid, 2009.

the rise of more "legally" distributed, self-released music on MP3.

Outlets such as the simply titled MP3.com, despite promoting themselves with major artists who had given MP3.com consent to distribute their songs, also served as a repository for thousands of artists without so much as a physical CD available on the market. After just 4 years of operation, though, the service was purchased by Vivendi Universal, and underwent an expected transformation that saw it cleaving closer to the dictates of that particular mega-corporation (and, consequently, dialing down its promotion of self-releasing artists.) Surviving discussion list posts about MP3.com are not entirely positive, such as Steev Hise's complaint that "…the only thing the company is about is MINING. Harvesting raw materials - the artists' work. And they don't need to even go to much effort to do it. It's as if I ran a mining company, but I didn't need to dig at all - the gold is jumping right out of the ground and into my pockets."[94]

Compared with MP3.com, The Internet Underground Music Archive (IUMA) was both more perceptive of how "unofficial" artists would be using its services, and significantly ahead of the curve in its understanding of the new audio technology. As early as 1994, before 'World Wide Web' was a household term, the IUMA existed on Usenet groups as well as file transfer protocol sites- as such, it provides a valuable, if under-reported link between the cassette networks and the full-blown digital music bonanza to come. As a consolation, the California-based organization was featured briefly on MTV and on a 1994 CNN business segment and as well. For the latter, proprietors Rob Lord and Jeff Patterson (of the band "Ugly Mugs") were joined in a chorus by - incongruously enough - a representative of the new age record label Windham Hill, who stated that "for record companies that don't know how to take advantage of this technology, yes, there is a threat- for those who understand how to utilize it, there won't be."[95]

---

[94] Steev Hise quoted at http://detritus.net/contact/rumori/200005/0021.html. Retrieved March 28, 2011.

[95] Katie Vogelheim quoted at http://www.youtube.com/watch?v=GT5LIEUJefM (retrieved August 5, 2011.) Also of relevance is the claim made in this video clip that IBM and Blockbuster Entertainment planned an "on-demand" CD manufacturing system for hard-to-find titles, a plan that was never implemented to any noticable degree.

Whatever gains were made through third parties like IUMA were consolidated and expanded upon by the rise of the "net-label," personal Web domains that offered full catalogs of compressed audio albums (typically available as .zip archives) and generally did not need to cede any aspect of their presentation to advertisers. Genre-specific net-label directories and word-of-mouth promotion (spread via sympathetic bulletin boards and the social networks that were not on the radar as of IUMA's heyday) have been sufficient enough to keep these labels a going concern. As with previous generations of "unofficial" audio, these labels ranged in scope from highly specialized to maddeningly eclectic, with some catalogs being formed completely from scratch and others being built from pre-existing archives of tape and CD releases (see the "Zeromoon" label of electronic and experimental music as an exemplar of the latter.) By now, the primary benefit of this kind of releasing (maximal recognition at minimal cost) should be obvious, yet there are other less commonly voiced advantages to this practice. For one, many net-label owners have pointed to the way they have increased the convenience of acquiring music, but some, like Clinical Archives' Alexander Lisovsky, also point to the ease of *disposing of* music from the labels: in a welcome moment of humility, Lisovsky shrugs that "certainly, there are many weak and disputable releases on C.A.," and that disappointing releases are "easy to throw out in [the] trash on PC…with a physical CD it is much more difficult."[96] It is this ease of disposability that provides a stern challenge to the net-releaser, and perhaps detracts from claims that net-releasing leads to an unprecedented dilution of sonic quality: sure, one can make a middling release available with greater speed than at any previous time in history, but its life span within a listener's collection will also be of an unprecedented brevity.

Digital Rusticity? The "Low Bitrate" Net-Release Movement

The audio file boom, as initialized by MP3 and sustained by more luxurious formats (e.g. OGG Vorbis, uncompressed .aiff and .wav files) has

---

[96] Alexander Lisovsky, email correspondence with the author, May 18 2010.

gone on long enough now that its own subculture of self-critical artists, typically overlapping with the larger self-releasing culture, has sprung up to tweak and test these formats' technical and aesthetic limitations. For example, the Russian net-label Microbit Records, formed in 2008, specializes in releases "devoted to low-bit music of all genres", with "releases [...] available as free download in MP3 and Ogg Vorbis format," and "...encoded in low bitrate (from 1 kbps to 64 kbps)."[97] Some of the releases also up the ante by being made available in monaural sound. Despite the apparent limitations of this concept, the label's roster boasts nearly 70 artists at the time of writing. As could be expected, much of this is post-industrial electronica, but there are enough surprises in store as well: the Microbit group Hobo (the only group listed without a presence on networking sites like MySpace or LastFM) play a punkish Russian-language blues, and Evgenij Kharitonov offers up a distressed form of concrete poetry made more unsettling by the sonic artifacts unique to low bitrate recording. Neizvestnost, a competent and fluid trance-rock unit, also turns in a rewarding release capable of overcoming the challenges provided by the label's *modus operandi,* perhaps even benefiting from the unnatural thinness of that particular sound (the group also features on the *Extreme Music From Russia* omnibus on the intensely selective Susan Lawly label.) Another net-label, 4m@-records - a sub-label of the Proc Records label - takes the 'low bitrate' aesthetic to a different level of tech-criticism by making its artists follow one simple criterion: the pieces they release must be no larger than the 1.44 megabyte storage space of the now-outmoded 3.5" floppy disk. The motivations for these types of releasing activities range from nostalgic reverie to a devious inclination to reveal the fallibility of techno-utopia, with, of course, the requisite smattering of in-jokes (see The Microbit Project's 4m@ release *Floppy Acid Keyboards Session Box Set, Disc's [sic] 1-6,* which pokes fun at both the phenomena of storage media and 'deluxe' collectors' items.)

What the releases from Microbit and 4m@ point to is nothing less than a kind of "neo lo-fi" for the digital age, a recognition of the fact that much of the "analog" lifestyle is well out of the price range of the average citizen: vintage analog keyboards, tube amplifiers and other workhorses of analog

---

[97] Available online at http://www.discogs.com/label/Microbit+Records. Retrieved March 22, 2011.

technology cost in the thousands of dollars, while the bill for their upkeep and repair can itself become a burdensome expense. Given such expenses, it is something of a conceit when a mainly analog-driven "lo-fi" recording act uses its equipment as a proof of its frugality and threadbare humility. So, it is increasingly up to digital outfits like Microbit to project those values in the music *they* release. Like much music that is consciously lo-fi (and not merely designated as such by the critical community), their radically 'bit-reduced' sound arrives at the ears like a "lost transmission" from some greater, more heroic age, or a document from some parallel reality- this sense of distancing paradoxically works to provide the listener with a more intimate or direct experience. Indeed, the limited frequency range and watery audio quality of low bitrate MP3s, complete with the infamous "digital artifacts" somewhat like the sound of aluminum foil quietly crumpling, wholeheartedly trade out sonic presence for distance. Seen in this way, their embrace is an attempt to re-introduce the kind of imperfection that necesitated active involvement on the listener's behalf; "blurry", distant or unfocused recordings have traditionally required a more attentive or ritualistic style of listening free from ephemeral distractions, which in turn was meant to produce that much more of a bond between performer and listener.

However, this type of recording and releasing also takes into account another dramatic shift that has taken place in 21st century listening habits: in an era where it is no longer necessary to court prospective record labels with "demo tapes" and the like, it is still necessary to provide would-be listeners themselves (rather than A + R managers) with a demonstration of some kind. This, ideally, deepens the artist-listener bond and secures them as a long-term supporter. To this end, the releases on Microbit and 4m@ make few demands on the listeners' time, but also demand minimal use of the computer-based listener's hard drive space. The bit reduction of these albums allows them to be downloaded very quickly on even a slow connection, and allows them to reside on any standard hard drive without crowding out other useful data. It's also worth considering that these releases can be heard without beckoning the listener into the cluttered digital wilderness of sites like MySpace (despite the aforementioned fact that the majority of these releasing parties still maintain their own pages there): all these features converge to make for a promotional "demo" that is as inoffensive and low-risk to the listener as possible.

For those who scoff at the advantages being provided by significantly reduced file sizes, it's also important to remember that the standards of speed and reliability for Internet connectivity are hardly level throughout the globe: in Microbit's Russia, for example, the percentage of computer users in the total population hovers around a maximum value of 50% (one source suggests that there are 59,700,000 Russian Internet users out of a potential 140,000,000)[98] which is the lowest estimate for much of Western Europe and Scandinavia. Naturally, these numbers take into account a sizable rural population, although urban Russia does not boast total connectivity either: among users in the cities, household Internet access is not a given, and the chosen environment for Web surfing may be an Internet café. Given the hourly prices charged at these cafes, and the fact that "in some cities [...] the highest speed people can count on is 256 kbps"[99] the ability to download music fairly quickly makes a little more sense. Put another way, urban Russia "might have passed the digital divide but still live[s] in the 'pre-broadband world with little or no access to YouTube and other traffic-sensitive online services."[100] Given such factors, it is a little more difficult to dismiss low bitrate releasing as a purely contrarian exercise meant to alienate audiophiles and 'scene' jumpers. Doing so puts the critic at risk of seeming chauvinistically unaware of foreign nations' infrastructural problems, State restrictions on media, and other mitigating circumstances.

Extensions Of The Net-Release: The Relevance Of Weblogs And Podcasts

One 'digital transfer' that should not go overlooked in this survey is the use of weblogs to achieve various ends related to audio dissemination. Some of these weblogs are free of charge along with a typical Google account; Google's Blogger service (acquired in early 2003 and unleashed in 2006 in its first beta form) currently accounts for a healthy percentage of the total share. While their ubiquitous presence on the Internet has since

---

[98] See http://www.internetworldstats.com/euro/ru.htm. Retrieved March 24, 2011.

[99] Available online at http://globalvoicesonline.org/2010/03/14/russia-mapping-broadband-internet-prices. Retrieved March 24, 2011.

[100] *Ibid.*

allowed them to be taken for granted, their ability to quickly link to any other site or file on the Web was a radical departure from what *Wired* co-founder John Battelle described as "hand-rolled" Web pages "using laborious HTML coding, [where] links were difficult to make."[101] Battelle's 2005 book *The Search* offers a brief encomium summing up the "pros" of blog usage, noting fears that "all that linking has attenuated the value of a link", yet saluting their "human-based classification schemes" that solve the problem of Web editing with the "Force Of The Many."[102] That "many" is apparently forceful enough to drive Blogger's Alexa ranking into the top 10 of all surveyed Web entities- but do these blogs have the to power to assuage the persistent fears of the "analog loyalists," or do Blogger and its siblings represent just another step into an abyss of cruelly diluted audio experience? While a resolute answer will not be given here, let's just say for now that these blogs do much to promote the cause of analog audio culture, by acting as exhibitions of all that was great and glorious about that age, at the same time that they digitally preserve it. This aside, it is worth looking at how blogs affect self-releasing culture as a whole.

First off, music blogs often act as proxy net-label "home pages" from which their entire catalogs can be downloaded, while fans can leave comments or sign on as "followers" in the best tradition of online social networks (detractors and ill-wishers can, of course, chime in as well, provided the hosting entity does not censor their comments.) If working in conjunction with a library service like the Internet Archive, or with file transfer services (e.g. Megaupload, Rapidshare), a great deal of audio material can be linked to from the main blog pages at minimal expense to the uploader. Again, many blogs focus more on the archiving and documentation of analog-era audio: materials that would otherwise languish, unheard and unseen, in personal collections, storage spaces or landfills. So, where these blogs are concerned, a spirit of non-commercial altruism is evident.

While many of the blogs employed for audio releases rely on stock

---

[101] John Battelle, *The Search: How Google And Its Rivals Rewrote The Rules Of Business And Transformed Our Culture*, p. 265. Portfolio, New York, 2005.
[102] *Ibid.*, p. 266.

design templates, and are hardly arresting visually, these humble coverings often conceal a hitherto unavailable wealth of information on self-releases, private editions and all things scandalously neglected. Along these lines, one of the author's favorites blogs, "433rpm" (433rpm.blogspot.com), formerly featured daily uploads of long-deleted items from the post-industrial cassette era, including a good deal that never made it beyond the borders of the Benelux nations. This appears to have been a severely time-consuming process, one that was only occasionally rewarded with very brief expressions of gratitude (typically a typed line or two) for the man-hours put into this project. Many such blogs do feature a link to donate cash via PayPal or some other method of electronic bank transfer, although my personal correspondence reveals that here, too, expressions of gratitude are few and far between. Yet these blogs keep proliferating in spite of slim rewards (even though many of the items posted on them are re-posts or duplicates of items that have appeared earlier on other blogs): the non-expectation of recognition or reward shows that the "unofficial ethos" of the previous generation is still alive and well within the daunting, exhilarating expanse of the info-sphere.

Another variation on the music blog comes in the form of podcasts[103], such as the ones parked at the popular podomatic.com, and those accessible via iTunes and other digital download shops. In many ways, the functionality of podcast pages mirrors that of audio blogs: both provide standardized RSS [real simple syndication] feeds for Web users who want to receive instantaneous notifications of updates to their content (the December 2000 introduction of RSS version 0.92, which permitted audio files to be included in RSS feeds, was one of the innovations that gave rise to podcasting in the first place.) Meanwhile, both podcasts and audio blogs mimic the "open for comment" nature of social networking sites by allowing "friends" or "followers" to provide various kinds of feedback on that content. Lastly, both serve as preservation sites for previous generations of self-released audio as well as promotional tools for its current manifestations. The ability to post video content at sites like

---

[103] This being a quirky portmanteau of "iPod" and "broadcast," many critics of Apple are reluctant to use the term, favoring "netcast" as an alternative. I do not intend to steer my readers towards a more Apple-centric culture by favoring "podcast" over "netcast," but merely acknowledge that, among audio laypeople, the former has become the more immediately recognizable of the two.

podomatic.com adds another dimension of interactivity, allowing the format to exceed expectations of being merely a digitally streamed "radio show" or playlist.

One notable difference between the two modes of audio dissemination can be seen in the role that the audio uploaders play: some do take the podcast seriously as the successor of the traditional radio broadcast, and play at being a host, with all that hosting entails (adding vocal transitions between audio tracks, providing anecdotal or critical supplements to the audio played, or acting as a mediator between a listening audience and a 'special guest.') Some uploaders simply offer audio without any additional guidance or intervention, although - unlike on audio blogs - the content can be streamed in the listener's browser software as well as downloaded outright. The former option is, naturally, adopted by radio broadcast outlets who hope to expand their reach beyond what their minimal wattage allows: most of the major broadcast players in the independent music or "free-form radio" milieu, such as New York's WFMU and London's Resonance FM, have regularly produced podcast facsimiles of their terrestrial radio broadcasts. Many of the archived shows can then take on another life by being traded throughout file-sharing sites.

Both the music / audio blog and the podcast have given music collectors an opportunity to present themselves not as some kind of perverse hoarders, but as serious archivists interested in the furtherance of their art. Too often the act of collecting is just a means towards correctly reciting a litany of respected names in the right company, an act that is now immortalized on the odd spoken word recording by Ralf Wehowsky, *An Archivist's Nightmare* (in which the primary audio content is the artist reciting the titles of over 1,000 records that he has recently acquired.) These new media, along with the peer-to-peer (P2P) file-sharing networks, have made it more difficult for those who view rare recordings as something to be handed down from a more experienced collector to a curious seeker who, presumably, does not know what he or she is doing and needs to follow the "correct" sequence of listening instructions. Of course, where P2P networks like Soulseek are concerned, users can still "ban" others from downloading pieces of their collection if the curious downloaders are deemed as unworthy neophytes. The "one-upmanship" of the hardcore collector can be preserved in such prohibitive ways, but those who tire of such virtual gatekeepers have plenty of other avenues available to them.

"One-upmanship" and de-physicalized audio would seem to be incongruous concepts, based on the observations of Luciano Floridi. He notes that music files are "typified, in the sense that an instance of an object (my copy of a music file) is as good as its type (your music file of which my copy is an instance.)"[104] On face value, this seems fairly accurate: digital downloaders cannot compete with each other in the way that record collectors often do, e.g. collector 'a' has an autographed copy or limited edition colored vinyl pressing while collector 'b' merely has the more common black vinyl pressing of the same record. On further inspection, though, even digital downloaders and their blogger hosts have found ways to reinstate a hierarchy of connoisseurs, and this is especially true when concerning analog media that is being de-physicalized and subsequently blogged. Arguments on blogs' comment sections can often be found stating that so-and-so was the "first" to upload a certain rare item, and therefore the secondary and tertiary postings should be treated as lazy attempts to ride on the coattails of the "originator." These arguments will then spiral into discussions of whose uploading job was better, and whose upload was truer to the essence of the source material: battles will rage over who has made their conversion from a 1st or 2nd generation cassette, or who has taken the care to upload at a more generous bit rate. The complaints about shoddy uploading jobs are perfectly valid from the perspective of those who wish to preserve audio for future generations, although the arguments relating to origination of posted materials do not carry as much weight: when dealing with digitally coded facsimiles of already existing materials, the word "original" is suspect enough, but stranger still is the desire to be seen as "first place" in a competitive race to inform the public about an essentially non-competitive culture.

Analog Vs. Digital, Or Objects Vs. Processes?

The backlash against the digital audio file, and its unique distribution systems, has taken much more sincere forms than, say, the playful

---

[104] Luciano Floridi, *Information (A Very Short Introduction)*, p. 12. Oxford University Press, Oxford / New York, 2010.

releasing of low bit rate recordings. That music in the 21st century is still being released on formats like acetate, albeit sporadically, is no fluke: in a world of immaterial music that is largely immune to the corrosive effects of the elements, physical formats with short life spans are released with the implicit suggestion that listening to them provides a richer, more meaningful listen. Acetates in particular, with their ability to be played back some 5-10 times before serious degradation in sound occurs, force the listener to approach them with the reverence accorded to any natural phenomenon on the verge of disappearance. Uncompressed audio files, on the other hand, do not undergo any steady process of degradation and (in yet another binary configuration) are either present or deleted- they can therefore be enjoyed *ad infinitum,* and ported to as many portable playback devices as the listener can afford to maintain. As far as the 'virtual' space of servers is concerned, some net-labels can still offer fairly high-quality, minimally lossy 320kps MP3 files, if they do not have the bandwidth to offer completely uncompressed formats.

So, with all the digital updates above adding a new dimension to unofficial audio, the question must be asked: has digital culture won the final battle against analog culture, and annexed the domain of DIY to all of its other virtual territories? Some may choose to see it this way, but the truth is rather less clean-cut: those with their hands deep in self-determined creative activities, and not merely observing these activities, tend to hybridize the two phases of technology in various different configurations. Contemporary cassette tapes exist whose contents are recorded completely with digital audio software suites, and there is always the aforementioned, still undefeated vinyl-philia of techno producers. In short, digital culture does not - following Brian Massumi - "erase or replace the actual" so much as it "redoubles" or "augments" it.

These hybridizing practices have not gone unnoticed among the cognoscenti who look into the audio world from the outside. There are now signs that, in spite of the continual expansion of digital communications, the anxiety and occasional bunker mentality resulting from their proliferation is beginning to recede; to give way to a more nuanced brand of thinking. Massumi writes the following in his thought provoking essay *On The Superiority Of The Analog:*

> Apocalyptic pronouncements of epochal rupture may sell well, but they don't compute. When or if the digital virtual comes, its experience won't be so dramatic. It will be lullingly quotidian: no doubt as boring as the Web can be.[105]

Note that Massumi is claiming "the digital virtual" is a state that does not yet exist: he counsels against conflating the terms "virtual" and "digital" since it "confuses the really apparitional with the artificial."[106] And after all, isn't this one of the greatest fears of the analog purists, that digitizing sounds, images, etc. banish them to some kind of ghost realm, where they can continue to "haunt" us but can no longer reach out and touch us? Or that digitization is a precursor to a terrifying dissociative state in which social engagement will be suspended for all but, presumably, a handful of master controllers? The "virtual reality" that conjures this old fear of apparitions is one where the mathematical model precedes the constructed world; the "hyperreality" investigated by Jean Baudrillard and his acolytes.

Another salient point of Massumi's is that "bodies and objects, their forms and contents, do not account for all of [actuality]...they do not catch the momentum...to look only at bodies and objects is to miss the movement."[107] From the conception of a sonic idea, to the discovery of the means (instruments) to project it, to its realization in performance or on record, there is a great deal of Massumi's "momentum": the few phases listed just now are the "map" rather than the "territory." This is particularly relevant when we consider how often the musical format becomes the primary battleground for determining the future of music full stop, setting aside the multitude of processes and interactions that precede and succeed the encoding of music onto a physical object. All the talk about the "warmth" of analog records, the "democratic" nature of cassettes, or the "utilitarian" nature of digital sound files makes it seem as though the formats themselves are dictating personality traits and plans of action. Certainly, the restraints and affordances inherent to each format play a large role in deciding what kind of content they carry. Yet it is

---

[105] Brian Massumi, *Parables For The Virtual (Movement, Affect, Sensation)*, p. 143. Duke University Press, Durham / London, 2002.

[106] *Ibid.*, p. 137

[107] *Ibid.*, p. 136.

overreaching to say that these formats effect or fully transform the personality of their users; that they can negate the host of ambient conditions that contribute to creative life and build a new type of artist from scratch. The Eugene Chadbourne that releases on CD-Recordables remains the same political rabble-rouser who also used vinyl records to convey his message, and if the CDr albums of Zan Hoffman contain any more or less of the characteristic experimentalism displayed on his numerous cassettes, then we should at least look for other variable factors in his lived experience before critiquing the format.

The time limitations on sound storage media might be proposed in a counter-argument; that format can indeed be the motor most dramatically altering musical character. Granted, these limitations have almost been abolished with the advent of the sound-file-as-format, and have certainly encouraged more flirtation with sonic styles that "breathe" or "unfold" at a more leisurely pace, yet short-and-sharp punk rock and jauntily quick indie-pop songs continue to be made in spite of this. Rather than just assuming that emancipation from time limitations leads to monumental works of ambience and noise, we should ask what else compels and inspires their creators to work in these idioms (after all, lack of time limitations could just as easily prompt one to record a 'virtual album' comprised of several hundred micro-sized pop vignettes.) Finally, one's attitude towards that much more universal time limitation - human mortality itself - is more likely to have a transformative effect on sound-making than the time limitation of the sound storage format: long before such a thing as sound recording existed, a great variety of sonic expression pondered and attempted to defy this fundamental fact of existence.

All told, there are numerous hazards to using the format as the sole, or primary, indicator of one's placement on the ethical spectrum of creativity, especially the misbegotten assumption that one always has multiple choices available when embarking on a new audio project (among other things, this ignores the large disparities that exist between national economies, and the contingencies that these disparities have placed upon non-essential activities like recording.) While the newer surge of digitized "immaterial formats" could, ideally, cause this "format-centric" tendency to flame out over time, we should probably not expect too much while the "concrete" formats remain in circulation and retain their power to embody commitments to abstract qualities (authenticity, tastefulness, etc.)

However, rejecting "format-centrism" is made all the more easy when we consider Massumi's argument that "digital sound is a misnomer,"[108] an argument that he expands upon as follows:

> It is only the coding of the sound that is digital. The digital is sandwiched between an analog disappearance into code at the recording, and an analog appearance out of code at the listening end.[109]

Broadening this critique to all forms of digital coding, Massumi insists that "*the processing may be digital...but the analog is the process* [italics in the original]."[110] This ineluctable fact means that kinesthetic and biological processes, so paradoxically upheld by "analogists" as the generators of spirituality that digital life cannot provide, will never be entirely out of the picture. The terror still exists that digital culture will become a more and more powerful adjunct to the rapacious control machine, yet one of the 'worst case scenarios' sustaining this terrifying vision - that of corporate slaves on a 24-hour lockdown within their computing environments, lulled into total passivity by their flickering screens - is already being phased out as of this writing. There is now more of an organic pushing and pulling between different types of, *pace* Massumi, "transformative integration" that involve digital devices inserted into all types of social environments.

Yes, the situation about which the Critical Art Ensemble writes is a distinct possibility (a "techno-revolution [...] designed to keep the body, but in a redesigned configuration that helps it adjust to the intensified rigors of pan-capitalist imperatives and to adapt to its pathological environment")[111]. But it no longer exists apart from countervailing forces, if in fact it ever did. The C.A.E's assertion that "science and technology are developed, deployed, and controlled by the predatory system of pan-

---

[108] Brian Massumi, *Parables For The Virtual (Movement, Affect, Sensation)*, p. 138. Duke University Press, Durham / London, 2002.

[109] *Ibid.*

[110] *Ibid.*, p. 142.

[111] Critical Art Ensemble, *Flesh Machine: Cyborgs, Designer Babies, And The New Eugenic Consciousness*, p. 7. Autonomedia, New York, 1998.

capitalism"[112] rings hollow in the face of mounting evidence, which shows that technological innovations can be produced by counter-cultural, even "radical" specimens of society, even if they may eventually end up serving the purposes of financial empire-building.[113] That the opposite also happens should be evident as well. Even if it were true that techno-science always begins its life cycle as the servant of total imperial control, we do not need to submit before yet another genetic fallacy, and declare "off limits" any tool or weapon originating in the laboratories of centralized authority. Refusing to even investigate how those tools can be used for de-centralized creativity, rather than for power consolidation, returns us to a binary conception of 'analog good' and 'digital evil' more pernicious than the binary coding of digital technology itself.

---

[112] Critical Art Ensemble, *Flesh Machine: Cyborgs, Designer Babies, And The New Eugenic Consciousness*, p. 7. Autonomedia, New York, 1998.

[113] The archetype for this remains Apple's Steve Wozniak and Steve Jobs, noted by author Tim Wu as "bona fide counter-culturals, with all the accoutrements- long hair, opposition to the war, an inclination to experiment with chemical substances as readily as with electronics...Wozniak, an inveterate prankster, ran an illegal 'dial-a-joke' operation; Jobs would travel to India in search of a guru." (Tim Wu, *The Master Switch: The Rise And Fall Of Information Empires*, p. 274. Alfred A. Knopf, New York, 2010.)

Hey, Mr. Post-Industrial Man:
The Swinging Sounds Of The Information Economy

The word 'industrial,' even when being spoken in the most emotionally neutral contexts, manages to carry with it a feeling of enveloping dread- it conjures imagery of uniform and zombielike processions of bodies, involuntarily drawn towards enormous grey cathedrals of noise and smoke, themselves barely discernible while standing against dirty, grey, polluted skies. Public reaction to all things 'industrial' is so bound up in this kind of apocalyptic imagery that the nations to which the West has outsourced its manufacturing capacity are now politely referred to as "developing" nations rather than "industrialized" ones. The association of factory life with extermination of the spirit, or with the replacement of immaterial values by machine-made products, has existed since factories themselves came on the scene. In more recent years, this bitterness has been compounded by the realization that "mechanical production has long since overshot the elementary goals of food, clothing, self-preservation and life [...] it creates new 'desires,' a measureless 'hunger for commodities' that is increasingly directed at artificialities."[114] With such somberness permeating all things "industrial," how exactly did this become such a popular "meme" for independent music production? Furthermore, why did it integrate so well into the networked cultures of correspondence art and home taping, which set their sights on the polar opposite of this dystopian image?

First off, given industrial music's place on the cultural timeline (1976-1984 being the more commonly cited 'golden' years of innovation) it may be helpful to realize how rapidly the great counter-cultural experiment of the 1960s and early 1970s spun out of control. For all of its good intentions towards humanity and the biosphere it inhabits, this experiment collapsed under the weight of its own contradictory presciptions for living: 1960s bohemians chastised those who went on an "ego trip," yet also demanded that they "let their freak flag fly" or indulge in displays of boisterous, presumably egoistic, un-restraint. Those who lived the "free" communal

---

[114] Peter Sloterdijk, *Critique Of Cynical Reason*, p. 437. Trans. Michael Eldred. University Of Minnesota Press, 1987.

hippie lifestyle to the letter left their societies open to infiltration by the type of snake oil salesmen and devious manipulators who had always dotted the American landscape: suddenly a girl refusing to enter into the tent of some self-styled "guru" could be condemned as "anti-love," rather than merely resisting the advances of that particular cad. The penultimate manipulator of hippie vibrations, Charles Manson, demonstrated how easily a collective projection of utopia could become a lust for Armageddon: the Tate / LaBianca murders carried out under his auspices were meant to ignite an American race war, after which Manson's "family" would emerge from their desert domain and reign over the war-weary human remnant.

When the 1969 Summer Of Love was nullified by the Manson murders (and soon echoed by the Altamont Free Concert disaster), the optimistic atmosphere of the previous summer was quickly clouded over by an eschatological mood. It was one that emboldened all kinds of conflicting tribal affiliations (e.g. bikers, black nationalists, and the expected hippie holdouts.) Each of them was eager to define the discourse of the new post-apocalypse America once the ashes had settled, and getting them all under the same roof for a rock concert was a recipe for instant aggravation. By 1974, all we needed for a master class in post-Woodstock disillusionment was Iggy And The Stooges' live LP *Metallic KO*. A generous portion of the band's live swan song is given to Iggy's suicidal audience provocations: he audibly invites violence from bikers probably thrice his size while critiquing the audience's ability to pelt him with debris (critic Lester Bangs, who attended both of the *Metallic KO* concerts in Detroit, has called this record " the only rock album I know where you can actually hear hurled beer bottles breaking against guitar strings.") Although the sequencing of *Metallic KO's* tracks doesn't quite make this clear (a 1988 re-model, *Metallic 2xKO*, helps somewhat), Pop was hospitalized for his biker taunting on the first of the two concerts represented on the LP. He returned for the second engagement, even after the bike gang known as the Scorpions had phoned the local rock radio station (WABX-FM) and threatened his life. Amazingly, given that Iggy's mere appearance for the second show was considered a provocation, the violence was not as intense as on the first night.

While it was an apocryphal event in comparison to the bookends of Woodstock and Altamont, it was still a fairly startling document of directionless violence being re-enthroned in youth culture (Iggy Pop would later boast on live television of having helped to "kill" the 1960s.) With proto-punk kamikazes like Iggy leading the charge, this violence became reinstituted as a catalytic force, and, in an ironic twist considering its own lack of focus, was seen as a means of staving off stultifying boredom and aimlessness. It wouldn't be long before even more spectacular outbreaks of music-inspired violence unfolded throughout the world, like the 1977-1978 European tour dates of the band Suicide: the documents of these dates (on a Blast First boxed set released in 1999) sound more like prison uprisings on a space station than proper live gigs. The punk rock scene, which counted the aforementioned artists as formative influences, proclaimed dystopian scenarios with an anti-traditionalism common to other 20th century avant-gardes, and with embittered chants of "no future." In doing so, they even upped the ante on the *ur*-punk poet Mayakovsky (who, though he may claimed "I have written *nihil* on everything that has been done before," was a *futurist* after all.)

It has been well over 40 years now since *Village Voice* first declared the death of the hippie, but still the cause of death remains a matter of speculative debate. Some of the debaters are more convincing than others, though. Shortly after the fallout from the Summer of Love, the urbanist Lewis Mumford wearily writes:

> Despite the well-founded dissatisfaction of the younger generation with the kind of life offered by the bloated affluence of megatechnic society, their very mode of rebellion too often demonstrates that the power system still has them in its grip: they, too, mistake indolence for leisure and irresponsibility for liberation. The so-called Woodstock Festival was no spontaneous manifestation of joyous youth, but a strictly money making enterprise, shrewdly calculated to exploit their rebellions, their adulations, and their illusions. The success of the festival was based on the tropismic attraction of 'Big Name' singers and groups (the counter-culture's Personality

Cult!), idols who command colossal financial rewards from personal appearances and the sales of their discs and films.[115]

While Mumford perhaps missed the point of what he calls "anti-art," and erroneously fused the motivations of Dada with that of "consciousness raising" 1960s U.S. counterculture, he reserved his strongest condemnations for the latter's irreconcilable aims: to him, what "seem[ed] like a withdrawal [was] only another form of active participation and submergence in the Power System [...] even Hippie costumes have offered a new market for mass production."[116]

The Dada comparison is useful here, though, since Dada shared some commonalities with the clandestine, yet influential music that violently inverted the "hippie" aesthetic (indeed, one of its founding groups, Cabaret Voltaire of Sheffield, took its namesake from the famed Dada salon in Zurich.) Just as the Zurich Dada scene was composed of refugees from the embattled nations of the First World War, the tenebrous, noisy, and international industrial music scene of the late 70s / early 80s was populated by refugees from the fallout of 1960s counter-culture. Indeed, one of the linchpins and indefatigable spokesmen of this culture, Neil Megson (reborn as Genesis P. Orridge), had serious hippie / boho credentials that he has even sought to reclaim in more recent years. Long before this would come about, though, GPO's group Throbbing Gristle catalyzed a musical movement that came to apparently purge itself of hippie consciousness. More accurately, the visceral impact of its electronic sound storms, and the darkly resonant subject matter, avoided the hippies' duplicitous attitude towards Mumford's "megatechnic society." Militarism, mechanical reproduction, survivalist austerity, suburban boredom, elaborate revenge schemes: no combination of underlying themes could have been farther removed from the evergreen, elfin paradise of hippie-dom. From Throbbing Gristle's Industrial Records stable in the U.K. to the Survival Research Laboratories machine performance troupe in the U.S., these thematic concerns surfaced in strikingly varied and nuanced ways.

---

[115] Lewis Mumford, *The Myth Of The Machine: The Pentagon Of Power*, p. 26. Harcourt / Brace / Jovanovich, New York, 1970.

[116] *Ibid.*, p. 367.

Once again calling upon the spirit of Dada, this new form appeared to *embrace* the manifold terrors of modernity, practicing "the art of declaring oneself, in an ironic, dirty way, to be in agreement with the worst possible things [...] produc[ing] an ego beyond good and evil that want[s] to be like its mad epoch."[117] This was industrial music's neo-Dadaist twist, and the shock theater of its progenitors' public announcements was made all the more effective by the sentimental pop culture that had preceded it. The philosopher Peter Sloterdijk's comments on Dada are easily applicable to the strategy of nascent industrial music culture:

> Between the mentality of the generals, who are respectably for war, and the mentality of the pacifists, who are respectably against it, the Dadaists erected a maliciously clashing third position, free of all scruples: to be unrespectably [sic] for it.[118]

This was where industrial music found its *métier*, in the adoption of lionized "mega-technic" tools by those who would otherwise be considered disrespectable and degenerate in polite British society, if not the whole of the industrialized world. Among the founding Throbbing Gristle membership alone, Cosey Fanni Tutti (*née* Christine Newby) had posed in pornographic magazines, Peter Christopherson had earned the sobriquet "Sleazy" for his voyeuristic approach to new media, and of course GPO had previously had his hands in every maligned subculture extant in Britain from the 1960s onwards. To see such people dressing themselves in *couture* military uniforms (not just the readily available army surplus ironically adopted by American hippies), while singing martial techno-hymns to "Discipline" and "Convincing People," was something quite different from seeing these stances furthered by people already ensconced in the respectable warrior or managerial castes. It must have been doubly confusing to see these déclassé anarcho-libertarians binding together the nomenclature of corporatism with the symbols of fascism: industrial albums were issued as ascetic, mock-corporate "annual reports," but also came graced with quasi-fascist insignias, e.g. Throbbing Gristle's white

---

[117] Peter Sloterdijk, *Critique Of Cynical Reason*, p. 392. Trans. Michael Eldred. University Of Minnesota Press, 1987.

[118] *Ibid.*, p. 393.

lightning bolt on a red-and-black background.

An appropriation like the latter is easily brushed aside as a frantic, arm-waving appeal for attention, especially given its similarity to the insignia once used by Oswald Mosley's British Union Of Fascists. Yet, tiny adjustments - in this case, changing the color scheme of the original from red and blue to red and black - pointed towards a deeper kind of inquiry. Red and black was simultaneously the color scheme adopted by all varieties of fascism (National Socialism, Franco's clerical fascism), *and* by just about every worldwide revolutionary movement, from Cuban *Guevaristas* to the Maoist 'urban guerrillas' of the German RAF [*Rote Armee Fraktion*.][119] By revealing the similarities between ideological systems, and the audiovisual devices they used for recruitment and agitation, industrial music drew a new set of battle lines: the "war" was no longer between socio-political extremes of Left and Right, but between those who wanted to impose systemic and absolutist codes for living, and those who wanted no limitations on expression. These qualities were seen as transcending specific political or economic systems.

Robbing The Information Bank

The industrial music made by Throbbing Gristle, SPK, et al., whatever its animating desires, possessed a uniquely disorienting and overwhelming force. Thusly it seemed to many like the sound of the Orwellian "boot stamping on a human face forever": the slow-grinding metronomic rhythms, frantic synth oscillations and "flat affect" vocalizations threw the listener into a locked-down panopticon where the enforced order was occasionally broken by jumbled radio and TV signals from the outside world. However, a little study reveals that industrial music was never just a doom-laden capitulation to total nihilism; a heralding of the individual's final defeat in the face of a much more well-

---

[119] Unsurprisingly, the RAF or "Baader-Meinhof gang" had their place in the pantheon of industrial subject matter as well: Cabaret Voltaire has at least one song named after the organization, and the group SPK originally took is name from the *Sozialistiches Patienten Kollektiv* (falsely accused, by the German media of its day, of regular collaboration with the RAF.)

organized power structure. While industrial culture's elements of negativity *could,* in isolated cases, cross over into self-parody, its model of resistance did provide an invigorating flash of hope (another interpretation of the TG logo) to the otherwise disillusioned.

Coming about at a time when the self-liberating ethos of the 'human potential movement' seemed like it was doomed to fail in its attempts to destroy the "inner policeman," this abrasive new art form took its cues from more skeptical adherents of personal freedom. Although his anarchic writing had provided no small amount of inspiration for the hedonistic 60s counter-culture, William S. Burroughs cast a disapproving eye upon the individualist trappings with which it masked its conformism. Even in the thick of the 1960s, Burroughs' interest was invested less in the 'hedonic engineering' of drugs than it was in non-chemical means of enhancement such as biofeedback, and at any rate he did not share the LSD missionary Timothy Leary's absolute optimism when it came to self-actualization through drug use: "95 percent of these people have no idea of what their 'own thing' is,"[120] he said of the ascendant hippie movement and their clarion call to "do your own thing." Writing in *The Job,* he also claimed that anything achieved chemically could be done with other means, encouraging the breakdown of verbal association lines through the application of his 'cut-up' technique (a kind of 'practical magic' based on the random dissecting and re-assembling of pre-existing texts) to writing and tape recording.

The Burroughsian approach remains, perhaps, one of the best working models of industrial culture's potential: although it was not averse to "destroying the inner policeman" through deep psychological self-inquiry, as was the hope of 60s group encounters like the Esalen Institute, it refused to believe that the "outer" policemen were invincible simply because they marshaled superior armed force. Their plan was to seize, decode, and re-appropriate the most sacred commodity of late-20th century regimes, that being information itself. Those who could detect the coercive messages occluded within the pop advertising, public service announcements and recruitment campaigns of State-sanctioned media could then radically alter

---

[120] William Burroughs quoted in *Literary Outlaw* by Ted Morgan, p. 387. Avon Books, 1990, New York.

the messages to their own ends. The use of camouflage clothing and record covers by Throbbing Gristle was a symbolic nod and wink in the direction of authorities who may have detected code-scramblers in their midst.

Because of this focus on the prosecution of the information war, a bit of confusion is bound to arise when introducing post-industrial music to students of sociology: in many ways, the original formations of industrial music cleaved very close to sociological definitions of what 'post-industrial' meant. The 'post-industrial society,' as sociologist Alain Touraine defined it in the early 70s, could be identified by its technological, programmatic elements and by its technocratic ruling class. Despite the misleading use of the Greek root *techne* [skill], this class was not composed of "technicians" in the traditional sense of being skilled laborers, but of managers tasked with administrative duties such as modifying behavior and socio-cultural attitudes. The State's legislative and policing functions had become more and more interwoven with the expansionist interests of corporations, an entanglement that dates back to at least the 1886 legal granting of "natural personhood" to corporations via the *Santa Clara County v. Southern Pacific Railroad* decision in the United States. Since large numbers of people were justifiably critical of how their rights in democratic societies were made secondary to the "personhood" and political influence of these institutions, control and streamlining of information became a high priority for the managerial class. Touraine, who did much to popularize the term "post-industrial society," recognized this as one of its essential features, going so far as to call the spread of "official" information a "parallel school."

The degree of importance that Touraine placed on information as a commodity cannot be overstated, as it is mentioned within his book *The Post-Industrial Society* numerous times. Here is just a sampling of Touraine's thoughts on the information economy:

- "This is how it is with bureaucrats: adept at change, agents of progress beyond doubt, but also often careerists, vain, distrustful, absorbed in their subtle stratagems and their desire to reinforce their own importance by holding back information, by fostering their own prestige in every way possible, and by defending the internal demands of the organization in opposition to its external purposes."[121]

- "The principal opposition between these two great classes or groups of classes does not result from the fact that one possesses wealth or property and the other does not. It comes about because the dominant classes dispose of knowledge and control *information*. Work comes to be less and less defined as a personal contribution and more as a role within a system of communications and social relations."[122]

- "A totalitarian regime reveals itself less by monopolizing wealth than by *the absolute control of information* in all its forms, from the content of the mass media to school curricula and the doctrines of youth movements."[123]

However, not everyone who figured into the original network of industrial musicians placed such value on the devious tailoring and withholding of information. In more recent times, Boyd Rice (the Colorado-based Social Darwinist whose psychoactive noise provided much of the genetic material for industrial anti-music) retrospectively criticized his peers in the movement for not seeing that modern regimes would rely on an information surplus, rather than an information shortage, as their primary mode of control: "…we're over a decade into the 'information age'…the sea change in mass consciousness has failed to materialize, as has the transfiguration of reality. Don't hold your breath for either."[124] However, this curt dismissal doesn't neutralize the fact that, even in a society where there is a State-endorsed information glut, concealed information can - and does - still exist. A tactical shift from outright silence and secrecy, to the false proclamation of a completely 'open' digitized society, does not mean that controlling agents want their methods and long-term goals to be known. As such, the 'information war'

---

[121] Alain Touraine, *The Post-Industrial Society*, p.58. Trans. Leonard F.X. Mayhew. Random House, New York, 1971.

[122] *Ibid.*, p. 61.

[123] *Ibid.*, p. 71.

[124] Boyd Rice, *No*, p. 88. Heartworm Books, Philadelphia, 2009.

ethos of industrial culture remains relevant for the present age- and, in a way, the stakes are now even higher owing to a fact that Rice himself admits: "…once something is in cyberspace it never goes away. It has a half-life beyond that of nuclear waste or Styrofoam."[125]

Rice often stands out as a contrarian dissenter, on this and numerous other issues having to do with industrial culture. Perhaps a more representative view of industrial culture's relationship *vis a vis* controlled information comes from Danny Devos, who, along with Anne-Mie van Kerckhoven, oversaw the manifold underground activities of Belgium's Club Moral. Taking into account not only the degree of information being released by the State, but also its targets, Devos says the following:

> If the 'controlling system' is targeting only one individual, the overload would be a possibility, because an individual would seldom have the opportunity to sort through it all. Unfortunately the 'controlling system' never knows for sure whom they are dealing with, and opponents have always proven more creative in finding ways to get the information they want. So neither way is foolproof. Speaking *as* a 'controlling system,' I'd say that giving no information at all is more effective than dropping bits of information that can lead a life on their own beyond your control.[126]

Devos' statements lend some credence to the author's personal view of industrial culture: it was imbued with a cautious optimism that authoritative measures may lead to unintended consequences, including ones detrimental to that overbearing authority. Coercive information *sui generis* is only enslaving when one believes it is opaque and "finalized" the moment it reaches its target audience. The challenge that the Burroughsian "cut-up method" posed to this institutional opacity took on a new life when the "home-taping" culture found it possible to make disruptive info collages and to freely distribute them. While this activity capably reordered news broadcasts and public service advertisements to its own

---

[125] Boyd Rice, *No,* p. 88. Heartworm Books, Philadelphia, 2009.

[126] Danny Devos, personal correspondence with the author, October 23, 2010.

ends, it also took an interest in certain types of *music* that were serving a clearly coercive function.

Elevator Activism

If the industrial offensive sounded like something you might hear in a Hieronymous Bosch nightmare remixed for the age of automation, it was also a testament to the technocratic society's defensive deployment of conventional forms of music: the constant utilization of music on advertisements, during the 'hold' periods of telephone communications, and in workplaces, was a measure taken in order to minimize discontent with the inorganic and impersonal environments where this music was broadcast (although it did little to create an illusion of organicity in these environments.) The term 'elevator music' came to encompass any music that had mass pacification as an end goal. Its pervasiveness caused critic Jacques Attali to write in 1977 that music "has replaced regular background noise, invaded and even annulled the noise of machinery"[127]- in doing so, it signified "the presence of a power that needs no flag or symbol: musical repetition confirms the presence of repetitive consumption, of the flow of noises as *ersatz* sociality."[128]

The Muzak Corporation, like Xerox and Kleenex, lent its imprimatur to an entire practice: that of scientifically tested, downright *pasteurized* sound. They therefore exemplified "emotional engineering" in this technocratic or managerial state. Also notable is the fact that the distribution system for Muzak recordings was even more hermetic than that of the tape underground, since their "demonstration albums were not available in stores, and were intended strictly for prospective clients and franchisers."[129] While much of Muzak's amniotic output was created "in house" by such composers as Dick Hyman (also an early booster of Moog synthesizers), they would become equally famous for their undeniably skillful neutering of popular rock songs, including those with an insurgent message: the

[127] Jacques Attali, *Noise: The Political Economy Of Music*, p. 111. Trans. Brian Massumi. University Of Minnesota Press, Minneapolis / London, 1985.
[128] *Ibid.*
[129] Joseph Lanza, *Elevator Music*, p. 285. University of Michigan Press, Ann Arbor, 2004.

frequency range of the originals was dramatically limited, instrumental substitutions were made (e.g. harp in the place of electric guitar) and any kind of vocal narration was conspicuously absent. The manipulative effect of this music, as well as its inhuman and ethereal quality, fascinated some musicians on the industrial fringe enough to re-integrate it into their own work. Subversive pop artists Devo, reworking a number of their more familiar songs on ther *E-Z Listening Discs* - and calling them "inframusic" in the process - had good things to say about this irrevocably synthetic medium. Devo founding member Mark Mothersbaugh notes that

> Muzak helped me shape my musical politics. When I heard Muzak versions of the Beatles, the Byrds, and Bob Dylan, my goal was to do the same to my own music before anyone else did. Our *E-Z Listening Disc* has an interesting history. We were writing Muzak-style versions of our songs before we even had our first album out [...] The first *E-Z* disc sold out so fast we that we did a second volume a couple of years later. Rock and Roll is so bankrupt that, out of desperation, they'll be mining those territories.[130]

Mothersbaugh's disdain for rock music was wholeheartedly shared by numerous other musicians from the industrial era, for reasons alluded to earlier: it boldly proclaimed its desire to defeat the "system" (itself never clearly defined) with a spontaneous and organic model of living, yet naively attempted to do this while replicating the "system's" mass organization and personality cultism. The endorsement of Muzak, or the apparently uncritical use of Muzak by musicians like Mothersbaugh[131], was one of the counter-intuitive strategies that distinguished industrial music from this previous mode of confrontation: instead of making loud protests against the technocratic State while "begrudgingly" making use of its machinery, industrial Muzak appropriators acted as if they *identified with* the technocratic State's control methods, making those methods seem

---

[130] Mark Mothersbaugh quoted in *Elevator Music* by Joseph Lanza, p. 205. University of Michigan Press, Ann Arbor, 2004.

[131] "Easy listening" aesthetics were also interrogated, with more blatant irony, when the band performed as the "evangelical" opening act ("Dove, The Band Of Love") at its own concerts.

all the more obscene.

At other times, the use of Muzak tapes in live performances - or simply use of the most prevalent *gauche* pop music of the day - initiated a jarring or exciting contrast with the sinister blasts of electro-chaos endemic to industrial music. Surviving recordings of the Slovenian group Laibach's first performances from 1982 provide a good example of how disorienting this mix could be: a peculiar Yugoslav brand of mood music and Dutch child star Heintje's "Aber Heidschi Bumbeidschi" act as bridges between terroristic vocal harangues and general martial clangor. This would be just one in a series of appropriations that were so deftly pulled off by Laibach, who inadvertently spoke for the larger industrial movement by saying

> The only way to stay partly outside the system is to speak the language of its ideology. The only way is to change yourself into your enemy and subvert the system...that is what we were doing before (under communism) and that is what we are doing now (under capitalism). We still continue to use the language of ideology as our own language.[132]

And so, the relationship of industrial music to 'elevator music' provides the unlikely key to this whole set of strategies. If something like the sculpted sterility of Muzak could be appropriated for anarchic ends, though it was officially designed to regulate moods and maximize productivity, then new tools like the cassette tape did not need to be feared as much. Simply put, there was little "authenticity anxiety" in the culture; this dread feeling that artists contributed to their own alienation in direct proportion to their involvement with new technology. Industrial music took to xerography, home taping, and even Super-8 filmmaking with a fervor unequaled by most other musical genres, and was shot through with the "communication / information above all" ethos of the contemporaneous mail art networks.

---

[132] Ivan Novak quoted in "Popular Music In The Second Yugoslavia," by Gregor Tomc. *Impossible Histories: Historical Avant-Gardes, Neo Avant-Gardes, and Post Avant-Gardes in Yugoslavia, 1918-1991*, p. 459. Ed. Dubravka Duric and Misko Sukakovic. MIT Press, Cambridge, 2003.

Something In The Air: Ambience And Ambiguity

> The factory was a body that contained its internal forces at the level of equilibrium, the highest possible in terms of production, the lowest possible in terms of wages; but in a society of control, the corporation has replaced the factory, and the corporation is a spirit, a gas.[133]

> - Gilles Deleuze

With the folding of Throbbing Gristle's Industrial Records in 1981 came the expected introduction of the critical term "post-industrial." Like other musical modes that have been designated as "post-", post-industrial music was not so much a refutation of the original set of techniques and ideals as it was a continuation of them in the absence of their most successful propagators. "Post-punk" suggested that the implosion of the Sex Pistols, The Clash etc. need not imply the termination of stereotypically "punk" proclivities, and so "post-industrial" was based on fairly respectful interpretation of the foregoing ideals: it was not an outright attempt at transcending of those ideals, as post-modernist thought may have been to modernism proper. What was interesting about this, though, is that the coining of the "new" genre name brought the music up to speed with the actual societal developments suggested by Alain Touraine: whereas the term "industrial music" mainly implied a critique of mechanization and obsession with the material gains thereof, calling the same music "post-industrial" was more appropriate for an art form that was critiquing the information economy and managerial state as well.[134] In this sense, it was arguably more effective than in the short-lived 'classic'

---

[133] Gilles Deleuze, "Postscript On The Societies Of Control." *October* #59 (Winter 1992), p. 3. MIT Press, Cambridge MA.

[134] It is also worth mentioning Lewis Mumford's distrust of historical consensus on the starting dates of the Industrial Revolution: "If the so-called Industrial Revolution, in the old-fashioned sense, could be said to have begun at any single point, it was in the mass production of printed words and pictures, in the new arts of engraving, and lithography." In other words, the beginnings of mass production were also coeval with the beginnings of the "information age." See *The Myth Of The Machine: The Pentagon Of Power* by Lewis Mumford, p. 169. Harcourt / Brace / Jovanovich, New York, 1970.

mode of industrial music, and the growing reliance upon the cassette underground (if not outright congruence with it) caused it to be more tenacious and to break with even more popular conventions of musicality. Not the least of these was the music's treatment of rhythm, and the absence thereof.

Industrial music's appropriation of mechanical rhythm, though owing a debt to the riotous rapture of disco, always had more subversive intentions. Some post-industrial artists, like the Spanish Esplendor Geometrico, made overdriven futurist rhythms their stock-in-trade. Die Form, the emissaries of intellectualized kink hailing from the French commune of Bourg-en-Bresse, also filled several self-released cassettes on their Bain Total label with deformed and submerged electro-dance beats.[135] However, it was the Slovenian industrial ensemble Laibach whose official statement on rhythm cut to the meat of the matter, in typically stern theoretical fashion:

> Disco rhythm, as a regular repetition, is the purest, the most radical form of the militantly organized rhythmicity of technicist production, and, as such, the most appropriate means of media manipulation. As an archetypal structural basis of the collective unconscious in a worker mass, it stimulates automatic *mechanismus*, and shapes industrialization of consciousness, which is necessary in the logic of massive, totalitarian, industrial production.[136]

The title of Grace Jones' 1985 LP, *Slave To The Rhythm*, certainly takes on new meaning in the light of these statements (*The Tyranny Of The Beat*, a 1991 retrospective compilation from The Grey Area label, also pays heed to this fact.)

---

[135] Only recently has the mania for all things "pre-Techno" unearthed these efforts- given the propensity for Techno DJs to hunt down artifacts that are pressed on vinyl, it is understandable that these cassette-based releases evaded recognition until the present age of Internet saturation.

[136] Laibach, "Perspective." From the Walter Ulbricht Schallfolien LP *Rekapitulacija 1980-1984.*

So, another innovation of post-industrial music - both within the cassette network and without - was its re-appraisal of "atmospheric" sound, and its rejection of the idea that modern music had to be beat-driven in order to be radical or revelatory. From the delay-effected primitivism of Zoviet France to the *noir* rituals of Sigillum S or Sleep Chamber, to the hypnagogia of Jim O'Rourke and Illusion Of Safety, post-industrial music found numerous ways to rescue ethereal sound from the faux-mystical domain of "New Age." That is to say, it ignored the existing dichotomy that suggested rhythmic music as "urban, active, socially engaged" and non-rhythmic music as "pastoral, passive, contemplative." Critically recognized "ambient music" had only been extant in popular culture for a couple of years prior to the first industrial music wave[137], yet this dichotomy was already in force, ignoring the less distinctly "electronic" strains of atmospheric music embodied by composers like Giacinto Scelsi. The skeptical, investigative attitude of industrial / post-industrial music worked in tandem with the long playback times of cassette tapes to make occasionally staggering musical documents: ones which evoked the ecstatic and agonizing "ambient" conditions that complemented the "rhythmicity" of urban architecture and production.

The post-industrial society has been defined, after all, not just by the rise of the information economy, but also by heightened sensitivity to changing atmospheric conditions: philosopher Peter Sloterdijk believes that in this age "man is not only what he eats, but what he breathes and that in which he is immersed...cultures are collective conditions of immersion in air and sign systems."[138] Life in the post-industrial age has become defined more and more by the human immersion in the immaterial and ethereal (categories into which 'information' ultimately falls.) From the relationships formed on Internet social networks, to the use of Sarin gas as a terror weapon on Tokyo subways, each shade of

---

[137] Brian Eno dates the "birth of ambient music" to the release of his 1973 collaboration with Robert Fripp, *No Pussyfooting*. See *On Some Faraway Beach: The Life And Times Of Brian Eno* by David Sheppard, p. 153. Chicago Review Press, Chicago, 2009. Somewhat confusingly, though, the "birth" is later claimed as coinciding with Eno's 1975 period of immobility, following a collision with a taxi cab (the release of the album *Discreet Music* followed this experience.)

[138] Peter Sloterdijk, *Terror From The Air*, p. 84. Trans. Amy Patton and Steve Corcoran. Semiotext(e), Los Angeles, 2009.

atmospheric immersion seems to have its own corresponding flavor of post-industrial sonic ambience. Once the huge smoke plumes of noise favored by artists like Maurizio Bianchi wore out their welcome (owing more to a swarm of imitative artists than to Bianchi's own efforts), more imperceptibly quiet forms of ambience began to appear, too. These hinted at the imperceptible but highly affective nature of viruses; be they the kind that disrupted computer communications or the new immunodeficiency virus that wreaked havoc throughout the post-industrial 1980s.

A defining characteristic of post-industrial ambience is its ability to disrupt the listener's customary experience of spatiality by making the "far away" seem close at hand. Ambience envelops and infiltrates in a way that, arguably, the quick and transient attacks of beat-based music cannot, and this is where musicians in the post-industrial milieu excel at shuttling both dreams and nightmares into waking consciousness. In both cases, the aforementioned Illusion of Safety have proven particularly adept: speaking on the piece "Trumpet Field" from the Illusion of Safety release *In 70 Countries,* member Dan Burke says it is meant to evoke "the kind of feeling you have when falling asleep at the wheel...or perhaps going in and out of consciousness after being kept awake and tortured for five days."[139] The record from which this piece is culled is an "unbiased observational documentary about torture," which, although Burke claims it offers "no answers...just a glimpse at the world of man," [140] does not fail to produce strong emotions against the practice under examination. The industrial strategy of stealth seems to apply to this recording: without the few torture-related dialogues that surface throughout the audio program, the flux of alternatingly repellent and attractive atmospheres would suggest nothing more than a natural order of things- even the ambiguous title would not be seen as a reference to nations in which torture was, at the time of release, being practiced. Yet the few hints offered are all that we need, and this makes the enveloping nature of the ambience all the more effective. What would have otherwise signified a harmless "something is all around you" now appends a much more sinister "...and there is no escape."

---

[139] Dan Burke quoted in "An Interview With Dan Burke Of Illusion Of Safety," *H23* #1 (Spring 1989), p. 18. H23, Pullman WA.
[140] *Ibid.*

Just as technocratic control spread like a "gas" or a "cloud," though, so did countervailing forces like the post-industrial, self-releasing music network. Unlike the musical genealogies that obsess over who "begat" whom, the literature of this underground (usually Xeroxed information sheets, or hand-folded and stapled info pamphlets) presented a formation of artists who appeared so chronologically close to each other, despite geographical difference, they were veritably "cloud-like" in their organization. In light of these developments, the online SoundCloud service (begun in 2007 as a means of distributing music akin to pre-existing Internet social networks) can be seen as an extension of post-industrial trails already blazed. Both the cassette network and the Internet were byproducts of what Arnold Toynbee called "etherialization": a state whereby "cultures that remain static and uncreative in the human sphere often promote ingenious technical adaptations and inventions, whereas more creative cultures transmute their energies into higher and more refined forms [...] their technical apparatus becomes progressively dematerialized."[141] It was appropriate that an "ethereal" non-rhythmic music would be such a feature of these networks.

Is Everything OK?

> A general unstated goal is to move away from the complacency around us, so we reject limits placed on us by our peers, institutions, and ourselves. Beyond *WAKE UP!*, we have no obvious social or political message (yet.) We would just like to produce, create, and perform.[142]

> - Dan Burke

William Burroughs' dictum *nothing is true, everything is permitted* - the

---

[141] Lewis Mumford, *The City In History,* p. 112. Harvest Books, San Diego / London / New York, 1989.

[142] Dan Burke quoted in "An Interview With Dan Burke Of Illusion Of Safety," *H23* #1 (Spring 1989), p. 19. H23, Pullman WA.

apocryphal last utterance of Hassan i Sabbah - was taken quite seriously by the more adventurous inhabitants of the post-industrial music landscape. In Burroughs' swashbuckling, achronological epic *Cities Of The Red Night*, seven different permutations on this saying represented seven different mythical cities. The twin cities of Naufana and Ghadis, "cities of illusion where nothing is true, and *therefore* everything is permitted,"[143] represented the idealized condition. In the city of Yass-Waddah, a cruel matriarchy (embodying Burroughs' occasional penchant for unhinged misogyny) "plots a final subjugation of the other cities...here everything is true and nothing is permitted, except to the permitters."[144] Numerous other transitional cities had to be passed through on the plgrimmage to Naufana and Ghadis, a journey that could "take many lifetimes."[145]

Realizing that the greatest victory of the control society would come with the extinguishment of the exploratory drive, the homemade counter-culture lashed out with an astonishingly intense arsenal of images, words, and sounds: sometimes this was presented in a breathless polemic fashion, but never anywhere close to the overconfident and exasperated tone of classic avant-garde manifestoes from the likes of futurists, Dadaists, vorticists, and so on. Within industrial culture, sympathetic underground pamphlets and international 'zines such as *Industrial News, Grok, H23, ND*, and *Force Mental* - many of which acted as forums to promote and review self-released cassettes - followed editorial policies whose only grounds for excluding something were if that something was *uninteresting*. At the very least, the contents of these magazines were not limited to musical trivia and taste-making: brief examinations of 'hidden history', subversive how-to articles and free-form, personal exegeses gave these periodicals their distinct patina of cool, yet embattled anti-conformity.

This aesthetic led to individual issues of these organs that could be almost perversely contradictory in terms of what they presented. The Belgian "kultureel strijdschrift" ["cultural battle 'zine"] *Force Mental* - partially the house organ of Club Moral - was so adamant in this

---

[143] William Burroughs, *Cities Of The Red Night*, p. 159. Henry Holt / Owl Books, New York, 1995.

[144] *Ibid*, p.158.

[145] *Ibid*.

conviction that one issue (#15) featured both an essay from left-wing neoist Stewart Home and a Charles Manson missive to the White House (along with an advertisement for the Manson-affiliated white separatist group, The Universal Order): two opposing poles of political orientation, if ever there were any. The remainder of the issue featured a highly informative text on Australian aboriginal peoples, visual evidence of serial murderer Ed Gein's ghoulish, decorative uses for human skin, and all manner of existential narratives from simultaneously frightening and exhilarating thresholds of experience (editor Danny Devos helpfully translated all of the multi-lingual text contributions into English.) Throughout all this, the underlying message is not one of uncommunicative shock, but one very similar to the message of networked art in general, i.e. knowledge of the peripheries is essential to knowing what the 'center' is (and whether or not that theoretical 'center' truly exists.) Dutch art critic Wim van Mulders, recognizing this fact, praises *Force Mental* in its 11th issue as superior to the "official" journals of art criticism: "I can read [...] in *Force Mental* contributions as interesting as in the prestigious, solid-based *Museumjournaal* (official publication sponsored by most of the Dutch musea...) I admit that *Force Mental's* approach is less pedagogical, unequivocal, and walks in its amoral freedom nicely between good and evil."[146] The magazine, if nothing else, echoed Dan Burke's earlier statement about resisting generalized complacency to a "t": the summary effect of its "amoral freedom" was to document a world where innate qualities of good and evil were mercilessly buffeted by chaotically shifting circumstances. The declared enemy, the Burroughsian "control machine," was that body of social institutions that saw its values as being irrevocably fixed and thus immune to these unpredictable circumstances.

Of course, the permissive attitude of the post-industrial tape and 'zine networks did not mean that every propagator of "non-mainstream" attitudes would have the laurels of greatness conferred upon them. Some participants in this culture did receive harsh condemnations in return for their transgressions, rather than support. This was the case with Chicago provocateur Mark Solotroff's Terre Blanche[147] project and its parent AWB

---

[146] Wim van Mulders, "Art Criticism: A Hatchet Or A Floorcloth?" *Force Mental* #11, p. 344. Club Moral, Antwerp, 1985.

[147] Solotroff recorded under the pseudonym "M. Sanderson" for the purposes of the Terre Blanche project.

Recording label, both of which draped themselves in the regalia of the eponymous South African pro-apartheid organization (AWB standing for Afrikaner Weerstandsbeweging, or Afrikaner Resistance Movement, of which the recently murdered Eugene Terre'Blanche was the ideologue.) Self-releasing artist Jeph Jerman, in the pages of Hal McGee's *Electronic Cottage* magazine, inadvertently set off a war of words when praising - with some qualification - Terre Blanche's skill as documentarians:

> I can even enjoy music backed up by convictions I disagree with simply because the whole package is so well thought out and constructed. Such is the case with Terre Blanche [...] I do not agree with their racial standpoint, which is one of white superiority, stemming from the daily lives of the members of Terre Blanche and their associates. If I lived in Chicago and was treated daily to threats of physical violence from Black and / or Hispanic neighbors, I too might develop a similar attitude.[148]

Jerman's comments, which could be interpreted as a warning that racially based hatreds can explode with sudden shifts in circumstances, is pounced upon in the letters section of the 2nd issue of *Electronic Cottage*. Lydia Tomkiw & Don Hedeker, of the group Algebra Suicide, write:

> Claiming one doesn't agree with the political point of view, but likes the music, makes as much sense as marching around in full Nazi regalia simply because "the color and texture of the uniform is nice, and the swastika makes a lovely graphic." It is still condoning the attitude and viewpoint, or at very least (but just as bad), condoning the vehicle through which the viewpoint is being supported and disseminated.[149]

The co-signers of this letter take an extra swipe at McGee by claiming this review contradicts his own editorial policy, i.e. that he reserves the

---

[148] Jeph Jerman, "Reviews." *Electronic Cottage* #1 (April 1989), p. 61. Hal McGee, Apollo Beach, Florida.

[149] Lydia Tomkiw & Don Hedeker, "Feedback." *Electronic Cottage* #2 (September 1989), p. 12. Hal McGee, Apollo Beach, Florida.

right to refuse "material that is counter-productive, needlessly negative, or derogatory."[150] Amusingly enough, the inside cover of the issue containing these protests contains a full-page ad for AWB Recordings, boldly advertising the *Sickle Cell* 7" record, and the issue following that one features another full-page ad for products in the AWB catalog. This internecine feud would reach its apex when Frans de Waard and Philip B. Klinger collaborated on a counter-AWB compilation cassette, which repurposed the initials of the South African organization and twisted them into an acronym for "anti white bastards." However, the larger issue, that of whether "everything is permitted" or not, has remained a burning issue for the self-released (and largely self-policing) audio underground. Burroughs, as the grand old man of counter-cultural American letters, had almost certainly not intended for his battle cry to be appropriated by those who were lending even tacit support to systems of control.

Terre Blanche's controversial recorded output (actually quite slim considering the furious rate at which post-industrial "power electronics" bands now release) was not limited to the *Sickle Cell* 7". A few additional releases revealed deeper levels of anti-black obsession: a 1988 cassette entitled *The New Slavery*, for example, "celebrates" the 1987 death of Chicago's mayor Harold Washington. AWB co-signees such as Slave State also offered variations on the apartheid theme (e.g. the cassette *White Land, White Rule*.) The single-minded viciousness of these groups' sounds, while not entirely distinguishable from any of their peers, paradoxically steer the music's message towards a queasy ambiguity: the music is so shrouded in ominous sonic fog, so shot through with echoing screams and FX-obscured incantations, whatever "triumphal" quality it might have had is defused. In the case of the Slave State tape, a "blind" listen, unencumbered by the visual cues provided by the packaging, fails to really point the moral compass in any particular direction: singer Thomas Thorn's excited, distorted yelps of *"white land...white rule!,"* even if intended as 'rousing oratory' of the fascist variety, could just as easily be heard as the panicked cries of someone lost in the wilderness and hoping to attract a rescue party. The steadily rolling waves of low-frequency electronics are open to equally subjective interpretations, capable of either energizing listeners or

---

[150] Lydia Tomkiw & Don Hedeker, "Feedback." *Electronic Cottage* #2 (September 1989), p. 12. Hal McGee, Apollo Beach, Florida.

rendering them insensate- but, as with the vocals, pre-cognition of the "political" content is needed to most dramatically shape the impressions received.

With this in mind, you could justifiably ask why groups with even a tincture of moral ambiguity are singled out for attack by their underground peers- why an "anti white bastards" tape "dedicated" to the AWB label, but not a similar one directed at those bands whose lyrics and texts are of a clear imperative nature? As hackneyed as Terre Blanche's approach is, it gives no explicit "marching orders." So, the complaint of Tomkiw and Hedeker arguably had as much to do with groups like Terre Blanche infiltrating or mocking the cassette "movement" than it did with their fascist aesthetics. The only problem is that, like mail art, Cassette Culture was (as claimed by Vittore Baroni) a *medium* and not a *movement*[151] - condemning Terre Blanche and company caused Algebra Suicide to fall directly into the trap laid for them, making them seem like *they* were in the wrong for being censors in an otherwise "open" culture. Mark Solotroff himself has shown little affinity with this culture, stating on at least one occasion that "I was always anxious to move on to records and CDs [...] I feel that it is of extreme importance to keep the quality level as high as possible with I.A. [Solotroff's newer project 'Intrinsic Action'] so that we will not be lumped in with the 'home tapers network.'"[152]

The enforced ideological ambiguity of groups like Terre Blanche and Grey Wolves[153] suggests that a third category of communication - pornographic titillation - should be considered in addition to the poles of "propaganda" and "reportage" normally brought up during arguments over the free flow of "extreme" cultural products. Long before the digital age trend for no-frills, narrative-free "gonzo" porn videos and hi-resolution

---

[151] Some dissent comes from Philip Klinger, a.k.a. PBK, on this issue: "That whole mind set [of Terre Blanche / AWB] holds back any hope for an evolving and positive 'movement' within the underground scene - it only provides more fragmentation - and my feeling is, at this point, we haven't even begun to explore the potential for expression using noise elements." http://media.hyperreal.org/zines/est/articles/freelet2.html. Retrieved October 21, 2010.

[152] Mark Solotroff quoted in "Intrinsic Action Interview #1". *Interim Report* #2. Shunya Suzuki, Tokyo, 1992.

[153] The(e) Grey Wolves once featured a member named "Crystal Knight," a blatant pun on the anti-Jewish pogrom of *Kristallnacht.*

"p.o.v." photo albums, pornography has had a long history of using some socially acceptable pretext of social or scientific research to aid its dissemination: art historian Therese Lichtenstein notes the existence of a German Institute of Sexology that cataloged visual evidence of sexual perversions for ostensibly documentary reasons, while there were also "sadomasochistic excursions in pseudoscientific pamphlets that contained illustrated stories of 'naughty' maids who 'deserved' whippings from their masters."[154] Like pornography, the final product also encourages a state of total sensory immersion and emotional detachment: the sizzling, febrile noise denies the possibility of focusing on some other stimulus, yet is never really anything more than a perspectival window onto a world of racial violence and terrorism. Though it clearly aims for affect, it demands no further analysis from the listener. Having considered all this, Mark Solotroff's post-Terre Blanche conceptual 'upgrade' to thematic concerns of violent sex / sexualized violence (as Intrinsic Action) seems like an appropriate career move.[155]

So, the question has yet to be answered: does William Burroughs' nonpareil libertarian approach allow even for groups that use this message of inclusion to promote *exclusion* (on grounds of race, class etc.)? Moreover, isn't the camouflaging of hardcore titillation as "documentation" or "research" consistent with the overall industrial ethos, that of revealing how different atoms of information can be combined to serve nearly any purpose, no matter how noble or nefarious? Even in a de-centralized social order favoring extreme permissiveness, individual preferences will still exist, and while no outright bans may be put into motion by decree or by design, unsavory ideas can be discredited to the point of irrelevance. Seen in this light, Solotroff's eventual rejection of the "home-tapers' network" as a means for transmitting ideas may have more to do with the network's own rejection of those ideas.[156]

---

[154] Therese Lichtenstein, *Behind Closed Doors: The Art of Hans Bellmer*, p. 90. University of California Press, Berkeley, 2001.

[155] Albeit another one that was questioned by Frans de Waard, as follows: "Mark Saunderson / Solotroff once said in *Chemical Castration* that 'I am not attracted to Whitehouse because of the violent sexual image they have.' And now he himself is taking part in it. I don't have much more to say on this issue- for me it's a clear case; it is just another image to be bought." Quoted in "Kommentar: Der Fall AWB." *SIAM Industrial Newsletter*, vol. 6 no. 1, p. 45. Translated from the German by the author. Society For Industrial Arts And Music E.V., Munich, 1993.

Whatever the true political coordinates of these groups and their allies may have been in the post-industrial 1980s, their sound work was fairly easy to replicate, and thus would have been negligible if not accompanied by the "whole package" that Jerman mentions. Compared with the harsh rigor of, say, Iannis Xenakis' electronic works - that predate these "power electronics" works by 15 years or more - this music calls for a politically incorrect bark to draw attention away from its dull sonic bite. Again, Sloterdijk has some pertinent thoughts on extremity that relate to the pose of constant agitation adopted by post-industrial music's terrorist "hard core":

> Isaac Babel's declaring that: "banality is the counter-revolution," also indirectly articulates the principle of "revolution," the use of horror as violence against morality explodes aesthetic and social latency, exposing the laws whereby societies and artworks are constructed. Permanent "revolution" demands permanent horror. It presumes a society that continually proves anew to be horrifiable and revisable.[157]

In the end, then, the problem is that Terre Blanche cannot, with their limited palette of skills, possibly hope to deliver sensations that are progressively more shocking or revelatory. Post-industrial groups like Illusion of Safety and Etant Donnes have stated, to some degree or another, a desire for their music to act as a "wake up call" for listeners, leaving themselves open to a similar criticism. Yet their audio-visual dynamic of ebbing, flowing seduction and repulsion is far more effective in terms of

---

[156] On the more extremist / transgressive fringe of post-industrial culture, the divide between "networkers / traders" and professionally oriented self-releasers was fairly pronounced. The teenaged Coup de Grace frontman Michael Moynihan complains "I can't stand all these people who write to anybody who writes them a letter. All this networking and cassette…junk. […] It's just as much a waste of time as anything else. Our business side weeds these people out. If people want to write to us, unless they say something that merits a response, all they'll get back is a printed catalog and nothing else." Quoted in *U-Bahn* vol. 2 no. 2, p. 6. The Arbeit Group, Madison WI, 1988.

[157] Peter Sloterdijk, *Terror From The Air*, p. 80. Trans. Amy Patton and Steve Corcoran. Semiotext(e), Los Angeles, 2009.

what *secondary, unintended* messages it can convey in addition to the artists' primary motive. The network of self-released music, one that prides itself on being "unfinished" and eternally reciprocal, seems like an appropriate place to insert individual works that are also "unfinished" and require an audience to "fill in" a multiplicity of meanings. Etant Donnes explains it succinctly: "I aspire to the spectators' soul…that is to say, I expect them to come and fill in my own vacuum."[158]

Not "In"dustrial: Adventures In The External World

In the process of 'winding down' this chapter, it would be wise to reaffirm the following: industrial and post-industrial music was, despite its cult level of acceptance, never a completely hermetic culture: for one, Throbbing Gristle's Genesis P. Orridge had initiated a series of street 'happenings' prior to the formation of TG, and later became a kind of gaudy Scaramouche of the post-industrial scene. Hand-duplicated cassettes and photocopied information booklets distributed by mail were only one aspect of a culture whose public visibility could, in certain circumstances, be downright hazardous for those who displayed their allegiance to it. The Laibach of 1980-1985 certainly raised the bar for 'industrial publicity stunts', when, as Eda Čufer recalls, they "…seemingly never took off the specially designed and quintessentially militant suits that were their signature. […] Living, working, socializing and performing in uniform, they not only *dressed* the part but their own identities became so subsumed by their Laibach personalities that they *became* their parts."[159] This culminated in a locally infamous TV appearance in which the group, in their militant attire, responded as a collective to an indignant interviewer's questions with answers such as "art is a noble calling that demands fanaticism." The public image projected on this show led to a formal ban on the use of the Laibach name, and on live performances, from 1983-1987.

---

[158] Etant Donnes quoted in *Wonderland* #1 by Yvan Etienne Et. Al., p. 59. Editions Wonderland, Besancon, 2000.

[159] Eda Čufer, "New Theater In Slovenia, 1980-1990." *Impossible Histories: Historical Avant-Gardes, Neo Avant-Gardes, and Post Avant-Gardes in Yugoslavia, 1918-1991*, ed. Dubravka Duric and Misko Sukakovic. MIT Press, Cambridge, 2003.

Elsewhere, the Club Moral organization seemingly did away with all but the most essential of private spaces. As Danny Devos describes it, the physical space known as Club Moral (of which the similarly named music group was just the 'house band') was like a more functional, post-industrial version of Andy Warhol's Silver Factory:

> Club Moral was located in an old factory building, about 1000 square meters large, several buildings around a courtyard, several floors. There were about 20 people, companies, bands, craftsmen who rented spaces there, all very cheap and extremely basic. There was a print shop, a car upholstery company, a ground-drilling company, a club of American military vehicle enthusiasts and some random figures in weird workshops, also artist studios and band rehearsal rooms. It looked a bit like a medieval fortress where everything was at hand. After a while I bought a 4x4 ex-Army ambulance, so the picture of self-sustaining unit was complete. And it is indeed true that we converted bare concrete spaces into living quarters. Maybe politics in Western Europe were so fucked up at the time that self-sustainment was more important, social structures were collapsing, so it was a kind of survivor attitude to build some kind of own self-supporting social mechanism to cope with what was happening around us.[160]

Finally, the cassette tape itself played an unlikely public role in the explication of post-industrial culture, thanks to the "cassette concerts" of the ebullient ex-Kluster / Tangerine Dream associate (and one-time Joseph Beuys student) Conrad Schnitzler. Schnitzler, despite his pedigree and potential for exploiting these "star" connections, remained one of the most steadfast proselytizers of hand-made music- he had self-released his music as early as 1971, hand-designing album sleeves for a record in an edition of 100. His *Kasettenorgel* [cassette organ], a home-built contraption that featured six stereo cassette decks internally wired to a single stereo output,

---

[160] Danny Devos, personal correspondence with the author, August 25 2010.

was an innovation that, much like Peter Christopherson's similar design for Throbbing Gristle, occupied a special place on the audio "cut-up" timeline between William Burroughs' early tape experiments and full-blown digital sampling. A more motile version of the same - a 'Walkman belt' attached to his body and connected to a helmet-mounted megaphone - allowed Schnitzler to more directly approach his audience (and vice versa), unconstrained by the boundaries of the performance stage. Indeed, plans for 'participatory' cassette concerts became more and more elaborate, and less a 'pure' performance of Schnitzler himself: with cassette recorders placed in the 4 corners of a live space, or in other positions throughout the room, audience members could become part of an impromptu orchestra (sound artist 'Gen' Ken Montgomery was the first Schnitzler-authorized 'conductor' of these performances.)[161]

Given Schnitzler's exploding of the idea that "Cassette Culture" was an "anti-social" enterprise, it's not astounding that he has been immortalized as a perpetually beaming, shiny-domed superhero in the independent comics of artist Matt Howarth. Of equal interest, though, is the fact that Schnitzler took like the proverbial duck to the 'water' of the cassette underground (and the subsequent CD-Recordable underground) even in spite of his 'serious' music pedigree: along with fellow Beuys student Dieter Moebius and Hans-Joachim Roedelius, he coordinated happenings at the Zodiak free arts club in West Berlin, and, as an outgrowth of the impromptu performances there, participated in an early incarnation (1969-1971) of the highly regarded electronic group Kluster. The deep space atmospherics and free-flowing electronic cascades of this ensemble would, in themselves, provide a lasting influence on post-industrial ambience while challenging the conventions of the unfortunately named 'Krautrock' scene. Schnitzler's ebullience and manic drive - the latter proven by a succession of 'regular' jobs in addition to an abundant musical output - likewise made him, up until his passing in 2011, a centripetal force in a

---

[161] Ken Montgomery, who went to early 1980s Berlin "on a whim" with his group KMZ, "fell in love with Berlin immediately, made good friends, and of course eventually met Conrad Schnitzler and hit it off with him. Conrad was a huge influence on me and it was through our mutual apreciation of Conrad that David Prescott [co-founder of the Generations Unlimited label] and I met up. I had planned to start Generations Unlimited, and already started recording what would be the GENCON LP [with Schnitzler]. David was working on his first LP and we decided to join forces and release our records together. It grew from there." Personal correspondence with the author, June 22 2010.

culture too often criticized for its insular grimness.

Escape From The Death Factory

This said, there should be no doubt that industrial music and post-industrial music has, to a greater degree than most popular art forms, tested the strength of the human spirit in an age of ironclad technocracy and conformity. Its quest to unshackle and purify information has revealed a modern propensity for cruelty, misdirected rage, and blind lust for short-term gains, among other deleterious attitudes- a bleak reminder that the rules of the game, in the age of techno-science, have not changed as dramatically as advertised. Some researchers from within this culture may have felt impotent in the face of such historically persistent breaches of ethics, and resignedly chose to join in the culture of exploitation. Many others chose to cultivate a trade in bowdlerized "industrial" merchandising that owed little to the original climate of research and reappraisal, and which was strikingly unreflective about its own potentiality: though Laibach's incisive criticisms of radical 'disco rhythm' applied perfectly well to latter-day industrial dance music, the 1990s brought about a trend for using the industrial beat as a backdrop to insipid bleats of romantic angst.

The hopelessly disaffected cynic is not exclusively a product of this culture, though: latter-day industrial fashion poses are usually just an externalization of pre-formed feelings of disgust. Meanwhile, the enjoyment of aesthetically repulsive or self-destructive art ("Happiness In Slavery," as the popular Nine Inch Nails song was titled) appears in numerous subcultures from over a century's worth of artistic development. So, when opposing "'classic' industrial culture" to "neo-industrial fashion," we have to look beyond the surface similarities in imagery, coded language and sonic affect: the difference is often a simple matter of choosing between distracting fantasy and engagement, between passive / submissive bewilderment in the face of technology and active appraisal of its more esoteric applications. The kitsch variety of industrial or post-industrial music can be identified by the extreme reverence it accords to symbols of mechanized destruction and "mega-technic" coercion, although there is no activating of any liberating potential that may come about by re-appropriating these symbols. At least a couple of 'industrial rock' bands have paid homage to the iconic scene in John Woo's *The Killer*, where actors Chow Yun-Fat and Danny Lee stand mere feet apart with handguns trained on each others' heads: this "Mexican standoff" image is understandably popular in a culture which too often reveres a static form of negative confrontation, and which - referring back to Renato Poggioli's assessment of F.T. Marinetti and the Italian Futurists - "is more interested in motion than in creation, gestures than acts [...] its creation often appears as a vulgar variant of aestheticism, and sometimes is reduced to nothing more than a kind of 'operation.'"[162] The dissatisfaction with this comfort zone of stasis, which is left behind for the cut-up zone of unforeseen consequences and continual reciprocation, is the spark igniting original industrial culture.

And so it seems that the cassette networks of bygone years are hard to imagine without a regular infusion of 'industrial' materials: few other subcultures were so determined to unleash a flood of sounds, images, and texts from areas of research that may have not even directly affected their disseminators. Whether this data was reporting on atrocities or mutating the banal into an intoxicating form of exotica, it was destined to form part of a larger media network based on self-determined creativity.

As to this culture's still-unrealized potential, it may help to look to Fluxus (one of the most important roots of industrial culture and networked art), for an example of what could result from all this treatment of "negative" materials. Describing the funeral of artist Robert Watts, Ron Rice notes the following:

> On October 17, 1988, assorted remains of the Fluxus group met in Pennsylvania to celebrate the death of Fluxartist [sic] Robert Watts. Watts himself had named the event 'FluxLux' and provided instructions before he died. These 'last rites' were, in a way, Watts' final performance piece. The mood was one of rejoicing – with music and dancing. It's funny- what goes around truly does come around

---

[162] Renato Poggioli, *The Theory Of The Avant-Garde*, p. 29. Trans. Gerald Fitzgerald. The Belknap Press of Harvard University Press, Cambridge / London, 1997.

again. It seems that an atmosphere of violence and negativity has set the stage for a renewed interest in the art of life and living. [163]

Industrial culture and networked art: united in the realization of 'life before death?

---

[163] Ron Rice, "Modern Morality Plays: Fluxus And Beyond." *H23* #1 (Spring 1989), p. 25. H23, Pullman WA.

Magnitizdat!
Can Self-Releasing Circumvent Censorship?

It has to be said, the spirit that animates history's more enduring artworks has been a particularly resilient one: it has been a force armed with the improvisational abilities that turn catastrophes into defining moments of creative brilliance rather than mere moments of collapse. Often the interventionist decrees of authoritarian powers have unintended positive consequences for the creative communities that outlive these edicts, since their injection of raw fear into the public consciousness can quickly separate vanity-driven dabblers from those who no know other way of life but art, and whose defense of that art is therefore carried out with a survivalist level of determination. In particularly extreme situations, where a possible death sentence hangs over any artist who dares to contravene official State ideology, a similar separation of wheat and chaff occurs whereby inessential content falls away from a creative work's core message. Yet as we glorify the resisting artist in this scenario, it has to be remembered that his or her struggles are only part of the story: in times when totalitarian power is in the ascendancy, it is busy piecing together its own narrative of heroism and resistance. As per the Czech dissident writer Josef Vohryzek, "...the totalitarian state has had to raise the policing function to one of the greatest virtues. In television films and propaganda programmes, it is no longer a worker or party secretary who embodies all the finest human qualities, but a cop."[164]

In writing this, Vohryzek almost certainly has in mind the Soviet-era Czechoslovak TV thriller *Třicet případů majora Zemana* [The Thirty Cases Of Major Zeman], which was especially notable for its caricature of the Czechoslovakian music-related subculture- one episode of the series goes after the local brand of hippie, derisively known as *máničky* ["mops"], not only portraying them as anti-social, cutthroat drug dealers but also as potential terrorists (the *máničky* in the 1972 episode 'Mimikry' eventually resort to hijacking a plane in order to escape to the West.) Such

---

[164] Josef Vohryzek, "Thoughts Inside A Tightly-Corked Bottle." Trans. Paul Wilson. Vaclav Havel et. Al., *The Power Of The Powerless*, p. 199. M.E. Sharpe Inc., New York, 1985.

adventurous hyperbole, whether or not it actually convinced anyone of the *máničky* threat to orderly society, illuminates the fear that authoritarian regimes have of public expression, and music in particular. The inspiration for 'Mimikry' was, after all, the local group Plastic People Of The Universe, despised by the puppet government of Gustáv Husák. The group, formed in the mold of psychedelic jesters like Captain Beefheart or Frank Zappa[165], was not even overtly political, yet was clearly seen as contravening Marxist-Leninist notions of duty and discipline. The hardliners' bafflement at how such groups could even exist in the 'workers' state' was adroitly answered by the writer Jiři Ruml: "it is unlikely that poets would ever enjoy the economic security they now have as skilled crane drivers; it is just that they would sooner 'raise spirits' than raise heavy loads."[166] Anyway, as the group's popularity expanded, so did the necessity to skirt around the law by performing in public gardens rather than official performance venues. The anti-Plastic People campaign of arrests, performance bans and the like eventually culminated in a 1976 show trial, which had the unforeseen effect of galvanizing the dissident movement around playwright (and notable Plastic People backer) Vaclav Havel: the 'Charter 77' document, circulated by Havel and several hundred co-signatories, lent its name to a larger movement that became one of the more prominent human rights organizations within Eastern Europe. Though their challenge to the State was largely energized by political events like the Helsinki Accords of 1975 (with its overtures towards self-determination and toleration of "fundamental freedoms"), the State's aversion to musical expression in particular also played a significant role in shaping Charter 77's resistance.

Before we continue any further down this road, though, it is important not to impose a single standard of oppressiveness on all of the authoritarian states of the post-WWII era. The 'Brezhnev Doctrine' of 1968 officially allowed countries within the Eastern Bloc to be independent in local affairs, provided the individual nations cleaved to the Kremlin's definitions of what constituted socialism and capitalism.[167] Within the

---

[165] The group's name is borrowed from a song off of the 1967 Mothers of Invention LP *Absolutely Free.*

[166] Jiři Ruml, "Who Really Is Isolated?", trans. A.G. Brain. Vaclav Havel et. Al., *The Power Of The Powerless*, p. 182. M.E. Sharpe Inc., New York, 1985.

[167] This was then followed by the amusingly named "Sinatra Doctrine" of Mikhail

socialist-aligned nations, there were different grades of police surveillance, differing opportunities for travel to the West, and different stages at which the production of insurgent media was curtailed. The "self-management" or non-Stalinist socialism of the former Yugoslavia, with its comparatively lax border controls and strikingly articulate, creative *avant garde*, was already far removed from the situation of a country like Romania. The latter was identified by such horrors as its suffocating *Securitate* police force, and by being the only country in the Eastern bloc to outlaw abortion as a means of dramatically increasing the population. Along with this, there was almost zero distribution of independent or avant-garde printed materials (to say nothing of self-released underground music), since even the rental of a typewriter required authorization from the "militia," once an exhaustive amount of personal information was provided. Part of the official State policy regarding these expressive tools read as follows:

> If the application is granted, the applicant will receive an authorization for the typewriter for 60 days. On a specified date, the owner of the typewriter must report with the machine to the militia office in order to provide an example of his typing. A similar example has to be provided every year, specifically during the first two months of the year, as well as after every repair to the typewriter. [168]

For a nation in which, during the 1980s, nobody "...was entirely sure what constituted a crime,"[169] and in which Nicolae Ceaușescu "for no obvious reason...suddenly began a campaign against yoga", the above edict actually seems somewhat banal. Yet it is representative of the ideological infiltration or micro-management that made any provocative creative act incredibly risky, if not outright lethal to one's self.

That anyone took such risks at all is a testament to mankind's almost

---

Gorbachev, named so because individual states were allowed to do things "their way" (a reference to the classic Sinatra tune "My Way.")

[168] Victor Sebestyen, *Revolution 1989: The Fall Of The Soviet Empire*, p. 165. Pantheon Books, New York, 2009.

[169] *Ibid.*, p. 164

biological restlessness when it comes to matters of self-expression and public recognition. In almost all nations of the former USSR, some small but indomitable group of cultural agents sought to erode the official narrative on pressing matters like economics, ecology, public health and, naturally, the possibility of unrestricted access to authentic culture. The *samizdat* publication - a Russian portmanteau of *sam* [self] and *izdat* [to publish] - has become, along with mail art, one of the key "unofficial" art forms of the post-industrial age, and a crystallization of the dogged persistence with which the era's dissident subcultures carried out their actions. Like the 'zine culture more familiar to Western readers, *samizdat* varied wildly in their content, from contrapuntal politics to transcriptions of classic literature to comics (notably, the superheroine Octobriana created by the Russian group Progressive Political Pornography.) Much like Western 'zine culture, the information within the publications' pages was usually given priority over the visual and tactile attractiveness of the publications, that is to say, their value is objects to be presented. Bindings and print quality also varied wildly, typically in accordance with what kind of materials could be obtained while under heavy surveillance (*samizdat* that were simply handwritten, for example, were not a total anomaly.) In rare cases, *samizdat* were even sold in something akin to a retail operation (i.e. the apartment of Budapest architect László Rajk): historian Victor Sebestyn recalls "*samizdat* boutiques" in Soviet satellite Hungary, where

> ...various publications would be laid out on a long table. The 'customers', whose names would never be taken, would say which magazine they wanted, and Rajk's team of 'copiers' would produce the texts in time for them to be collected the following week. It was a remarkably efficient system.[170]

The practice of *samizdat* eventually became so well known that it gave rise to related clever neologisms and code words, such as *tamizdat* (*tam* being a term in Slavic languages for "over there," thusly meaning publications and recordings smuggled in from Western countries.) When the practice was

---

[170] Victor Sebestyen, *Revolution 1989: The Fall Of The Soviet Empire*, p. 149. Pantheon Books, New York, 2009.

transposed to a different medium - magnetic tape - it was re-dubbed *magnitizdat*. Prior to this method of audio distribution, there were other stunningly improvisational means of making unofficial recordings: the Lithuanian music writer Mindaugas Peleckis notes a phenomenon known as *roentgenizdat* or "on the bones" records, named as such because discarded X-ray film was the medium onto which the spiral grooves were etched.[171] "On the bones" jazz records or "ribs" were a staple of Soviet underground nightspots of the 1950s, and were originally created as a response to austerity conditions during the foregoing world war (the format survived into the punk rock era as well.) Their lifespan, similar to that of other volatile media like acetate disks, was quite brief (perhaps an upward limit of a month and a half), and official recognition of the medium in 1958 led to the expected spate of new prohibitions and imprisonments. The authorities themselves seem to have gotten in on the act, as well, since some "ribs" exist that are little more than "audio traps" meant to ensnare Westernized youth: some records might feature a few tantalizing moments of rock 'n roll that were then abruptly terminated by a scolding voice repeating the official Party line about rhythm-fueled degeneracy.

Not all unofficial audio products from the Soviet era were as esoteric or as low-fidelity as the "ribs", though. The early circulation of magnetic tape reels within the USSR seemed like it would be a great boon to freedom of expression: instead of circulating insurrectionary ideas through the shaky medium of *samizdat* carbon-paper transcriptions, whose content could not be altered, all variety of speeches, music etc. could now be circulated on a re-writable medium. Some *samizdat* were prone to fall apart or crumble after minimal use, as well, giving them the colorful local euphemism *bibula* [toilet paper] in Poland. In addition, the creation of *magnitizidat* reel-to-reel tapes was already less fraught with risk than the publication of *samizdat:* Soviet regulations on paper duplication were more tightly controlled, and "access" to photocopying equipment meant getting clearance to pass through double-locked, guarded, steel doors. Only in 1989 could the *L.A. Times* report that the Soviet Ministry of Internal Affairs "'wanted to relinquish control over the acquisition, storage and operation

---

[171] Some helpful visualizations are available online:
http://www.kk.org/streetuse/archives/2006/08/jazz_on_bones_xray_sound_recor_1.php.Ret rieved February 23, 2011.

of copying equipment,' admitting that photocopiers are now standard office equipment and not really the grave threat to state security they were once perceived to be."[172] By contrast, anyone was permitted to own a home tape recorder (despite their daunting purchase price), and "magnitoalbumy" or tape albums tended to be years ahead of what the state-owned record company, Melodiya, was allowed to produce. For example, the first rock music LPs within the USSR appeared as "magnitoalbumy" prior to Melodiya's flirtations with the rock idiom.

All was not smooth sailing, though, when it came to the availability of blank recording media in the Soviet era. An outright ban on blank media would have been a tacit admission that a larger community of dissent existed than what was claimed by official propaganda, but other means of restriction could be applied in place of a blanket ban. One method was to classify cassette tapes as "luxury items," as was done in Latvia and elsewhere- governmental authorities could limit perceived insurrectionary practices by pricing these media above what most citizens could normally afford, while not betraying their paranoia quite as much as they would have by disallowing their sale altogether. Cassette culture stalwart Lord Litter confirms this practice as being widespread in the former East Germany, where a single blank C60 cassette could cost $12 U.S.[173]

As the reader can probably also surmise, getting cassettes past the customs inspectors of the USSR provided its own challenges. At least one would-be networker, who advertised in the back pages of *Electronic Cottage* magazine, included instructions on how to write his name and mailing address in Cyrillic characters- the presumption here was that this would seem less suspect than parcels sent from abroad with the name and mailing address written in Roman characters. Importing original copies of mass-produced Western albums into the Soviet republics could be done by bribing the right officials, or by the intrigue of CIA agents, while much popular music could be recorded from picking up shortwave radio broadcasts. The propagation of Cassette Culture was a different story. On one hand, more difficult since the nature of that propagation involved so

---

[172] Michael Parks, "Soviets Free The Dreaded Photocopier." *L.A. Times,* October 5, 1989.

[173] See "Here Comes The Rest Of The World!" by Lord Litter, *Electronic Cottage* #4 (July 1990), p. 19. Hal McGee, Apollo Beach, Florida.

much direct contact rather than going through 'black market' intermediaries. No information has surfaced about covert operations to smuggle handmade cassettes into the USSR: the small and scattered worldwide audience of Cassette Culture consumers was difficult to pin down ideologically, and not as profitable as Beatles records would have been for an enterprising black marketer. On the other hand, much of the work flowing through the cassette underground was likely to confound censors and inspectors: though a cassette of Anglo-American rock songs would have invited immediate suspicion, what could be said for a tape of pure noise or hyperactive audio collage work, with visual accompaniment to match? While it could be interpreted as counter-productive chaos, one could just as easily argue that such sounds promoted acceptable socialist / anti-traditionalist sympathies in the vein of early Russian Futurism.

Because of this, hysteria over the banning of musical imports may have been limited to the West's commercial output. Enough communication did exist to organize concert events and tours for Western 'underground' and 'alternative' artists, especially as the reforms of the 1980s emboldened some within the artistic sphere. During this heady period, it was not impossible for unconventional groups like the Sugarcubes to bounce into Lithuania from Iceland (by 1988, local authorities were far more likely to be concerned with the *Sąjūdis* movement's repeated calls for restoration of Lithuanian as the official language and full disclosure of Stalin-era crimes.) Lord Litter, in conversation with East German artist Jorg Thomasius, also notes that

> ...when approached about how it is possible to make 'forbidden music behind the Iron Curtain,' Jorg is quick to dispel the myths in these words: "these words are absolute, but the reality is not. Behind the Iron Curtain it was possible to make contacts with others in the West." [...] "Forbidden" is also perhaps too exotic a word to describe Jorg's actions. For years Jorg worked with "Das Freie Orkester" [The Free Orchestra], who performed in small spaces around East Berlin. While it was technically forbidden, it was possible; one need only take the necessary precautions not to attract too much attention. For example, when the Free Orchestra split the bill with

Gen Ken Montgomery, the posters that had been designed
deleted the reference to Gen Ken as an American artist."[174]

As the Brezhnev "Sinatra" doctrine became more prominent in the later
Soviet years, it would not be inconceivable for travelers throughout the
Eastern bloc to exploit the somewhat less oppressive conditions in one
Soviet colony in order to transport audio artworks to another.

In general, when confronted with binary 'good vs. evil' configurations,
in which each side accuses the other of utmost evil, we also have to be
wary of absolutist propaganda (regardless of which two political foes
happen to be locking horns at that particular time.) While oppressive
regimes abroad may legitimately be designated as such, invocations of
their absolute evil nature are a time-tested ploy for diverting attention
away from the 'home' country's own failure to maintain a passable
openness of expression. One recent manifestation of this transference of
blame has come about upon China's ascendancy as 'global power': news
stories of the Chinese obsession with crackdowns on the World Wide Web
have been manifold, especially as regards their battle of wills with the
Google search engine. If we date their censoring efforts to the late 1990s,
though, we find that the Anglo-American alliance is not exactly averse to a
bit of such 'filtering' when this suits its own needs (more on this later.)

From The Workers' State To The Nanny State: Music Censorship In The U.S.A.

Censorship within the modern United States is a topic with its own
rich history, understandable considering the amount of communications
innovation that sprung from the American landscape. This history has its
own curious precedents for determining what types of works are worthy
of censorship. For example, the *United States vs. One Book Called Ulysses*
trial of 1933 had a darkly comic outcome: the lesson of the *Ulysses* trial was
that something could be perceived as art if it had an "emetic" function
(moving the viewer to sickness) rather than an "aphrodisiac" one (moving
the viewer to arousal.) This decision seems to still carry some weight today

---

[174] "Jorg Thomasius: After The Wall Has Fallen," by David Prescott. *Electronic Cottage*
#4 (July 1990), p. 17. Hal McGee, Apollo Beach, Florida.

when trying to draw boundaries between socially redeeming artwork and prurient materials:[175] explicit sexual content in films and on television has not been permitted nearly as much as the portrayal of extreme violence and mayhem. Movie theaters showcasing violent slasher fare could be found in nearly any middle American suburb, while theaters specializing in x-rated films of an "aphrodisiac" nature quickly found themselves unwelcome except in crime-infested urban neighborhoods.

When video rental stores such as Blockbuster Video began to compete with theaters, the same formula basically applied: "emetic" films a-plenty dotted the shelves, featuring all manner of torture and death, but "aphrodisiac" pornography was disallowed from the chain marketing itself as "family-friendly." We can only speculate as to why emetic violence and horror is given precedence in the American entertainment landscape; among these speculations is that these forms of entertainment engender a kind of productivity-increasing fear in society, while purely erotic entertainment encourages a state of blissed-out languor. Any central authority would want its citizens to remain productive and motivated, and presumably this authority feels that graphic depictions of macabre and monstrous evil, intense battle, and the like are more likely to provide a collective sense of urgency and a greater economic output in turn (ironically, the pornography business itself remains defiantly lucrative.) The objection to erotically inspired hedonism, seen itself as a precursor to all variety of nihilist and chaotic tendencies, leads to encouragement of cultural products that promote traditional martial values.

Perhaps because of this general situation, censorship within the U.S. has often been a complex affair involving collusion of both the private and public sectors, or of business and government. When certain media, such as motion pictures, were in their infancy, it was alliances between private organizations such as the National Board of Censorship and The Film Trust (itself comprising the then-largest producers of motion pictures and Eastman-Kodak, the largest producer of film stock) that took the lead here, rather than any high court decision or Congressional influence. Author Tim Wu notes that, through them, "not only scenes involving lewdness could be banned...even scenes that, for instance, made burglary seem easy

---

[175] Confusion can obviously arise when an artwork encourages *both* of these responses.

could violate the imperative of moral uplift."[176] As with much future censorship in the U.S., these organizations were simply imposing their own ideological orientations upon viewing audiences, acting in a pre-emptive manner that required no input from concerned audiences and no surveys of what filmed scenarios the viewing public actually found reprehensible. The Film Trust even went so far as to see itself as, more so than the government, the custodian of proper American values, boldly claiming how "it was due an exemption from the law because, as a private regulator of free speech, it was performing a public service."[177] Incidentally, the 1915 federal district court ordering the dissolution of the Trust also marked a turning point for American film, in which its innovations became competitive with those of Europe for the first time since the medium's inception.[178]

The primary thrust of censorship within the United States, applicable to nearly all of the artistic disciplines, has been the elimination of obscenity. Setting aside, for the moment, the fact that such concepts as "obscenity" and "indecency" are often subjectively defined yet expected to be universally intuited, it is interesting to note how the vigorous moral campaign against obscenity differs from attempts to contain dissenting political opinions. While these are still plentiful in the U.S., they are dealt with more by being conspicuously ignored, by not being given "equal time" to be aired on the corporate media networks, or by simply being mocked, caricatured, and misrepresented. These combined methods have been seemingly adequate so far, though a succession of more vaguely applicable laws concerning 'enemies of the state' lie in wait to finish the job. At any rate, U.S.-style censorship attempts prior to the Global War On Terror focused more on corruption of public morals than on political speech (perhaps betraying the elite's cynicism towards its citizenry, who were deemed largely incapable of following political discourse.)

---

[176] Tim Wu, *The Master Switch: The Rise And Fall Of Information Empires*, p. 70. Alfred A. Knopf, New York, 2010.

[177] *Ibid.*, p. 72.

[178] In all fairness, though, the infrastructural damage done to the European continent during World War I also needs to be taken into consideration here: while American film in the 1910s was more diversified than any other film industry on the globe, American film studios did have the luxury of not being requisitioned for use by national armies.

A similar form of cynical condescension has been a regular feature of the American patrician class when it comes to the issue of parents and youth: the former are assumed to be too busy with their daily duties to protect their children, who are constantly prone to uncritically absorbing both emetic and aphrodisiac forms of entertainment. The Parents' Music Resource Center, launched in 1984 by a group of senators' wives, managed to have a series of high-profile Congressional hearings held on the subject of obscene pop music, and pioneered the now commonplace phenomenon of placing warning labels on record albums. The PMRC, like many lobbying groups, was notable for its monocausal approach to a multi-faceted phenomenon of youth degeneracy, seeing the free access to profane, lurid, or violently themed music as being the root cause of social quandaries. In other words, this music was *not* something that merely reinforced or articulated the long-standing feelings of unrest or helplessness coming from the ambient conditions of modern life. Initially formed after Tipper Gore - wife of former Tennessee senator Al Gore - discovered her daughter had been listening to Prince's onanistic ode "Darling Nikki" from the *Purple Rain* LP, the group quickly carved out a place for itself in an American decade that was brimful of moral panics. The title of Gore's book-length PMRC manifesto, *Raising PG Kids In An X-Rated Society*, hinted both at the group's *modus operandi* and at their alarmist strategy: 'society' as such was *already* lost to obscenity, rather than merely in danger of having its morals corrupted.

The early success of the PMRC's campaign took many Constitutional libertarians by surprise, although it should not have. The First Amendment does, after all, prohibit Congress from abridging the freedom of speech, yet it makes no provisions for industries that bow to a perceived public demand to modify their product. This was the case for the film regulating organization National Legion of Decency, noted by author Tim Wu as "an entity wholly independent of government, its power over an industry deriving from that industry's own self-imposed structure."[179] If it did not, the attempts to lobby Congress to pass a prohibitive 'blank tape tax' should have already alerted music fans everywhere that industry collaboration with the government was a threat to self-determined creation of recorded

---

[179] Tim Wu, *The Master Switch: The Rise And Fall Of Information Empires*, p. 122. Alfred A. Knopf, New York, 2010.

audio. In fact, the 'tape tax' bill in question (HR 2911) moved through Congress only because of a trade conducted with the PMRC: the RIAA's president at the time, Stanley Gortikov, was not sold on the prospect of record labeling and felt it would have an adverse effect on sales- however, the RIAA capitulated to the stickering practice when it realized HR 2911 would easily pass in exchange for - as author Barry Miles recalls - "suggesting a notice on potentially 'unacceptable' records and [going] along with the PMRC's concerns about hidden messages and backward masking on records."[180]

So, what would prevent the PMRC from limiting themselves to their stated mission of being an information service, and not using the United States Congress to instigate a full-scale prohibition on the sale of "obscene" materials anywhere, anytime? The closeness of the PMRC's public relations people to that august body raised many a skeptical eyebrow within the music community (Gore's partner Susan Baker was the wife of former Treasury Secretary James Baker) as did a PMRC "blacklist" that overstepped its boundaries and included songs that did indeed raise the flag of aforementioned political dissent. The PMRC's proposed rating system, unlike the Motion Picture Association of America's extant rating system, did not merely suggest an age range for which certain material might be appropriate, but targeted certain categories of lyrical content: records would be rated "V" for "violent," "D/A" for mention of drugs and/or alcohol, "X" for "profane or sexually explicit" or "O" for "occult." Also unlike the MPAA's rating system, the PMRC ratings would - as suggested by their arch-foe Frank Zappa - stigmatize music performers as being people who actually aspired to live in ways that their hyperbolic lyrics suggested. Film actors, as the story went, at least had the defense that they were involved in fictional portrayals, while musicians were unfairly assumed to be *not* engaging in self-parody, fantasy, or fictionalization of their own lives. For these reasons and more besides, the needling punk activist Jello Biafra (forming part of the anti-PMRC spearhead alongside Zappa) derided the organization for trying to appear like "just a consumer advocate group in the spirit of Ralph Nader."[181]

---

[180] Barry Miles, *Zappa: A Biography*, p. 334. Grove Press, New York, 2004.

[181] Available online at http://www.theroc.org/roc-mag/textarch/roc-10/roc10-08.htm. Retrieved February 19, 2011.

Yet the PMRC was not incapable of fighting fear with fear, and raising the crescendo of panic every time their detractors attacked them for violating Constitutional principles. For example, claiming that a threat is something we have "never dealt with before" is a time-tested way of causing fear of the alien to bypass a more rational assessment of a threat's validity. The PMRC deftly attempted to massage the "explicit lyrics" threat into public consciousness by bestowing such a sense of novelty upon it: for example, in a debate on the television panel show *Crossfire*, one representative of the organization stated the case for the PMRC's work by stating "suggestive lyrics aren't new...*AIDS* is new...3,000 kids under 16 *a day* getting pregnant is new."[182] Regardless of whether or not such data had been distorted or outright fabricated by the group's representatives, it seemed that they underestimated the "rockers'" ability to articulately confront the PMRC's assumptions about the degree to which music warps impressionable minds. The PMRC saw in the rock and rap world their own *máničky* or bumbling degenerates, and it was only appropriate that Zappa, a guiding influence on the original Czechoslovak ne'er-do-wells, would counter-attack with acerbic candor, with an unanticipated command of legal proceedings and of the real psychological effects of mass media. For example, in his televised *Crossfire* debate (one of many on the subject of censorship in the mid-1980s), the composer raised a pertinent point about the full extent of pop music's influence on public attitudes:

> Let's take a look at one statistic: 99.9% of all the songs that are broadcast on the air, or that appear on television, deal with the subject of love. They don't deal with sado-masochism or chainsaw sex. If the lyrics were really so effective, wouldn't the world be filled with love, since that's what we hear day in and day out?[183]

With resistance coming from such unexpected quarters, the PMRC perhaps sensed a losing battle in the 'war of panics', and was eventually forced to defend their own position *vis a vis* censorship. Representatives

---

[182] *Ibid.*

[183] Available online at http://www.youtube.com/watch?v=H28SNdvBstA&feature=related. Retrieved February 9, 2011.

from the PMRC tried to assuage the fears of the American public's libertarian die-hards by rejecting the practice of "prior restraint," or the regulation of music at the production level. These fears were not unjustified, since contested albums like the Beastie Boys' *Licensed To Ill* were already being denied distribution by their label (CBS) unless certain songs were deleted and others had their lyrics altered. Nevertheless, the PMRC's aim was - according to the official line - to merely initiate a ratings system that would warn parents and other concerned authorities of content likely to warp the vulnerable minds of teenagers and pre-teens ("mechanisms for choice in the marketplace," in Tipper Gore's terminology.) However, the contemporaneous fear among recording artists was that the PMRC's proposed rating system would cause a "chill factor" severely limiting distribution. Much in the same way that a film's 'x' rating carried with it a toxicity that urged theater chains to keep their distance, loud warnings against prurient content alienated music retailers with a reputation at stake. This situation persisted into the 1990s as supermarkets like WalMart began to constitute a greater share of the music retailing pie (especially in markets where said retailer was the centerpiece of the local economy.) During one of Jello Biafra's numerous harangues against the PMRC, he also noted how chain shopping malls in the U.S. would "[send] down memos saying they will evict any store that sells any record with any warning sticker on it whatsoever...some of these [record] stores are located nowhere but in chain shopping malls, so their choice is, blackball some heavy metal, blackball the Dead Kennedys, or you can lose your lease, Jack, and go out of business."[184]

Herein lies one reason why the networks of self-released music managed to skirt the PMRC's most sustained efforts: not relying on retailers to disseminate their work, Cassette Culture was practically a non-entity in the eyes of the shortsighted censors, who did not conceive of other distribution channels beyond the over-the-counter purchase, or promotional methods beyond MTV airings and radio broadcasts (one would think that their knowledge of heavy metal distribution would at least have put them in touch with that culture's heavy emphasis on international tape trading.) The much maligned "Washington wives" of

---

[184] Jello Biafra, "Talk On Censorship: Letter To Tipper Gore," from *No More Cocoons* CD, Alternative Tentacles, San Francisco, 1992.

that organization, also intimately connected with the nation's captains of commerce[185], seem to have had no idea that a music culture existed where trading and gift giving were the norm for distributing works. Ironically enough, much of what traveled through the Cassette Culture circuits would probably have induced fainting spells among the PMRC membership: French performance artist Jean-Louis Costes' screamed outbursts of porno-terror and scatological absurdity put the slick innuendo of Prince to shame (although Costes would get his chance to provoke good old-fashioned moral outrage when touring through North America in more recent years.) Likewise, we can only surmise what the family-focused organization would have thought about the youthful crop of producers within the contemporary cassette scene: for a watchdog organization that spent so much time trying to monitor youth habits of music *consumption*, it spent surprisingly little time looking after youthful *production* of objectionable material. While the majority of mid-1980s American youth were not as resourceful or as aesthetically cruel as the 15-year-old Michael Moynihan (of the post-industrial terror unit Coup de Grace), even a few such youthful cells would have likely provided them with cause for alarm.

Of course, the point here is not to show how Cassette Culture provided an outlet for full-bore prurience and dementia at a time when it was under greater scrutiny than usual (even if Cassette Culture did occasionally produce a bumper crop of prurient materials.) Rather, the point is to show that, in the event that groups like the PMRC gained more censorious control than they ultimately had, music production in the U.S. would not have suffered as much as the music *business* would (and even the latter's suffering might now be called into question, at a time where a "parental advisory" sticker often makes a recording more desirable among thrill-seeking audiences who aren't legal minors.) The PMRC's focus on preventing 'youth' from buying objectionable records, while it was obsessive, would have been too narrow even if it had removed such records entirely from the retail landscape. The 80s network forming around self-released cassettes circumvented not only retail stores, but also traditional live performance spaces (some such spaces, like Ken Montgomery's Generator space in New York, served both as makeshift

---

[185] Coors Brewing Company, Domino's Pizza, Blockbuster Video and American Airlines were among the corporations providing support for the PMRC.

retailers for the cassette underground and as performance venues.) Much like the current state of music in the wake of the post-Internet music industry crash, revenues for artists would likely still come in from live performances, from wearable merchandise (which could also be self-produced by artists with access to silk-screening equipment), and from the donations of an audience who felt they were buying into a common ideal rather than simply paying an isolated artistic representative of such. In an alternate universe where the PMRC successfully lobbied the federal government to keep shopping malls free of over-the-counter obscenity, it would have eventually had to intervene in the activities of the postal system to staunch the flow of audio alternatives: an act that would have plenty of citizens questioning the real differences between censorship in the U.S. and that in the Soviet Union.

Some Cautions About Digital Resistance

The present era of digital dissidence must seem, for those who have lived through prior epochs of information repression, like a veritable *Age d'Or* of transparent expression; a long-awaited time in which the censors finally get their comeuppance and have every form of *verboten* expression slip through their grasp, with said expression proliferating in an untold number of online domains. The alleged anonymity of Internet transmissions has seen libertarians of various stripes extolling that particular communications medium for reasons that go far beyond the scope of this book: its promise of free expression without immediate repercussions, however real or illusory it may be, has been credited with fomenting a recent spate of coordinated protests and revolutions that, ostensibly, would not have happened in the old world where communication was less instantaneous and de-centralized. The reported usage of the Twitter "micro-blogging" service to assist in the Iranian "Green Movement"'s uprising of 2009 is one heavily cited example of techno-dissidence operating at a velocity that confounds police forces. This echoes the 1979 Iranian revolution, also aided by populist communications technology, which swept across that country (cassette recordings of the Ayatollah Khomeini's speeches provided much of the ideological content rallying the anti-Shah base.)[186] At the time of writing, Egyptian demonstrators calling for Hosni Mubarak's resignation even wave placards thanking Facebook (in one instance, spray-painting the social network's name on a wall in Tahrir Square) for providing a bit of bonding cement for that insurrectionary movement.[187]

However, the euphoria over this supposedly uninhibited communication is no longer universally distributed, if indeed it ever was. Slowly but surely, a number of contradicting opinions have begun to emerge, articulating an intense cynicism towards the simplistic, binary view that posits the Internet as the exclusive tool of the dissident population and corrective violence as the sole available weapon of repressive governments. Author Evgeny Morozov, in a recent volume, takes great pains to counter the brightly burning enthusiasm of the "cyber-utopian" contingent with a number of more nuanced, grimly realist claims. One of his primary arguments is that many repressive governments, in the 20th century and beyond, have relied upon different combinations of information allowance and restriction, which themselves fluctuated in accordance with the political climate, rather than upon a blanket dispensation of coercion and terror. Referring back to the twin literary classics *1984* and *Brave New World,* themselves regularly used to illustrate the two different poles of "social control through absolute freedom" and "social control through absolute repression", Morozov chides any and all who believe in a State that will rely solely on one controlling mode or the other:

> To assume that all political regimes can be mapped somewhere on an Orwell-Huxley spectrum is an open invitation to simplification; to assume that a government would be choosing between reading their citizens' mail or feeding them with cheap entertainment is to lose sight of the possibility that a smart regime may be doing both.[188]

---

[186] One of the popular slogans surrounding these cassettes' distribution was "we are struggling for autocracy, for democracy, by means of xeroxracy."

[187] This appears to have been done both as a celebratory acknowledgement of the social networks' potential, and as a nose thumbing at the government after they ordered the shutdown of all Internet access on February 4, 2011.

[188] Evgeny Morozov, *The Net Delusion: The Dark Side Of Internet Freedom,* p. 79. Public Affairs, New York, 2011.

In this respect, the Cultural Revolution of Maoist China - the near-total, State-endorsed denial of arts and entertainment spearheaded by Mme. Mao in the mid 1960s - stands out more as a brutal anomaly than as the logical endpoint that all expression-limiting regimes will eventually arrive at. Over the long term, the victims of this policy of total cultural austerity developed a variety of exotic tics, nervous conditions and psychological disorders, and any dictatorship hoping for longevity cannot rely forever on the support of a culturally desiccated populace. Mao Zedong's own paranoia of communications technology also seems like a relic now, in an age where Internet counter-insurgency sites and their psy-ops 'cyber war' complement any political struggle already be raging in the streets and public squares. Mao famously had his paranoiac fires stoked when the erstwhile liaison to Moscow, Yang Shang-kun, tape recorded the 'Great Helmsman' without his approval: Mao "did not want any record kept of what he said and did, unless it was carefully sanitized...in the old days, he would light a match to telegrams once they were sent."[189]

Morozov cites the example of East Germany as one where affordance and restraint was more shrewdly balanced to serve the regime's purposes. His study on the subject reveals a conclusion similar to the one drawn by Jorg Tomasius above: contact with the West was not blocked in every single instance, and indeed much in the way of Western cultural transmission was allowed to act as a sort of release valve from daily pressures. As Arthur Schopenhauer wrote in the mid-19th century, this release valve caused "every discontent [to be] immediately relieved in words...indeed, unless this discontent is very considerable, it exhausts itself in this way."[190] Sure, the Amiga record label acted as the sole outlet for commercial music releases in the country, but elsewhere Morozov notes a GDR where East Germans "were not particularly interested in tracking the latest news from NATO...instead they preferred soft news and entertainment, particularly American TV series [...] even the leading Communist Party journal *Einheit* acknowledged that *Dynasty* - known in Germany as *The Denver Clan* and the most popular of the lot - was widely

---

[189] Jung Chang and Jon Halliday, *Mao: The Unknown Story*, p. 499. Anchor Books, New York, 2006.

[190] Arthur Schopenhauer, *Essays And Aphorisms*, trans. R.J. Hollingdale, p. 152. Penguin Books, New York, 2004.

watched."[191] At the very least, unlike their neighbors in Czechoslovakia, East Germans did not have to wait for the latest exploits of Major Zeman to provide them with a night of mindless home entertainment.

Essentially, the East German authorities had apparently wagered that a populace given free access to banal Western entertainment would long for the material comforts on display, but would not have a similar yearning for human rights and governmental transparency. For champions of these latter concepts, it is poignant that the authorities' wager paid off in so many instances. Not too far away geographically or on the historical timeline, the Hungary of János Kádár proposed something similar with its *gulyáskommunizmus* ['goulash Communism']: consumer goods and amenities were allowed to flow to a greater degree than in other Soviet colonies, in exchange for a silent acceptance of the Russian occupational force and secret police, and other limits on publicly voiced dissent. The *'samizdat* boutique' introduced earlier was a product of the *gulyáskommunizmus* era, although the audience for this kind of alternative culture was sparse at the point when the quantity and variety of material goods was still attractive (and before Kádár lapsed into more traditionally Stalinist thinking.)

Morozov's complaint extends also to the assumption that the Internet is essentially a "one-way" street as far as freeing up information concerned: the attempt to draw a direct line from *samizdat, magnitizdat,* or "ribs" to the Internet ignores the crucial fact that authoritarian bodies can, and will, use the Internet as a propaganda organ as well (Morozov helpfully notes that "there was hardly any pro-government *samizdat* in the Soviet Union...although there was plenty of *samizdat* accusing the government of violating the core principles of Marxism-Leninism.")[192] As the number of new net-labels and music blogs increase, offering up an unprecedented eclectic stew of free-form audio styles and alternative opinions, it's all too tempting to believe the central authorities will continue napping while the electric, polyglot partying goes on around them: even the official website of the Chinese Defense Ministry features a section for free music

---

[191] Evgeny Morozov, *The Net Delusion: The Dark Side Of Internet Freedom,* p. 63. Public Affairs, New York, 2011.

[192] Evgeny Morozov, *The Net Delusion: The Dark Side Of Internet Freedom,* p. 46. Public Affairs, New York, 2011.

downloads. The infiltration of anti-American nations by post-modernist, Western culture, sculpted by ad agencies and design firms as much as by State players, has gone on for too long to remain unnoticed in newer manifestations. As a result, authoritarian forces will probably become more resilient and capable of speaking the media language once exclusive to the West, even absorbing its po-mo advertising tricks of sustained irony, self-reference and hip detachment. If one thinks the merger of a seemingly purposeless aesthetic with a purposeful ideal is impossible, they merely need to look to the example of Christian-oriented record labels such as Tooth & Nail, which have successfully harnessed the cool, laconic detachment of American indie rock to the more demanding tenets of Christian living.[193] Silly as it may seem to pronounce it here, the production of audio recordings with a State-crafted totalitarian message, yet marketed as "alternative" and accompanied by self-effacing, consciously messy design motifs, may not be too far off. With government employees from China and elsewhere regularly appearing on online social networks to counter international denunciations of their policies, it is not inconceivable that audio-specific networks, net-labels etc. could become infiltrated as well.

Another significant protest of Evgeny Morozov (although certainly not unique to him) is that Western agencies have been too quick to claim credit for their technological innovations' role in collapsing authoritarian regimes. Much historical distortion has been employed here in order to anoint the U.S. and her allies the with role of the downtrodden peoples' savior, extending even to the practice of *samizdat* (my colleague Mindaugas again reminds me that this practice was already in effect since the 1850s, nearly a century before the establishment of the CIA and the other governmental agencies that claimed to have given it a major push during the Soviet era.) Disastrous decision-making on a local level, rather than foreign subterfuge, leads more often to the crumbling of authority- the Soviet system in question was arguably dealt as great a blow by Russia's military expenses (e.g. its protracted involvement in Afghanistan) as it was by mass enticement to Western norms of behavior. Nor is that gross military expenditure - counting both the loss of human life, and the

---

[193] One example of this success is the debut of Tooth & Nail group Underoath's 2006 LP *Define The Great Line* at #2 on the Billboard 200 charts.

disproportionate size of the defense budget - the magic key that provides all the answers to all the questions concerning the Soviet collapse. Such seismic events owe themselves to a steady accretion of originally unrelated factors, themselves spanning the whole breadth of human activity from cultural expression to political agitation.

Meanwhile, one surely unwanted side effect of Western commentators' vociferous praise of the Internet, and their proprietary attitude towards all activities occurring on it, has been a premature curtailing of its revolutionary power in countries where it is being seen as a growing threat to the prevailing order. In the same Iran in which the Twitter 'revolution' was supposed to have played such a dramatic organizational role, the Gmail service has already been banned, and native citizens returning from abroad are often grilled by customs officials about their social media accounts (and, we can assume, any dissident 'friends' linked to those accounts.) As the 2011 protests in Egypt's Tahrir Square mounted into something more formidable than expected, the Mubarak regime demanded the complete shutdown of Internet services.

In the end, it seems difficult to completely disagree with the Cassette Culture elders who see the Internet generations as terminally distracted and lacking the consistent drive necessary to provide momentum for an underground or oppositional movement. The old indie culture stalwarts who cry out against instantaneity are occasionally justified in criticizing the blazing velocity of this communications medium, seeing that the substitution of raw speed for communicative depth rarely leads to cultural developments of any lasting value. Tragically, some of the most passionate communication within the digital playground of free music blogging, net-labels etc. is reserved for distractive and destructive ends - "flaming" others in the community - rather than for encouraging new productions and collaborations. We have already seen how arguments on the ubiquitous message boards and comments sections of music blogs can develop around trivial matters, such as one blogger's re-posting of a digitally ripped, out-of-print underground cassette that had already been uploaded to another blogger's pages. The astute reader will note how such attempts to demand personal credit for a collaborative archiving enterprise are incongruous with the ideals already laid out for Cassette Culture and beyond. This situation is poignant not just because it sees innate human selfishness arising in a culture that attempts to contradict this quality: such internecine bickering often provides an invaluable service to authoritarian forces, who are quickly learning to manipulate an information surplus to their ends in the same way that they previously manufactured information shortages. The aforementioned fact that the Internet has demonstrable potential as a pro-authoritarian tool (whereas previous forms of networked media were rarely used as such) gives added weight to these critiques.

One thing that remains painfully unsaid, in the recent writings of Morozov and fellow skeptics, is that the digital 'West,' too, is capable of such authoritarianism, after a fashion. Following this realization, we'd do well to consider whether the prospect of a global Internet democracy is being promoted by Western governments because it advances the cause of human rights and free expression, or because it makes for a planet-wide populace of the kind described in the former East Germany, i.e. one more content to escape into consumer trends and insignificant TV dramas than to make serious demands of their elected leaders. Suspicion of Western motives for praising the Internet's liberating effects should arise when considering the West's disapproving attitudes towards a good deal of the democratic elections to have taken place in the 21st century: from Russia to Palestine, the democratic process has been enacted only to entrench the local interests of those nations, and the Western (primarily American) anger over these results is telling. It is more pliant consumer societies that are ultimately hoped for here, not just nations that promulgate a kind of Jeffersonian democracy. This is why self-released music, be it net-releases or home taping, will likely never be endorsed by Western governmental agencies with the same fervor that they have accorded to the Internet: its emphasis on trading, free distribution etc. makes it sit uneasily in an economy based more on accumulation of purchased goods. Said accumulation is regularly equated with "freedom" in those volatile nations not currently being permeated by Western influence, and it is the actual freedom of expression promised by self-released media that is, in this strangely inverted scenario, seen as a sideshow to the "liberating" ritual of unreflective consumption.

Hopefully, future debates about censorship will be made without using "the Internet" as a stand-in for the whole range of expressive freedoms. The new generations of freely downloadable net-releases provide their own benefits, i.e. allowing sound-hungry audiences huge archives of music at little or no cost, but this availability does not signal the end of censorship at the hands of authoritarian governments, corporations, or any alliance of social institutions aiming for consolidation and expansion of their power. Given, technological advancement is presenting unique challenges to some of the most pernicious forms of censoring: the simplicity of making and distributing a net-release is a major blow to the governments, boards, trusts etc. that may engage in the choking practice of "prior restraint." Regulating expression at the production level has become progressively more difficult as self-determined culture has progressed from cassettes, 'zines and *samizdat* to net-releases, weblogs and digital video files. Certainly, the wielders of power could always attempt something similar to the typewriter laws issued in Ceaușescu's Romania, by confiscating home computers and requiring a permit to even rent one. Yet this would quickly become a very messy operation for anyone wishing to seize this little bit of creative freedom from individuals that may have no other affordable outlet for their expression. Moreover, few present-day rulers want to meet with the kind of violent end that the aforementioned tyrant did.

As we close out this discussion of expressive freedom, though, it's also important not to equate "freedom" with a condition of total amorality: the realm of self-released music does have its own moral values to uphold: avoidance of passivity, personal growth through direct communication, and the personal stamina to "hear out" people whose ideas may initially seem too extreme or unrefined. This is, admittedly, an abridged list, which is hopefully rounded out by some of the other research conducted in this book. However, the last item on this list is of special interest here: this ability, more so than just the resourcefulness and industrious of the self-releasing audio artist, is what separates them from their authoritarian opponents. The relative autonomy of their production and distribution methods is still radical in much of the modern world. Yet, the permission of contradicting views, and the acknowledgement that one's ideals are only made stronger if they are seen as not living in fear of contradiction, is a motor that has driven cultural manifestations before self-released audio, and will continue to drive newer ones still.

We cannot easily condemn past regimes for, say, cracking down on their *máničky* while at the same time demanding that autonomous subcultures flush out their more negative constituents. On a whole, the self-released musical culture has been remarkably restrained in situations where it could have adopted more of a censorious attitude: from the racist / nihilist-chic of cassette-era groups like Terre Blanche, to the self-defeating profligacy of Kenji Siratori's CDrs and 'Non Quality Audio' net-releases (both the subject of a later chapter), this culture's numerous antagonists have been allowed to continue with their most deleterious activities, for a simple reason. Taking a cue from Durkheim's notion of crime as having a social function, this culture "see[s] in deviant behavior a systematic stabilizer of the code of conduct as a whole [...] deviant behavior (even where it confers no direct benefit on society) may be symptomatic of dysfunction in the inherited code itself."[194] In other words, the self-releasing culture promotes itself as a censorship-free zone because the occasional ingress of intellectual laziness and aesthetic offense encourages individual and collective improvements among those affected by these transgressions. The deviant fringe artist in this culture acts not as a mere scapegoat, who exists to make the mildest virtues and most mediocre creations of the other participants shine by comparison: rather, the deviant artist's existence challenges those of mild virtue and mediocre creative skill to truly hone their craft. Furthermore, the decision to permit their deviance goes deeper than just a reflexive, contrarian wish to "not be like" preventive forces as varied in their methods as the Securitate or the PMRC. These bodies, who look to crush their moral and political opposition with "chilling effects," with "prior restraint" and other censorious methods may have tremendous short-term success in doing so, even success that stretches across multiple human generations. However, such overzealous authority also lays bare the cowardice and inflexibility that contributes to their eventual downfall.

---

[194] John Gray, *Hayek: On Liberty*, p. 45. Routledge, London / New York, 1998.

Mister Modular:
In Conversation With Vittore Baroni

Choosing a single artist to illustrate the transition from networked visual art to networked audio art, i.e. the "Cassette Culture," is no easier than choosing an all-encompassing representative for the former type of art. Few feel qualified to act as a spokesperson for the admittedly varied intentions of others, and, as already stated, there is an almost universal reluctance to promote oneself as the "head" of anything in this culture. Especially on the European continent, where the most radical art collectives (e.g. Surrealism) have splintered into competing factions while under the mismanagement of paranoiac leaders, no one with a job to do is particularly eager to waste their otherwise productive time on internecine squabbling about whom deserves what title. So, in these situations, those who are just the most enthusiastic about their work, and its place in a larger creative milieu, end up becoming "ambassadors" by default.

Yet settling for an ambassadorial role does not have to mean compromising one's personality entirely, or withdrawing from making one's own output. If one promotes the creative works of others with enough manic energy and enough conviction, it seems only natural that those works would end up influencing and shaping the character of the 'ambassador,' until he or she is compelled to make yet more works that combine the collective nature of influence with the nuances of individual experience. An excellent embodiment of this dual artist / ambassador role comes in the form of the Italian artist Vittore Baroni's "badge show" in 1981, a one-man "walking exhibition" in which the artist strolled through Forte dei Marmi with his white overalls encrusted in badges designed by fellow networkers. While the exhibition was explicitly intended as a showcase for the works of 200 different artists, it also furthered the individual intentions of Baroni: "every day at 3 p.m., I covered the short distance from my house to the Forte dei Marmi Municipal Art Gallery, as an ironic statement against the gloomy and provincial cultural policy of my town [...] I do not like the usual gallery show arranged for the usual small crew of art freaks; I prefer to work for a non-art audience, so I performed my 'live show' for the fun of smiling passer-by."[195]

Taking his international approach into consideration, it seems contradictory to speak of Vittore Baroni as an "Italian" artist- yet, whatever his own opinions on being tacked to a local 'scene,' Italian representation in the communities of mail art, and its related networked art forms, has been conspicuous. As Baroni's countryman Ruggero Maggi states, "this could be attributed to movements like Futurism, which, without doubt, contributed very strongly to the development of some art ideas, such as active collaboration between artists, using postcards, letters, etc [...] also in part this could be contributed to the Italian artists...[rather] to their soul[s]."[196] If the work of Baroni and his collaborators is any indication, then the Italian mail art contingent was also quite active in their own immediate vicinity, fueled by a mania for communicative creation that could have kept them comfortably busy if no international contacts had ever been made.

As one of the central organizers of the audio-visual arts collective TRAX (alongside the late Piermario Ciani), Baroni was responsible for an eclectic, yet oddly cohesive aesthetic that took post-industrial commercial design, rock 'n roll, Futurism, and indie comic art into its orbit. Before even encountering a TRAX-related product in the flesh, one was already dealing with a multiplicity of possible meanings: the TRAX moniker itself was taken from the word "track" (carrying multiple interpretations such as 'evidence', 'footpath' etc.) with the substituted "X" at the end implying a bit of mystery or unpredictability. The actions carried about by TRAX did have a *je ne sais quoi* about them, especially when considering their oscillation between whimsical and transgressive attitude from one action to the next. Yet this very unpredictability was what stimulated further interest in the works of the TRAX collective- their professional presentation and consistent sense of humor (read: lack of high seriousness) may have placed them in a no-man's land between the gallery and the commercial book / record sellers, since nobody could know how to properly market this material. In retrospect, though, it seems like that was the point- to show how surprisingly fertile the "no-man's land" could be; to show just how many creative people existed who could otherwise not have

---

[195] 1981 flyer advertising Vittore Baroni's "Badge Show". Personal collection of the author.

[196] Ruggero Maggi quoted in "Ruggero Maggi," *N D* #10, 1988. *N D*, Austin, Texas.

their work translated for presentation in the institutions mentioned above.

The precursors to the TRAX project were already, like Baroni's "badge show," taking the question of public recognition and irreverently mining it for creative materials. Ciani's imaginary band, The Mind Invaders, existed in images but never performed or recorded (when they did, it was to deflate listener expectations with a single dial tone on the *Onda 400* 45rpm EP.) Posters, lyric sheets, and even audience questionnaires were designed for the project, whose methods veered mischievously close to the 'hype machine' of the mass media: The Mind Invaders simply took things one step further by 'hyping' an immaterial band rather than an actually existing band that was short on substance. Meanwhile, Baroni's own Lt. Murnau project (done in collaboration with Jacques Juin, of the French / German mail art project Llys Dana), made indecipherable cut-ups of Beatles records[197] and released them on a VEC Audio Exchange cassette entitled *Meet Lt. Murnau*, while concealing their identities behind masks that bore the likeness of silent film director F.W. Murnau. The masks, of course, made for a situation in which anyone could assume the identity of Lt. Murnau and make their own similar (or not so similar) audio works. Given the already established "horror film" theme of the group, Piermario Ciani suggested that their act of creating "plunderphonic" music (well before that term came into circulation) was a way of "vampirizing" sounds.

In 1981, Ciani and Baroni combined their efforts and the TRAX project soon sprang to life with a manifesto that, among other things, announced, "we are not artists, because art is a word that means everything and nothing," and "we inherited from everybody, but we do not owe anything to anyone." It may have been that this rejection of obligation actually led to TRAX' higher-than-average quality of DIY workmanship, rather than providing them with an excuse for consummate slacking: denying the mantle of the "artist" (along with all its subsets- actors, writers, film-makers etc.) allowed for TRAX members to view raw creativity from a number of different angles. People could sculpt for themselves a personality ranging from laboratory technician to superhero (and, yes, a "Traxman" comic book was designed by the collective's third co-founder, Massimo Giacon.)

---

[197] For what it's worth, Vittore Baroni notes that sending away for his Beatles Fan Club membership card was one of his first experiences with "networking."

Disavowing the title of "artist" was not novel, since "networker" had already been suggested as an alternative term that more encompassed the aims of participatory creativity- yet the TRAX collective added its own special flavor to this shifting of priorities. Each TRAX member was assigned a "unit number" (with numbers 1-3 going to founders Ciani, Baroni and Giacon): while the numbers ascended in accordance with the point in time that a new member joined the project, they did not otherwise indicate a member's degree of importance relative to other Units. On the recruitment process of new Units, Vittore Baroni states the following:

> The aggregation of the various Units took place as a totally spontaneous process, and not as a consequence of any formal request. TRAX never engaged in actions of propaganda with the precise objective of increasing the number of collaborators. TRAX did not research an uncontrolled and inherent growth, but rather an expansion based on the accordance of methodologies, on the mutual respect of the participants, on direct contact and voluntary collaboration, without bonds of any kind. The TRAX units never met to formulate a rigid plan for the development of the project.[198]

So, in the best tradition of "industrial" art, the nomenclature of regimentation and depersonalization was utilized for means that were *antithetical* to further regimentation and depersonalization. A "unit", furthermore, implied an useful object whose plasticity could be further manipulated upon contact with an audience member from outside of the TRAX circle- modern life was already filled to bursting with "units" for storage, refrigeration, heating, calculating, waging war, etc.- so why not a "creative" unit as well? Referring to the TRAX membership as, say, "operators" may have successfully conjured a similar post-industrial atmosphere, but it was the attractive ambivalence of "unit" -which could apply to inanimate objects, single humans and multiple humans alike- that successfully conjured a post-industrial climate in which media of *exchange* were once again taking center stage. Interestingly, this "modular" creative system did not require an exclusive allegiance from any of its Units in the

---

[198] Vittore Baroni quoted in *Last Trax* booklet. TRAX, Bertiolo, 1988.

way that a major record label might with one of its subjects. Units were free to launch their own enterprises concurrent with their TRAX membership (and many have done so to an unprecedented degree, with Frans de Waard and Masami Akita being just two Units who feature elsewhere in this volume.)

Despite some statements of the first three Units, in which they declared themselves to be dead set against artists' questing after originality for its own sake, the artifacts left behind by the collective are decidedly unique for their era. You would be hard pressed to find, for example, another creative person or persons who had designed a bag of inedible polystyrene "snack food" to accompany a cassette release.[199] Nor were many other networkers (in either 'mail art' proper or the audio world) experimenting with fashion, as was the case with the "Modular Gear" project of Baroni and Maria Teresa Ronconi- these ultra-modern artifacts were capable of being given multiple uses, e.g. earrings could be 'recycled' as accessories for the modular handbag. Even those products which might seem "conventional" by comparison, like compilation cassettes with accompanying booklets, xerography and customized boxes, were made less so by the content animating the familiar concept. The stentorian noise of industrial music rarely harmonized with goofy audio *bruitisme* as it did on TRAX compilations (despite some of them being ostensibly restricted by theme, e.g. "Technodeath" or "Videogames For the Blind.") For all the resistance to the authorship of new narratives, TRAX proved what networked art was capable when firing on all cylinders: there was an illusion of originality that TRAX projected by injecting those stories already told with new attitudes, new meetings between individuals, and new modulating circumstances.

In lieu of writing a detailed history of the TRAX project, it seemed like it would be a better idea to personally contact Vittore Baroni and ask him about some of the more common recurring themes of that project, as well as his considerable level of involvement with the mail art and networked audio communities. The results of our email conversation are reproduced below.

---

[199] This was TRAX project 0981, the "Trixi" crisps designed by Ciani and Giacon. These were handed out at a vernissage along with a blue-colored cocktail.

++++++++

I'm curious how much impact the mail art network had on the early tape / cassette audio underground- did you notice a lot of crossover between artists in these two cultures? In other words, were there many artists who divided their time equally between sound works and more visual / tactile mail art pieces?

From my point of observation, probably a more European-oriented perspective, there was surely some overlapping between the two worlds, but not that many individuals who split their time *equally* between mail art and music. Usually there was a rather marked bias in favour of either the visual/textual or audio expression. Anyway, in the late Seventies and early Eighties both the mail art community and the tape network were well aware of their reciprocal existence, but the two circles never mixed completely, and not in big numbers. In this sense, the TRAX project (similarly to Rod Summers' VEC cassette series in The Netherlands) was a quite rare, deliberate and protracted (1981-1987) effort to mix the two communities. I just happened to have a deep interest in music, as well as in mail art and other street level cultural expressions, just like my TRAX partners Piermario Ciani and Massimo Giacon. Many postal artists were not very interested in producing music, and many home-tapers were not that much into making art or willing to trade their efforts, even if they had to create the graphics for their cassettes and catalogues.

I guess that approximately 10-20% of the cassette musicians took their interest in mail art beyond the simple swap of products and promotional material. The same goes for the mail art crew, not more than 10-20% of the regular participants in the postal network produced their own cassettes or other audio works. The reciprocal involvement tended to be rather temporary, limited to a few projects, but there are some exceptions worthy of note: the whole Neoist (anti)movement for example, born out of the mail art milieu (through postal art legends David "Oz" Zack and Istvan Kantor/Monty Cantsin), included several individuals active in mail art, cassettes, video and other media. Monty Cantsin was an early prototype of an "open pop star" or "multiple name": anybody could call him/herself Monty Cantsin and produce music or art under this name (Graf Haufen in Berlin, Pete Horobin in Scotland, Istvan Cantor in Vancouver, tENTATIVELY a cONVENIENCE in Baltimore and several others produced Neoist cassettes and vinyls with their home labels, mostly circulated in mail art circles). My own Lieutenant Murnau project (1980-1984) was also created with a "multiple name" strategy in mind, with the added "rule" that any music released under that name had to be created by reassembling existing music: a ghost band that acted like a vampire, sucking life from the bodies of work of other composers (a trend later commonly known, after John Oswald's master works, as 'plunderphonic' music).

I remember purposely trying at the time to proselytize among tape musicians, getting them interested in the mail art phenomenon by trading or mailing out free copies of my own *Arte Postale!* magazine, TRAX audio-visual releases or my audiozine on cassette [*Area Condizionata*.] So it happened that certain fanzine makers started to publish graphics by mail artists, articles on mail art, a few of them became involved in the correspondence network. A few examples of 'zines, all from the early eighties, are M.R. Pillar's *Real Shocks* (issue 2 has Lt. Murnau on the cover), *Stabmental* by Geoff Rushton (better known as John Balance, r.i.p.), William Davenport's *Unsound*, the German *The 80's*, the French/German *Llys Dana / Le Point D'Ironie*, the Italian *115/220*, *Onda 400*, *50%* (all by Piermario Ciani) or my own *Lieutenant Murnau* 'zine (10 issues). Even well-known musicians from the first Industrial/ New Wave scene dipped their fingers in mail art: Throbbing Gristle and Cabaret Voltaire members, Nocturnal Emissions, Merzbow, Deficit Des Annees Anterieures, Die Form, etc. With TRAX, we tried to take the best from the networking oriented music and mail art scenes and mix them together. Our audio-visual packages usually included a cassette compilation plus a booklet or set of postcards and less conventional small art objects, in the tradition of Fluxus "flux kits". TRAX also tried to instigate interferences and collaborations among the authors, so that the final "modular product" would be as much *about* networking as a by-product of networking tactics (the vinyl album *TRAX - Xtra* of 1982 is a good example of collective creation).

If I scan my collection of hundreds of cassettes from the tape network era, though there are a lot of wonderful and "arty" products, it is not easy to come up with names of other labels with a fifty-fifty mix of music and (mail) art: the VEC series, Graf Haufen/Hapunkt Fix's Artcore Editions in

Berlin, probably just a handful of others. Going more in detail, though, you may find many single authors who produced a unique blend of networking art & music. Keith Bates (UK), for example, is a gifted musician with a fully equipped home studio who has organized several mail art projects in the last twenty-odd years, but also produced mail art-related cassettes. Bates sometimes contributes to mail art events and publications with fitting songs inspired by the theme, just like I did with the group Le Forbici di Manitù when in 1992 we recorded the song *Let's Network Together*, a 7" vinyl single included in issue 63 of *Arte Postale!* magazine, intended as a sort of "un-official hymn of the networker" to be played before the start of each Congress taking place around the world during the ground-breaking *Decentralized World- Wide Networker Congress 1992* project. Other musicians/mail-artists who produced seminal "networking audio" works or compilations are Gerald Jupitter-Larsen/The Haters, Chuck Welch/Crackerjack Kid, David Zack, Mark Bloch, Nicola Frangione, Henryk Gajewski, Alex Igloo, Minoy, Peter R. Meyer, John M. Bennett, etc. I often fiddled with the idea of assembling a CD anthology of the most historically relevant mail-art related sound works, but I never got around to producing it.

You noted that about 2/3 of the planet did not end up contributing to the mail art network in its heyday, so I'm guessing that a similar percentage holds true for those who were originally doing home-taping and the like. However, among those that did participate, what kind of demographics were involved? My own dealings with present-day enthusiasts of 'experimental' music have put me in touch with everyone from affluent doctors to people living in squats / autonomous centers, people 5 decades apart in terms of age, etc....so I'm curious what you noticed about people's backgrounds when you first started collecting material for TRAX and exchanging audio material?

My well-grounded impression is that while the mail art community has always been (and still is) a very heterogeneous mix of people of all ages, professions and social status, the tape musicians, at least the core group in the early years of the phenomenon, were a much more uniform set, at least in their age range (from teenagers to twenty-somethings.) Mail art, since the very beginning, has accommodated in its ranks professional artists, art students, simple onlookers, even people who had never tried to make art or write poetry before this experience. The first seminal articles on 'art by correspondence' appeared around 1969, on the pages of well known art magazines like *Art in America* but also in *Rolling Stone*, and this is very revealing of the parallel (underground) popularity that mail art always enjoyed both among art professionals and young amateurs. The tape network, on the other hand, evolved mainly from the bedrooms and garages of young people who were inspired by the punk do-it-yourself ethic to start their own first musical project or a small label.

Yes, a portion of the tape networkers were also aficionados of synthesizers, krautrock and "serious" contemporary experimental music: people who grew up in the cult of Klaus Schulze and Tangerine Dream and who could well have been in their thirties or even older in 1977. This more specialized circuit however was not as widespread as that of the younger musicians that related to rock, new wave, punk, garage, industrial and lo-fi weird music. I was twenty-five years old when I started TRAX in 1981, and I always had the perception that most of my correspondents were more or less my age or a few years younger. This was confirmed by the many close encounters I had with tape musicians, through visits to my home by contacts travelling in Italy or during my trips around Europe. In London, particularly, I had the chance to meet various tape producers: typically they had just left their relatives and were living in squats with very little money. To them, buying some postage stamps to send out their tapes (or to make mail art) instead of buying a good meal was often a brave gesture, and because of this it was even more meaningful.

I should also ask- how willing were people to disclose personal or background information? I know there was a practice in this scene of sending "audio letters", you know, talking on tape to other correspondents and telling all kinds of intimate details about your personal life- but on the other hand, I imagine there were also some participants who were a little more guarded, who decided to just let their works alone form the 'mental picture' of who they were...correct me if I'm wrong!

Of course, I speak only from my own experience- that may differ substantially from that of other networkers. In many years of tape trading, I must say that I have received only a handful of "audio letters"- it was usually more the case of handwritten notes accompanying the cassette. A written letter is so much more practical as a reference, if an answer is expected, so I see "audio letters" as the odd and quite uncommon device used mainly to offer a more intimate and "physical" introduction for distant contacts that you may never have a chance to meet in person. Now that I think of it, though, probably I did not get that many "audio letters" because the musicians might have thought I (being Italian) would have understood only a few bits of their chatter... it was probably a practice more diffused among people of the same mother tongue (but I never got one in Italian!).

Sincerely, since almost all the tape networkers were male and I happen to be hetero, I never felt a big urge to know their intimate lives and feelings. At the same time, apart from the predictable halo of mystery that people involved in "esoteric music" and the like sometimes employed for greater effect, I never felt a particular reticence from the part of my contacts about their personal experiences. Quite simply, any question asked would usually be answered, and these were customarily concerned with a swap of addresses, info about distribution and magazines, collaboration projects, musical equipment, musical tastes, etc. The fact that in the early Eighties I was one of the very few journalists in Italy championing Industrial and noise music on the pages of national magazines like *Rockerilla* and *Velvet* (and too many underground 'zines to mention here), probably gave me a different perspective of the tape network. Besides the swaps and contacts spurred by TRAX and my other projects, many groups would send me promo material for review, and I had the chance to interview and promote artists that often crossed from tape to vinyl to a more "mainstream" kind of popularity. This resulted in my various postmen probably hating me for the impressive amount of envelopes and small packages that I received any working day of the week.

So the magazines you mention working for, was this your official 'day job' at the time of the TRAX project? I'm wondering if doing work for them provided you with more opportunities to engage in your other creative work (for example, having access to all types of office machinery and professional contacts etc.), or if it was just a nuisance which 'got in the way' of your creative output?

During the TRAX years, I graduated from the University of Pisa with a thesis on William S. Burroughs, I studied languages (English, Danish, German, French) but I never really wanted to teach or embrace an academic career. The journalistic work has always been a sort of "third job" for me, I still do it out of passion and I only write what I like to write. Specialized rock magazines pay very little (when they pay you at all) and with the amount of books and recordings I buy regularly, I was already happy when the income from my writings could pay for my cultural "habits". I always helped my parents in the family job (running a hotel in the fashionable seaside resort of Forte dei Marmi, on the coast of Tuscany), until a few years ago when they retired and the place was rented. Since that was only a summer job, I also had other "normal" jobs for a living, like running a small jewelry shop for a few years. I was always very practical and I knew from the start that writing alone could not support a family (I have a 16 year old son now). Even when in 1996 I founded the small press AAA Editions with Piermario Ciani, I had little hope that this could become a full-time occupation. In fact, after publishing over thirty books, we decided to stop, national distribution just does not work for a small publisher and through our website we could only sell a handful of copies.

I always did my journalistic work from home, as a free-lance contributor. I did not feel like moving to a big city like Milan or Rome, where all the big magazines have their headquarters, so that's why I always remained a semi-professional. I would interview bands through the mail or by phone, in pre-Internet times, or on the occasion of concerts. In this activity, and for the kind of articles about obscure bands I always favoured, of course the tape network (and mail art) contacts proved to be very useful, always suggesting new names and ideas to pursue. I always saw my work as a journalist, and also as editor for AAA and other publishers, not as a nuisance but as a great chance for cultural enrichment: you really do get "inside" a record or an artist if you write a review or an article about it, so the effort was always doubly repaid (a broadened knowledge of the subject and a little money on the side of it).

I do not feel like a "hired hand" in my journalistic work, even if I do not want to compare my stuff with the much more literary output of people like Lester Bangs or Richard Meltzer, I have done my bit with creative reviews (purposely without listening to the record, inventing it from scratch, etc.), interviews with imaginary bands, etc.

What was the daily working situation like for the other TRAX founders?

TRAX was founded after a brain-storming, actually a meeting in a coffee bar one afternoon while attending a new wave festival, between Piermario Ciani (who thought up the name TRAX and the main guidelines, hence he was TRAX Unit 01), me (Unit 02) and Massimo Giacon (Unit 03). We lived in different towns with hundreds of kilometres between us, so we were mostly "networking" through the mail and phone, meeting only a couple of times a year. We met through exchanges of our 'zines and fortuitous contacts in the musical underground. Then there were a dozen other TRAX Central Units (persons who produced at least one TRAX item) and approximately five hundred TRAX Peripheral Units in seven years (persons who participated to at least one TRAX project). Piermario (sadly deceased from cancer in 2006) was helping out in the family business at the time, a small bakery, by delivering the bread early in the morning and taking care of the administration. He was also working as a freelance professional photographer and graphic artist mainly for local rock bands (collectively known as The Great Complotto), so his home in Bertiolo, a very small village in the country near Udine, was always an intersection of interesting creative people: punks, comics artists, etc. He was behind many underground projects, fanzines, festivals and exhibitions, plus the conceptual band Mind Invaders. Massimo, a few years younger than me and Piermario, was still a student at the time, just starting his career as a professional comics artist (on the pages of national magazines like *Il Mago*, *Alter*, *Frigidaire*) and playing with his own band Spirocheta Pergoli (later I Nipoti del Faraone) weird songs, *a la* Residents, that were a stable presence in TRAX products. Giacon turned out to be the more successful of us three, in his artistic career: he still publishes comics and illustrations (in fact, I just reviewed his last graphic novel *Boy Rocket*), but he has worked a lot as a "neo-Pop" gallery artist and as a graphic designer of objects for top studios and firms like Memphis, Swatch, Alessi.

Since we're discussing Massimo's comics work, I'm interested in the role comics played in the TRAX releases- this seems to be a fairly unique feature when compared with other cassette releases of the time, or other 'mini multi-media' offerings (actually I can think of few 'indie' labels, period, who have released comics-and-music packages.)

Even before I learned to read, I was an avid consumer of comics, and I never really stopped, it is a form of verbo-visual expression that fits perfectly with my own range of tastes, just like rock music or horror movies. Rock and comics both represent, for people born in the Fifties like me (but also for later generations) a form of intrinsic and instinctive revolt to official culture: the perfect media to express dissent and to explore or create new languages. Massimo Giacon was of course a big comics fan, to a lesser degree also Ciani and other TRAX collaborators, so when the TRAX project took shape, it seemed very natural and obvious to include Giacon's comics in most audio-visual products (as well as his music.) In addition to single short stories and illustrations also by other comics authors (like Johnny Grieco or Davide Toffolo), we created a serialized "long story" of the adventures of the superhero Traxman. With Giacon's drawings and my own scripts, this appeared in various TRAX booklets and catalogues in a black and white version. Later, we perfected this story in a re-drawn colour version, that was serialized in the pages of *Tempi Supplementari*, a nationally distributed magazine published as a supplement to the trend-setting *Frigidaire* (a magazine that in the early Eighties revolutionized the Italian comics scene, introducing to a large audience new authors like Pazienza, Tamburini, Liberatore, Mattioli, etc.) The Traxman adventures were a sort of spoof thriller-sci-fi epic that both parodied the stereotypes of characters like Spirit or Superman and included the main TRAX players (me, Ciani, Ciullini, Ayers, etc.) in fictionalized form. It was a meta-comic that assumed whole new meanings if you read it knowing the history of the various TRAX members... Unfortunately, just when the Traxman adventures were ready to be collected in book format, *Frigidaire* found itself financially in bad waters, so the project was shelved.

I do not think anyway that TRAX was the only tape label interested in comics, there were many in DDAA's French Illusion Production, Charles Burns designing the graphics for early Sub Pop items also comes to mind (when Sub Pop was still a small zine releasing cassettes!), I'm sure there are many other examples. Actually, in 1984 with materials from my collection I curated for the town art museum of Forte dei Marmi the exhibition *Nuvole Rotolanti* ("rolling clouds", the comics' balloon being nicknamed "cloud" in Italy) that was a wide exploration of all kinds of interferences between rock and comics. Massimo Giacon was one of the guests performing at the show, the Spirocheta Pergoli 12" EP *TRAX 0784 - Fuzzi Bugsi tumpa il bongo!* was published as "catalogue" of the event, and the record was based on a story that Giacon had just published in the monthly comics magazine *Alter*. I was very disappointed by the book by Ian Shirley *Can Rock & Roll Save the World? - An Illustrated History of Music and Comics* (SAF, 2005), because it failed to even mention Giacon, Igort, Carpinteri, Archer Prewitt, a whole load of artists/musicians that produced an incredible wealth of work on the thin line between comics and music.

Mainly I wonder what the Italian attitude was towards comics at that time-namely, if it was viewed as a "lower" art form like it is here? To make the parallel with home taping, is it something that, in the 1980s, would have been used by people of an 'alternative' or 'subcultural' mindset rather than by professionals?

Yes, of course in the Eighties comics as a medium were considered much less important and "respectable" than it is today, yet at least in Europe there is a long tradition, going back at least to the mid-Sixties, of influential intellectuals and cultural figures (like writers and essayists Umberto Eco and Oreste Del Buono) that have studied and promoted the Sequential Art of comics as culturally mature, actually a relatively new form of expression that was almost born full-formed: Outcault's Yellow Kid, McKay's Little Nemo, Herriman's Krazy Kat are masterpieces of graphic and lyrical invention that from day one could count as fans people like James Joyce and Gertrude Stein! Of course, we must get rid of a habit towards generalization here, since (like in music, literature and all the other media) there have always been "low" forms of very popular, banal and standardized comics as well as high-brow "author's comics" (as they call them here), plus all the stops in-between. There was surely an independent and underground comics scene in the Eighties, just like there was one in the Sixties (Crumb & *Zap* friends) and Seventies (the *Metal Hurlant* school), but these are just small slices in a very big cake. Most people listen only to certain genres of music (be it rap, rock, electronics, classical, reggae, jazz, opera, etc.), and similarly there is a very varied and complex comics audience for a very varied and complex market and cultural landscape. Like Giacon, I am not interested only in the tradition of underground and independent comics, but I pick my favourites from the whole history of comics, starting with Mickey Mouse and Popeye.

Having said this, I should probably also note that our relationship to comics here is a love-hate one...they are still seen as a cheap, anti-intellectual, pandering medium, and yet they are also our "national literature" since almost every successful comic is adapted into a mega-hit film. Almost the exact same situation occurs in Japan, where 50% of the available printed materials are comics...

There will always be the bigot that thinks that rock is only mindless noise and comics just dumb sub-literature for spoilt children, but, generally speaking, I think that luckily these are more and more just commonplace opinions of the past. In Europe the comics market is not so dualistic as in the USA (superhero vs. indie comics) or Japan (*manga* vs. all the rest), it is a much more varied scenario where often authors that would be considered "difficult" in the US sell as much commercially as certain superheroes. We tend to see the phenomenon of cine-comics (mostly adaptations of superheroes) as an inevitable side-effect of the popularity of the medium, but there is a widespread concordance on the fact that, for example, *The Watchmen* is a masterpiece in print, while the filmed version is just a so-so curio (in the same way that *Sgt. Peppers* is a milestone album in rock history, while the film adaptation by the Bee Gees...). Anyway, what was underground fringe culture yesterday (rockabilly outsiders & the lot) is mainstream pap today (Satanist rock on MTV), so old categories must always be brought up to date. Too much popularity for the comics, which on one hand is very positive for those working in the field, has already put into motion strange forms of exploitation. The "graphic novel", for example, has won its battle and can now be found in good quantities in all the Italian bookshops (and not just in specialized comics stores), as it has been the case in France for at least the past two decades, but the market has already been saturated by cheap and uninteresting books produced by publishers who smelled some money in the new format.

I'm noticing, with the TRAX releases, there is a certain emphasis on fun, whimsy, and play- did you ever find this difficult to reconcile with the more "industrial" projects you undertook, like the Area Condizionata / Italiano Industriale compilations? I ask because these days, the general assumption is that "industrial" equals intense meditation on suffering and paranoia, fetishization of social evils etc., although some people still focus on its more 'positive' side ("ecstacy through noise overload," "out-witting the control machine," and so on.) Put more simply, did you see that much of a big difference between working on the more playful side of networked audio, and the more "industrial" side of it?

Well, things often aren't what they seem from a seat in the stalls, if you visit the backstage. I have had the chance to meet a large number of the first wave of Industrial musicians, and though the image they projected was that of dark and mysterious explorers of all things forbidden and excessive, they were usually mild, gentle and well mannered persons. Plus, most of them had a very good sense of humour. If you analyse at close range the work of Throbbing Gristle, the blueprint for Industrial music, there's a lot of intentional black humour in there, including sarcastic tricks played on the more gullible portion of the audience. A certain Industrial band, that I will leave unnamed, would not miss a single episode of the notorious UK soap opera *Coronation Street*...

Anyway, we did not want to limit TRAX to a single aesthetic or to a single musical genre, the project was very open to all kind of styles and trends, what kept it together was the precise "modular" structure of the products, rather than the homogeneity of the contents. So the harsh Industrial sounds of M.B. or the apocalyptic cut-up collages of Cabaret Voltaire's Richard H. Kirk were just one piece of the puzzle, and could be joined together with Giacon's comics or the spaghetti pop/new wave sound of the bands from The Great Complotto. Since nobody seemed to do that (punk compilations on punk labels were only for punk bands, etc.: how boring!), I took a sort of malicious pleasure in mixing the cards, marrying taboo and playful subjects: weren't we supposed to "break the rules", as counter-cultural operators? Our attitude was of the "fuck 'em if they can't take the joke" kind, we had nothing to lose after all.

My own Lieutenant Murnau project was a very deliberate attempt to mock the "serious" stereotypes of Industrial Culture (not for the fun of it, mind you, but rather to suggest that it was time to move on to other levels of "seriousness"), while at the same time trying to enrich Noise Music and plunderphonic collages with atypical romantic overtones, associating the sound compositions to hidden aspects of the very interesting life of the German movie director Friedrich Wilhelm Murnau and the mythology of his expressionist work (*Nosferatu, Faust, Sunrise, Janus Head*, etc.)

I guess industrial music, like that which you've mentioned, still holds a fascination for me because the more romanticist or mystically-oriented acts have harmoniously co-existed with more 'cognitivist', or more existentialist ones (and, sometimes all of these tendencies have inhabited a single person at different stages in their career!) To an extent, I feel like the same is true of the 'cassette underground' as a whole: it felt as if people were, for the most part, temporarily putting aside their ideological distinctions in order to clear out a space for all marginalized people to be heard. However, I suppose that conflicts (particularly 'wars of words') did arise from time to time- was the policy within the underground to just take a 'hands off' approach to these situations, to ignore them until the opposing sides had exhausted themselves? Or were there ever attempts at intervening in inter-artist conflicts?

Like the mail art network, of which I have been part for over thirty years, the "cassette underground" was pretty much a collaborative affair, it was in the mutual interest to keep the web of contacts peacefully growing (more contacts, more interesting sounds to swap, more chances to be heard and sell a few cassettes...) There was no competitiveness but rather a tendency to help each other in any possible way (through musical collaborations, reviews in magazines, etc.). Conflicts were therefore kept to a minimum, that's how "social networking" still functions today. You don't notice that much infighting in Facebook and the like: to flourish, the network must be (or at least seem) a very safe and pleasant place.

This said, cassette makers and industrial musicians were persons like all the rest, so it was inevitable that, like in any large group of people, now and then conflicts of different nature may arise. But I remember very few such cases, and all of small importance. Maybe the only episode that I can think of now that fuelled a collective outcry is when William Bennett circulated (obviously with provoking intentions!) an over-the-top racist "manifesto" of Whitehouse music[200]: on fanzines and correspondence

---

[200] This merits some further explanation here, since Whitehouse's claims in the aforementioned statement (e.g. that they represented "the most violent music of the new Right") did indeed become a polarizing issue within the nascent post-industrial underground. Danny Devos of Club Moral recalls the situation as follows: "before we started publishing *Force Mental* [magazine], AMVK [Anne-Mie van Kerckhoven] had been doing the layout for a magazine called *Data*. *Data* was financed by the University of Antwerp, and it focused on experimental theatre- three 'zero' pre-issues were made. Then there were plans to really start, and expanding the content to other kinds of experimental art and media. At the time (around 1981) the uprising of the new Right was a much discussed item, so the *Data* team decided to make the first issue a theme issue on that subject. The idea was to have different opinions on the subject, as seen by different artists, authors,

exchanged at the time, many took their distances from him, while a few supported Bennett's views and others considered the text just a silly prank. More generally, though, in retrospect it is in fact quite surprising that there seem to have been so few altercations (even in heavily "politicized" Italy) between artists that were openly promoting extremely radical and often diverging ideological stances.

OK so, as you've said, there's at least one parallel we can draw between 'cassette networking' and the present-day phenomenon of Facebook / social networking websites. Come to think of it, the whole 'multi-user personality' concept of Luther Blissett, etc. has been given new life on these sites...anyone can assume whatever identity they choose (and for whatever purposes!) if they are clever enough to make it convincing...

From Dada to Punk and onwards, multiple names and fake identities have been used for various purposes (even illicit and criminal ones, I'm afraid, and in large numbers). Anyone can do that, but it's a completely different (and much more difficult) thing to utilize a collective name to give life to a meaningful creative project. Otherwise, it's just like wearing a different t-shirt or showing a new tattoo.

Do you feel there is any experience from your cassette curating / trading

---

playwriters, filmmakers working in experimental art in one way or another. It would include any point of view, without judging if it was good or bad, as long as it was recognised and featured in several projects by the artists/authors. At that time Whitehouse promoted themselves as 'the most violent music of the new Right', so it wasn't too much of a big step to invite them to contribute and write a piece about that. In between, *Data* remained in limbo due to lack of finance and disagreement about how to continue. That's when we decided to start our own magazine, with AMVK and I as chief editors and various artists/authors as contributors. The idea and the outcome of *Force Mental* were explained in the first issue, and some of the collected material for *Data* issues was published. So as a matter of fact, it was us who asked William Bennett to write a text about 'the most violent music of the new right' and what we published was what he sent us." (personal correspondence with the author, August 18, 2010.) William Bennett claims that the piece in question, which recycled many of the favorite talking points of the racist Right, was meant to be followed by two more companion pieces in which "essentially the texts were the same but the euphemisms were different- substitute words like 'imperialist', racist, 'state oppression,' 'colonialist' etc. for the [derogatory] ones contained." (William Bennett quoted in *Interim Report #2*, Tokyo, 1992.) Since neither of those installments in the series was ever published, it remains unclear whether a multi-part parody of social control mechanisms was the intent or not. Also of interest is that the original issue of *Force Mental* containing Bennett's piece also features an similarly incendiary piece from Devos on the facing page.

experiences that can NOT be replicated by being in an online social network? Do you feel that the online networking experience is lacking that 'special something' which attracted so many people to mail art and to networked audio?

There are certain similarities as well as big differences between the networks based on correspondence (but also phone calls and physical meetings) of the Seventies-Eighties and today's so called "social networks" based on the Internet (MySpace, Facebook, Skype, Twitter, etc.) The most obvious difference is that, although all these networks function as "open" arenas for anybody who is interested in taking part in the action, the Web sees the participation of *millions* of individuals, compared to the hundreds or thousands of regular participants in the postal circuits. Of course the "analogue" networks were therefore more "specialized," formed by people with much stronger interconnections and shared interests, plus that experience involved investing some time and money (in postage stamps, art materials, cassettes, queues at the post office, etc.), while a message on Facebook may take you just a few seconds in a Internet café.

Anyway, it would be unfair to compare the two forms of networking trying to establish which one is "best" or "more special": they both have their positive and negative sides, and there is no reason why you should not utilize different forms of networking simultaneously or in a complementary way, for example taking advantage of Internet to distribute cheaply and more effectively invites to "physical" exhibitions of mail art ("flash mobs", to give another example, are collective events that use the web to organize physical events and performances.) I never felt as if I had "lost something" when cassettes went out of style: I love changes and evolution (cds, Mp3s, what will come next...), there is so much more you can accomplish and get to know through the Web (can you imagine researching and writing your book with a typewriter?). And then, there will always be revivals for good things, a cassette collection may even become a valuable rarity, it's fun to re-evaluate what you were into when you were young, yet I prefer not to look back too much.

I find with TRAX (and with some of the other handmade / networked art collectives) that there are interesting paradoxes in the work: for example, you were working with photocopied art that could be replicated thousands of times over, yet instead of being impersonal this stuff seems to have had a very intimate "from-me-

to-you" quality to it.

Paradoxical is for me a great compliment and a very positive adjective. I always loved that line from Walt Whitman, the author of *Leaves of Grass*, when he said: "I contradict myself? I contradict myself!" With TRAX we were quite deliberately staging a *parody* of industrial (in the sense of mass-marketed) products. The "modular" theory behind TRAX meant that our products could often be fragmented and reassembled in different combinations: this was intended to be a creative option, to include some form of participation from the part of the buyer, but it also reminded you of the factory assembly line. So this is why the TRAX graphics, after the imprint given by Piermario Ciani to early products, tended to be very neat, bold black and white, a bit cold and hi-tech: to suggest a mass-produced product, even if it was a limited edition of a few hundred copies or less. It's a bit like the Fluxus kits that looked like boxes from the shelves of a supermarket, yet included small hand-made artists' publications and objects.

There's also Ciani's quote that "TRAX set out to produce as much as possible and involve the greatest number of people," yet in the final estimation, it looks like the project attracted a small core of demonstrably talented, dedicated individuals rather than a huge mass of vaguely committed people favoring quantity over quality.

Of course, if you compare TRAX with today's "social networks", five hundred or so authors involved in seven years (of which less than twenty became active Central Units), it is really a small number of participants. But anybody can register on Facebook just like anybody can participate in a mail art exhibition, while we made it very clear from the beginning that TRAX was *not* a mail art project. Contrary to the "unwritten rules" of mail art, we were producing items intended for sale (even if we never really made any money out of them, we barely covered our costs through the sales) and we were making a *selection* of the participants, according to the taste of the TRAX Unit curating a certain item. For each TRAX project, we would invite only those contacts that we thought would be more appropriate for the given theme. Then, we would include and reproduce only the visual and audio works that lived up to a certain standard. Each time, there was probably as much material that remained unpublished as what ended up in the final product. Each author would often contribute several audio tracks or visual pieces, so we could select just what we liked most. I do not think that the "democraticity" of networking should get in the way of the quality of the product you offer for sale: who could be happy about buying (or trading) an "open" but lame audio compilation? TRAX wanted to involve the greatest possible number of people from all the corners of the world, yet retaining a quality standard and a commitment to the proposed theme.

I think most readers will notice, by now, that TRAX was not merely a "cassette label", nor was it an organization for which all of its various activities were just part of an elaborate promotional campaign to sell recorded works. So, from what I can see, TRAX ignored the standard promotional model of record companies etc., in which you have to go through a ritualized sequence of steps in order to make a proper 'communion' with your favorite artist or to really 'understand' them: watch the video, then buy the record, then go to the concert, then get a concert t-shirt and 'tour only' souvenir disc, and so on. It seems, in contrast to this, that attendance at any given TRAX-related event, or acquisition of any given TRAX product, would be able to give you a good understanding of the project's aims- you didn't have to own the entire discography or all the collected writings to gain inspiration. Is this a fair assumption for me to make?

TRAX was something completely different from a "cassette label" (or a "record label", since we also released a few vinyls). It was more a "networking project", something a bit unheard of in 1981. We were often described as an "international group", for lack of a better definition. I saw it really as an artists' collective, with members spread out in different countries, rather than as a commercial enterprise: there was no single headquarters, since there were many TRAX Central Units (in fact, a potentially limitless number of Central Units). Certain products would be released and circulated only by the Central Unit who created it: for example, I only had my own participant's copy of the TRAX "Of Poland" cassette. The (rather utopian) idea behind this plan was that TRAX could have snowballed and become a "cultural strategy" adopted by thousands of authors worldwide...

Yes, each TRAX "modular product" tended to be an experience concluded in itself, with a main theme ("X rated", "Black Xmas",

"Anthems", etc.) and the response to this theme from a varied sample of authors. Yet, since the format of the products was always variable, as well as the names of the participants, we were trying with each project to present something new and unexpected. We did not have a large audience - how could we, with limited editions of a few hundreds copies? - but our buyers and "traders" were a very faithful group, they tended to collect each new release.

If, after all this, someone should be curious to hear a TRAX project, I must point out that "unofficial" free downloads of some of our cassettes and vinyls have appeared in blogs here and there on the Web, so with a quick search and a little luck you might be able to listen to the quite rare (and quite funny) Spirocheta Pergoli 12" or to the *TRAX - Xtra* LP, recorded "at distance" by ten musicians in a web of crossed and modular postal collaborations. Besides, a couple of years ago I started a series of official TRAX reprints with *TRAX Red Night / Notterossa*, two cds released by the Italian label Small Voices (the original cassette dedicated to William S. Burroughs remastered on disc 1, plus a different mix of the original tapes on the second disc). After this luxurious and costly package, in pure TRAX style, I decided to produce the following reprints, always with added bonus tracks and new graphics, as free digital downloads and very limited "collector's edition" cds, with the help of Sandro Gronchi's label Radical Matters and of the musician Gianluca Becuzzi (a.k.a. Limbo, Kinetix, etc.). You can find the free download of the *TRAX Anthems* album reprint (original LP and cassette with alternative versions of various national anthems, plus a brand new hymn) here: http://www.radicalmatters.com/asp/web_editions.asp. The next reprint, scheduled to appear in 2011, will be of the *Xtra* album. I still write for the rock monthly *Rumore* and for various other magazines, and I have published eight or nine cds as part of the eclectic group Le Forbici di Manitù, the last one *L'Isola* (Snowdonia, 2010), dark songs and ambient / shoegaze instrumentals based on a gothic short story written for us by horror queen Alda Teodorani. The next project by Le Forbici di Manitù will not be a normal recording but an "open album" freely circulated on the Web and based, you guessed it, on a concept of modular networking...

From Nijmegen With Love:
Frans de Waard

For quite some time now, whenever cultural observers have hoped to demonstrate how radical freedom of expression enriches society (or accelerates its decline), they set their sights on the Netherlands. The perceived liberal and tolerant thrust of Dutch culture (with "Amsterdam" often substituted erroneously for the nation as whole) has become a constant mantra on the lips of good-time libertarians and utopian dreamers.[201] Conversely, it remains a favorite *bête noire* of the neo-conservative ideologues who believe that such freedoms are the province of degenerate ingrates who "owe" their relaxed lifestyle to the "full spectrum dominance" of U.S. military might- and whatever the case, a hostile takeover by reactionary religious forces will be the ultimate outcome of this societal laxity. If there's one thing held in common between both sides in this eternal struggle, it's that they regularly fail to uncover more nuanced and innovative Dutch cultural contributions outside of the Cannabis Cup, public bicycles, and sex shops that would qualify as "underground" in other social climates. It would be stretching it to say that mind-blowing *Nederhash* and other only-in-Amsterdam vices play no role in shaping Dutch popular culture, but it would be even more foolhardy to claim a hard causal relationship between, say, the time one spends languishing in local hash bars and the quality of one's creative output. William Burroughs once remarked that dreams were as mundane as the average dreamer, and I'd submit that this applies to hash-induced dreams as well. As is the case with any thriving center of artistic production, an above-average degree of personal freedom means little without above-average personalities to harness it- and the modern Dutch audio world, to its benefit, has had no shortage of those.

---

[201] A rebuttal from the interviewee reads as follows: "you could wonder how much of that is true in the current political climate, since 9/11. We saw the murder of a populist politician (where one could wonder if he was right wing, since [despite] being openly gay, he was as well defending sexual freedom and women's rights against fundamental Muslims) and Geert Wilders, who is less concerned with those rights and is outright xenophobic. His party had 1/6 of all votes and will be part, most likely, of the new goverment." (Personal email correspondence with the author, September 9 2010.)

Perhaps another historical feature of Dutch life - the ever-looming possibility of disastrous flooding - is just as important to note as the much-hyped permissiveness of the city centers. This, combined with the population density of the country, has necessitated ambitious projects such as the *Zuiderzeewerken* system of dams and drainage, or the innovation of the man-made "throw-away island," meant to part river waters during the construction of sluices for the Haringvliet dam (although both these projects were initiated only after prior disasters.) Resourcefulness and self-sufficiency have proven invaluable for keeping much of the Netherlands afloat, and they have also been key traits of the more successful and acclaimed Dutch musical personalities (although they would probably not attribute it to any sort of 'national character'.) From the radical political autonomy of the punk-jazz Ex collective, to improv percussionist Han Bennink's skill for making instruments out of quotidian junk like pizza boxes, there seems to be an innate knack among Dutch musical outsiders and eccentrics for making do with whatever is available (and the myth that most Dutch residents have the money to support professional music careers is another one which should be dispelled immediately.)

There is still a refreshing disregard for using others' rulebooks to communicate highly personal experience, which has manifested itself not just in the sound, but also in methods of musical distribution, releasing and broadcast. This is especially evident since the early 1980s, when a few intrepid spirits established a parallel independent infrastructure of cassette labels and pirate transmitters, in an attempt to accommodate the rising wave of hungry musicians armed with newly affordable recording technology and unorthodox topical material. Even with a *curriculum vitae* of adventurous music behind them, no one could exactly count on courting interest from the few independent record labels on hand (the majors, meanwhile, were still struggling to reach a consensus on how to best package and present "new wave" before its neon light flickered out.)

As just a quick tour through Internet discography sites will reveal, the Netherlands were not alone in taking up the mantle of the nascent Cassette Culture, but they did account for some of its most avid proselytizers. One of these was a young Nijmegen native, Frans de Waard, also a founding member of the oddly organic post-industrial troupe Kapotte Muziek. His

Nederlandse Cassette Catalogus, one of his first forays into 'boosting' the scene, was one of the earliest precursors to the Internet 'discog' resources mentioned above- although it did not double as a marketplace or as a forum for music-related commentary, as its online equivalents now do, it did provide an invaluable means of sifting through a plenitude of cassette releases that were becoming too numerous to keep track of without a resource of this kind. Divided into two different index sections (one for labels, and one with postal contact information for individual artists), the *Catalogus* at the very least suggested a national scene in which Amsterdam did not hold a creative monopoly: towns such as Breda, Leidschendam, Nieuwegein, Amersfoort, and Maastricht all had tape label representation (in addition to the more populous centers of Rotterdam, Den Haag and Utrecht.) Among these diverse locales, labels such as Kubus Kommunikaties, Soft Joke Productions and Limbabwe offered an equally diverse variety of musical styles (although not without some overlap between each other: artists in the Netherlands, as in most other countries participating in the home-taping network, were rarely under obligation to make their works available through a single label.)

In more recent years, the 'no frills' approach of the *Catalogus* has been reprised in the text-only *Vital Weekly* newsletter maintained by de Waard, an outgrowth of his erstwhile involvement in the Staalplaat record label, distributor, and performance space. In this newsletter, he and a rotating cast of other contributors provide a feel for what's worth keeping and dismissing in the swelling underground of post-industrial, self-determined music. As a reflection of the Internet age, it is, unlike the *Catalogus,* no longer an exclusive resource for this kind of information- yet it remains one of the few information sources to which creators of home-duplicated media can send their work and have it evaluated seriously (de Waard sets down a few ground rules, i.e. that people not send more than 3 releases for review at one time, or send releases without contact information included on them- those who do so anyway may find their records' "reviews" are largely reminders for them to properly follow instructions.) De Waard's straightforward attempts at providing constructive criticism are often pitted against the more cerebral and discursive reviews of guest contributors, like the somewhat opaque noise theorist "jliat," leading to especially humorous results when the two end up reviewing each other's works.

As this discussion with de Waard should make clear, involving oneself with the world of networked art on one level (e.g., publishing a fanzine related to its activities) often involves an ineluctable slide into involvement with other communicative media, such as radio shows, or the organization of various concerts and congresses. This phenomenon has surfaced again and again during the course of my researching this book, so we can't really say that de Waard is the definitive example of "networked media multi-tasking." Yet he remains one of the more accessible specimens of this kind: in stark contrast to the conceptual proclivities of cassette network alumni like Achim Wollscheid and Giancarlo Toniutti, de Waard spends less time developing a cognitive framework for the kind of art that he instinctually gravitates to. For him the praxis of seeding sonic ideas and watching them grow is, apparently, of more importance than a tight framework, and no further justification is needed beyond this intense affectivity, it seems. His is an approach that networked and self-released audio would be poorer without.

++++++++

What's the first instance you can remember of seeing / hearing a "homemade" recording in the Netherlands? Was this something that was made locally, or imported?

I used to keep a list of all cassettes I bought, straight from the beginning, and although I lost the list ages ago, I'm very sure of the first two entries on that list. The first was 'The Squats' and the second was *From Brussels With Love.* 'The Squats' was Nijmegen's first punk band, started in 1979 (I think), and I was in the same class as the drummer. I didn't look like a punk, but I read the right fanzines and bought mainly Dutch punk rock, simply because it sounded more what I liked, I guess, rather than because it was a nationalist thing. In the most important fanzine of the Netherlands, *Raket*, I read something about people releasing cassettes of punk rock and experimental sounds and that seemed a great thing. So, in the local record store, they had this Squats cassette that I bought there, rather than from my class mate (for reasons I no longer recall), and almost immediately I also bought *From Brussels With Love,* an international compilation from Les Disques Du Crepuscule. This happened in 1981. I read about that tape in a new magazine from The Netherlands called *Vinyl,* and my musical interest had already moved away from punk to post-punk, new wave and experimental/electronic music. That first issue (the magazine was famous for the inclusion of flexi-discs) had a very negative review of that, but a positive article on the label. Since I was into all things Factory Records, that tape seemed a must have, and it was. The quality of the music, the selection of the artists and the presentation was a real eye-opener. It gave me the idea to do this myself too- to make music and release tapes, although it didn't happen until 1984. Until then, I was on the consumer side of things and collecting information about Dutch labels, which led - in late 1983 - to my first publication: *De Nederlandse Cassette Catalogus,* a list of all labels and their releases.

Can you tell me more about the catalog- namely, how many copies did you print up, where was it distributed, and how many people were initially interested in reading it? Did it include reviews or biographies of artists, or was it mainly just a listing of everything you knew at the time?

My father loaned me some money to get 1,000 copies printed, and it got quite good media coverage. Alternative and overground papers wrote about it, and it led to various radio interviews on the subject of releasing cassettes. I didn't sell that many, maybe about 500 or so. Later editions were published by Stichting Stopcontact and then by the official Dutch institute For Pop Music. It was just a plain list of label names, addresses and their releases, no reviews or biographies. Perhaps that would have been a better idea. But I do think it was fairly complete. I wrote to all the labels asking for the listings, and they tipped me for other labels etc.

Around the time of cataloging all this material, what kind of trends did you notice in cassette recording? I think today's assumption is that all people doing 'homemade' or 'do it yourself' releases were people who preferred either more extreme material, or perhaps more 'psychedelic' material. However, I assume that not everyone was approaching it from the post-industrial side of things- were there also a lot of participants who just wanted to have a 'pop' band, yet wished to avoid big record labels?

I picked [a tape] from the shelf and browsed it just to refresh my memory, and the majority of the releases were by "home tapers" as we called them back then. Guys twiddling knobs on a synthesizer for an hour, and so on. Then there are quite a few who dealt with punk music, since that was a DIY movement, and only a very few are other music, mainly pop. I think back then the idea was that if you were in pop band, you wanted a real record deal. Those bands made tapes, but just a demo to get gigs or a contract. They were not included in my catalogue, since it only had tapes that Rik Publik could actually purchase. But the majority of them were 'experimental music', mostly guys by themselves (as far I could tell no girls at all, or working with men/boyfriends, like Ding Dong) or more experimental rock bands, like Nasmak (the best known of the lot.)

This is a commonly recurring complaint, that the tape 'scene' was almost exclusively male- do you think this was because fewer women were really interested in doing home recording / releasing, or for other reasons? One would think - especially with the recent DIY art and design boom, as evidenced by sites like etsy.com - that this method of production would be more appealing to younger women, especially those who are critical of the perceived male orientation of 'major' consumer culture.

Actually, I have no idea why this is the case. I tried to find the answer for years, but failed. I can't have think of a good reason why this is all male dominated, but it is. Ding Dong was the best-known Dutch label, and the best selling. They were run by the artist couple Van Kaye & Ignit. Ignit also had a radio show on national radio and she was the main person of the label. They divorced, I think, and left music altogether, I think. They released more easy electronic pop music, and did a great thematic compilation on Film Noir.

Was her radio show dedicated to self-released material (and was there any other program in the Netherlands that was)? I've read about some other 'free radio stations' of the 80s (Radio Dood, Radio Patapoe etc.), I wonder to what extent they relied on material from the cassette underground.

No, her program was not really about self-released material, just records and some tapes. There was a great program called 'Radiola Improvisatie Salon' by Willem de Ridder, who played tapes produced at home, and who was more instrumental to promoting the world of tapes. The free radio thing is a bit harder to discuss: they had a limited reach with their transmitters, so I never heard Dood or Patapoe. From what I know about it, they were indeed very radical as to what was playing. The local illegal radio called radio Rataplan was very left wing, and each minority had their own program, but [there was] very little music. I had a program there with experimental music, vinyl and tapes, but the whole radio [station] hated it, because of the musical content. It was a different kind of station than Dood or Patapoe: more like Radio 100, from Amsterdam. Very informative for the squat movement.

Why the hatred of your show- was it because you weren't focusing enough on political issues related to the autonomous scene? It seems to me that promotion of independent art and music production is as valid a political statement as anything.

I totally agree, but unfortunately the progressive political minds don't like the real progressive music- just sub-standard alternative rock. Still do, actually. There were other music programs, focusing on, say, hard rock or cosmic music, but we got the shit. My co-host was a pretty well regarded man at the station, so we got away with it. Otherwise, I don't think it could have lasted long.

I recall reading about de Ridder's show also; wasn't it his policy that he would play anything that he received at the station? How successful do you think his experiment was?

Yes, that was his policy: '*I have here an envelope from Frans de Waard and there is a cassette, which I will now play for 5 minutes*', without previously auditioning the tape. I thought that was a great concept. He had this on national radio, for 30 minutes on Friday night at the pop station, and every month (on Sunday afternoon) for 2 hours on the classical station. It was pretty successful, I guess, for what it was, but perhaps the celebrity of de Ridder helped. He's still "world famous" in the Netherlands.

So, when did you decide to 'take matters into your own hands' and begin actually distributing tapes, rather than compiling information about them and playing them on the radio?

I sent some of the booklets to foreign magazines for review, and one of them was to a German guy named Graf Haufen (who oversaw a label of the same name, Graf Haufen Tapes, the band Falx Cerebri, and his fanzine *Die Katastrophe*). I was already corresponding with people elsewhere, and he told me he compiled two cheap compilations called Katacombe, and asked me to compile the third one, with just Dutch industrial and experimental acts. Since I knew plenty of people I did, and that started my label [Korm Plastics], and my project Kapotte Muziek, since obviously I had to enclose a track of myself. That was October 1st, 1984. It was KP3, since in good Factory Records tradition I thought I shouldn't start with KP1. Later on, I added my cassette catalog as KP1, and *Archive*, another magazine of discographies, as KP2.

Before the Staalplaat shop began, were there any shops in which the sale of these homemade products was possible? I don't mean necessarily 'record shops', but any sort of multi-purpose store, gallery, boutique, etc....I always hear the urban legend about how industrial or noise cassettes were for sale in select sex shops in Japan, for example, but I've never been able to either confirm or deny that.

I'm not sure, as [Staalplaat] was around since 1982, so I immediately started selling to them. There was in 1984 also a shop at V2, an artist run space in 's-Hertogenbosch. And there was one in Rotterdam called Kasset, I believe, but that didn't last very long. In Amsterdam there were other shops, which indeed sold clothes and books, but nothing sex-minded. Remember, in the 80s the feminist movement was very left wing, so was the cassette movement, and things like pornography were closely monitored. When such things arrived, say the *Sex and Bestiality* release[202], Staalplaat had a hard time defending that. When I was in Japan for the first time (2001), I didn't see any of that either.

More important for me than the fetishistic audio content of some releases was the status of these tapes as 'fetish objects;' these rare and special things that only a few people knew about (not to mention people knowing very little about the artists

---

[202] Actually a series of compilation cassettes, rather than a single release, issued by the French label Bain Total. Compiled by Die Form's Phillipe Fichot, the cassettes' thematic content is mostly in line with the cruelty-laced eroticism evinced by his own flagship musical project.

behind them, either)...it seems that when the creators realized this format had a potential to be a kind of fetish item, they also began to experiment more with the packaging, wrapping the cassettes in special artworks and so on. Can you remember any early instances of this "objet d'art" packaging style, and do you have any favorites?

I must admit that packaging was not the strongest interest I had. A famous bread company in the Netherlands once advertised *"the thing you throw away is the package."* The musical content was always more important. The objects were always a bit of a nuisance for people like me who had so many tapes. Some of them were nice, like the milk carton thing by Doxa Sinistra and the *One Hour For Spits* compilation packed in a bathing sponge, or the pillbox [design] of *Assemble Generale 4,* but where do you keep them? One thing I always hated was the video boxes: too big! The other thing that always bothered me going to cassette fairs (which were actually quite frequent in the mid 80s) was that the people who didn't like the music always bought a tape with a nice package, just because the package looked so nice. The three examples I mentioned were also about great music. I'd rather have a nice, informative booklet like *From Brussels With Love.*

Well it's no secret that a lot of these cassettes came with a lot of supplemental informative content as well: stapled booklets or small magazines and so on. Don't you think that this was another thing attracting people to the homemade cassette format: not just a chance to hear music one could not hear elsewhere, but to receive kinds of information one could not receive elsewhere? Especially with acts that were born from the Industrial tradition, there was a tendency towards including text collages of strange and esoteric news items, or image collages with a similar effect. Also- regarding the cassette fairs you mentioned: obviously I'm too young to remember or experience things like these first-hand, so I wonder what these were like. Did they feature live performances (musical or otherwise) in addition to the selling / trading of cassettes? Were these any more prominent in the Netherlands than in another country?

Usually it was with concerts, performances, book selling- a very 80s "youth house" thing to organize. I was too poor as a student to travel abroad to see what they were like, but I'm sure they were held in other countries too. I organised one at a student club who dwelled [sic] in money, so they organised an independence day in the afternoon with this fair, where I had a stand as a label and in the evening concerts by THU20, The No-listics, Prilius Lacus and Death Pact - the very first time I played a concert with my friend Sjak van Bussel (now of Antenne Records and DJ DMDN) as Death Pact. In between, a copious buffet was served which was talked about for years to come. Some people, like Roel Meelkop (who played with THU20) still remember. But that was an exception.

I'm curious also about the prolific nature of many cassette artists (although many of these, like Merzbow, became just as prolific with the issuing of 'professional' releases.) What do you think was the attraction to releasing, say, 10 or more tapes by one's own project in a single year? Did people feel it was necessary to release this often to remain 'in the spotlight,' or was this extreme production a kind of commentary / parody of mass media?

That I think is a difficult question, as it deals with the motivation of why people choose to do what. I assume in most cases it was that 'work is constant', and they cared little about 'moving on', or 'doing just one thing and then move on', but rather wanting to be 'involved' all the time. Lots of labels were doing compilations, so it was a good way to be in the loop if you had new music to present. I don't think it was commentary or parody. It was very much outside the real world of sound production: away from studio budgets, marketing etc.

Since you were selling or trading a lot of tapes by the more 'ultra-active' artists, what did you notice about people buying them: would people buy every single item released by a certain artist of this type? Were there a lot of 'hardcore collectors' even at that stage of the game?

I didn't sell that many tapes, I gather, but after a while I had a certain range of customers who would buy every new thing. But what is a "lot?" 10? 1000? More like 25 than 100, I'd say. Once you had a reputation as a label to watch out for, you were in. However, a lot of labels didn't want to gather any reputation at all: for lots of these labels it was a hobby, something to do in the evening hours. Make some music, release a tape. More than now, it was, I think, a situation where people go for an entire label, rather than one artist. Even then, I don't think anybody collected everything by Merzbow.

Since you mention labels were important to potential collectors of this material, here's another label-related question: was it more common for an artist to approach you and say "I want to release something on your label," or was it more common that you personally invited people to participate in it?

Here again, it would be a combination. Since one had a label, people would approach you, and depending on what you wanted as a label, many releases, not so many, you said yes or no. Some people choose to release everything offered to them. For my own label, I didn't accept everything. Sometimes you'd be inviting people that you thought were great, but perhaps already 'too big.' In my case, it was Bourbonese Qualk and Controlled Bleeding, who wanted 10 free copies as payment, which in 1985 I thought was an excessive demand- but I did [release them]. Merzbow just mailed a track, and one copy as payment was ok, as it probably was with everyone else [he sent work to.]

I've noticed that a significant amount of material from your past projects is freely downloadable now, thanks to various music blogs. I've also noticed that some people have an attitude of hostility towards these blogs, merely because they make it too "easy" to find the obscure, out-of-print material that they struggled to find just a few years ago: many people think that music fans will have a greater connection to their music if they're involved in this time-consuming ritual of hunting for it. How do you stand on this issue?

I find that hostility odd, very odd. But then again, I don't collect collectable items- I like to hear music. So I think it's pretty good that the blogs exist. In the 80s, you perhaps did 25 copies of your tape, because you thought no more people than that were interested, and perhaps these days no more than 25 buy your CD. These days, music is separated from the medium (cassette/vinyl) and is a digital file. Unfortunately for some, myself included as a label boss, people think that a digital file is free. With music that is released these days, and blogs immediately offering that for free, I can only say that I think this is very counterproductive, as labels will eventually stop investing in releasing new music. That is a trend I don't like. But for all that great, old, lost music that is too obscure to release on a CD, it's a good alternative to get out to young people and let them hear it. I am not an object lover, I don't prefer cassettes over vinyl, or vinyl over tapes etc. Music is made to be heard, and if possible right away. Music should also not be about collecting as many MP3s as possible, but about actually being heard.

The Whole Hog:
Interview With Al Margolis

Until the industrial experiments of the late 1970s, and the mutual rise of DIY music-making technologies around this time, it was difficult to find press coverage of an "everyman" character who dabbled in electronic music (let alone listed this as their profession.) Sybaritic dandies like pre-*Discreet Music* Brian Eno were the public image of the "electronic musician": singular polymaths who could appear on a concert stage resplendent in platform boots and rouged cheekbones, yet be equally comfortable giving off-the-cuff university lectures on cybernetics the next day. Such characters were seen as the progenitors of a splendid tech-utopian daybreak yet to arrive, and the use of synthesizers, rhythm machines, or even Revox tape decks was an unequivocal comment on future possibilities more than it was ever a reflection of present-day reality. The android affectations of Kraftwerk took this futurism to even greater extremes, simultaneously playing off of existing *kitsch* stereotypes of a completely automated future, and embracing those stereotypes as a model to be emulated. Not to be outdone by the feather boa-draped arch-poseur Eno, or by a quartet of uniform Teutonic mannequins, the Afro-futurist album artwork for Herbie Hancock's 1974 LP *Thrust* is another example of the "electronic musician as outer space pioneer," showing the electric piano / synthesizer virtuoso using his keyboards to pilot a bubble-domed spacecraft over a fantastic moonscape.

Exceptions, as always, abounded- from the spartan, mass improv efforts of Musica Elettronica Viva to the synthesized voice experiments of the poet John Giorno. And, to be fair, Brian Eno's guest turn playing synths on Nico's *The End* does temporarily ditch the futurist sensibilities for street-level, existential howls of here-and-now psychic torment. Yet the concept of "electronic music" as being the plaything of a patrician elite, or of untouchable prodigies with highly developed frontal lobes, was not an easy one to shake off until the receding 'shock of the new' coincided with the greater availability of electronic instrumentation.

The gregarious Brooklynite Al Margolis is the central member of If,Bwana and the founder of the Sound Of Pig tape label (his newer Pogus Productions solidifies the gains made by S.O.P., featuring innovators like Pauline Oliveros, among others.) While referring to him as an "everyman" seems a little bit inappropriate, given the sublime, amorphous quality that If,Bwana tracks can muster (and the broad sonic palette that comprises the swelling S.O.P. catalog), it is clear that Margolis is a world away from the image of the electronic musician as a sci-fi aristocrat from beyond the Milky Way. This is not just because his regular chat sessions with scene magazines made plentiful references to mundane things like a "day job," but because his self-effacing nature precludes any feeling that he needs his work to validate some sense of greatness. When not confessing to *Electronic Cottage* how "I'm not great at making plans," he insists to readers of *ND* that "I'm not a real salesman"[203] (this in spite of the *ND* interviewer, Das from Big City Orchestra, noting that S.O.P. is one of the "most reviewed labels around."[204]) Ads for the S.O.P. catalog could also be regularly spotted in local music broadsheets of the period, such as *Sound Choice* (whose decision to review cassettes and "proper" LP releases in the same column space was a surprisingly rare editorial move.)

Margolis is also, unlike countless other musicians who have used the Big Apple as a muse, loath to let his work be defined by the part it plays in the larger New York mythos. Though Margolis maintained a roster of local allies during the mid-'80s heyday of cassette networking, including Sue Ann Harkey (Audio Letter) and Paul Lemos (Controlled Bleeding), his attempts at "scene-making" took a decided backseat to his unwavering habits of tape dubbing and networking. Nor does Margolis' music exude what would be critically recognized as a New York "vibe"; that stereotypically anxiety-ridden, oblique and half-intellectual / half-visceral approach that found its way into everything from Talking Heads' jitter funk to the hypermodern experimentation of John Zorn and his 'downtown scene' colleagues. Though he maintains the city's high standard for eclecticism in many different ways (by curating a full spectrum of music styles and anti-styles on his labels, and being a capable multi-instrumentalist) he has other priorities than advancing the Gotham

---

[203] Al Margolis quoted in "Sound Of Pig Music" by Das. *N D* #8, p. 8. *N D*, Austin, Texas.
[204] *Ibid.*

mystique. If anything, the music of If,Bwana was and is a trans-Atlantic phenomenon, part of the autodidactic post-industrial culture that ignored local, generational peer pressure and got to work building a sonic vocabulary that would overcome localized linguistic conventions.

Kindred spirit Frans de Waard describes the music of If,Bwana as "beyond ambient, before noise: in a grey area in between all of this, but with maybe more hints to modern classical music than one should guess."[205] This is a fair summation: Margolis' works often took full advantage of the longer playback times that cassettes offered, with 20-30 minute electronic pieces slowly unfolding in a fashion similar to the genres de Waard mentions (but without the endless improvisational fillips of electronic 'prog' jams, or the calculated cruelty of the more long-winded 'power electronics' assaults.) Having cut his teeth on purely electronic material, Margolis later updated this aesthetic in arrangements for voice and acoustic instruments, occasionally approaching the robust minimalism of a composer such as Giacinto Scelsi. His is a respectable contribution to the ambience already described in this book's chapter on post-industrial aesthetics: meaning, ambience as active immersion and enhancer of everyday consciousness rather than as a glorified escape hatch from the same. Although the literally hundreds of titles in his S.O.P. catalog do not follow exactly the same trajectory, with some attempting go-for-the-jugular noise, others playing with humorous, pataphysical tape assemblages, and still others sailing into jazz improv waters (see Amy Denio's *No Elevators*), most of them[206] manage to present a sound not available in great doses elsewhere. As with other old standbys of the cassette network, S.O.P.'s wild variance, along with its indifference towards manifestoes and extra-musical distractions, was its defining characteristic. Whether one sees this as a diletannte-ish lack of direction or as a mission to fill a vacuum left open by the rest of the recorded audio world, many S.O.P. alumni have since risen to the highest possible echelon of 'experimental' music.

The following conversation with Al Margolis, though it takes more than two decades after his being appointed the "cassette godfather," shows

---

[205] Frans de Waard quoted at http://www.vitalweekly.net/488.html. Retrieved Octiober 21 2010.

[206] Here I have to confess to not hearing the complete Sound Of Pig catalog, and so will have to settle for this partial judgement.

an individual who still labors tirelessly at making unorthodox audio attainable (in both the sense of being affordable and comprehensible.) Margolis' various endeavors have not held out the possibility of a brilliant future like a carrot on a stick, tantalizing audiences yet retracting the promise at the end of the show. Instead, they have attempted to yank that future vision into the present, to make it more open and engaging.

++++++++

(note: recording cuts in here abruptly, Al Margolis leads in…)

There's been a kind of gap in terms of cassette knowledge- there's a generation in between myself and what's around now, who don't know anything about it, or so it seems. And then there's a younger crowd who know a lot about that stuff…over the last few years, it's interesting how it's gone from being almost totally ignored to having a little more information.

There's probably people who are 21 or younger who have more knowledge of this material than myself, just by virtue of having more free time during the day to do research, and to visit blogs which are uploading a new cassette's worth of material (or more) every day.

Well, it's funny because I still sell S.O.P. cassettes to people who want them- the cassettes now, the masters are all 20-plus years old and the dubbing decks are not what they were. I'm actually in the process now where, whenever someone orders a cassette, I dump them to computer, burn them to CD-R and I make a cassette of *that* for them. So, whenever someone orders 10-15 cassettes I'm both happy and pissed off (laughs)…especially with things I haven't done before, it's like "ahhh, shit…" If people buy two or three at a time, it's cool, but I've actually had people who want a whole lot at one time and it's like, well…if you order it that way, you're never going to get it, because I'm just going to be overwhelmed. I also do this on the computer I do my current work [on], so I'm switching between dubbing tapes and doing my own music.

I should probably ask what caused you to be involved with cassette-based music in the first place.

Actually, I always wanted to be a musician- but it took a long time for me to get into 'weirder' music, more experimental stuff. The way I really got into it, for starters, was through either *New York Rocker* or *Soho News*, I can't remember...it was more devoted to post-punk / new wave stuff from around the country, even though it had 'New York' in the title. Through reading that, I found *Op* magazine, which was originally based in Olympia, Washington. It was a big, newsprint-sized magazine at first, and they decided from the outset to just do 26 issues, one devoted to a single letter of the alphabet. It was pretty wide-ranging, it went from pop bands to classical composers: one issue could cover Fela [Kuti], Fred Frith, the Feelies....I think I first started reading it around issue 'E' or 'F', and that was the first time I saw anything [written] about cassettes, [or] people who were just doing cassette stuff. In the first issue I saw there were 5 or 6 tapes being reviewed, and by the last issue there were whole pages' worth of cassette reviews.

Something just struck me about these people, so, I kind of started just writing people's addresses down and getting contacts, getting cassettes as well. I was playing in a kind of poppy, post-punk type band then, and I wasn't really even thinking of recording much at that time. But that's when the Porta-studio first came out, and I ended up getting a Fostex X-15. We all quit our jobs at the time- the band wasn't going anywhere, so we bought a synthesizer and tried doing something different. But I screwed up a tax return at the time and owed the government some money, so I thought 'well, I've got to pay these fuckers a few hundred bucks, so let me buy this X-15...' and that's how I got to doing my own recording- I think New Year's Day of 1984 was the first recording of experimental music I ever did; the first If, Bwana track. At that point, I'd been buying cassettes from people for a couple of years, and it just dawned on me that if I started a label, then I'd have something to trade instead of spending money (laughs.)

Would you say the majority of the tapes' actual distribution came about through trading? What was the percentage of people paying money for these releases at this time?

I basically started S.O.P. in '84, like October or so- I had 3 or 4 cassette releases by the beginning of the following year. But during the heyday, the biggest time, I went through about 3,000 cassettes. If my recollection is correct, it was about a third of each- I sold about a thousand, traded a thousand, and just "promo'ed" another thousand. At that time, we had maybe 250 cassettes in the catalog, so 3,000 sounds like a lot, but it's really about 10 of each title [laughs.]

Were you recording as If, Bwana before creating the label, or did your personal recording run parallel with the label's creation?

Well that first track was in 1984, and the first If, Bwana cassette [*Freudian Slip*] was S.O.P. #004, so it was pretty much concurrent- I started recording as If, Bwana about 6 months before the first cassette came out. It took me a few months to get my shit together, but they were fairly concurrent, actually.

The place where I worked with my father was like a textile company, and I was a shipping guy- that year when I said I was selling about 3,000 cassettes in the year, I had dubbing decks with me at work. I had 3 dubbing decks and, during the course of an 8 hour day, I could probably dub 15 cassettes a day, and then I'd come home and do the same at home, so I'd essentially be dubbing all day.

One of the first choices I had to make with the label was, do you go out and mass-produce a few hundred cassettes, or do you decide to do it yourself? Back then, to produce a couple hundred cassettes was still a couple hundred dollars...

So, you could go to a small-run duplication place if you wanted?

Yeah, they had those, and they'd do all the printing for you- I can't remember off hand, but I think that if they did the whole job for you, 200 cassettes may have been $200-$300. Or, hey!- you could go out and buy a dubbing deck for $100-$150. That was the choice for me. I ended up getting more and more dubbing decks over time- and I must tell you, dubbing decks now that cost about a hundred and fifty bucks are not as good as the ones that cost that much 20 years ago...I found one recently that was just a piece of crap [laughs.] I bought one like that, and probably within 6 months the doors had popped out and it was eating tapes...

Did you usually produce a set quantity of tapes before you knew what the demand would be, or did you do one-off tapes 'on demand'?

It's not the same thing quite as it is now- with Pogus I do a 1,000 CD run and it's easy enough to just bang out 100-200 promo copies from that. But if you sent me a cassette and I decided to release it on S.O.P., then I'd definitely make 15-20 copies for you personally, right away. I'd just go ahead and make a quantity of stuff, since there were a lot of magazines (*Op / Option, Sound Choice*) and radio stations like WFMU to send stuff to. There was 'x' amount of people to trade with, too- so as soon as a tape came out I'd at least make 20 or 30. A lot of people either had a little bit of distribution, or there were tons of little fanzines that would review things, like *FactSheet Five, ND, UnSound*...those were the blogs of the day, really. I tell people that nowadays I could do a 1,000 CD run and just give them *all* away, owing to the number of blogs and little Internet radio stations. Thankfully there wasn't quite so much back then, but there was a fair amount of little 'zines back then.

So, I'm trying to run a label, I'm trying to keep it going and so making enough dough so that it pays for itself would be fine- I'm not sitting here making a living by running my label. But on the other side, the big record companies have been so stupid, because giving away and trading music was always your free advertising- at one point during the tape / cassette days, the record companies just decided 'oh, we're losing money, people are stealing all this music,' and that's when they went to Congress and got them to either put a tax on cassette decks or blank tapes. And it's like, ok, yes I'm swiping stuff from you because I can't afford to buy every record I might want, but you're still getting the sales at some point- and in typical, never-ending record company fashion, half the things we were taking were out of print....you know, does this story sound familiar? And now they've run into an industry that has way more money and is more central to our economy. When they ran into the computer industry, that's when they got nailed. As a small label, I'd like it if you buy a CD, but I'd just assume you share it- if someone's ripping it off, it's the nature of the beast and it doesn't really bother me. However, there's a certain point where, if everything is free and there's nothing to sell, then how do you sell something? If you steal DVDs and rip everything off of them, at a certain point these guys go out of business. The Criterions of the world, for instance, who have to spend 'x' amount of money to make all this stuff available- if you steal all their stuff, then they go out of business, then there's nothing to steal. So, it's a weird conundrum.

At the very least, it seems like subscribers to independent labels are more likely to do their own promotion for that label in proportion to how much they consume, and to try and compensate in some way when they've received material for free- by uploading positive reviews and so on.

Well that's why I never get bent out of shape over this- I'd rather you hear the music and do what you do, there's no way I'll be making a living out of it anyway, so it's not a question of money. I'd much rather you hear the sounds- for most of the guys in the pop world who make a living, it's through live gigs and merchandising, not through music.

Were there any 'top sellers' on S.O.P. that you can recall?

If what people are buying *now* [from the S.O.P. back catalog] is an indication of what they were buying *then,* the biggest sellers I have now are Jim O'Rourke's cassette [*Some Kind of Pagan*] which was one of the first things he ever put out, the Big City Orchestra one was pretty big when it came out, *Massacre of the Innocents,* Debbie Jaffe's stuff as Master / Slave Relationship, the Merzbow / John Hudak split, some of the Jeph Jerman things…some of those things weren't necessarily 'big' then, but since those projects are still going on, some of those things get ordered fairly frequently these days. At a certain point, maybe I was glutting the market as well…after cassettes #175-200, maybe my interest wound down, and a lot of the 'zines were folding- *Option,* following on the heels of *Op,* became a fairly commercial type of magazine and the magazines like *ND* and *Sound Choice* came out less and less. I was putting out more stuff, but there were fewer places to send it to.

Although I liked everything on the label, I think there may have been certain things I liked more than others and 'pushed' more.

Were you on good terms with everyone on the label, or were there any 'fallings out' or conflicts of interest?

Actually, the only person that seemed to be a pain in the ass over time was Brian Ladd of Psyclones- it wasn't any kind of big difficulty, though. This was when Hal McGee started his *Electronic Cottage* magazine (looking at homemade music as a kind of electronic folk music), where I was called the "cassette godfather." Brian was quoted in this or some other magazine, saying something like "cassette godfather?! I remember when he was buying cassettes from *us*" [laughs.] It was just something kind of stupid like that. But just in terms of contact / dealings, I never had any problems with him, he put me on some compilations through his Ladd/Frith label. But that's the good thing about the mail, you didn't have to have *instant* communication with people!

Speaking of instant communication, are there artists on your label that you still haven't met face-to-face?

I haven't met most of them! It really was from around the world, although I did gigs in different areas....I met [Jim] O'Rourke in New York years later. Out of all the 300 cassettes, most of those people were elsewhere.

What was some of the first international contact you had with your label, and at what point did this contact begin?

S.O.P. #9- within the first 10 releases, there was a German guy, Der Akteur- then the tenth and eleventh [cassettes] were some compilations which had some international people represented on them....Muslimgauze, Het Zweet, English and French stuff from #20 onwards. So, pretty early on. I think part of it was also buying compilations from other people, which had addresses printed on them, so I would write to them saying that I'd like to hear more.

I always wondered if there was one particular 'Johnny Appleseed' character who went to continental Europe (or came back from there) with some tapes, or if this activity sprung up simultaneously in different countries.

I think the same impulse sprang up there, and in Japan, right from the get go, or at the same time- I don't think any one continent really 'started it.' Barbara Moore, who used to run a store called Bound / Unbound, had a lot of old Fluxus things on cassette- and S Press out of Germany had cassettes of sound art and sound poetry even before the beginning of the cassette network (1980, or late 1979 even.) So, again, I don't think it was a matter of the United States just doing it and then [home taping] taking off over there. It was a practical medium once you decided you weren't going to do a record. And some of the early things, before the 4-track tape decks and stuff...people like R. Stevie Moore who were doing pop songs, it was harder to do than just doing noise compositions, since there was a tape lag.

Since we're talking about the cusp of the 1980s, do you feel the Industrial movement was really the main impetus for the first wave of cassette releasing, or were there other movements that also fed into the desire for cassette releasing?

Early on, whoever was doing cassettes was coming from totally different places- whether you listen to early S.O.P. stuff or other labels, you would have these really strange compilations, featuring industrial music, noise, jazz, pop, folk stuff- it was totally wide open. I think at that point it was just independent music, non-commercial music. You could have an If, Bwana, or have Don Campau doing a pop tune, you could have totally weird things by people who were totally incompetent. Over time, it splintered to the point where there were [genre-specific] compilations of industrial or pop music or whatever. Throbbing Gristle was an entry point, but for me it was more of the DIY / punk thing- I played guitar for a long time and was growing up in the 70s, but was never a good enough guitarist to be in a band, yet still wanted to play. So the punk-ish thing wasn't solely about chops, it was about spirit and ideas and the whole thing. So that, more than industrial, is probably the prime mover for a lot of things- at least for me.

I think there's a misconception now that most of what was released on cassette at the time was industrial or power electronics, music done with distorted shortwave signals and so on- maybe the current vogue for this material is leading people to believe that.

Well there *was* definitely a lot of noise on cassette, and I think that's because it was just the simplest thing for people to do, on a certain level- and it interested people too. I remember when I went from recording to Fostex 4-track, to recording on 8-track reel to reel: it was basically the same as the material I was doing before, but I now had more tracks to play with. I think the first thing I released on 8-track was "They Call Me Bwana." There was one guy who I traded with, I can't remember his name off hand, but when I sent the guy a cassette of this stuff- he said, I don't know how he meant to say it, but it came across as "now that you have 8 tracks, why aren't you doing music [laughs]?" It wasn't necessarily that I didn't like doing song-based stuff, but why would I change just because of *that*?

Over time, I did get more stuff that was noisy. But there were all kinds of other things too- as I said, it was just a non-commercial format. And at one point, I think there actually was a fanzine called *No Commercial Potential*. And that's really what it was all about- you did what you wanted to do, but I was always amazed when I ran into someone who thought doing cassettes, being a small fish in a smaller pond, was a way to make a living.

Actually, you know what- I've been working for a few different record companies for almost 20 years, so I *have* been making a living, and in some respect it's been because I ran a cassette label and managed to parlay that into other things- so I guess I should shut up and claim that there *is* a 'way in' through cassettes, just weirder than I ever thought it would be!

At any rate, what you lose in commercial potential seems to be compensated for by the large pool of like minds to trade with and correspond with.

Sure, plus you learn how to tell people "I can't stand your project" in a really nice way…and that was always the funny thing, I got tons of people writing me all the time, and some of it was great, some of it was crap. So you learn really early to tell people "I'm not really interested in your project" without insulting. Every once in a while, I'd get a letter from people where they were really crying out to know the truth [about the rejection of their work], at which point you could be more straightforward.

Did you ever have to turn down submissions to S.O.P. on ideological grounds?

I don't think I ever did turn down anyone on ideological grounds- there were definitely some people out there doing things that were questionable, I suppose, that weren't necessarily neo-Nazi stuff. And some of that stuff was to shock, anyway- noise with concentration camp imagery and all that crap. Maybe I didn't travel quite in that circle, exactly.

I think the sameness of much of that material ended up being more offensive than the actual content intended to shock...

If anything, I think what tended to offend me was the people who did the crank phone call kinds of things. That kind of thing was just stupid and childish, embarrassing people who didn't know they were being embarrassed, and so on.

   [...recording cuts abruptly again...]

Now you're like in your 3rd generation of cassette people- this was 10 years ago now, I remember 'Gen' Ken Montgomery telling me that he went to Buffalo to do a speaking gig talking about the cassette network, and meeting someone who was doing her research on the cassette stuff. Apparently, when they had the conversation, he mentioned a bunch of people she had no clue about and she mentioned a lot of people he had no clue about. A couple years back at a big bookstore here, there was also a big cassette show dealing with current labels, in conjunction with the No Fun Festival- Thurston Moore did the opening talk, and it was all about newer labels like Hospital and American Tapes, and all that stuff. But the guy curating this had no clue about older stuff. So, I saw this thing and got ticked off, Ken did too- if you're going to call your show the 'history of the cassette network' and it only reaches back to 5 years before....that's where I get a little antsy or pissed off. If you want to call it the 'current cassette revolution,' that's fine, but when you're skipping a couple of generations, and you don't seem to know shit as a curator....mmm....not good.

What about artwork for your cassette releases- was there a standard template that everyone adhered to, or was design completely left up to each individual artist?

The only template part really tended to be the [label] address section- I was no artist, I'll tell you that. I encouraged anyone who wanted to do their own cover stuff to do it, because if they didn't, and left it up to me...they got what they got [laughs]! But I tried to do my best to be as creative as possible...I've heard tell of some funny conversations about my crappy artwork, I wasn't actually privy to them but I heard about them afterwards, people making fun of some of the stuff. But if you had a chance to do your own cover and instead give it to me to do, that's life baby! I have really bad handwriting too....you didn't want me writing stuff on your cover (laughs.)

Surfing The Polywaves: GX Jupitter-Larsen

According to [Edward] Lorenz and others, chaotic systems are not only astonishingly sensitive and responsive, but also surprisingly resilient and self-regulatory over the long term, and ultimately very robust. [...] Two Boston research teams who analyzed the fluctuations that characterize the rhythms of healthy and diseased hearts found, at both the macro and micro level, that health appeared to be synonymous with chaotic disorder, and disease with simpler, more orderly, heartbeat patterns.

-Reg Morrison [207]

The term "chaos" is a word that is heavily used in writing on avant-garde audio culture (this author's included), and is often used interchangeably with a cultural definition of "noise" (i.e. some subjectively unpleasant sound.) Both chaos and noise have more information theoretical definitions relating to their status as non-communicative information, from which their apparent "uselessness" derives and also gives rise to the cultural definition of both as a kind of information waste product. However, in the same way that silences can be communicative spurs to action, noise or audio chaos plays a catalyzing role: Gregory Bateson's famous pronouncement on noise was that "all that is not information, not redundancy, not form, and not restraints, is noise- the only possible source of *new* patterns."[208] So, just as chaotic activity can regulate biological systems as in the example noted above, it can also prevent cultural production from stagnating.

Nonetheless, having been attributed to just about every type of sound

---

[207] Reg Morrison, *The Spirit In The Gene: Humanity's Proud Illusion And The Laws Of Nature*, p. 235. Cornell University Press, Ithaca NY, 1999.

[208] Gregory Bateson, *Steps To An Ecology Of Mind*, p. 416. University Of Chicago Press, Chicago / London, 2000.

whose complexity outpaces the best efforts of the critically minded listener to groove on it, the evocative power of "noise" or "chaos" as a genre marker is becoming more and more attenuated by the day, to say nothing of its taxonomic accuracy. And, let's be frank: much of the sonic art that is either lauded or derided as "chaos" really is just material featuring advanced complexity of design rather than total inchoateness. Densely layered (or just surprisingly novel) "chaotic" compositions, from the early innovations of 12-tone music to the boisterous audio cartoons of John Zorn, have often relied on formal scores and could thus easily be performed / recorded in the same manner twice- the latter composer, when not scoring outright, has also integrated pre-performance rules into his game pieces that, although allowing for vastly different interpretations from one performer to the next, still keep the possibilities within the realm of the finite. Along similar lines, generative computer music - that variety which 'plays itself' after some deft coding by the computer operator - rarely ventures into unrepentantly chaotic territory, more often it is a kind of "nonrandom disorder" in which the music may continually fluctuate and exhibit unusual dynamic shifts, but is still constrained within certain audio parameters during the programming stage. For the uninitiated, listening to such music can take on the bewildering effect of riding on a train where everyone else is conversing in a different language- but failure to comprehend that language doesn't mean that, for those who do understand it, things aren't proceeding in a purposive and ordered manner.

Having said all this, there are still forms of sound in which chaos seemingly reigns, and in which, like Morrison's irregular beating of the heart, that condition is not necessarily a bad thing: while it's still open to debate who the merchants of 'true' chaos are, there are numerous sound artists who have discovered means of make strangely compelling art that relies on the irrational gesture temporarily displacing the rational one. The twin positivist tendencies of demonstrable growth and progress are thereby ignored in order to tread the apparent roads to nowhere. It should come as no surprise, given the qualities of self-released music already introduced, that so many of these artists join in the amorphous "unofficial" networks to further challenge and modulate their own perceptions. The "noise" of these networks - the massive number of releases available, or the intensely non-sequential manner of discovering who's who and what's what in the culture - fits like a glove over the very noisy audio contents of certain releases.

GX Jupitter-Larsen, known most widely for sculpting mountains of impossibly loud, saturated sound as The Haters, is one of these artists, and perhaps one of the more celebrated members of the international noise community that owes its spread to the use and abuse of unofficial releases and handmade media. His frequent invention of neologisms like "polywave" and "the totimorphous," put forward as guiding principles behind his work, are spoken about with serious academic candor in spite of their implausibility or subjectivity. Jupitter-Larsen has often said things to the effect that he was more concerned with changing his own mind than with changing those of others. This is a hallmark of the chaotic operative in an ordered society that relies on total consistency of ideology and looks upon sudden revelations and 'changes of heart' as being insincere attempts to hide something or to evade criticism. In a 1994 interview with the magazine *ND*, though, he reveals that he could care less about such societal evaluation of his activities, stating that "society isn't the only game in town; so human experience shouldn't be limited to it. Just because I'm at a concert doesn't mean I'm a member of a band, or the audience for that matter."[209] Also claiming to be from "nowhere in particular" in the same piece, he conjures up images of the pre-societal nomad that has existed in smaller and smaller numbers since the dawn of the agrarian revolution. While his clamorous noise works, especially during the 1990s, have placed him at the forefront of that field, his highly conceptual performances, involving activities like "watching mud dry" or watching television in front of a separate group of spectators, solidify his status as a kind of internal nomad as well: following personal whims wherever they may lead, and without any explicit invitation for others to draw the same conclusions or even to follow in the first place. Jupitter-Larsen's *New Sounds Gallery* radio program, broadcast from Vancouver's CFRO radio throughout the 1980s, was also a key public exhibition of what period sound artists were capable of, and was allied with other period shows such as Peter Meyer's *Nattövning* and Joe Schmidt's *Home Taper Show* (both of which traded broadcast material with *New Sounds Gallery* in order to

---

[209] GX Jupitter-Larsen quoted in "The Haters." *ND* magazine, spring 1994, p. 16. *ND*, Austin, Texas.

further their own respective experiments.)

In lieu of a full biographical portrait (which I don't feel the artist would want included, anyway) I've included this brief interview with Jupitter-Larsen in the larger narrative of this book, as it offers some unique insights into the practice of networked audio throughout the 1980s and 1990s. Of special interest is the analogy he uses to describe the distillation of post-industrial music into more abstract forms come the 90s, and his personal take on the value of novelty in the sound milieu. Last, but not least, his thoughts on "art as a statement" are very much in sync with the motives of many other self-releasing audio creators.

++++++++

I'll start off simple (although hopefully not too clichéd): at what point in your creative life did you first decide to work with the medium of audio recordings? Was there a certain kind of information that you felt could only be conveyed through recorded sound, rather than through some other medium?

From the very start, actually. I never thought sound would ever be my main format, but it had always been important for me to be able to explore my ideas in all possible media. Some details are just expressed better in some media more so than others.

So when you first began to experiment with sound, were you already aware of a larger network of people also working with similar material, or did you feel yourself to be more or less alone / isolated in that regard?

I felt completely isolated. I knew of nothing else. Back in 1980 I just gave my records away at punk shows or sent them off as mail art. I was completely out of the loop when it came to what the kids in the industrial scene were up to. It wasn't until 1982, when a mail artist in Texas passed one of my records along to Maurizio Bianchi in Italy. MB then contacted me directly. It was soon after that when MB told Merzbow about me and the three of us started trading like crazy.

Anyhow, it was because of my correspondence with MB and Merzbow that I finally got plugged into a scene that was slowly becoming what we now know as Cassette Culture.

For readers who haven't heard work of yours from that period, what kind of recordings were you making?

Mostly tape collages of things falling apart. Some field recordings too. Again, with stuff falling apart.

What originally led you down this particular path? For example, was it a matter of finding these types of sounds personally enjoyable to immerse yourself in, or finding them useful as a metaphor for the state of culture and society at the time, or something more complex than either of these?

At first, I just really enjoyed these types of sounds. Then, over time, things get complicated. Metaphors become fetishes, fetishes become metaphors.

Speaking of Masami Akita [Merzbow], I recently translated a piece of his on 80s audio networking, in which he discusses your past involvement with New Sounds Gallery? How closely tied in was that show with your aforementioned tape-trading activity?

New Sounds Gallery was a radio art show I did from 1984 - 1988. There was some tape-trading going on, but mostly it was a venue for artists who wanted to do radio-specific pieces. Call-in shows, game shows, radio plays, all-night sound sculptures; stuff like that.

I was wondering if, making the kinds of sounds that you do, you found the self-released cassette medium too constricting in any way (for example, having to deal with extraneous 'system noise' / tape hiss etc.)? Having said that, were there any instances where you exploited these limitations themselves and transformed them into a kind of creative / conceptual raw material (while it's not related directly to your work, I'm thinking of the Reynols release which is built up completely from the sound of overlapping 'hisses' from blank cassettes...)

It took a while, but after a few years of tape trading I finally started mixing my sounds with the tape hiss in mind. Instead of fighting it, just make the hiss part of the complete piece. The tapes started sounding much better after that.

To this point I haven't discussed the performance aspect of your work with the Haters- did cassettes ever play any role in these performances: using pre-taped materials to form part of the show's sonic component, and so on? (I also seem to remember one show of yours that involved a number of de-tuned radios being shoveled from one waste receptacle into another, and so I wonder if you did anything of the kind with cassette players...)

During the 80s, cassettes were often used in live performances. These early performances had less to do with sound and more to do with theatre. My first real use of sound on stage was to be a timing mechanism. I just wanted my performances to last about 20 minutes, so I played one side of a C-46 cassette. The sudden start of the noise would let everyone in the audience know that the performance had just begun. Likewise, the abrupt end of the soundtrack unmistakably marked the finale. Everyone understood this application, regardless of whether they had been told the meaning or not. In the 90s, I started using live sounds more and more, and I didn't need to use the cassette any longer on stage.

I notice that cassette trading / production seemed to taper off notably in the '90s as well- not the least because there was more of an 'indie label' infrastructure by that time, offering to release larger factory pressings of work by people who had been active in these clandestine networks throughout the 80s. I guess that would also be one reason why veteran artists from the tape underground didn't have as much use for the newer, 90s DIY media such as minidiscs or CD-Rs (Maurizio Bianchi being a major exception there)- but what's your personal take on this situation? Did you find the newer digital DIY media to be less useful or necessary than what came before it?

There were different factors involved. A few of the veterans might have been put off by the new digital formats, but I think most were just creatively burnt out by the 90s. Then, the Cassette Culture of the 80s gave way to the Noise scene in the 90s, and by the time of lot of the older guys wanted to get back into things, they found themselves turned off by the decisively noisier work being done by these newcomers. If I could use art history as a metaphor, it was as if Surrealism had become Dada instead of the other way round. For myself, personally, the newer digital DIY media has its place. I really don't mind it one way or the other. And I for one, preferred the more abstract, minimalist, harsher sounds that have been dominating the scene ever since.

The above brings me to another odd observation about people in these respective scenes, and their way of interacting with the public- I've noticed an almost ceaseless back-and-forth battle over the last decade, about whether or not it's 'appropriate' to be performing live music, noise, whatever, merely as a single person with a computer (or some other digital sampling workhorse) as the sound source. Looking over documents from the prior 'cassette' culture, I haven't noticed nearly as much venom directed at artists who would just perform with a tape deck(s) as the primary sound source- any idea why this might be, other than the fact that there are simply a greater number of people now tilling the 'underground audio' field than before?

Comes to a lack of moving parts. The whole thing is psychological. The eye has domination over any performance. If an audience member sees movement of any kind, even if it's just the spinning reels of a reel-to-reel, that's a physical action and therefore a real performance. If someone sees a guy behind a laptop, there [are] no moving parts. It therefore isn't a physical action, and therefore not a real performance.

It could probably be argued that there's still some performance aspect to at least some of the 'computer' gigs in which overwhelming blasts of light, fog and other visual distractions compensate for human bodily movements.

You would think so, but such overwhelming blasts of light, or fog, or whatever only seem to reinforce the idea that nothing is going on when a laptop is involved. Again, it has to do with a perceived lack of physical movement by the performer. Since the audience perceives the guy sitting or standing behind the computer as not doing anything, the staged visual distractions only work to underscore this perception.

Anyhow- as you were saying before, the 90s underground audio world upped the 'intensity' quotient of the sounds being made; do you feel that anything else radically new came about in this era in terms of ideas and presentation? If anything, I notice a lot of 'digital-age' updates on the earlier networked audio concepts (e.g. the 'exquisite corpse'-style compilation where raw material is manipulated by a sequence of different artists...)

The dialogue is ongoing. None of the ideas were really all that new even back in the 80s. The newness isn't important. What is important is the vivaciousness of the debate going on. To revisit, rework, and reinvent the concepts involved. This is how ideas stay meaningful and relevant in the here-and-now.

Since we've determined the techniques going into these various works aren't anything new, what about the subject matter / thematic content of the post-'cassette boom' crop of independent artists? Do you think the increased amount of vigorous debate has led to an increased variety in the themes that people are choosing to bring to the table (or just a better articulation of pre-existing themes)?

Oh migoodness YES! Especially when you compare the Noise scene of the 80s and 90s to the industrial music scene of the late 70s. Let's face it; the Industrial scene had a pretty narrow worldview. Cassette Culture of the early 80s was broader with all the different types who got involved. It was a much more open network. Noise in the 90s might have been harsher in attitude and aesthetics, but people could pretty much express whatever fetish or obsession they might have had, in any way they wanted. There really weren't any rules with what was right or not. Sadly, I can't help but feel the Noise scene of the past 10 years has become more about style and less about attitude.

I should also ask if there's been any significant incidences in which this ongoing debate prompted you to re-evaluate or your own work...

The notion of variation-of-a-theme has always been the basis of everything I do. For me, art has never been about making a statement. It's been about making a journey. So everything I've done has always been a work in progress. By that very nature, I'm constantly re-evaluating my work.

Do you feel that the emphasis on 'style' over attitude you mentioned has some correlation to artists in this field favoring short-term goals over a life-long, perpetual journey?

I'm sure that's always the case when style is picked over substance.

PART TWO
PAUSE: New Challenges

A MiniDisc Autopsy Report
(And Other Thoughts On Format Failure)

When dealing with technologies that have run their course, it's easy to forget how quickly and resolutely we became absorbed in utopian hopes upon their arrival. In the throes of full-blown tech mania, we anthropomorphize the beloved instruments and view them as regular companions rather than as extensions. Yet, once these instruments are supplanted by something yet more alluring in its promises, we can spend all day rationalizing away how we "always knew" the former technology would come up short in the end. It was, after all, just another time-devouring diversion that the military-industrial complex designed with the purpose of quelling dissent. Or, at the very least, it provided a sad substitute for "authentic social experience" while "mediating relationships" in a way that proved detrimental to all but the shadowy design and marketing squads who brought it into the world.

If there were a hell for technologies, I imagine it would reverberate day and night with the sneering condemnations of such retrospective 'experts,' who would appear as talking heads on one of those *VH1* programs designed to instill a false sense of our having progressed from the pop culture fascinations and technological raptures of prior decades. Inconveniently for these experts, though, enough evidence points back to their having as much of a stake in technological infatuation as anyone. Like old love letters unearthed during a routine search for some less emotionally resonant object, such pieces of evidence occasionally surface to remind us of the starring role we played in initiating and sustaining this state of techno-rapture: as much as we would like to see ourselves as the passive, blameless targets of mass hypnosis, things were never this simple in reality. Like any wild love affair, we became swept up in it to the point where boundaries between subject and object melted away, and each partner managed to deeply influence and alter the other's daily functioning. And like any wild love affair to have ended with some degree of dissatisfaction, we violently deny believing that *this time* utopia would be realized through this joyful dissolution.

A fine example of an exhumed love letter is the first Japanese print ad for the Sony Walkman, introduced in 1979 (at the time, it was pitched as a "walking stereo with hotline".)[210] In the ad, both a twig-thin young dancing queen of Western origin and an older Japanese traditionalist (he sports a monk's tonsure and white *yukata*) share a TPS-L2 Walkman on a nondescript public thoroughfare. In a typical bit of humorous self-effacement, the older Walkman enthusiast is saddled with the bulkier pair of headphones, and appears as if he's straining not to pass judgment on the ecstatically hip-swaying youngster clad in tube top and animal-print scarf. It must be a difficult task, since the girl's vivacity borders on militancy, especially in the way she grips the Walkman unit and thrusts it towards the camera, while opening her mouth in an expression somewhere between a manic laugh and a scream of defiance. While the older gentleman takes care to not be defined by his listening apparatus, it's hard to imagine the younger spokes-model *without* one; removing it from her would be like a bloody amputation rather than just a 'taking away' of the object. It would be Jimi Hendrix appearing on stage *sans* guitar, or a habitual roller skater switching into a pair of loafers (and, as the story goes, the Walkman was partially inspired by observations of Californian roller skaters.[211])

The image is overlaid by a comparatively bland text about how you can now take your home stereo outside with you, which is a kind of redundancy when the striking image has already stated this much- yet that doesn't appreciably dilute its utopian excitement. All the ingredients for the vaunted "better world through technology" are there: there is the solution of a previously irresolvable problem (the problem of sharing music in public without disrupting others routines, solved via the multiple headphone outputs of the TPS-L2.) There's the suggestion of harmonious coexistence between clashing traditions and aesthetic inclinations, made possible by a clearly demarcated zone of non-competitive play and

---

[210] The 'hot-line switch' was so named because it would instantly suppress the volume of the music being played through the headphones, and make it easier to hold conversations.

[211] Admittedly, this is only one of the anecdotal 'origins' of the Walkman design: others have suggested Sony co-founder Akio Morita's dislike of trans-Atlantic flights, or have ascribed its creation to a totally spontaneous revelation accorded to original Sony founder Masaru Ibuka.

discovery- after all, as Johan Huizinga notes, "play is older than culture"[212] and can still be fallen back upon in times where it seems culture is erecting its own formidable barriers to interaction. Sony's advertising schemes would export these utopian potentialities all around the world, with a variety of similar campaigns- for a while, it seemed the ads' utopian fiction would provide a strong enough counterweight to the more cynical fiction proposed by 'nanny state' functionaries (e.g. that the Walkman would cause people to retreat into isolated, anti-social tech-cocoons.)

But then, just as easily as we baby new technologies, wrapping them in swaddling clothes and bestowing achingly cute nicknames upon them, we kill them like unwanted pets. Of course, the word "kill" is never used with great frequency when we are dealing with the termination of things we once loved: in the case of pets, we "put down" a deliberately drowned kitten or a lethally-injected old dog, in the case of technologies we "discontinue" or "retire" them. And at this point a harsh light is cast on our disingenuousness: all throughout the other stages of the tech-companion's "life cycle" it has been treated as a human equal (or even a superior), being talked to or coaxed or cajoled as if its lack of verbal response was just the tech's way of playing "hard-to-get" rather than evidence that it lacked consciousness. Now, in the "retirement" stage, the original rush to anthropomorphize these devices can be explained away, in a way that Bruno Latour expertly describes: "the word anthropomorphism always implies that such a projection remains inappropriate, as if it were clear to everyone that actants on which feelings are projected were actually acting in terms of different competences."[213]

---

[212] "Play is older than culture, for culture, however inadequately defined, always presupposes human society, and animals have not waited for man to teach them their playing." Johan Huizinga, *Homo Ludens: A Study Of The Play Element In Culture*, p. 1. Beacon Press, Boston, 1955.

[213] Bruno Latour, *Aramis: Or, The Love Of Technology*, p. 226. Trans. Catherine Porter. Harvard University Press, Cambridge / London, 1996.

Learning To Love The MD

"I like pizza pie, I like macaroni / but what I love is My First Sony"[214]

-'My First Sony' advertising jingle, circa mid-1980s

Upon relocating to Japan for the first time, one of my first notable purchases was a ridiculous-looking orange compact bicycle with wheels 14 inches in diameter (purchased with parking issues in mind, a thorny problem familiar to just about anyone who commutes to a major Japanese train station by bicycle.) My first non-essential purchase worth noting (which long outlasted the soon-to-be-stolen bike), was a Sony MZ-R900 MiniDisc Walkman / recorder. Unlike the bicycle, it came in a variety of sophisticated color schemes, of which I chose a deep, metallic red. Although the 'MD'[215] hardware and blank recording media was still virtually nonexistent in the U.S. (ditto for pre-recorded MDs), I was now thrust into a world where blank MDs could be bought at virtually any supermarket or convenience store across the country, and high-end playback or recording equipment could likewise be found in the most modest department store's electronics section. This was still a couple years before the practice of mp3 downloading would produce its well-documented effects (documented even further in this volume, of course), and so the possession of an MD player still conferred certain advantages upon its owner that weren't enjoyed by the rank-and-file of compact disc listeners. For one, the ability to record sound at different bit rates meant that a single MiniDisc could record or play back a few albums' worth of material before any kind of reloading took place. The MD's attractiveness also owed itself, admittedly, to its clandestine nature when compared to the other then-popular forms of music transport. For live music enthusiasts, a palm-sized MD recorder could fit inside of an empty 'wide' pack of clove cigarettes, and could then be safely smuggled inside a

---

[214] The Spanish-language version of the same provides an interesting point of comparison: *"Me gusta cantar, andar en un pony / pero prefiero 'Mi primer Sony.'"* Sony's marketing aces had clearly arrived at the conclusion that kids in Spanish-speaking nations relished active play, while their American counterparts would rather sit around and gorge themselves on fatty foodstuffs.

[215] The terms "MiniDisc" and "MD" will be used interchangeably throughout this essay.

concert venue, where a tiny microphone snapped into its 1/8" analog line input produced a satisfactory document of the evening's entertainment. The same input could also accommodate any electronic instrument, providing a fine way to record rough sketches of musical ideas before they evaporated.

Other noteworthy features abounded. A slim, rechargable NiMH [nickel metal hydride] battery powered the unit for up to 21 hours of playback time or 8 hours of recording time, and an extra AA battery could still be plugged into a pair of contact points on the bottom of the player. A 'track program' mode allowed for re-programming the sequence in which you heard tracks on a pre-recorded MD. A 'melody timer' interrupted the listener's music program with an alarm at a pre-determined time (which seems like a fairly trivial addition until you've experienced the sleep-inducing effects of a longer-than-average Japanese train commute.) A wand-like remote control unit, connected to a pair of stock Sony headphones and capable of being clipped to a piece of clothing, was also equipped with a backlit display on which the user-programmed titles of songs would scroll by. And, for the particularly active listener, a skip-resistant "G Protection" caused the reading laser to, when dislodged, regain its position some 10 times faster than previous designs of portable disc players, making the inevitable bumps and jostles on the street (and, once again, the train) easier to deal with.

The MiniDisc itself was, whether this was the intent or not, a handsome hybridization of the two most popular recording media to precede it: the cassette (the MD also featured a plastic outer shell or cartridge) and compact disc (a 64mm, magneto-optical disc sealed within the cartridge.) The design therefore suggested a marriage of practical concerns, like longevity and security, with fashion sense- the reflective gleam of the small disc was nicely complemented by shells of different opacity, color, and texture. It was emphatically present even though it was close to being nothing at all, and so - even during its protracted death - it still bore the physical appearance of an "emerging" technology.

With all of these things working in its favor, the question has to be asked- why did "MiniDisc Culture" not succeed "Cassette Culture" as a means of music networking? Why was there no insanely prolific R. Stevie

Moore or Merzbow of the MiniDisc, or, why, in fact, didn't the original artists ever consider adding a MiniDisc release or two to their vast catalogs (which already seemed to span every other conceivable home audio format?) Especially in the 'avant' end of the culture, where the critique of new media and the unlocking of its hidden potentiality are such going concerns, it would seem the MiniDisc would be adopted more than it really was. On that score, there is really just one title that is still a talking point to this day: the MD simply titled *MiniDisc* by Gescom, which did, admittedly, make clever use of the medium's "shuffle" or randomized playback function. The radically synthetic music itself induced an uncanny, hallucinatory feeling that the MD player was inventing the sound in real time rather than playing back the "fixed" contents of a recording. The mid-late 90s crop of new, street-smart 'computer music' was notable for its high-velocity transmission of discreet audio events, which coalesced or self-organized in a way that seemed to escape the intent of the programmers. Gescom's MD was an occasionally frustrating, but mostly rewarding example of this tendency, a rich new vocabulary that a number of other artists could have applied to their own releases. Just as the slow-spreading dread clouds of Maurizio Bianchi's music complemented the kinesthetic effect of watching the slowly, steadily turning spools of a cassette, Gescom's fleeting and chimerical sound particles seemed tailor-made for the MD (and vice versa.)

Other experiments with the medium abounded, but next to nothing materialized as a commercially available or even "underground" product. More commonly, MD technology was employed in the making of a final product but hardly ever *was* that final product. The sound artist Paul Dickinson (as well as the author) made use of both the MD recorder's generous battery life and, more importantly, its motion sensitive recording function, to make recordings of themselves talking in their sleep. As hinted at above, the shock-resistant features and featherweight portability of MD players were also very useful for professionally recording concert performances (not just "bootlegging" them.) For similar reasons, MDs could be utilized in live performances which relied partially on a pre-recorded 'backing track' as part of the performance, with little worry about magnetic tape suddenly getting devoured or a disc skipping (*a la* the nightmare scenario that effectively ended the lip-syncing careers of Milli Vanilli.) And, speaking of Merzbow and Gescom, the membership of both units[216] used an MD recorder to lay the tracks for a scathing noise LP entitled *Satanstornade*, still one of the more compelling documents of that non-genre.

One thing may help to give some closure to those fretting over the death of the MD, and that is the medium's inability to ever become a truly international phenomenon. As we've already seen with the Cassette Culture of old, its robustness owed itself in part to its international character. Audiocassettes in the 1980s were widely available throughout Europe, the Americas, and Asia, and were thus not seen in these countries as a 'specialty' or even 'novelty' medium. The initial fears over introducing radical new playback equipment turned out to be unjustified (audio outlets in the U.S. reportedly "...thought the [Sony] company was crazy trying to sell a $200 stereo that didn't even record.")[217] It is necessary, for the purposes of this investigation, to return to the MiniDisc's conceptual birthplace in order to determine the exact causes of its failure on foreign soil.

A Brief Tour Of The Akio Morita Format Cemetery

The Sony legacy, as embodied by the corporation's celebrated co-founder[218], Akio Morita, has become almost synonymous with the Japanese Economic Miracle that typified the nation's brightest post-War years. While the camera business, as exemplified by Nikon, deserves proper credit for initiating the transition away from Japan's being perceived as junk peddler to the world, Morita's Sony was not far behind. Morita has been called "...perhaps the most effective public relations man for 'Japan Inc.,'"[219] which is high praise indeed, and even though it tacitly

---

[216] Russell Haswell, one half of the Satanstornade project, has also featured in Gescom's revolving membership.

[217] Thomas A. Harvey, "How Sony Corporation Became First With Kids." *Doing Cultural Studies: The Story Of The Sony Walkman*, p. 133, ed. Paul DuGay, Stuart Hall Et. Al. SAGE Publications Ltd., London, 1997.

[218] Masaru Ibuka can more properly be called the founder of Sony, despite the public acceptance of Morita as being a kind of ideologue for the company.

[219] Ian Buruma, *The Missionary And The Libertine: Love And War In East And West*, p. 235. Random House, New York, 1996.

acknowledges "Japan Inc.'s" notorious inflexibility and defiant sense of exceptionalism, these were qualities that Morita tended to alternately embrace or reject in different circumstances, rather than adopt wholesale. Partially due to his efforts, the present alluring image of Japan is not one of a hermetic, time-frozen archipelago, but one where the iconic "*geisha* with a mobile phone" runs free, or where a highly selective acceptance and "remixing" of international commerce enhances its national uniqueness rather than erodes it. Regardless of their veracity, these images remain a staple of tourism bureaus everywhere.

Morita's attempts at playing to both sides of the local / global divide have not always resulted in a smooth reconciliation. On one hand, once Morita's firm's success entitled him to act as a spokesman for the Japanese work ethic (and Japanese ethics as a whole), Morita could say with a straight face that "there were no wars in Japan during the country's period of virtual isolation from 1603 to 1868"[220] and that "...our labor relations [...] have a kind of equality that does not exist elsewhere."[221] On the other hand, Sony was often criticized locally for making too many concessions to internationalism, and especially for its radical sense of 'non-place' (the company's name is itself a portmanteau of the American expression 'sonny boy' and the Latin *sonus* [sound].) The somewhat inaccurate boasts from Morita, and his attempts at appeasing both nationalists and globalizers, may seem to have little relevance to the discussion at hand, but no "who killed the MiniDisc" mystery should be written without taking into account the attitudes of its primary marketers.

At least one defense of Morita is necessary, namely that blaming him alone for all of the corporation's missteps would be fallacious: while Sony's General Audio Division exemplified the contemporary Japanese trend of being obsessed with market share above all else (one popular Sony rallying cry was "*BMW- Beat Matsushita Whatever* [the cost]"), it was hardly the originator of this consuming obsession. And, to his credit, Morita even took a starring role in denouncing the market share battles that, due to their ferocious competitiveness, became known as *Sekigahara*

---

[220] Though Morita may be refering to wars between nations, the Tokugawa period mentioned did feature its share of local uprisings and conflicts.

[221] Ian Buruma, *The Missionary And The Libertine: Love And War In East And West*, p. 236. Random House, New York, 1996.

(the decisive battle which helped cement the reign of Shogun Tokugawa.) Morita's occasional return to traditional values, on the other hand, could still be seen as a contributing factor to the Sony's more well-publicized errors: this staunch traditionalism once led him to nearly disown his son upon hearing that he was courting a pop singer.

For a titanic corporation whose last quarterly earnings statement, as of this writing, totaled over $78 billion, you really wouldn't expect Sony to have many glaring weaknesses- yet the organization's history of rolling out new recording and playback media has not always been a smooth ride. The prestige that often came with innovating new products (the Trinitron TV set, for example) was followed soon enough by reverse-engineering efforts by competitors that yielded comparable products, manufactured without the additional expenses of research and development that Sony had borne. Elsewhere, a few high-profile Sony properties have, like the Concorde, shown that technical superiority alone cannot guarantee any technology's survival in a marketplace that does not exist free from political corroboration or from the interference of lobbying groups.

Starting with the introduction of the BetaMax videocassette in 1975, Sony did experience a couple stinging defeats in the 'format wars.' BetaMax was the first home video format to hit the market, yet the cartridge was both smaller in size and technologically superior to the clunkier VHS tapes that would soon jump into the fray courtesy of the hated Matsushita, Philips, and other manufacturers.[222] Unfortunately for Sony, this would be one lesson in technological superiority not being able to carry the day all by itself: most home video consumers simply wanted the format on which the greatest available number of movie titles had been released, which just happened to be VHS. One such loss was probably humiliating enough for Akio Morita and his acolytes, but history would repeat itself yet again in 1987 with the introduction of the digital audiotape, or DAT. As Fredric Dannen tells it, "...the [record] industry had already resisted the LP, the cassette, and the compact disc [...] chances were good that DAT would prove a boon to business" (Dannen makes sure to add the caveat "foresight is not one of the record industry's

---

[222] Here, Sony's claims of technological superiority came from a better horizontal picture resolution and reduced video noise when compared with VHS. However, even in the early days of its competition with VHS, it offered an inferior amount of recording time.

strengths.")[223]

Once again, sheer technological superiority was supposed to make DAT the reigning home audio format: music would be recordable and reproducible without any type of distracting surface noise. Adding to Sony's would-be fortunes this time around, the issue of available pre-recorded tapes would, ideally, be remedied by a high-profile sale of CBS Records to Sony: allowing Sony to press DATs at will from CBS' massive back catalog would, in theory, help to prevent a repeat of the BetaMax failure.[224] Like the MiniDisc, DAT experienced some success as a professional recording format, but a major - and arguably decisive - blow would be directly struck against the format this time by the record industry itself, of which CBS was a major component. Technological superiority worked against the DAT by putting fear into record executives concerned, as always, about their bottom line: perfect facsimiles of existing digital recordings appealed to them even less than the already widespread practice of copying to vulgar audiocassettes. As such, the major record conglomerates demanded that home DAT equipment be manufactured with built-in "spoilers" or microchips that would prevent digital-to-digital recording. Once again, a technology meant to eliminate scarcity was running up against an industry that clearly benefitted from a manufactured condition of such. Whereas the major recording industry had previously failed in its attempts to institute the blank audiotape tax, the rise of new digital threats to its sovereignty successfully resulted in a piece of legislation known as the Audio Home Recording Act of 1992 (which amended the extant copyright act of 1976.) The result of the new "spoiler" or copy protection scheme was to increase the manufacturing cost of DAT players, making them unaffordable to the majority of consumers.

Completing this trinity of doomed formats was, of course, the MiniDisc, although it can at least be said that Sony succeeded on its home turf with this format (the American record industry's hostility towards the

---

[223] Fredric Dannen, *Hit Men: Power Brokers And Fast Money Inside The Music Business*, p. 318. Random House, New York, 1990.

[224] Strangely, though, CBS president Walter Yetnikoff was one of the label bosses violently opposed to post-LP formats that would allow for home taping. Prior to the January 1988 sale of CBS to Sony, Yetnikoff was on the frontlines of the battle to have Congress impose a tax on blank tapes.

DAT made the cultivation of "home turf" absolutely essential.) MD equipment first hit the streets of Japan in November of 1992- mere weeks after the Recording Industry Association of America celebrated the institution of the Audio Home Recording Act. The MD was still very much a going concern by the time of my aforementioned relocation there (in mid-2000.) It can even be said that Sony won hands down over Philips' competing product of the day, the digital compact cassette, which was retired in the fall of 1996.[225] When Japanese friends and co-workers wanted to give me mixes of their favorite music as a goodwill gesture, or wanted me to listen to recordings of them speaking English (hoping that I'd offer helpful critique and corrections) they would invariably give it to me on MD. This was done, with no exceptions that I can remember, without first asking if I was in possession of an MD player. Given this product saturation on the local level, the MiniDisc provides an interesting study in the failure of globally marketing goods and services. From the evidence we have to work with, the format seemed to be very much built around the time-tested aesthetic preferences of Japanese consumers, those consumers' social habits, and even the nation's saturated, modular urban infrastructure. None of these things could be said to have an exact equivalent anywhere else in the industrialized world, and so Sony's efforts at globally marketing this quintessentially Japanese item did not guarantee success.

Little Giants & White Light: How Japanese Aesthetics Built Up And Tore Down The MD

Those ever-crucial and almost exclusively Japanese aesthetic preferences have always provided a jarring contrast to those aesthetic values propagated in the more utility-obsessed parts of America and Europe. Reams of writing on trans-Pacific relations make special note of the Japanese acceptance of smallness / compactness as a thing of beauty, and this long before the introduction of consumer electronics: the Korean writer O-Young Lee claimed that the Japanese had a head-start on the computerized "age of reductionism" via this inclination, which is

---

[225] The irony here is that the initial showdown between MiniDisc and DCC, which did boast a less 'lossy' compression algorithm than the MD, drew fire away from the primary thrust of Sony's marketing campaign, i.e. the MD as a replacement for the analog cassette.

manifested in "Japanese fairy tales [...] featur[ing] 'little giants' who turn needles into swords, bowls into boats...in contrast to such characters of Western folk legend as Paul Bunyan."[226] With such a rich history of finding 'the great in the small,' there would be quick acceptance of radical miniaturizing solutions like switching from transistor / resistor-based technology (even though Sony pioneered the transistorization of the radio) to one centered on integrated circuits: this was the design coup behind the original Walkman. The modern variations on this penchant are enshrined in the term *kawaii,* or exaggerated cuteness and innocence, which is such a pronounced feature of Japanese advertising and marketing that "...Japanese [...] can go down a department store aisle of merchandise at a rapid walk, and identify which items are Japanese-designed and which are foreign without breaking stride."[227] Respected Japanologist Boye Lafayette de Mente warned in the mid-'90s that "the Japanese attachment to cuteness does not appear to be weakening as a result of Western influence,"[228] and that assessment held true for MiniDiscs throughout their tenacious existence in their home country. Seeing them arrayed on the shelves of a local Tsutaya[229] branch, in every available color combination and every available pattern from polka-dotted to zebra-striped, MD display racks seemed almost indistinguishable from the candy aisle in a grocery supermarket. Their status as the most compact of the existing recordable media ratcheted the 'cute' factor up another notch, guaranteeing a lucrative side market in accessories for organizing MiniDiscs and displaying them in one's own home.

The compactness of MiniDisc hardware and software was not just a concession to the reigning *kawaii* aesthetic, but was based on more practical spatial considerations as well. Even in the era of the vinyl LP, alternate formats for Japanese albums were being experimented with in an attempt to maximize music collectors' living space: albums of 7" flexidiscs, packed into information-rich booklets, were one alternative to the more imposing

---

[226] O-Young Lee quoted in *Thriving On Chaos: Handbook For A Management Revolution,* Tom Peters, p. 15. Alfred A. Knopf, New York, 1988.

[227] Boye Lafayette de Mente, *Japan's Cultural Code Words,* p. 196. NTC Publishing Group, Lincolnwood, Illinois 1994.

[228] *Ibid.*

[229] A Japan-wide "culture convenience club" aimed mainly at the market for video and audio rentals.

12" vinyls. 3" cd singles, which usually came housed on a plastic tray in rectangular 'long boxes' with flip-top lids, were another popular alternative to the 5" CD maxi-single. So, when the prospect arrived of completely immaterial music formats, ported around by devices even more compact and lightweight than the stalwart MD player, these new gadgets were also primed for success in the Japanese market. It was the American firm Apple who, in a cruel betrayal of their former collaborators (the acclaimed Apple PowerBook 100 was a joint project of Sony and Apple's Industrial Design Group), would rapidly accelerate the MiniDisc's downward plunge into irrelevance or use by "special markets."

In February of 1998, one *Wired* writer could confidently snort in an article on the MiniDisc that "...the real cassette tape and CD killer is already out there. Just ask the thousands of college-age music pirates who daily download MP3-compressed tunes from the Net for free."[230] However, this attitude betrayed the Stateside bias of that writer: another source would report two years later, and with equal confidence, that Japanese skepticism towards the Internet was much higher than in the U.S. "Japan will not catch up without embracing the Internet,"[231] warned the authors of *Can Japan Compete?*, while claiming that "Internet diffusion [...] is low in Japan, with only about 17 million users as of March 1999, compare with at least 92 million in the United States...twenty percent of large companies (those with 7,800 employees or more) are not connected to the Internet."[232] This may be a testament to Japan's superior amount of on-hand conveniences, lessening the need for online scavenger hunts, or there may be more complex reasons for this disinterest: either way, it was clear that "the Internet" could not bear the lion's share of the blame for killing physical home audio formats in Japan.

So, it was not the sudden availability of nearly endless, quasi-legal music downloads that made other physical formats less attractive in Sony

---

[230] Available online at http://www.minidisc.org/wired_hype.html. Retrieved on July 10, 2010.

[231] Michael E. Porter, Hirotaka Takeuchi & Mariko Sakakibara, *Can Japan Compete?*, p. 168. Perseus Books, 2000.

[232] *Ibid.*, p. 167. This diagnosis is perhaps contradicted in the book's conclusion, when the authors claim "cyber start-ups are clustering in Tokyo's Shibuya district, which translates to Bitter Valley and is now fashionably called Bit Valley" (p. 187.)

country, but the importation of a playback device that embodied the stereotypical Japanese reductionism and cleanliness even more than the previous generations of the Walkman. The models now referred to as "classic," their stark white faces embedded with a small view screen that further accentuated this seraphic glow, were perfect fits in a consumer culture where "white" was now synonymous with tastefulness and ageless sophistication. Japanese consumer life takes place largely under an incandescent sky of intensely bright halogen lamps, where products from skin whitener to white chocolate are in abundance- one amusingly named shopping center in Osaka's Umeda district is called "Whity," and the nationally observed "White Day" is a companion to Valentine's Day, in which males are expected to present their sweethearts with gifts of that color. Sure, heretical figures have always existed among Japan's more traditionalist aesthetes- Jun'Ichiro Tanizaki's *In Praise Of Shadows* is filled with scornful attitudes towards bright electric lights and "polished tile," and especially questions the "need to remind [ourselves] so forcefully of the issue of our own bodies" when in a bathroom where "every nook and corner is pure white."[233] Yet Tanizaki and the rest of Japan's literary giants hold little influence on a youth-dominated consumer culture that sees its own positive or progressive ideals in this incandescence, and who thus came to love the little ivory bar of portable music as much as they had the previous innovations of Sony and friends. Tanizaki, quite the pessimist when it came to Japanese youth, lamented how "the conveniences of modern culture cater exclusively to youth [...] the times grow increasingly inconsiderate of old people."[234] Anthropometric innovations in technology, which made them equally usable by young and old, would have meant little to this embattled aestheticist. Tanizaki would also hardly be surprised that the youth assisted in "killing" previous generations of utopian gadgetry with no hesitation, given the irrelevance placed on the culture of their elders.

The MiniDisc's sad failure to become an international phenomenon can be ascertained from early 21st century gear reviews: one of the earliest reviews of the market-cornering iPod serves as a good example, noting in

---

[233] Junichiro Tanizaki, *In Praise Of Shadows*, p. 5. Trans. Thomas J. Harper and Edward G. Seidensticker. Leete's Island Books, Sedgewick, Maine, 1977.
[234] *Ibid.*, p. 39.

its opening lines that "the newer generations of portable music players have moved a long way from the previous standard of portable compact disc players."[235] As you can see, neither MiniDisc (nor DCC or DAT, for that matter) are mentioned as points *en route* to the latest technological standard, nor was it uncommon at all for reviewers outside of Japan to draw a straight line in their tech chronology from CD player to iPod. Such binary thought creeps into all other areas of our critical lives, and so this is to be expected when using the CD player as a metonym for all pre-iPod devices, with their dependence on a 'physical' playback medium and on a plenitude of moving parts.

The iPod featured no recording capability, but did feature synchronicity with iTunes software and thus a high degree of convenience when organizing music libraries (later Sony Hi-MD models attempted a similar degree of PC connectivity with the SonicStage software, with more recent developments to the software coming after enlisting an Apple defector - Tim Schaaff - as senior vice president of software development.) The blanket popularity of that device, in absence of a "record" feature, is an important point to take note of, since it gives lie to the theory that far more audio consumers exist than audio producers. Even in this golden age of the "pro-sumers" who may not have any intention of fashioning their home recording dalliances into a career - but who are nonetheless schooled in basic production techniques - the consumption and collection of audio seems to be a greater "draw" for owners of electronic audio equipment. The hybridization of consumer and producer roles, on its own, has not been enough to instill a 'will to creativity' in those who are perfectly content to observe the unfolding cultural landscape without personally intervening.

Apple's recognition of the "pure consumer", and their larger share of the overall home audio market, was one factor that helped elevate it to its status of i-hegemony, but the endlessly recited mantra that it was a "triumph of *design*" truly helped to seal its fate. Richard J. Pew's definition of design ("the successive application of constraints until only a unique product is left"[236]), with its hinted emphasis on extreme reduction of

---

[235] Author uncredited, "Apple iPod and SONICblue Rio Riot Portable Music Players." *Computer Music Journal* Vol. 26 No. 3 (Fall 2002), p. 115. MIT Press, Cambridge MA.

features, seems to have been the model for the iPod and for most other Apple products of the new millennium. Despite understandable complaints about the high prices these items commanded, and the subsequent criticism that the cost was a sort of "admission fee" to an exclusive club of brand-name loyalists, the Apple products of the new millennium were definite achievements in the field of physical anthropometry. Though they weren't immune to a condition of ubiquity lessening their attractiveness, their symmetry and solidity were of a high standard, and did not assume that the initial users would be of a similar technical proficiency as the designers (a problem that had haunted the earlier designs of Apple co-founder Steve Wozniak, particularly his CORE remote controller unit.) The interface of the original models was as simple as that of early coin-operated gaming consoles- the controls' constraints outweighed the affordances to the point where very few mistakes could be made in day-to-day operation, and despite the sentimental value still given to my old MZ-R900, I have to concede that even it is an unnecessarily complex icon of "featurism" when held up against the "classic" iPod's intuitive controls. For those unfamiliar with those controls, they were no more than a single 'click wheel' and center button, along with a 'hold' switch that prevented unintended adjustments to volume level or other variables controlled by the click wheel.

Shed No Tears...Inspiration Endures

Perhaps, in the previously imagined 'hell for technologies,' the boundless space would reverberate with more than just the condemnations of once infatuated consumers who claim they won't get fooled again. There would be not just an infinitude of self-righteous denunciations, but also an infinitude of misplaced praise: you'd have Bill Gates lauding the proud conceptual originators, Sony, as being "an unsuccessful maker of Japan's first electric rice cooker" who pulled themselves up by the bootstraps and became "a world leader in consumer and business electronics."[237] And, of course, there would be the unfolding drama of

---

[236] Richard J. Pew quoted in *The Psychology Of Everyday Things* by Donald Norman, p. 158. Basic Books, New York, 1988.

[237] Bill Gates, *Business @ The Speed Of Thought: Using A Digital Nervous System*, p. 5.

Apple's success to observe- a parade of pomp in which the company would reach dizzying heights of self-righteousness and would be lucky enough to have their moral duplicity unobserved by the public at large. They did, after all, delegate their manufacturing functions to China all while tooting the horn of a "Californian" design culture informed by ethical (read: ecology-sustaining and humanitarian) concerns. They were so successful in this that they could even form an alliance with pop music's own doyen of "righteous causes," U2's Bono: special "U2 Edition" iPods would come shipped with the band's catalog of songs pre-loaded onto the unit, and a silhouette of Bono at the mic would even be used as the stock "artist icon" on the function menu of the iPod Touch. Like other bastions of "ethical" consumerism - say, Starbucks, for example - they would "sell products that claim to be politically progressive acts in and of themselves [...] political action and consumption become fully merged."[238]

But now we are right back where we started: in the early 1980s where the Walkman was supposed to bring together oppositional cultures, and where utopia was conjured by the then-novel concept of enjoying a self-contained, "private" audio world in the public sphere. As the ad designs would remind you, consuming the Walkman really was an act of producing: that is, producing a new mode of interaction where the *jouissance* of private listening combined with the excitement of chance encounters while "out on the town," excising the sense of isolation from the former activity and the feelings of de-centeredness or sensory overload from the latter. It was a win-win situation in which cultivating a private / personal "lifestyle" would also have a positive effect on the ambient conditions of public / communal life. All the same, it is strange to see these devices, which act as the relaying systems for art, being trusted with bringing about a utopian condition while the art itself plays a secondary role- the situation brings to mind the Heideggerian laments about techno-science's centrality to the Western outlook on life. One proof of this can be found in the new categories of "artist" cropping up in the 21st century, like the iPod playlist selector, who do not need to have an understanding of what certain artworks reveal, and do not relegate themselves to a position where "the artist remains inconsequential as compared with the

[238] Slavoj Žižek, *In Defense Of Lost Causes*, p. 430. Verso, New York, 2008.

work...like a passageway that destroys itself in the creative process for the work to emerge."[239] Instead, their works of data compilation and tabulation are fairly egotistic exercises meant to highlight and promote the of uniqueness of their creators' lives- a phenomenon that has led to a proliferation of journalistic fluff pieces in the vein of "What's On Barack Obama's iPod."

As such, maybe the non-existence of a "MiniDisc network," or any artistic movement that acknowledges it would be impotent without technological progress, is nothing to mourn (and my own sentimental attachment to the MD is, in the final estimation, also an attachment to a time in my life that buzzed with many other new possibilities.) Collaborative artistic ventures like "Cassette Culture" did not, after all, develop from a pool of individuals who "suddenly" became creative once this technology became widely available: they developed around people who would channel their energies into any technological outlet that better facilitated the flow of that energy. As creators, we will survive the "putting down" of once beloved technologies, but will not so easily survive the extinguishing of inspiration itself. Too often we find ourselves in a situation where creative inspiration is contingent upon the arrival of new technologies, forgetting that inspiration causes *their* emergence, as well.

---

[239] Martin Heidegger, *Poetry, Language, And Thought,* p. 40, Trans. Albert Hofstader. Harper & Row, New York, 1971.

We're All Outsiders Now:
In Defense Of Pretense

To date, placing one's work outside the realm of conventional musicality has done little to prevent the arising of new and problematic classifiers. Waving the flags of radical heterogeneity and denying 'ownership' of sounds, while insisting that people may interpret those sounds in any way they please, has not done away with the construction of catch-all containers to aid in those activities so loathsome to musical romantics, like the purely 'hobbyist' interest in music. This situation reaches its tragicomic apex with those styles that most determinedly call for the dissolution of boundaries (e.g. 'noise', 'free music'.) Regarding noise in particular, academics like Ray Brassier have condemned "…the failure to recognise the paradoxes attendant upon the existence of a genre predicated upon the negation of genre."[240] Having recognized this paradoxical condition, though, even Brassier has no greater ease escaping from it: in his essay titled "Genre Is Obsolete," he still must call upon the genres of "…dub, glam-rock, musique concrète and electro-acoustic composition" in order to describe how they "are conjoined in a monstrous and exhilarating hybrid"[241] that is the music of "To Live And Shave In L.A."

Whereas noise at least has a stable meaning in information theory that can be used in lieu of its "cultural" definition, some genres exist merely to designate, or promote, a *mindset* of the artists in question. One of these tenuous genres, "outsider music," fits into our larger discussion of self-determined music for a number of reasons.[242] Perhaps foremost among these is that, when cataloging audio recordings that are released in the most autonomous fashion possible, it seems foolish to only focus on the economic restraints that have led to this practice. At some point, we also have to consider artists for whom social interaction with any kind of recording industry middleman - be it a studio engineer, label

---

[240] Ray Brassier, "Genre Is Obsolete". *Noise And Capitalism,* p. 62. Arteleku, Madrid, 2009.

[241] *Ibid.,* p. 65.

[242] I will refer to outsider music by that name for this essay only; the point of which is to jettison the term once its instability has been thoroughly revealed.

representative or manager - is made physically impossible by quirks or defects in the artists' own personalities, or a general "asymmetry" with regards to present-day society. Now, sharp deviation from normative behavior is certainly not absent among the established elite of the music world: even the most fawning hagiographies of rock 'n roll's heroes admit occasionally to these musicians' inclinations towards megalomania, paranoia, obsessive compulsion, and so on down the line. Just the literature on musicians' voluntary dives into madness (particularly by means of substance abuse) would be enough to keep readers busy for years. Yet these artists have, by and large, been able to rein in their respective manias and phobias just long enough to maintain the business relationships that are the *sine qua non* of being a big-league entertainer. Moreover, many of these conditions were themselves implanted or exacerbated by the intense public exposure that comes with the career, and so these artists remain in a different category than those who have struggled with debilitating conditions from birth, or from the early stages of socialization.

These major league artists are also more appropriately identified as "rebels", or people who come to some realization of their incompatibility with the present "system," and decide to agitate against it. A rebel can certainly be considered one form of "outsider," because he or she forfeits the benefits that could come from being more fully integrated into the dominant "system" (and also gambles on the hope that future benefits will be accrued when their oppositional activities become popularized.) The category of people officially recognized as "outsider musicians" are not really as much of a counter-cultural force, either because they are blissfully *unaware* of the "system" altogether, or because they define such adversarial forces in their own terms. At the very least, they are not properly counter-cultural until a support group of critics and patrons advocates on their behalf, explaining how these artists unwittingly embody everything that is against the reigning hegemony. According to Michelle Boulé and Irwin Chusid, one-time hosts of WFMU radio's *Incorrect Music* show:

> If there's such a thing as the opposite of being 'cool,' that's what these artists are. They don't *know* from cool…cool was never an option. Cool wasn't something they considered and then decided 'it wasn't them.' These people

are on another plane of existence where 'cool' is not a factor.[243]

Despite the respectful tone that Chusid takes here, in a news segment on the *Incorrect Music* program, its hosts are shown donning sanitary gloves and "dumpster diving" for discarded audio and video cassettes - the only form of "public" distribution that most of these recordings will see. The show, during its early 21st-century run on WFMU, thus placed "outsider music" in the realm of kitsch, yet the artists presented on the show were, for the most part, not treated as pet freaks. Although the on air presentation did not shy away from presenting this collected material as a comedic product, condescension was usually reserved for artists who themselves adopted a condescending or sanctimonious tone. Other would-be offenses - such as inability to carry a tune, overdriven sentimentality, inflated sense of greatness - were regularly dismissed, if not outright encouraged. Disqualification was not in the cards so long as the submitting artists were not perceived as "straight" people playing at being "weird," or as attempting to enter the "back door" of fame by exuding a studied, deliberate badness.

By all accounts, the *Incorrect Music* portrayal of the "outsider" is of a sincere folk artist operating within the suburbs of post-industrial society, an individual whose all-consuming obsessions are simply pursued with more emotional fervor and less moderation or rationalization than the mainstream would normally allow. Yet even in recorded music, perhaps the most populist area of the arts, obsessions are more welcomed when the obsessive artists realize their place in the grand scheme of things. Art critics like Clement Greenberg have long cautioned that sincerity is not enough, nor is the sincere belief in one's own current artistic mode as the "best":

...some people dare to say that rock music is as good as Schubert, even better. At least they are being sincere. Sincerity in the truth is always a good place to start from. I say it's double-edged because it is often used as an excuse

[243] Irwin Chusid quoted in http://www.youtube.com/watch?v=5AcPIi-U26w. Retrieved on August 15, 2010.

for not trying to find out why Schubert is so good. [...] It becomes an excuse for copping out on the effort of going back to works of the past.[244]

It is the "incorrect musicians'" confidence in the profundity of their banal lyrics, and the timeless romanticism of their very ephemeral musical arrangements, that provides the odd mixture of hilarity and empathy so common upon hearing their works: they are like the musical equivalents of the eternally grinning garden gnome. Yet, it is difficult to see the artists themselves as the sole originators of traits like runaway optimism. They are, in the end, just affected by the mass media's reassuring proclamations to a degree that not even those media had intended. These are the people who have taken the proclamation of "anyone can be a star" seriously; those who have unreservedly placed faith in the mass media's palliative reminder that "being true to oneself" will confer a literally unlimited number of rewards. Or, as Greenberg suggests in his famous essay on kitsch, "the axioms of the few are shared by the many...the latter believe superstitiously what the former believe soberly."[245]

Sometimes the process of line blurring is even stealthier than what Greenberg might suggest. Certainly, there have been absurd moments of musical novelty that have stolen the popular imagination: David Seville's "The Chipmunk Song," Rick Dees' "Disco Duck," and the musical spin-offs from the insipid "Crazy Frog" ringtone are not dissimilar in tone from the many animal-oriented tunes showcased on *Incorrect Music* (e.g. Lille Eris' "Jeg Vil Ha En Lite Hund.") Period "exotica" reveling in the imagery of tiki, voodoo, and monster movies is now chuckled at for its divorce from serious attempts at social transformation, yet Michael Jackson's horror-themed "Thriller" remained one of the most wildly successful singles of the 1980s (and Jackson's status as one of the first heavily-featured black artists on MTV did add a bit of social transformation to the mix.) Lastly, many of the uninhibited patriotic songs that come out of the "incorrect music" stable are hardly even a degree removed from the compositional and lyrical quality of "God Bless The U.S.A.," the best-selling single of Lee

---

[244] Clement Greenberg, *Homemade Esthetics*, p. 95. Oxford University Press, New York, 1999.

[245] Available online at http://www.sharecom.ca/greenberg/kitsch.html. Retrieved September 14, 2010.

Greenwood that became the *de facto* anthem of the 1991 Gulf War.

Although much of the music above has been done on home-recorded cassettes, CD-Recordables, etc., another notable medium for this music is the "song poem" record. It is not a pure self-release since it involves the collaboration of a shady group of middlemen. These are referred to by enthusiasts of the medium as "song sharks," named so because they solicit potential musicians with advertisements promising to make a professional demonstration recording of their mailed-in poems, sheet music (or both) after a hermetic process of "professional evaluation." Of course, nothing is ever rejected in this "evaluation" process. The "sharks" then exploit the acceptance of the "accepted" artist by mailing out a more explanatory (and usually persuasive) request to fund the process of recording the submitted work. As Phil Milstein of the The American Song Poem Archive explains it:

> The next twist is perhaps the trickiest of all, for even the dumbest perch in the pond knows that in the music industry, if you've got a salable commodity then companies will pay *you* for access to it. Instead, the song-poem company must convince the song-poet that she should pay *them,* typically to the tune of $200 to $400 [...] The company suggests that its fee constitutes merely the "seed money" required before it can begin to develop the lyric into a finished record, and represents but a small portion of the total costs involved. In fact the fee - or so claims the literature - is levied not so much for the revenue it will bring the company but rather as a "show of good faith," a demonstration that the song-poet believes strongly enough in the quality and potential of her handiwork to deem it worthy of financial risk. The truth, of course, is that the fee covers a lot more than just a "small portion" of the costs: it subsidizes the entire overhead and profit for that record, and so once the record is produced and manufactured the company has already gotten from it everything that it can. It is of no further value to them.[246]

---

[246] Available online at http://www.songpoemmusic.com/what_is.htm. Retrieved September

So, the final product here, usually a stack of promotional records or tapes returned to the songwriter, is all we have in terms of an "edition" or "pressing": though the music here is not self-released, it is clearly "unofficial" since serious discographies will not take note of these records, and serious music outlets will not stock them.

Music recorded in this style is not, in most cases, even written or recorded by the "song poet," but by a revolving cast of technically skilled studio musicians who, as evidenced by the 2003 documentary film *Off The Charts: The Song Poem Story,* can manufacture a complete recording within an *hour* of receiving the song lyrics in the mail. This can result occasionally in a bond between the song-poet and the studio interpreters, or in disgust at the studio's misinterpretation of the work (in the past, many letters have been published on Milstein's site attesting to this disconnect.) Or, in the rare case of the enigmatic Rodd Keith, this collaborative process can result in the studio musician becoming elevated to a kind of star status themselves - Keith's habit of recording nearly all his song-poems on a mellotron was unprecedented for the music industry of his time, and these innovative pieces have been compiled on the prestigious Tzadik CD label.

The odd friction between two different sets of creative individual - the starry-eyed song-poet and the faceless but competent studio pro - is a modern tragedy all unto itself. Although it's also evident that absurdist comedy can arise from this relationship, as shown by the now infamous late 70s attempt by John Trubee to call the "song sharks'" bluff and write a song-poem too willfully terrible for them to accept. As the legend goes, his psychotic LSD fantasy "Blind Man's Penis" was given a reverent reading - and delightfully incongruous country-western backing - by Nashville vocalist Ramsey Kearney. This unlikely marriage has become, not entirely undeservedly, one of the most well known song-poems on record, appearing on numerous official and unofficial mixes of "outsider" music.

The various "incorrect musicians," and song-poets in particular, have been seen as an example of some great American "return of the repressed": private obsessions becoming public in a most lurid and unexpected way.

15, 2010.

Another plausible theory, though, is that obsessive yearning is the very defining characteristic of the nation. As such, it's tempting to say that these artists' songs of zealous approval for American society's *kitsch* elements do more to harm its cause than the marketable, political anger of groups like Rage Against The Machine, for these songs showcase a society where "...the narcotic side of inert stupidity belongs to the very possibility of late technological psychopathology...the pleasures reflected in and invented by industrial forms of leisure."[247] Take for example the late Wesley Willis, a chronic schizophrenic native to Chicago, who issued dozens of virtually identical CDs featuring his superhero fantasies, obscene rants, and concert reviews, all spoken and yelled over keyboard presets that remained virtually unchanged throughout a full CD program. When he ends a bestiality-themed ditty with a shouted endorsement for the local fast food franchise, it provides as acidic a commentary on standardized culture as any confrontational punk rock jeremiad.[248]

Willis is a particularly relevant case, since the sheer audacity of his approach bridges the gap between two different varieties of outsider, particularly the way in which the phantasms of his mind vie for lyrical space with his ruminations on fast food and mundane consumer needs. The outsider type already mentioned, a sort of willfully naïve and critically immune personality, could probably still pass for a member of "straight" society - at the cost of rejection by its cultural avant-garde. A second type of outsider, more embraced by that avant-garde, inverts that scenario. These artists are afflicted with serious mental illness, or a tragic inability to be recuperated by post-industrial society, a fact that sometimes (but not always) manifests itself in their musical style.

Like so much that has already been stuffed in between the covers of this volume, the phenomenon of outsider music owes its popularity to a number of contradictory audience attitudes, each of them hoping to hold a privileged position when it comes to discussing the form's legitimacy and meaning. For many, the perplexing array of styles commonly categorized as "outsider" are little more than one part of a perverse entertainment

---

[247] Avital Ronell, *Stupidity*, p. 89. University of Illinois Press, Urbana / Chicago, 2002.

[248] This is undoubtedly also the opinion of Californian punk mainstay Jello Biafra, who released several of Wilis' CDs on his own Alternative Tentacles imprint, and appropriated the Willis track "Rock 'n Roll McDonald's" for his own live performances.

program- maximal communicative distance between the artists and this segment of their audience is usually maintained, although that audience does enjoy the occasional titillating thrill of seeing these performers if and when they hold concert performances. For this segment of the outsider audience, the purpose of this music is its simple illustrative reinforcement of their social or intellectual superiority.

So, the natural counter-balance to this extremely patronizing clique of fans is the group that finds the perceived deficiencies of the outsiders to be, in actuality, advantages: by virtue of being exiled to this ill-defined "outside," the artists are free from any pressing social obligations and can thus comment more honestly and lucidly about the state of the modern world. This seems, at least, to be the driving force behind the ongoing adoration of unassimilated 'man-child' songwriters like Daniel Johnston, or of Miguel Tomasin, the Down's Syndrome-affected vocalist and drummer of the Argentinian experimental trio Reynols. At any rate, for the considerably more reverent portion of their audience, listening to outsider music is a spiritual program for getting rid of oneself, to cast off the hang-ups and neuroses that the lionized outsiders almost effortlessly resist. While the ironically-distanced, social-climbing hipsters may use recordings of outsider music to affirm their own place in society, the more respectful aggregate of fans uses this music to cut up and reinvent a defective, inherited sense of self. To view this situation in terms of song-poems: the former group tends to stick to those with more 'wacky' and alien subject matter (see especially Caglan Juan Singletary's "Non-Violent Taekwondo Troopers" and his musings on "kung-fu bicycles"), while the latter would embrace just about any recording "created by everyday people who are, for once, willing to sidestep their normal routines and in so doing risk failure."[249]

The entertainment oriented group of outsider fans can be satisfied by artists who adhere to a couple of simple precepts. Firstly, the outsider artist must be one who fails to live up to some previously-existing standard for performance or recording etiquette, and yet remains totally oblivious to this fact (doing otherwise would, of course, would make the

---

[249] David Greenberg, liner notes to *The Human Breakdown Of Absurdity: MSR Madness Vol. 3*, Carnage Press, 1987.

entertainment value very short-lived.) The mumbled Elvis impersonations of the out-of-shape Swede Eilert Pilarm, or the scatological tirades of Wesley Willis (who composed his Casio-driven tunes as a means of combating the demonic voices in his head) can comfortably fit this bill. An extra bonus here is the artist's assumption that there is not only nothing wrong with this awkward presentation, but that it is in fact already leading to a life of fame: the Rolling Stones-obsessed singer-songwriter Paul "Super Apple" Muralia, who prefaces his few found compositions with detailed "stalker" monologues directed at Keith Richards, is one example of the faulty perception of one's actual social standing.

For the latter grouping of more spiritually concerned music aficionados, "outsider" can be a stand-in for a number of other artistic inclinations towards childish regression or primitivism (provided that the artist does not personally acknowledge these characteristics as such, or consciously attempt to 'make a statement' by deliberately deploying them.) The music is therefore a sort of *bruitisme* exonerated from meeting serious standards of tonality, compositional rigor, conceptual rigor, or production quality, yet succeeding in spite of not clearing some (or any) of these hurdles. The stereotypically reclusive musician Jandek, who oddly pressed all of his recordings onto 'proper' factory-manufactured LPs and CDs rather than cassettes and CD-Recordables, is often lauded as the very incarnation of authenticity for foregoing production flourishes and playing in a severely disjointed style. He plucks single guitar notes that, although seemingly random, always coalesce to create a sense of dislocation nearly uniform throughout his deep catalog of songs. He slowly and hesitantly sings clipped phrases that, though too obtuse to seem like they reference any specific event, develop a sense of uncomfortable, enveloping initimacy. Like the somewhat more tuneful and jaunty Daniel Johnston, Jandek is the subject of a loving bio-pic - *Jandek on Corwood* - and, on those rare occasions when he performs before a public, gets to perform alongside musicians with more knowingly avant-garde inclinations.

Ascent Into Madness: Insanity And The Avant-Garde

Actually, the occasional musical marriage of *bruitisme* with the 'serious' avant-garde, or at least the appreciation of the former tendency by the latter constituency, is something that transcends this particular medium, if not the arts themselves. Overly educated philosophers, for example, have often been credited with merely returning to the way of perceiving the world that comes naturally to young children: the philosophical act of 'unseeing,' or realizing that things aren't quite what they seem, is not that unlike the way in which small children familiarize themselves with the world. Both seem to inhabit a world where wonderment, or ungraspable wisdom, is every bit as valuable as the empirically tested knowledge. Yet philosophers are just one category of people who operate in more of an exploratory mode than what might normally be acceptable for "grown adults." The mentally ill are another category of individuals who have been put forward as being closer to an authentic, sometimes prelapsarian, ideal. André Breton, while acting as spokesperson for Surrealism, thought enough of them to applaud them in his first *Manifesto Of Surrealism*. Upon witnessing the hallucinatory phase or *attitudes passionelles* of hysterics, as photographed by Jean-Martin Charcot in his clinic, Breton writes:

> I am willing to admit, to some degree, that they are victims of their imagination, in that it induces them not to pay attention to certain rules -outside of which the species itself feels threatened- which we are all supposed to know and respect. But their profound indifference to the way in which we judge them, and even to the various punishments meted out to them, allows us to suppose they derive a great deal of comfort and consolation from their imagination, that they enjoy their madness sufficiently to endure the thought that its validity does not extend beyond themselves. [...] They are honest to a fault, and their naiveté has no peer.[250]

Breton is so taken with "madmen," in fact, that he suggests "Christopher Columbus should have set out to discover America with a boatload of them."[251] Breton and fellow Surrealist Paul Eluard thought so highly of

---

[250] André Breton, "Manifesto Of Surrealism." *Manifestoes Of Surrealism*, p. 5. 1924.

hysterics that they commemorated them with a 'fiftieth anniversary' essay ("Le Cinquantenaire de l'hysterié," 1928), acknowledging the year in which Charcot first solidified his theories on the hysteric state.

Breton's defense of the hysteric state was not an anomaly within Surrealist thought, but the very apotheosis of it: Breton insisted on trying to achieve trance states and hypnotic slumbers as a spur to creative action, as well as generally any activity that defied rational thought or "critical sense." It is telling that Breton implicitly links states of madness or irrationality with the mental state of children, claiming that "...a hunger for the marvelous, as we could still revive it in childhood memories" was "...a violent reaction against the impoverishment and sterility of thought processes that resulted from centuries of rationalism...we turned towards the marvelous and advocated it unconditionally."[252] It was doubly invigorating for Breton, activist iconoclast that he was, to champion a malady that was still being seen in Charcot's time as a punishment for some past transgression. As Michel Foucault writes on the 19th-century pathology of hysteria, "...what had been error would become fault, and everything in madness that designated the paradoxical manifestation of non-being would become the natural punishment of a moral evil."[253]

An equally influential "madman" lauded by the Surrealists was Gérard de Nerval, one of the 19th century's major literary precursors to Surrealism alongside Isidore Ducasse. Nerval is widely remembered for the quintessentially Surrealist act of walking his pet lobster Thibault, on the end of a blue silk ribbon, throughout the Palais Royal gardens in Paris (an act that Nerval defended by noting how the lobster "didn't bark" and knew "the secrets of the sea.") Although he was diagnosed in 1841 with 'acute mania' rather than hysteria, Nerval was a perfect vehicle for Breton's missionary promotion of "madness" as being a state of *superior* awareness relative to bourgeois society's moral outlook. This was in part due to Nerval's track record when compared to his would-be rebellious contemporaries. Though his bohemian fellows in the wake of the July

---

[251] André Breton, "Manifesto Of Surrealism." *Manifestoes Of Surrealism*, p. 5. 1924.

[252] André Breton, *The Autobiography Of Surrealism*, p. 63. Marlowe & Company, New York, 1993.

[253] Michel Foucault, *Madness And Civilization*, p. 158. Vintage Books, New York, 1988.

Revolution (known as the 'Jeunes-France' or 'Petit Cénacle') affected all the cosmetic trappings of rebellion, namely "long hair, beards, Renaissance cloaks and doublets, and *outré* synonyms such as "Petrus Borel The Lycanthrope"[254], they were soon enough regarded as Byron-esque poseurs more interested in lifestyle affectation than creative output (this should sound very familiar to anyone who has grown up with a music-based subculture of the 20th or 21st century.) It was Nerval who "remained faithful to [the] transgressive energies [of Jeune-France] to the very last"[255] while his more publicly 'visible' contemporary Théophile Gautier ended up as a librarian to the Napoleonic regime. As with the hysterics, Nerval simply refused to believe his storied eccentricities were worthy of being called a clinical illness, and persisted with them in spite of an official diagnosis- he even turned the tables on his doctors by likening them to a priesthood demanding confessions of guilt (a point that was probably not lost on Breton, who loathed the Catholic church and the medical establishment in almost equal measure.) Nerval saw himself as a 'political prisoner,'[256] and insisted "if the mind has to become completely unhinged in order to place us in communication with another world, it is clear that the *mad* will never be able to prove to the *sane* how blind they are, to say the very least!"[257] Indeed, the Surrealists' proposed marriage of 'feminine' hysteria, as represented by Charcot's patients, and the 'masculine' mania of Nerval, still provides a valid model for modern-day of the mythical outsider. Characters like Nerval, through his sonnets and novellas, were not only able to demonstrate a highly unique artistic sensibility, but were able to defend themselves in an articulate manner against their accusers.

The only problem with simply equating outsider musicians with "madness" is that many present-day sufferers of mental illness do not, for whatever reason, fall under the rubric of "official" outsider music. A good deal of the officially recognized outsider musicians have a mental disorder, such as chronic depression or schizophrenia, that gives their work its characteristic sense of being suspended between real and imagined worlds

---

[254] Richard Sieburth quoted in *Selected Writings*, Gérard de Nerval, p.xiv. Penguin Classics, New York / London, 1999.

[255] *Ibid.*

[256] Namely, he was a victim of "doctors and police inspectors whose job it is to keep the field of poetry from invading public thoroughfares"- see *Selected Writings*, p. 348.

[257] *Ibid.*, p. xx.

(and those mental worlds can themselves vascillate between being celestial or infernal realms.) Yet here we run into trouble already: certain groups from the industrial / 'noise' music underground have featured clinically depressed or disturbed members, yet do not qualify for outsider status on the basis of these disorders alone. The chronic depression (and eventual suicide) of Atrax Morgue's Marco Corbelli, or the schizophrenic membership of an early SPK lineup, are items not often considered in critical attempts to delineate an outsider aesthetic. In fact, much music from the darker and more aggressive genres remains conspicuously ignored, even when the musicians' mental struggles terminate in catastrophe.

Critics can be justifiably skeptical when surveying extremer-than-thou districts of, say, black metal music, considering that the genre is now packed with artists who claim to have hellish visions or to be driven by spirits- more often than not a public relations move necessitated by being in such an overcrowded 'scene.' All the same, there is a certain critical bias towards *bruitisme* that manifests itself in less harmful ways: the disarming sweetness of a Daniel Johnston, or the vulnerability conjured by Jandek's sad and laconic songs - something akin to handling an aged photo or brittle, crumbling hand-written manuscript - are for now the preferred modes of "outsider-hood." This is interesting, because it seems to betray a kind of "outsider morality" posited by the anthropologists of this unstable genre: an inherent goodness that has the power to hold up a mirror to society... but not to violently upset it.

This critical consensus can also be witnessed in anthologies of "outsider" visual art, for which the norm is currently something like Henry Darger's whimsical, panoramic depictions of pre-pubescent wonderlands. It is far removed from the realm of archetypal outsider / lunatic Antonin Artaud (another Breton favorite), "under [whose] influence, collective texts of great violence where published at the time."[258] Reading Breton's praise of Artaud, though it comes with reservations, is almost like reading a glowing contemporaneous review of some black metal transgressors: his work "meant to be sharp and gleaming...but gleaming like a weapon."[259]

---

[258] André Breton, *The Autobiography Of Surrealism*, p. 85. Marlowe & Company, New York, 1993.

These contradictory ideals, though both basing themselves on assumptions of mental instability, take us farther away from figuring out what is really meant by "outsider music."

Out Of Time: The Trials Of The Cult Hero As *Übermensch*

While the intoxicated madman is one popular model for the "outsider," yet another is that of the sovereign individual who was born at the wrong time (and who may still end up being classified as "mad" because of a persistent belief in ideals that are too archaic or futuristic.) Their advanced skills in interpretation and expression are so superior to the average man's skill in these areas, that this superiority becomes converted into a deficiency. This in itself is baffling, given how "average people" regularly latch onto pop stars who are seen as being beyond their reach, though this probably has more to do with those stars' physical embodiment of certain ideals than their intellectual capacity for conveying ideas. Gustave LeBon writes:

> At every period there exist a small number of individualities that react upon the remainder and are imitated by the unconscious mass. It is needful, however, that these individualities should not be in too pronounced disagreement with received ideas. Were they so, to imitate them would be too difficult and their influence would be nil. For this very reason, men who are too superior to their epoch are generally without influence upon it. [260]

No more concrete example of these tendencies may be found than David Tibet of Current 93 (*neé* David Michael Bunting in Batu Gajah, Malaysia.) C93, his flagship musical project, has alternately been pegged as "apocalyptic folk," "post-industrial" or, yes, "outsider music."[261] None of

---

[259] André Breton, *The Autobiography Of Surrealism*, p. 85. Marlowe & Company, New York, 1993.

[260] Gustave Le Bon, *The Crowd: A Study Of The Popular Mind*, p. 79. Dover Publications, Mineola NY, 2002.

[261] The term "outsider" is used on multiple occasions in David Keenan's watershed editorial

these is entirely accurate, since elements of these styles - as commonly recognized - bleed into each other in ways that are not exactly duplicated outside of this particular project. The single apparent criterion for adding a musical element to the C93 *ouevre* is its ability to send a shiver up the spine, and so warped Gregorian chants, bucolic passages of acoustic guitar, and ectoplasmic electronics all slide in and out of the mix to evoke a woozy sense of parallel reality. The eschatological vocals, delivered in a tone that is crisp and cutting ("gleaming like a weapon?"), work to prevent the mind from drifting too far into this swirling nebula of sound. However, the imagery conjured by the lyrics, which have in the past been culled from personal visions of Tibet, has its own set of uniquely disorienting effects.

Even before his music is discussed, Tibet's artistic associations have identified him as a character of very unique predilections and convictions: he has counted among his allies the neo-pagan electronic artists Coil, the penultimate modern surrealist Steven Stapleton (a.k.a. Nurse With Wound), the Spenglerian noisemaker and kitsch enthusiast Boyd Rice, and Tin Pan Alley archivist Tiny Tim.[262] All of these have also worn the mantle of "outsider-hood" as well, which has chafed their skin to varying degrees: while these artists have been misunderstood by both the avant-garde and the masses, most of them have shown no desire to be taken into either fold. This rejection of recognition is a far cry from the yearning of song-poets, or Jandek's famous attempts to sell "25 LPs for $50." Combine this with an inversion of the public perception of the artist as someone who is crushed by society to one who regally floats above it, and you have some of the main ingredients for a third category of "outsider," the cult hero in the guise of *Übermensch*. Though born at the wrong time, it's still assumed that they have some Nietzschean superhuman qualities (e.g. relentless drive towards affirmation, instituting numerous "thou *shalts*" in the place of "thou shalt *nots*".)

---

on Current 93 ("Childhood's End" in *Wire* # 163 (September 1997), p. 35-37. This was one of the first features on the group to appear in a regularly circulating 'newsstand' magazine.

[262] Of Tiny Tim, Tibet has superlative words to say. He was "one of the most moving and profound people I've ever met [...] I was the last person to speak to him on the phone [...] he was the greatest genius of popular song ever. It's tragic that people still perceive him as some kind of one-hit comedy turn." Quoted in "Childhood's End" (see above) p. 35.

One of the commonly accepted facets of post-structuralist thought is the idea that a "minor" form of creative activity is necessarily a "political" one- in the act of claiming to represent an otherwise unrepresented aspect of humanity, or of creating an identity rather than just expressing one, an artist's work becomes a political struggle for affirmation. What can be said, though, for artists who - while "minor" in their unique aesthetic sensibility or system of beliefs - deny having an interest in reaching the public at large, much less an interest in politics? David Tibet, though his works are now widely distributed and highly regarded by a cross-section of music fans, claims that this state of success was never intended:

> Steve [Stapleton] and I always thought [the recordings] would be sent into the wilderness, as no one would care. Apparently people do, either by loving what we have done, or hating it. I do it because I am driven to do it. I [also] translate Coptic because I am driven to do it. [263]

Tibet then admits that small-scale approval is not unwelcome, but he firmly rejects that approval (or rejection) of any kind is an influencing factor:

> I have met many friends through what I have done. And friends always help us in our self-inquiry. I am interested in what people who know me think of my work, but only inasmuch as I am also interested in what they think of my new cat. Finally the work is ONLY for me. If those who know me make comments on it, I reflect on them deeply; but they don't affect what I would have done. If fans like my work, I am happy. If they don't, I am equally happy.[264]

Unlike many artists who stand indifferent to public opinion, though, Tibet does still feel obligations to external forces: they just happen to be not of this world. In fact, Tibet's spirituality seems to trump any sort of political self-affirmation as the impetus for his work:

---

[263] David Tibet, Personal email correspondence with the author. July 27, 2010.
[264] *Ibid.*

> Who is driving me? Well, I think everything comes from
> God. We all have our appointed tasks and are called to
> manifest it / them as best we can. God will judge what I,
> and we all, do. There is no posterity to which we can leave
> anything. Everything returns to him, praise and damning
> equally.[265]

As exemplified by this statement, Tibet's spiritual commitment is not an ironic affectation, and thusly makes things more complicated for anyone attempting to use his work as an illustration of larger societal tendencies (e.g. people of 'religious' orientations are not typically creators of unusual music, nor friendly collaborators with would-be spiritual adversaries.) Complicating matters further still is the fact that Tibet has undergone a number of transformations in the nature of his beliefs, some of which have never been accepted by his audience as sincere:

> Even when the music became more explicitly 'Christian'
> (or at least Gnostic / heretical Christian) I noticed people
> still thought I was 'Crowleyan' and that the Christian
> statements were 'ironic'. So I, finally, can have no
> influence over what people think of me or my work -
> which is as it should be![266]

It should be noted that the serious, defensive tone of Tibet on display here does not give us much of an appreciation for his biting, counter-critical sense of humor. Showing just how little he cared for the "cult hero" title, and for courting acolytes at the expense of personal creative development, Current 93 once released a peppy piece of *ersatz* dance funk ("Crowleymass") that implicitly ridiculed the prevailing view of C93 as emissaries of eldritch grandeur and fearsome occult insight. Tibet's spoken / rapped vocal on the song, with its mock-tough refrain of *"don't give us no sass or we'll kick your ass...'cause we're the heralds of Crowleymass"* speaks volumes for his weariness of having these characteristics ascribed to him, especially his supposed inflexible devotion to the grand magus in the

---

[265] David Tibet, email correspondence with the author, received on July 27, 2010.
[266] *Ibid.*

song's title. An added swipe comes via the album's listing of personnel, which credits a player of "Wickedest Guitar In The World" (a play on Aleister Crowley's own period reputation as the wickedest *man* in the world.) The great irony here is that, even with a satire as blatant as this, Tibet claims to have still received letters praising him for saluting the "Great Beast" in the dance-pop style: a hitherto unaccomplished feat that he could now add to his catalog of magickal deeds. Of course, those who saw this to be Tibet's first stab at humor were maybe not looking hard enough: in all likelihood, an artist without a funnybone would not have re-cast Enid Blyton's beloved storybook character Noddy as a tragic "Gnostic icon."[267]

The existence of someone like Tibet provides a conundrum for all varieties of Outsider Fan: he clearly lowers his emotional defenses in order to describe himself and his worldview more clearly, a point in common with the more certifiably naïve artists in this quasi-genre. Yet he reveals himself using vocabulary and concepts that are unfamiliar to the majority of this post-modern listening audience. For many in this pool of listeners, the mere act of being able to "describe the world" is scoffed at as an impossibility (critic Terry Eagleton acidly comments that post-modern criticism "consistently denies the possibility of describing the way the world is, and just as consistently finds itself doing so.")[268] The post-modern promotion of cultural hybridity has also led, rather unfairly, to a condition wherein the very word "purity" raises censorious eyebrows- in an odd leap of logic, the hope of artists like Tibet to achieve a "pure" creative state is likened to to the insidious 20th century conflicts over genetic and national purity, or is at least seen as a kind of spiritual hypochondria.

The high erudition that Tibet projects on the subjects of religion, innocence, visionary states etc. is often misinterpreted as "snobbery" or, more damning still, "pretension." Even if this were a true condition, which I doubt it is, "pretension" itself is a stance worth re-examining, since it does not automatically imply condescension towards others (or exploitation of

---

[267] Current 93's 1986 album *Swastikas For Noddy* elaborates on this concept, and is the first to fully break with the 'post-industrial' soundtrack of Gregorian chant and electronic noise that identified the band earlier.

[268] Terry Eagleton, *The Illusions of Postmodernism*, p. 28. Blackwell Publishers, Oxford, 1996.

others' gullibility.) My friend Leif Elggren, a Swedish artist who has made power and authority one of the central topics of his work, argues that pretension can be altruistic (i.e. a willful sacrifice of one's personal reputation that in turn inspires others) or can act as a self-fulfilling prophecy: if one declares themselves to be king of their own imaginary territory, as Elggren has done with his long-running Elgaland-Vargaland project, they may just find that the line between pantomimed power and actual power becomes less visible. In this respect, he mentions how so many positions of actual power are themselves based in pretension, "invoking their divine right to rule."[269] Elggren, with a Saab engine filter as his crown, has now assumed all the functions of a "real" king other than legislative power- but there is a more important point here than just the ability to generate respect and power relationships by fiat. According to Elggren, "it is not silly, like a lunatic or an artist, to put a paper crown on your head and claim yourself a king or whatever."[270] Refering to a Swedish expression for pretentious speech ("talking through one's nightcap"), Elggren also states

> ...talking through one's hat has also, sometimes, meant something special and exclusive [...] in extreme situations where desperation or fear has struck those in power (in the school yard, at the bank, in court or the offices of government), the singer, the oracle, the prophet, or the poet has been summoned, perhaps even the madman.[271]

In *equating* the artist or poet with the 'lunatic' and the 'madman,' rather than just suggesting that others' madness provides a fount of inspiration for artists (e.g. Charcot's hysterics), Elggren is essentially saying "we're all outsiders now." We can infer here that all creative acts are potentially pretentious to someone somewhere, and so a life totally lived on the "inside" would mean one where every action is done in the name of pure utility, not carried out by irrational and "pretentious" attempts to live a life the likes of which haven't been seen before.

---

[269] Leif Elggren, *Genealogy*, p. 134. Firework Edition, Stockholm, 2005.

[270] *Ibid.*, p. 42.

[271] Leif Elggren, *Physiological Frequencies* (page unnumbered.) Gallery Niklas Benelius, Stockholm, 2009.

Imaginary Music

Being designated as an outsider means that an artist often has no obligations to please society at large, since the 'outsider' tag is likely to stick- yet it also means a lack of available capital and social resources that can approach total privation. When the challenges of the latter condition begin to outweigh the liberating benefits of the former one, making *any* kind of music can border on the impossible, yet the fantasy of concretizing one's hopes and dreams in an end product still remains. Out of this comes a tendency that we could call 'imaginary music', in which an individual may, like Elggren and his kingship, promote herself or himself as being a professional artist despite a lack of legal recognition. The would-be artist provides some aspect of the presentation, like a curiosity-provoking set of 'press materials', or an advertisement for an album yet to be delivered, and leaves it to the imagination of the audience to conjure up the musical content.

The act of "issuing" a non-material offering does have its precedents in the more officially accepted avant-gardes, such as Yves Klein's infamous 1958 exhibition in the nearly empty Iris Clert Gallery - an act which essentially saw Klein selling the air in the gallery to the patrons. The Yugoslav conceptualist group Gorgona translated this type of action into the realm of self-publishing: the Gorgona artist Dimitrije Bašičević, a.k.a. Mangelos, was put in charge of an "immaterial" edition of the *Gorgona* anti-magazine which never came to pass (the reader can probably already see the humor in a sadly "unrealized" edition that was intended to be immaterial in the first place.) Closer to the musical realm was the "invisible LP" of Berlin's Die Tödliche Doris, whose content was meant to materialize upon simultaneous playback of their previous LPs *Sechs* and *Unser Debut* (both featured an equal number of tracks, themselves with equal running times.)

While all of these actions are interesting on their own merits - especially when considering how invisible "non-items" elicit responses from the material world just as easily as concrete artifacts would - their intentions differ greatly from amateurs operating outside the boundaries of any recognizable "art world." The elusive character known as Mingering Mike, originally based in Washington D.C., is one of these colorful amateurs: while never having done anything more than a few rudimentary bedroom recordings (which were not released until very recently), Mingering Mike advertised himself as a soul music superstar through a massive portfolio's worth of hand-drawn LP covers (many of them shrinkwrapped to add an extra illusory sense that they contained actual music inside.) The "records" themselves were constructed of materials like cardboard and had their "grooves" hand-drawn onto the imaginary playing surface. Adding to the drama, hand-written reviews (unanimously positive) were affixed to the records along with hand-made price tags and even stickers indicating which "hits" were featured on that particular LP. These singular objects were discovered by the record collectors Dori Hadar and Frank Beylotte in a flea market record bin alongside more legitimate, playable records, and the rest, as they say, is history: once these works were scanned and posted online in 2003, Mike's wish for stardom came true (even if the granting of this wish was somewhat belated, and it meant he would now have to deal with the "outsider artist" designation.)

Mike's LPs are not just a promotional vehicle for himself, but also aggrandizements of his close friends ("The Big D" is one guest singer who routinely shows up on the album art), and at any rate, they create an elaborate alternate reality based on the social struggles of the early 1970s (Mike was at the time hiding from the Selective Service, and his prolific number of hand-drawn records were one way to alleviate the boredom of "lying low.") As "time capsule" pieces of anthropological interest, they are every bit as valuable as the commercially available artifacts from this time- putting three or four of Mike's works back to back gives an immediate impression of a world where kung fu films and calls for social unity, *a la* period singers like Curtis Mayfield, are in the ascendancy.

In all cases, Mike's work is - like the artists showcased on *Incorrect Music* - a perfect example of the formula "more 'x' than 'x' itself": his emulations of "authentic" soul superstars can lock onto that music's mythical essence moreso than its pioneering acts are able to, simply because he does not have to do anything *but* capture and distill that essence: not being anywhere close to the media apparatus of megastardom, he has no need to craft a separate image for talk show appearances, to make dramatic stylistic adjustments when sales forecasts look grim, or to dilute the message with one-off experiments meant to appease a "crossover market." Mingering Mike's forgeries are therefore not that different from the works appearing in the original cassette underground, or even David Tibet's work as he imagined it would be (not) perceived: there is no assumption of *any* critical community or audience for it, and with that comes something approaching a "pure" form of creative freedom. Those who work with a total ignorance of the above factors often provide the strongest test for whether or not an idea's essence can survive- that is to say, when it is being revealed in all its blinding nakedness.

The potential for new "Mingering Mikes" has mushroomed with the rise of the Internet and online social networks, which - like the Italian "Mind Invaders" project of the early 1980s - can inject a bit of excitement and mystery into a stagnant scene even without a marketable recording. Although the act of intentionally misleading people can be called into question, it's still too early in the game to write off these new exemplars of imaginary music as dumb, pedestrian pranks. For some, the validity of ideas has to be given a trial run before being aired in forums where physical contact is made, and so these outlets serve their purpose as a meter for gauging others' acceptance or hostility. Many can scoff at the phenomenon of "manufactured social acceptance" as a sad stand-in for the real thing, but this technique is used to great effect now - via 'viral' advertising - by major corporations the world over seeking to sell product. It is something which runs the risk of becoming their province alone if others on the "outside" do not find ways to use this special kind of pretense to their own ends.

++++++++

If we conceive of artistic genres as being containers, then perhaps it would be useful to extend this metaphor a little bit: after all, containers are useful means of storing and preserving, yet are rarely impervious to the ravages of time. Storing volatile contents in a container only accelerates this process. When studying and reviewing the sounds that "outsiders" make, far too much emphasis is placed on the inner lives of the artists in question, and any sonic component seems to be an afterthought. Much in the same way that "new" musical genres arise merely when new hairstyles or modes of dress are adopted by the players of an already existing style, the gatekeepers of outsider audio do not require musical novelty so much as novel twists in the artists' biographies. Once delineated in this way, the *music* of the outsider is used as one illustration of the artist's status as a troubled soul: it is a single element in a larger pattern of eccentric and unpredictable behaviors, and therefore not to be taken as the central focus of character study.

The continually fluctuating definitions of inside and outside will continue to change as societies continue to update their knowledge of pathology. This occurs as the moral imperatives, that often contribute to classifying certain behaviors as either sick or healthy, change themselves: for example, Sylvére Lotringer reminds us of "the decision in 1974 by the Psychiatric Association to drop homosexuality from their list of 'deviations.'"[272] This is to say nothing of other disproved practices like deducing "criminal types" from the careful study of phrenology. These fluctuating pathologies and prejudices make for a genre that will have little fixity to it, and little precise meaning for future generations: it is one which makes even the maddening explosion of electronic dance music sub-genres seem clear-cut in comparison (because, again, here we at least have a certain foundation of uniform sonic characteristics to help with the classification process.)

The sheer volume of artists that can be potentially labeled as outsiders begs the question: how much of an "inside" really exists, and if "outside" is code for "minority status" within a larger population, well, a nearly infinite number of minority predilections can be invented based on all sorts of criteria from ethnic heritage to personal preference in breakfast foods. Could it be possible that the "inside," or a group that succeeds in embodying normative conditions at *all* times, is the true minority here (and thus the true set of the population that should feel excluded or alienated

---

[272] Sylvére Lotringer, *Overexposed: Perverting Perversions*, p. 44. Semiotext(e), Los Angeles, 1988.

from the authentic conditions of life?) When Leif Elggren writes that "I really do support a pretentious attitude in art, and I do believe it is of great importance,"[273] he is reminding us that being pretentious, going "outside," and being a creative person are all one and the same thing, while being "inside" means confining oneself to an ever narrowing prison.

---

[273] Leif Elggren, *Genealogy*, p. 120. Firework Edition, Stockholm, 2005.

Rated "L":
Limited Audiences Only

The marketing psychologist Robert Cialdini, in a jeremiad against the manipulators of false scarcity, helpfully notes "the idea of potential loss plays a large role in human decision making. In fact, people seem to be more motivated by the thought of losing something than by gaining something of equal value."[274] This is certainly confirmed by a number of instances both within the art world and without. In the world of championship sports, for example, audiences will become more critical of mistakes made by their favored team when they are defending a championship won the previous year: they will exhibit more angst over the possibility of "passing the torch" than they would have over an initial championship run that fell short. The same holds true for very real, bloody territorial conflicts: the Finnish Winter War of 1939-1940 saw the homeland defenders repelling an invading Soviet army three times the size of their own defense force. Lastly, recorded music is no exception to this principle. From Philadelphia to Stockholm, the retail shops that have survived in the MP3 era have been the ones stocking plenty of artifacts that were legitimately on the verge of extinction, or erroneously perceived to be on the verge of extinction.

If the selling prices of records on the discogs.com marketplace are your main source for determining who rules the musical roost, you'd be forgiven for thinking it's a very strange world we live in. Just navigate yourself to the website's 'most expensive records' list for the 10th of February, 2010, [275] where a disproportionate amount of chart-toppers come from the bleakest peripheries of the industrial music subculture. Through this list we can marvel at the $1,051 price tag accompanying a Les Joyaux De La Princesse box set, $831 commanded by a Genocide Organ 7" *single*, and $754 for another LP by the same group. Not to be outdone, the comparatively benign hip-hop artist Mistafide fetches over $4,000 for a 12"

---

[274] Robert B. Cialdini, *Influence: The Psychology of Persuasion*, p. 238. Harper Collins, New York, 2007.

[275] See http://blog.discogs.com/2010/02/top-100-music-w-highest-selling-price.html. Retrievd March 2, 2010.

single of "Equidity Funk," and Keefy Keef's own eponymous 12" rakes in nearly $1,200. Various house and disco obscurities also drift ashore on this list, with all the combined musical styles perhaps saying more about discogs.com's pronounced electronica bias than about music fandom as a whole. Despite the very wide chasms in aesthetics and ideology separating the items on this list, their voracious collectors (at least those I've met personally) have at least one thing in common, in that they see their collecting activities as fulfilling a valuable socio-historical role. Namely, they feel that they are ferrying these objects across the river Styx into a new era where these artifacts' distinct attitudes and messages will be better appreciated. Thus, the high costs paid for niche-market curios can be justified as being somewhat small in comparison to the glory reaped in the end- glory gained for helping the standard-bearers of one's own lifestyle to survive a perceived dark age of ignorance.

Upon closer inspection of the items on this list, though, one thing becomes readily apparent: the records swapping hands for 3 and 4-figure dollar sums are often much more than just 'records', *per se*- they can occasionally be painstakingly constructed, lavishly packaged display pieces not merely meant to be heard, but to enhance the music's metaphorical content by allowing the owner to participate in a bit of immersive role-playing. Take, for example, Les Joyaux De La Princesse's boxed set *Exposition Internationale - Arts Et Techniques - Paris 1937*. If you were to see it outside the context of one's own record collection, it would seem like a private, bittersweet collection of correspondence and hard-won memorabilia: sepia-tinted photographs, pamphlets sealed with stickers and fastened with gold braids, postcards, rubber-stamped envelopes and a replica photo album from the pivotal event around which the music (burned to comparatively humble CD-Recordables) is themed. As for that thematic content, The 1937 Paris Expo saw the pavilions of both the Soviet Union and Nazi Germany erected across from one another, in a dark foreboding of the coming clash of totalitarian powers: artistic invocations of such crucible moments in history, arriving before outbreaks of apocalyptic fury, are a hallmark of the 'neo-folk' or 'martial industrial' circles that LJDLP inhabit. It's precisely the reverence for the mythical periods in which these moments are situated, periods in which heroism trumped banal materialism and celebrity, that inform the creation (and deliberately limited availability) of packages like this one.

However, acts like LJDLP hardly have a monopoly on the 'album-as-artifact' approach. If we take a train away from the smog-choked industrial music district and its abattoir shrieks, alighting at the glittery and pulsating nightclub district, we find that the latter can certainly keep pace with the former where inventive album housings are concerned. The special edition of the Pet Shop Boys' recent album *Yes*, loosely inspired by Gerhard Richter's mid-60s color block paintings (*192 Farben*, etc.), is advertised like something you'd expect to find in an Ikea showroom. The design notes for the deluxe 11-vinyl set beckon to us with "smoked Perspex box with magnetic outer fastening," "Pantone colour printed outer sleeves, with full colour inner sleeves," and "Giclée print and insert featuring colour key and credits." Sexy! Elsewhere, a not totally dissimilar group of U.K. electro-pop heroes are already traveling the contemporary art museum circuit with a prime example of 'album as artifact': Peter Saville's notorious 'floppy disk' design for New Order's 12" single of *Blue Monday*, complete with its original conceptual blueprints, has a starring role in the museum catalog for *Sympathy For The Devil: Art And Rock And Roll Since 1967*, the Chicago Museum of Contemporary Art's 2007 survey of parallel developments in visual and audio art. Its alleged status as the 'highest-selling 12" single of all time' lends credence to the theory that novel packaging pays off when it engages sonic, visual, and haptic senses all in equal measure. Bernard Sumner's lobotomized vocal on the original song, and its cold *"one-two, one-two"* synth-bass chassis implied a world where digitalization would soon take command, a world where the song's flamboyant and festive disco influences were remorselessly coded into binary signals. The specialized, die-cut floppy disk record jacket (which featured the band's name and song title coded as colors rather than printed alpha-numerically) perfectly mirrored the strange allure of the song's impersonality and flat affect. Unsurprisingly, the record has now had its shelf life extended even further by being a prototype of 21st century "retro-futurism."

Specialized *objet d'art* packaging also strikes a deep chord with groups who see themselves as the misunderstood vanguard of modern aesthetic life. One of its effects is to reverse recorded music's nearly unchecked trend towards greater portability, making music once again something to be presented in one's own inner sanctum, where it is contemplated and revered only in the company of close confidants. Especially when genres like 'neo-folk' / *folk noir* are concerned (a genre with which the *discogs.com* list alumni Joyaux de la Princesse, Der Blutharsch and Death in June are allied), these objects should serve as crystallizations of a romantic idyll / ideal based on pre-industrial handicraft, or on notions of Heideggerian authenticity and its attendant hostility towards *art pour l'art*. They become the totems of a culture that, in this case, is like an early 21st century echo of the early 20th century's romanticist *Wandervogel* youth groups. Those groups' reclamation of individual sovereignty via the *Waldgang,* or hike to the forest, has merely been replaced with an internal journey or 'psychic quest' more akin to the kind outlined in Herman Hesse's novels. Still, one highly limited release by Der Blutharsch, *Fire Danger Season,* plays upon neo-folk fans' inclination toward both of these exploratory tendencies: the otherwise inessential music of the release comes in an embossed leather army satchel, accompanied by a leather CD wallet also embossed with oak leaves and iron cross- suitable for playing at field marches and *Waldgänge* alike. The "prohibited" nature of the release's martial symbolic content only adds to its desirability, as it does with much fetishistically packaged music.

The 'reactionary modernism' of neo-folk music hardly marches in lockstep with the more personalized philosophical imperatives of the sound arts scene, although here is another area where unique housing for recordings contributes to their total sensory impact. Here we occasionally find the packages acting as a challenge to the listener rather than as a seductive come-on (although the possibility of seduction by challenge is never out of the question, either.) This recalls pianist Cecil Taylor's famous admonition to listeners to make preparations before listening to his music – a fact that has raised the ire of peers like Branford Marsalis, who acidly remarks that he doesn't try his hand at fielding baseballs before watching a ball game. A selection of handmade releases from the fringes of 'Cassette Culture,' sound art, and psycho-ambient music have taken Taylor's prescription for listening one step further. That is to say, certain releases have required their owners to perform ritualized, preparatory actions before any kind of listening process can take place. The chaos-embracing sound / performance artist GX Jupiter-Larsen, who has his own history of producing such packages, also claims "...there's an impractical side [to hand-made releases]." He mentions just a few such instances of the impracticality aesthetic:

> A 1993 cassette release, entitled *Yasha* by MSBR (Molten
> Salt Breeder Reactor) aka Koji Tano, was packaged in a
> snapcase coated with layers of foam. Not easy to open at
> all. The artist and label that epitomizes the difficult fetish
> in tape the most would have to be AMK [Anthony M.
> King], and his label Banned Production. AMK loves
> packaging. Since the 80s, he has never wanted any two BP
> releases packaged alike. His White Hand *Prologue/Epilogue*
> cassette came in a tarpaper matchbox. His John Hudak
> tape *Slumbrous Breathing* was packaged in leaves. His Tac
> *Try My Hand* cassette, one of his favorites, was attached to
> a block of concrete. His Daniel Menche release, *Dark
> Velocity*, is a cassette in between metal sheets riveted to
> wood. It takes power tools to get it out. In fact, with many
> Banned Production releases, one has to practically destroy
> the package in order to access the contents. Even then,
> with almost all BP tapes, the cassette label is
> inconveniently glued over the holes. Meaning one has to
> cut or rip the label off the tape in order to actually play it.[276]

A little supplemental research shows that Jupitter-Larsen's inventory
is just a small sampling of what this underground network is capable of-
my friend Jessika, once an employee of the Anomalous Records store in
Seattle (r.i.p.), even claims to have encountered one grisly 'art edition'
cassette packaged inside the dead husk of a roadkill animal. In all
seriousness, though- what these examples of 'difficult' packaging suggest
is that elaborately hand crafted (or artfully damaged) packaging of
recordings can function as critiques of the instant gratification common to
the information age. A symbolic bit of risk or work is required, whether
aided by means of power tools or a strong stomach, in order to secure the
eventual reward of music. Considering that some of modern sound art's
influence comes from the enlightenment-through-endurance methodology
of 1970s body art and performance art, this attempt to kinetically involve

---

[276] GX Jupitter-Larsen, personal correspondence with the author, July 2009.

listeners makes more sense. While this usage of custom packaging seems far removed from the introspective contemplation accorded to the striking *objet d'art* packages of neo-folk and martial industrial music, they do have just a little bit of kinship: both cultures are, in their own way, dead set against a world in which art is no more than a 'mirror' commenting upon the present set of circumstances. Right down to the materials selected for a sound work's packaging, art should provide an opportunity for an exit from the house of mirrors.

However, it may be a little premature to assume that *any* artist favoring art editions over conventional packaging is providing us an altruistic service. In the estimation of Robert Cialdini, anyone can be a 'compliance practicioner' wielding artificial exclusivity and scarcity as powerful 'weapons of influence': this is especially true in romantic subcultures like neo-folk, where scarcity is often equated with uncontestable ideological purity and occult wisdom. Meanwhile, for the more heavily populated electronic dance music cultures, in which only micro-variations on the season's musical theme are permitted, producers still need a way of distinguishing their product from dozens of others, and so custom packaging is often no more than a gamble on securing a larger piece of the market share. Producers of hopelessly limited art editions, whatever their intentions, are not naïve: they know that they are working in a field that relies, moreso than most professions, on converting emotional response into financial benefit. They know that emotional responses to claims of scarcity and exclusivity will regularly take precedence over more complex cognitive processes, forcing panicked consumers to commit quickly. The more cynical music producers out there are surely also aware of the music speculator market, and speculators' propensity to invest in the kinds of items mentioned in this piece: just note the number of artfully-designed, limited vinyl albums that now come with bonus CD-Recordables or 'download cards' featuring the same material as the record, so that collectors won't have to downgrade their resale value by actually placing them on a turntable.

It's impossible to guess at the intentions of musicians who favor the more unorthodox packaging schemes, and to say whether their actions are done as a means of self-affirmation, as a gift to their fans, or as a boon to commodity fetishists. If the latter is the case, though, specially packaged releases are a considerably more expensive investment in the first place: speculators buying them for the purpose of resale stand to make a minimal profit, if any, because of this. If we look at the single most expensive record to sell outside of the discogs.com microverse (the autographed copy of John Lennon and Yoko Ono's *Double Fantasy*, presented to Mark David Chapman shortly before his slaying of Lennon) the factors of random / chance occurrence and historical circumstance affect market value more than any type of extravagant packaging on its own.

To be sure, many of the same artists who employ *objet d'art* packaging to deflect attention away from their mediocre music have taken this into account, too, and some play up the sinister or revolutionary nature of their own personae as a calculated P.R. strategy (when not outright fabricating these personae.) After all, the obsession with the musical 'other side' of inflammatory public icons, from Charles Manson to Louis Farrakhan, has elevated their cachet among record collectors. Therefore, emulation of criminal or anti-establishment archetypes seems like another good way to ensnare some extra listeners and speculation-minded buyers. The fusion of specialized packaging with the development of personality cults has, over time, proven an irresistible approach for the world of industrial 'noise' music- the result has been a glut of absolutely worthless, fatigue-inducing recordings, more offensive for their condescending marketing than for the re-heated "taboo" content. Our friends Genocide Organ are right there in the thick of the "they might be *real* insurgents!" trend, teasing us with a paucity of available background information and with records wrapped in Confederate battle flags (yes, this is the one that went for $831.)

In those cases where artistic focus is diverted towards crafting more potently glamorous and rare fetish items to house audio recordings, it doesn't seem too far-fetched to believe the quality of recorded sound will suffer. Cialdini remarks that, where such objects are concerned, "the joy is not in *experiencing* a scarce commodity but in *possessing* it [...] it is important that we do not confuse the two."[277] While he doesn't explicitly condemn people who favor the latter option, he does suggest that making scarcity the *sine qua non* of emotional or spiritual gratification is a mistake.

---

[277] Robert B. Cialdini, *Influence: The Psychology of Persuasion*, p. 267. Harper Collins, New York, 2007.

Still, the allure of the rare object has not abated and probably will not so long as the idealistic or aesthetic approaches of the releasing artists are themselves scarce. And so, the issuing of "limited editions" remains a staple of most music-related undergrounds: the limited edition is a concept that applies to the most mundane of packages as well as to the more lavish ones mentioned above.

Signed, Sealed, And Delivered

"Signed and numbered" editions are another attempt to "resacralize" items that collectors may not find so desirable otherwise. The return of the cassette tape as a 21st century recording medium, however contrived or sincere, suggests that many have sickened of the CD-Recordable and its kin, and will only go for these items if they come with a verifiable extra degree of personalization (or 'resale value' for the slightly more cynical.) This situation has only been spurred on by distrust of dubiously "rare" CD-Recordables whose exact number of circulating copies cannot be proven or traced, and so hand-written numberings ("#1 of 200") and corresponding signatures are an easy way to regain the trust of skeptical consumers.

When considering how personal signatures help to authenticate these products, it is worthwhile to consider the populous Asian nations that still rely on a variation of the personal seal as a method of authentication (e.g. China, Taiwan, Korea, Japan.) In Japan, the *inkan* or *hanko*, a rubber stamped circular seal that features the Chinese pictograms constituting the owner's surname, is considered a legally admissible form of "signing" official documents. The seals are professionally made and governmentally regulated (they must also be registered and certified in a municipal office to carry any real authoritative weight), with particular emphasis place on the circumference of the seal and the lack of extraneous / decorative elements apart from the 'name' pictograms. It is interesting that this method of verification is so widespread- clearly the attraction to these seals is "the promise that each successive impression will be the same."[278] Critic Hillel Schwartz finds it "peculiar, that our modern culture of the copy

---

[278] Hillel Schwartz, *The Culture Of The Copy*, p. 219. Zone Books, New York, 1996.

should opt instead for the authority of the signature, since no two signatures by the same person are exactly the same."[279] Indeed, the rubber stamp in the U.S. has been stigmatized as a device of thoughtless bureaucracy: consider the term "rubber stamping" as used in politico-speak, which refers to the official passing of controversial laws with seemingly no scrutiny from the people approving their passage.

This comparison of signing vs. stamping may seem like a meaningless aside, but it does have broader implications for our discussion of authenticity. The inhabitants of the Far East are often viewed by the Western "mainstream" as being, simultaneously, plagiaristic raiders and incorruptible preservers of national (read: original) character.[280] In the realm of record collecting, though, these two different modes of authentication both serve the same function and are both welcome: both methods *consummate* the listening experience and lend a sort of "official permission" to engage in that experience. This stamp of approval is actually more valuable when "unofficial" recordings are concerned, since the expanding world of self-released music is beginning to offer more opportunities for devious counterfeit items claiming to be issued by the more respected artists.

The myriad forms of signature and hand numbering, however, are not immune from the scheming of counterfeiters, either. Forging signatures on limited edition tapes or CD-Recordables can lead to at least some short-term profit before the counterfeiter is found out (admittedly, the ability to publicly register complaints on online marketplaces like discogs.com and Ebay makes the repeatability of certain scams more difficult.) As you can probably tell from the list of sentimentality-provoking objects noted above, the underground is not without its fanatics who "want to believe" and may be as content to own an unverified signature of their favorite artist as the "real thing". Placing the entirety of, say, neo-folk fans into this category would be overreaching and insulting, but it can't be denied that this music aims at intense emotional reactions- as do professional rip-off artists.

One thing should not go unnoted in this discussion of signatures, and

---

[279] Hillel Schwartz, *The Culture Of The Copy*, p. 219. Zone Books, New York, 1996.

[280] This is not solely a Western projection, but exists on an intra-Asian level as well, with the Chinese being just as critical of the Japanese tendency for emulation rather than origination (a sentiment that was at its peak during the Sino-Japanese war.)

that is their ability to function as aesthetic devices rather than as 'mere' methods of authentication. I have here a self-released CD-r recently issued by the sound artist John Duncan, in which a circular tin opens to reveal a bone-white disc whose only adornment is the artist's uniquely curving signature in black marker. When combined with the disc's bracingly intense and austere contents, it is easier to understand this signature as part of the *gestalt* of the presentation: the brutally linear signature, like the music itself, seems static and even supine until the listener / viewer achieves a certain level of non-distraction. In many creative forms, the signature is an obligatory element that must, nevertheless, not intrude upon the viewer's contemplation of the artwork's simulated space: just look at any painted landscape or classical piece of portraiture. However, with the mail art practice of "artistamps," the statement of *existence* dovetailed into a statement of *creative intent*, while also managing to have an ornamental quality. Self-released audio works, as well, have the potential to achieve this: the signatures adorning handmade media can rise above their status as bureaucratic "proof" and can subtly enhance audio information with visible means. Put simply, they can be a significant element to further the means of the artwork, rather than a sign of authorship or as an otherwise useless appendage. This practice of aestheticized signing has gone on long enough that many artists, such as the mail networker Ruud Jansen, have considered using the compact disc as a "canvas" upon which to paint (although Jansen's CDs contain no playable audio.)

Holy Blood, Holy Grail: Scarcity And Sadomasochism

In Marina de Van's 2002 film *Dans ma Peau* [In My Skin], the protagonist becomes fixated on exploratory self-mutilation after being wounded in a minor accident at a party. As the romantic relationship with her banal partner recedes, the frequency and intensity of her private, bloody rituals increase. Near the film's end, she approaches a pharmacist in an attempt to buy formaline for preserving a severed piece of skin- he refuses, but, without knowing the full extent of her fixation, gives her helpful off-the-cuff tips for tanning it. Her subsequent admiration of this object, which she holds up against her bare neck and smiles at as if it were a fine necklace presented to her by her now-insignificant lover, betrays no explicit suggestion that she will stop her rituals- even with this dramatic sacrifice of herself to herself. Some recording artists have also used a highly personal type of forensic evidence to give their fans the authenticity they crave (though this may not be their primary intention): the habit of artists signing or smearing recorded artifacts with their own bodily fluid is an unequivocal way of "putting themselves into the work," of literally liberating the artist's "inner workings" and of allowing the consumer's purchase to act as a sort of Communion rite rather than a mere exchange of cash for goods. Again, the focus is on re-sacralization of the mundane, although the relative extremity of this act raises a different set of questions regarding the real relationship of the collector to the artist.

The esoteric electronic group Coil was one of this elite of bloodletting authenticators. For most of their career, Coil built their listenership on a solid foundation of enforced secrecy and highly unpredictable music (from sweet, nocturnal madrigals to overloaded, frenzied exorcisms), but they also excelled in the design of *objet d'art* packages like those mentioned earlier: everything from hand-painted, LP-sized boxes to bottles of absinthe. If some of these items have gone missing from the discogs.com list, it is because these multiple editions now command prices too high for even the biggest spenders frequenting that busy marketplace.

It is perhaps Coil's reputation as a changeling group that made them so in demand on the "signed-and-numbered" market to begin with: following the group on a release-by-release basis was such a chaotic endeavor, aided only in later years by frequent text updates from the group, that owning signed copies of their work probably had a more reassuring effect on listeners than it would for collectors of a "normal" genre-based music group. That is to say, a recognizably "human" signature anchored the group in this world even during their most celestial flights of musical fancy, and made the collector feel that they had, in a way, domesticated this alien intelligence in human guise.

So, the existence of a Coil "trauma edition" (an LP packed in a plain white sleeve on which Coil founder John Balance had slathered his blood during an alleged episode of possession)[281] provided this kind of artist-listener bond to the *n*th degree. More than this, though, the edition implicated a certain segment of the Coil audience in a sadistic enterprise of demanding yet scarcer totem objects from their newly domesticated musical animals. The fact that the record cover was designed in a fit of demonic possession could also be seen as a pun on a second meaning of possession: the one that Cialdini earlier opposed to experience. Subsequently, it could be seen as a prime example of confusing the love of possession with the love of experience. The same album was released in a number of editions from digipak CD to "conventionally" autographed LP, so the owner of the "trauma edition" would have to construct a particularly strong rationale for why possessing Balance's sanguine fluid provided such a unique thrill: was it really because it contributed to the Coil listening experience, or was it because it provided the ultimate evidence of ownership and sadistic triumph over the tortured artist? Balance's decision to make this item available likened the collector to a spectator at the Roman arena, where "the old practice of religious blood sacrifice was given a new secular form"[282] and whose frequenters reveled in "rituals of extermination [...] sensations sufficiently sharp enough to cover momentarily the emptiness and meaninglessness of their parasitic existence."[283]

Other variations on the blood-drenched edition are scattered throughout the audio underground, each hoping to outdo the other in the exhibition of "authenticity through pain," and each managing to temporarily invert the master / slave relationship between artist and collector. The formerly "sadistic" artist, who forces the hapless audio addicts to sacrifice the fruit of their labor, becomes the exhausted and wounded victim of continual demands for further elucidation and / or stimulation. At the very best, the artist-as-victim may experience some therapeutic benefits from his or her recorded abreaction, but this is never guaranteed. The Texan doom metal band Senthil, whose former guitarist "Wretch" took his own life, have released a cassette (*Crypticorifislit*) that

---

[281] The title in question is *Musick To Play In The Dark Vol. 2* (Graal, 2000.) 26 copies of this edition are supposed to exist, lettered A-Z. Unlike other Coil items of a highly limited nature, no literature exists stating that this record comes with a certificate of provenance.

[282] Lewis Mumford, *The City In History,* p. 229. Harvest Books, San Diego / London / New York, 1989.

[283] *Ibid.*

was allegedly covered in the blood of all participating band members, as was the 2007 cassette *Septisemesis* (this one upgrades the morbidity with a bonus razor blade commemorating the ritual.) The former, featuring a vocal style that results from an alleged self-strangulation with chains, is so permeated by despair that some listeners claim the music finally turns itself inside out and enters into the realm of comical self-parody.

Such a dire release has a certain feeling of "one-upmanship" about it, daring other underground shock merchants to try something yet more transgressive without risking institutionalization, permanent disfiguration or some other unenviable fate: so, it can be argued that the releasing artists are holding the whip even after submitting themselves to an unnecessarily painful ordeal. Yet to their listeners, and not their direct competitors in this macabre game of "chicken", the secret thrill lies in the bloody process of the artists' martyrdom, and the more intense acts of suffering are enjoyed on their own merits, not so much for their place in the rankings of artistic self-flagellation. In other words, the willfully suffering artist remains an instrument of the sadistic voyeur's will regardless of how well these artists master their peers.

Suffering through the recording process, and consummating this process with one's own shed blood, is still a relatively unique act even within the darker corners of self-released audio, although it does fit into a larger history of voyeurs and martyrs: for example, a literary figure no less than Yukio Mishima confessed to having his first orgasm upon viewing a copy of Guido Remi's *St. Sebastian*.[284] If this attitude seems more prevalent now than ever, it is partly because the cultures where it takes root have retained the messianic message of religion while doing away with its ecstatic ritual content: for those who are romantically minded, vague creeds of technological progress and "casual" church services are anathema precisely because of their all-inclusiveness and their promise of omnipresence (of God, instantaneous telecommunications, etc.) Die-hard romantics recoil from any such embrace, since possessing the omnipresent would be essentially meaningless and leave no room for a hierarchy of "soul-edness". Collectors of artifacts from the neo-folk underground especially recognize this, but also, with their yearning for *"other lives and*

---

[284] See Camille Paglia, *Sexual Personae*, p. 246. Vintage Books, New York, 1991.

greater times[285] [of constant, mortal challenge]," reject the lack of thrills and challenges that come from a state of omnipresent security and convenience. William James noted that "the sovereign source of melancholy is repletion...need and struggle are what excite us"[286] while Schopenhauer remarked "after man had consigned all pain and torment to hell, there was nothing left for heaven but ennui,"[287] and so even the return of psychic terror via "trauma editions" and other such releases is a welcome release from a world of comfortable stasis.

Schopenhauer, in his ironclad pessimism, posits his own type of scarcity: that of people who find "pleasure in the beautiful, true delight in art."[288] He admits that the joys of experience will trump the joys of possession in only a select few, "because it demands rare talents, and even to those few it is granted only as a fleeting dream."[289] The desire for scarcity itself seems to be getting more and more popular: otherwise the demand for the more "extreme" fetish objects, be they blood-soaked cassette tapes or even CD-Recordables covered in patches of the artists' skin (anything is possible!), would not exist. A hope still seems to exist that full human potential will be reached when 'x' number of fabulous, rare artifacts have been attained, and at that point possession will become an "experience" of greatness- a transubstantiation from rare recorded artifacts into the body and mind of their original creators.

The problem with a fetishistic mindset is that it is predicated almost entirely on belief rather than knowledge, and with these conditions in place, manipulators and fakes of all kinds may thrive: again, what better type of consumer to rip off than those who "want to believe" they are receiving an authentic, signed, limited edition, and who will refuse to seek out any verification that might deny them the blissfulness of having captured such a rare bird? As in a consensual sado-masochistic

---

[285] This refers to a refrain of the Death in June song "Runes And Men," appearing on the 1987 NER LP *Brown Book*. Widely recognized as one of the pivotal records in the neo-folk genre, it set the nostalgic / melancholic tone for much of the subsequent music in this vein.

[286] William James quoted in *The Myth Of The Machine: The Pentagon Of Power* by Lewis Mumford, p. 343. Harcourt / Brace / Jovanovich, New York, 1970.

[287] Arthur Schopenhauer, *The World As Will And Idea*, p.198. Everyman, London, 1995.

[288] *Ibid.*, p. 200

[289] *Ibid.*

relationship, all the involved parties here get what they want…but for how long is this relationship sustainable? Moreover, when real traumas in the collectors' lives begin to eclipse simulation of such (via identification with others' private terrors), will this relationship still be meaningful?

Big Time Scarcity

It's easy to condemn those on the fringe of audio culture for the manufacture of artificial scarcity, and for using these methods of manufacture to artificially inflate popularity. We'd be wise to remember, though, that artificial scarcity is not the sole province of the underground. Major media conglomerates have used these same artificial conditions in order to promote their own pet projects: the major label "star system" is just the concept of scarcity applied to human personality rather than static objects (though, make no mistake, consumption of these objects' "unlimited editions" is the end goal here.) Part of the appeal of recording stars, as projected by their accompanying P.R. machines, is the utter uniqueness of their act- what's more, it is often implied in the sales pitched for these stars that consuming their uniqueness is tantamount to celebrating uniqueness *in general.* Recognizing uniqueness in its particular forms, be it Michael Jackson's moonwalking the vocal range of Yma Sumac or Luciano Pavarotti, leads to an implicit condition of "universal uniqueness," and so we as consumers are once again being sold the idea that our fandom is an "active" or "participatory" one that is helping the world to change for the better.

In some cases, we can concede that the scarce traits being promoted are, if not unique, then certainly rare enough to warrant some kind of attention. There will, in all likelihood, never again be another singing and dancing star who keeps a pet chimp named Bubbles, holds interviews from atop a tree on his private ranch, and can make the slightest of eccentricities (e.g. a single sequined glove) seem like transcendent icons of ingenuity. In other cases, though, this advertised singularity is demonstrably false, and pop consumers find themselves buying into the idea of *"brand-as-belief"* just as easily as the stylistic rebels of the deep underground. The adoption of artistic pseudonyms by those who would otherwise have "normal-sounding" names is just one component in a program of manufactured distinction, a distinction that often owes itself to the acumen of an editorial team, as in the recording studio process of "comping" [creating a composite out of multiple recorded "takes"].

Elsewhere, the legal framework for protecting this distinctiveness (e.g. the California Celebrities' Rights Act of 1985) also hints at its fragile nature; otherwise such protective measures would not need to be taken to enforce exclusive rights to the reproduction of a celebrity image. The "brand-as-belief" concept asks us to politely ignore these behind-the-scenes machinations, and also to synthesize possession and experience in unnatural ways. The corporate marketing of these musical automatons is not that different from the "brand-as-belief" ploys used to sell Coca-Cola, in which the brand is not only "the taste, the curvy bottle, and the logo" but also "the set of consistent emotional and visual connotations that the drink carries by merit of a century of advertisement...it is simply an experience."[290] As marketing becomes more and more "interactive," courtesy of online playgrounds related to the products in question, this illusion seems more and more like an objective reality, where "direct, broadband experience [...] will enable the company to circumvent the retailer and create a brand as experience far more compelling than that in the physical store."[291]

However, setting aside the debatable claim that there is a set of consistent emotional responses to Coca-Cola, the "experience" being suggested here is nothing more than a simulacrum or representation of experience: if consuming a bottle of Coke provides the user with a feeling of having bonded with hundreds of millions of Coke drinkers worldwide, it is a pure fantasy projection of the consumer- such an experience would be logistically impossible in reality. The sensory experience of tasting the high fructose corn syrup is real enough, as is the tactile sensation of clutching the bottle and watching the rays of the sun reflect off of its pallid green surface. So, I will concede that owning an object can be experiential, but the experience that is *supposed* to be conferred by that ownership - the experience that is promised by its marketers - is more often than not

---

[290] Philip Evans and Thomas S. Wurster, *Blown To Bits: How The New Economics Of Information Transforms Strategy,* p. 162. Harvard Business School, Boston, 2000.
[291] *Ibid.,* p. 164.

confused with representation. Wherever we turn, we can't escape the fact that "fetish" recordings rarely have the magical power to conjure even a hallucinatory state similar to the promised experience.

This is where certain elements of the sound arts culture, for all of their inscrutability in the eye of the typical music consumer, manage to escape this trap. Daniel Menche's *Dark Velocity* tape, mentioned above, may "represent" hard work with its stentorian package design, but it also literally *requires* hard work to be released from its metallic prison with power tools. The music is not merely "challenging" because of its saturation and relentlessness, but because it reverses the usual order of possession and experience suggested by orthodox sound recordings: instead of being promised a simulacrum of an experience after hearing a record, an experience *precedes* the act of listening and influences the way that the sounds will be interpreted. "Influence" is the key word here, since the way in which sounds are interpreted can be a powerful influence or catalyst of future experiences, be they conversations, altercations, dreams, etc. It seems healthier to approach them this way (e.g. as tools for *gradual* re-organization of the present lived environment) than to make them function as *instant* portals to a distant past, future, or "other life."

This brings us back to the cassette networks of the 1980s: for all their other shortcomings, they realized that the total experience of creating and consuming sound was to take precedence over a fetishistic valuation of a single part of this process (e.g., the collection, appraisal, and hierarchical ordering of scarce recorded artifacts.) Only in recent years, with retrospective (or "necrospective") distancing, has the focus on that single element become more important, along with the rise of the speculator market. By all accounts, Cassette Culture was as much about the joy of correspondence, chance meeting, collaboration at a distance and numerous other processes that were crystallized in the final product. When lavishly constructed packages were designed, or when intimate inclusions like signatures and hand-made artworks were included along with the "main course" of the audiotape, this was done not purely in a competitive spirit of "one-upmanship," but as an acknowledgement of the "art as gift" ethos described by Vittore Baroni. It was "a desire to astonish akin to the *potlatch* of the American Indians, a will to make game of the pretentiousness of official art and to operate in the opposite direction to the dominating market system, to recover a more playful and purely spiritual expressive dimension."[292] So, these self-releasing communities, based around the dual interpretations of art as being both *gift* and *game*, were defined by the "feeling of being 'apart together' in an exceptional situation, of sharing something important, of mutually withdrawing from the world and rejecting the usual norms" and thus "retain[ed]...magic beyond the duration of the individual game."[293] The *potlatch* ritual shared these characteristics with the networks of self-released music, but also shared another key characteristic that opposed them to scarcity worship: in both scenarios, gifts were given away to show the strength of the giver, i.e. that they could survive perfectly well without these objects. In the *potlatch*, gifts might be gleefully and ceremonially destroyed to prove this very point, while *objets d'art* delivered to some distant recipient in the tape network might not meet with a reply (although, ideally, failure to reciprocate could bring about a definite loss of personal honor.)

We will never know conclusively if John Balance, who departed in 2004, experienced magical rapture or ecstatic release in the act of spattering album covers with his own blood, as Marina de Van's character in *Dans ma Peau* clearly does. However, both this real-life act of mutilation and the fictional scenario show how individuals can, while engaged in very literal self-preservation, also attempt to grasp for something beyond themselves. Sacrificial offerings are the result of their actions, but the processes leading to the results were transformative, whether or not the proof of their trials became items of public interest. In these cases, an "unproductive expenditure" equals a reaffirmation of vital existence, a fact that lies at the core of most enduring artwork. Both the simple sacrificial act of recording and releasing music on one's own, as well as violent purging actions like the ones mentioned, can bring about a set of circumstances preferable to the prevailing experience of reality. It is important that this creative spark not die out: for, where art and music are concerned, all other forms of scarcity should be secondary to this "common" will to live.

---

[292] Vittore Baroni, "Art As Gift (It's A Net, Net, Net World)," Sentieri Interrotti / Bassano 2000: Crisi della rappresentazione e iconoclastia nelle arti. Derive Approdi, Rome, 1999.

[293] Johan Huizinga, *Homo Ludens: A Study Of The Play Element In Culture*, p. 12. Beacon Press, Boston, 1955.

We Have Never Been Extreme:
Promotion Through "Anti-Promotion"

The issue of being recognized for one's work is probably one of the greatest dilemmas faced by artistic "alternatives" to prevailing ideologies. Public acknowledgement, on one hand, is absolutely crucial for securing contacts that will provide support for further works, and for enabling connections with those like-minded individuals who make life worth living. On the other hand, being a recognizable public figure does not automatically confer an advanced comprehension of self or reality, or the transcendence of them. In the words of Dave Prescott, of Generator Sound Arts:

> Art remains an impossible mystery to so many, and yet possible for so many more. I was brought up with this "Beatlemania paradigm," and it has taken a long, long time to realize that one's amount of recognition simply isn't important. Recognition is not a function of art, but of hype.[294]

Although it may seem bizarre in a television-oriented culture that views massive fame (and total deprivation of privacy) as a kind of birthright, there are still many creative individuals who prefer the selective recognition provided by the small, dispersed audience that comprises the "underground" networks. Unfortunately, since this "underground" classifier is tossed out with the same casual disregard that is used for the delivery of once shocking swear words, we might benefit from a brief remedial lesson in what it means to whom.

The terms "underground" and "extreme" have been conflated in recent history, with both of these designators being broadened to fit a number of

---

[294] Quoted in "The Dave Prescott Interview" by Al Margolis. *Electronic Cottage* #3 (March 1990), p.35. Apollo Beach, Florida, 1990.

different contexts where art and/or entertainment is concerned. The former term has largely been used to give a positive gloss to the aesthetic qualities of invariance and one-dimensionality (in cases where those qualities weren't already seen as a good thing,) and has been successfully marketed towards audiences for whom, as the phrase goes, "too much is never enough." Meanwhile, "underground" has now become a term that could be applied to just about any slightly unpopular manifestation of culture, and some could argue that its potency has also been severely diluted as a result: once the designation for culture that was created in defiance of an established political order, trafficking in "underground" activities carried with it a greater-than-average risk of dispossession, incarceration, and whatever other forms of intimidation could be wielded against its purveyors and consumers. Now, since the ascendancy of "underground" as a marketing term, these myriad risk factors do not come into play nearly as often, although the suggestion by the marketers is that a *financial* risk is being taken, rather than a political risk. It is this sense of determined sacrifice on the "underground" artists' behalf that provides the necessary *frisson* or 'edge' for that particular work. In other words, the "underground" label provides consumers the sexy sense of participating in something that will *potentially* explode onto the world stage at any given moment, but for now is confined to the consumption habits of an avant-garde, elite target market.

When the critically panned 1990s rapper Vanilla Ice made a 2005 bid for career rejuvenation entitled *Platinum Underground*[295], we can safely guess which version of the "underground" he was attempting to court: the one seeing itself as having more eclectic consumer / lifestyle choices than the mainstream, and not the more activist "underground" associated with political dissent and disruptions of the prevalent ideological order. An embarrassing listen to the album pretty much proves this to be the case; like other records by mega-sellers who have suddenly fallen out of favor, it "ret-cons" the artist's previous mega-fame as being a false image of his/her persona meant to test the loyalty of the leaner, meaner, more committed underground core who are still "down" with the artist despite the dismissive howls of "wack" and "played-out" from the more fickle and

---

[295] The title alludes to the artist's ability to reach 'platinum seller' status (over 1 million albums certified as 'sold' by the Recording Industry Association Of America), while still retaining the authenticity that comes with rejection of mainstream attitudes.

disloyal mainstream. Once a recording is trumpeted as being "under [the] ground," the earth / soil metaphor also extends to that recording's existence as a reclamation of long-buried "roots," forgotten by either the artist or by the musical community in general.

Nowhere is the attainment of "underground" credentials more prized than in certain segments of the heavy metal music world. Because of the wide range of radical and non-centrist positions that comprise this music, there are definite activist strains of underground activity that put their agents at the mercy of the risk factors outlined above. Yet, in terms of the sheer volume of metal produced and consumed, the music does issue something of a challenge to the "underground = unpopular" equation. One of the most popular online portals into the heavy metal realm, the Encyclopedia Metallum, can boast of entries for nearly 75,000 bands (42,393 of which are still active) and an active member base of almost 236,000 (we can presume the number of casual browsers dwarfs this number).[296] An exclusive or elitist segment of society, that doesn't wish to be contaminated by outside forces, does not necessarily mean that movement is too highbrow or inaccessible to popular taste.

As an experiment in gauging metal's appeal to the masses, just pick any city on the face of the globe that can sustain an infrastructure for regularly presenting live concerts. Note the audience capacity of the venues that host metal events, and compare this with the same for, say, any strain of live jazz (if it is represented at all.) Except in very rare instances, you'll probably find metal shows are happening more often, and packing in anything from a few hundred to 80,000 souls into the halls and outdoor arenas that showcase them. Meanwhile, jazz performances are more infrequent and only reach an upper threshold of a few thousand spectators when in full 'festival' mode. On face value, the reasons for this aren't that difficult to discern (although some generalizations have to be made): the median age for metal consumers tends to be lower than that of jazz aficionados, and youth are generally more responsive to visceral, bombastic musical styles that make clear lyrical allusions to rebellion. It's also possible that the regular lauding of jazz as a "quintessentially

---

[296] Highly subject to change, of course. See http://www.metal-archives.com/stats.php. Retrieved August 16, 2010.

American art form" probably does it no favors among a young, scrappy, cynical audience already looking beyond the U.S. for inspiration. In the 'band stats' for the Encyclopedia Metallum, we can pick from, for example, 3,537 Brazilian bands alone: about a fourth of the U.S. grand total.[297]

By looking beyond the Anglo / American sphere of influence, though, we also start to come across those "undergrounds" which have not come to their subterranean status because of a voluntary act of exclusivity or elitism. The caustic subgenre of black metal, given its very well-publicized track record of causing blasphemous offense (e.g. the Norwegian band Gorgoroth's infamous Krakow concert in 2004),[298] and its implication in isolated incidents of criminal mayhem, has been outright banned in countries like Malaysia, meaning that the only underground that can feasibly exist is an activist one. In other words, merely associating with the 'scene' on any level is a political act, whether one likes it or not. On the European continent, though, things are a little less clear-cut: a consumer or 'lifestyle' underground certainly exists (and we'll get into the often perplexing vicissitudes of this underground in a moment,) yet it must differentiate itself from a co-existing activist underground built up largely from denizens of the neo-pagan, nationalist Right and its *Blut und Boden* ethics. The friction between the two undergrounds is evident, although there are occasional syntheses, and common working methods: which include among them a fondness for deliberately obscure releases.

Vampires Basking In The Sun: *Les Legiones Noires* And Other Collectible Monsters

> "*This is the kapitalist [sic] release for American fuckers... those who weren't able to get it in '95. This is the reason why I wanted no artwork. This is the last pressing and your ultimate chance to get it...but anyway, I think so few of you really deserve*

---

[297] See http://www.metal-archives.com/browseC.php. Retrieved on August 16, 2010.

[298] "'*On stage there was blood everywhere. About ten decapitated sheep heads and naked people, alive, on large crosses. Everyone was painted with 100 liters of sheep blood. Also there were Satanist symbols everywhere. One of the hanging female models fainted and an ambulance had to be called,*' TVP director Andrzej Jeziorek told VG.*" See http://www.aftenposten.no/english/local/article723414.ece. Retrieved on August 16, 2010.

> *it, as you're unable to reach my world of Night and Sorrow.*
> *We'll meet in Hell anyway... Destroy your life for Satan."*

-"Meyhna'ch", liner notes to Mütiilation's *Vampires of Black Imperial Blood* re-release

Whether you find the above statements to be hilarious, chilling, offensive, or pretentious, there's no denying that their writer has left his own indelible imprint on the larger world of unofficial audio. As a key figure in the deliberately obscure French black metal clique known as *Les Legiones Noires* [The Black Legions], Willy "Meyhna'ch" Roussel has built up a ravenous cult following with a bare minimum of pubilc relations apparatus. By issuing provocative statements like the one above, he has managed to drive a sharp wedge between the casual consumer and the long-term defender of the faith. Stranger still is that Roussel has accomplished this not by achieving mainstream exposure, but by wholeheartedly embracing the self-releasing aesthetic. With little more than a catalog consisting mostly of demo cassettes, some cryptic maledictions in sympathetic fanzines, and a single-digit number of concert performances, Roussel and the other self-styled "legions" in the French circle have captivated the imaginations of an audience starved for unmediated, (if overwhelmingly negative) communication, while draining the bank accounts of those collector fanatics willing to pay in the thousands of dollars for their hyper-limited recordings. Oren Ambarchi, the inventive Australian guitar and electronics operator, is rumored to own one of the largest black metal collections on his home continent, and thus provides as authoritative a voice as any on what gives the LLN their unique standing:

> My favourite BM releases are the ones that are super raw, minimal and ecstatic. There's also the allure when something is hard to get a hold of - the more difficult it is to find a release, the more I seem to want it, and it's always exciting when it's difficult to access info on an artist. That mysterious element is always a plus - not unlike the NZ Xpressway cassettes and early Japanese noise cassettes from the early '90s that I would buy from RRR. That's something I miss about the pre-Internet era - having to

really search for this stuff (& growing up in a place like Sydney, Australia didn't help matters.) My fave French Legions release would have to be Belketre's "Ambre Zuerki Vuordhrevarhtre" demo. The Belketre release is completely crazed and unlike anything, some of it reminds me of [My Bloody Valentine's] "Loveless" mixed with Mauthausen Orchestra and free jazz. Most of the other Black Legions releases are much more conventional, but this one really stands out - totally weird and devastating. The Moevot project must be mentioned as well of course. The idea that metal kids are listening to this stuff in their bedrooms is really incredible.[299]

Ambarchi's estimation of the bands listed above, though he doesn't apply it to the full pack of LLN artists, affirms how their appeal came about: not only through a uniquely twisted sonic approach, but also through a paradoxically successful brand of "anti-promotion." Certain communicative habits common to the individual units within the collective, such as bracketing the universalist concepts of "world" and "humanity" in mocking scare quotes, or titling compositions with the defiantly unpronounceable words of an invented language, helped to establish the mystique that the Legions still enjoy in the underground. This intoxicatingly weird clique was notable for recording hopelessly limited cassettes and vinyls with astonishingly (and often intentionally) poor sound quality, possibly meant to sound like what an alien civilization might find on an archeological dig once the Legions' much-prophesied "Black Holocaust" had consumed the planet. The near-total lack of self-promotion on their behalf has given them an elevated standing in an overcrowded metal scene, while countless bands that go through all the "right channels" of P.R. work remain ignored and without acclaim. This is not to say that the LLN units don't deserve a little bit of acknowledgement for creating a standout product: what Barry White or Isaac Hayes were to the satiny love ballad, these sinister anomalies are to the careening, psychopathic miasma of over-saturated shrieks and roars.

---

[299] Oren Ambarchi, Personal email correspondence with the author, August 18 2010.

The French circle's infamy is an even more impressive feat when you consider that many of the original LLN releases were advertised and sold as 'demo' cassettes, and remain classified as such on the authoritative Encyclopedia Metallum. Traditionally 'demo' cassettes have been transitional products suggesting the possibility of a more elaborate work-in-progress that will come about once better working conditions are in place. As such, demo tracks are recorded with the intent of securing the backing of a record label, radio airplay, live gigs or - ideally - all three. The works of the LLN tend to render the term 'demo' superfluous, though: there's little difference, in either recorded content or creative intent, between this grim circle's hand-dubbed demo cassettes (complete with photocopied, B+W foldout artwork) and its handful of releases on other formats. The line between unofficial and official release becomes blurred even more when considering that many of the aforementioned demo cassettes have been bootlegged into oblivion- a fate that was, in the past, usually reserved for mass-market LPs and CDs.

To further understand the enduring appeal of LLN's radical approach, it's important to consider their strategy of 'promotion-by-disappearance,' accomplished by tantalizing audiences with only hazy, low-resolution glimpses of the artists. The Black Legions' "public image" haunted like the smile of the Cheshire Cat- leaving an unsettling impression behind as the body responsible for it evaporated. Yet many saw the cultivation of this apparitional image, though it was so close to being nothing at all, as uncomfortably akin to the overground concept of 'hype.' the Finnish underground's zealous promoter Mikko Aspa reminds us:

> In the early days of [my] band, I highly disliked the posing of the traditional metal. Including black metal. You also have to remember the times of the mid-late 90s black metal, when suddenly people for the first time had access to the internet, and you could find a vast amount of band websites where each project had only created a logo, band photos and pretty much nothing else. [Their] music was still non-existing, but the "image" was already done.[300]

---

[300] http://diabolicalconquest.com/interviews/clandestine_blaze_interview_with_mikko.htm. Retrieved August 8, 2010.

Aspa (who will be dealt with in more detail soon), can be faulted for many things, but can't be faulted for doing what he has criticized above. The burly, crop-headed Lähti native has done everything in his power to aid the stereotypically "extreme" aesthetic, short of forming his own political action committee: he has participated in or fronted over a dozen projects dealing with doom metal, black metal, grindcore, power electronics, or some suffocating, malevolent hybrid of these different styles. He has delegated a thematic 'workload' to each project, so that each one will dig its fangs deeply enough into the meat of some modern taboo: 'Clandestine Blaze' mainly stomps on Judeo-Christian mores, 'Nicole 12' flirts with pedophilia, 'Creamface' catalogs other deviant sex practices, and so on. As could be expected for material of this nature, Aspa releases and distributes it himself through a multitude of personal imprints, on a combination of homemade tape / CD-Recordable releases, and professional LPs. Rather than maintaining a single clearinghouse for extremity, he again delegates a label each to one style: 'Freak Animal' Records represents electronically manipulated harsh noise, while 'Northern Heritage' ladles out huge helpings of raw black metal. This activity has carved out a position of authority for Aspa within these various undergrounds, but authority alone will not convince LLN spokesman 'Wlad' that he deserves to be chastised for disingenuous promotional methods...or for much of anything, really. To wit:

> No one can judge us because we don't belong to the "humanity." We are so far from it that they can't even understand what we are, they can just FEAR us because we are the face of their own death when they will return to the dust and emptiness they came from [...] even if we had problems with the police, nothing will stop us—nothing can stop us.[301]

One obvious retort to this would be: well, what about economic limitations? At this point, it seems as though 'Wlad' has truly persuaded

---

[301] 'Wlad' quoted in "Vlad Tepes: Awaiting The Forthcoming Black Holocaust. *Kill Yourself 'Zine*, Vol. 2 No. 4 (1995.), p. 15. Anus Company (place of publication unlisted.)

himself of his own immortality, as he believes he stands above "human" financial issues as well:

> Money is a human concept. As Black metal is in essence a Satanist's music, money shouldn't be earned with it. As I said before, Black metal will return to darkness, and it has nothing to do with human worms and money anymore. So Vlad Tepes will never make money with their music.[302]

As one intrepid interviewer points out after eliciting the above quote from 'Wlad,' his cult group Vlad Tepes was asking $10 for their then-new demo cassette *War Funeral March* (twice the usual mid-'90s asking price for an item of its type.) It's a question that gets brusquely pushed aside in the original interview, and one that is still not resolutely answered.

Although the members of the LLN (who are mostly now inoperative) are not technically classified as such, there is a subgenre of black metal known as "suicidal / depressive" BM, which seems like the logical endpoint for all these "anti-promotional" tendencies. Like the Skoptsy sect of imperial Russia, it's hard to imagine it lasting for more than a generation if it's successful in its aims,[303] which would seem to include the self-destruction of its entire listener base. This is particularly morbid when considering that, before "suicidal" became shorthand for a more drone-heavy, dysphoria-flavored style of playing aided by cavernous reverb effects, the black metal scene already had a history replete with dramatic suicides (the shotgun suicide of Mayhem singer Per Yngve Ohlin, a.k.a. "Dead," remains the watershed event in this regard.) Cultural critic Dominic Fox expertly frames the attraction to "suicidal" music, in which

> ...depressive thinking is simultaneously intensely lucid and intensely blinkered: ruthlessly and brilliantly reductive, it is able to demolish any consoling counter-argument by referring it immediately to the ground zero

---

[302] 'Wlad' quoted in "Vlad Tepes: Awaiting The Forthcoming Black Holocaust. *Kill Yourself 'Zine*, Vol. 2 No. 4 (1995.), p. 15. Anus Company (place of publication unlisted.)

[303] The Skoptsy sect practiced castration in the belief that it would return them to a 'pure' lust-free state antedating Original Sin. The reader can probably surmise why this was harmful to their further propagation.

of its own originary devastation. [Depressive thinking] is monotonous in the same way that Xasthur's music is monotonous, endlessly circling around the same motifs. The world it composes is one in which the light of the world has gone out, and every being formerly illuminated by that light now stands with every other in a common obscurity.[304]

As Fox suggests, every sonic characteristic of this music reinforces the brutally repetitive and time-devouring nature of depressive thought and / or suicidal ideation. Black metal recordings from the "suicidal" peripheries utilize a miasmic production style that makes it difficult to even place the era in which the recording was made. Alternating melancholic and enraged tremolo-picked guitar riffs create an impression of noxious clouds wrapping themselves around the listener. Screamed, howled, and growled vocals are submerged far lower in the mix than they would be for more conventional, ultra-compressed pop and rock tracks, and so identifying unique words and phrases is next to impossible (a task not made any easier now that the phenomenon has gone global, with lyrics being recited in a number of mother tongues.) Like its not totally dissimilar cousins in the realm of 'dark ambient' music[305], it relies on maintaining this enveloping atmosphere at the expense of highlighting the timbral distinctions between different sound sources. Whether intentional or no, the sonic effect is to conjure a pre-rational world not governed by humans and, consequently, by modern humans' privileging of specific meanings and messages over vague affect. The endlessly repeating and whirling guitar arpeggios, girded by pulsing mechanical 'blastbeats,' seem to dissolve time itself, or wrest the human organism from a world where time is numerically quantified- again, returning the listener to an age where time was only marked by the onset of desire and the satiation thereof. After all, the concept of clock-based time was, as Marshall McLuhan notes, given a great push by the medieval monasteries, a natural enemy for black metal if ever there was one.[306]

---

[304] Dominic Fox, *Cold World*, p. 48. Zero Books, Hants, United Kingdom, 2009.

[305] Unsurprisingly, a number of the projects under *Les Legiones Noires* banner either play exclusively dark ambient music, or a mixture of black metal and dark ambient.

[306] See Marshall McLuhan, *Understanding Media: The Extensions Of Man*, p. 135. Signet, New York, 1964.

It's easy to call the myriad flavors of black metal music ('raw', 'suicidal', etc.) the result of unfettered nihilism, yet doing so leads us to yet another one of the paradoxes in this culture. The nihilism espoused by these musicians, especially those in the "suicidal" camp, is closer to Christian asceticism than the original Nihilist intellectual movement of the 1860s, described elsewhere as "...a critical approach to virtually everything... uninterested in debating art or beauty, preferring the harsh reality of empirical knowledge to the feeble efforts of romanticism, sentimentality, or philosophy."[307] When Vlad Tepes expresses a desire to withdraw from constructive human activities until the coming of the "Black Holocaust" (if they were ever serious about this), it is not entirely different from the anomie of a devout Christian who silently, grimly bides his time until the Second Coming of Christ. The farthest fringe of metal may indeed be "uninterested in debating art and beauty," but they are steeped in romanticism (as evidenced by the adopted Gothic salutations of LLN and others), and not likely to use "classical" Nihilism's critical capacity as a weapon to develop new ways of living. Inviting listeners to "destroy their lives for Satan" may be a strange promotional strategy, but it is only a more exaggerated version of other extremely ascetic creeds-what's more, teasing consumers with a threatening intimation that "they don't know what they're getting into" has been a successful tactic of pop culture marketing for some time, luring happy thrill-seekers to purchase everything from carnival funhouse tickets to mouth-burning hot sauces "from hell."

When not dwelling on suicidal minutiae, black metal and its underground relations have a pronounced *homicidal* streak that reunites it with the world of politics. However, even the scene consensus on this penultimate misanthropy, and who is most deserving of it, is divided. When considering that the genuine extremity of these attitudes often disqualifies these artists from any type of "official" releasing and distibution network, this is something that bears a closer look.

---

[307] Mark Leier, *Bakunin: A Biography*, p. 203. Thomas Dunne Books, New York, 2006.

"We Hate Everyone Equally!" The Question Of "Egalitarian Misanthropy"

For all of Mikko Aspa's enthusiastic transgressions, he and his has fellow travelers in Finnish black metal have not yet achieved the local notoriety of another countryman - the 'deep ecologist' Pentti Linkola - known for his unequivocally harsh pronouncements on the human condition. Given the eminently quotable, pugilistic character of his texts, it would be surprising if at least a few in the underground of black metal, power electronics, etc. did not have a Linkola title proudly displayed in their libraries. Linkola's controversial 'calling card' statement on the population crisis will be familiar in many circles, but it is worth reprising here anyway:

> What to do when a ship carrying a hundred passengers has suddenly capsized, and only one lifeboat is available for ten people in the water? When the lifeboat is full, those who hate life will try to put more people onto it, thus drowning everyone. Those who love and respect life will instead grab an axe and sever the hands clinging to the gunwales."[308]

As shudder-worthy as Linkola's statement has been to optimistically minded humanists, it is difficult to classify him as a pure nihilist of the "small n" type described above (indeed, a sub-heading to one of his scorching essays is "there is no place for nihilism in this world.") The thesis of his more radical writings, stated repeatedly in a number of minor variations, is that "the greatest threat to life is more life," and even a cursory look at his writing shows his fanaticism to be motivated by a need to protect extant lives at the expense of prospective lives- a more committed misanthrope would simply encourage any and all life to "get out of the way". Having said that, reaching such a conclusion does require one to read beyond his essay entitled "Bulls Eye," an emphatic spitting upon the graves of the 9/11 attacks' victims. Likewise, his claim that "business [...] is severely disrupted when people battle with each other" (is the arms industry not a 'business?'), and his suggestion that wars

---

[308] Pentti Linkola, *Can Life Prevail?,* trans. Eetu Rautio, p. 135-136. Integral Tradition, UK, 2009.

should begin to more effectively target civilian populations of young women and children, as if they are not doing so already. Even with such misanthropic hurdles to overcome, though, Linkola soon returns to mourning the fact that "...among masses of billions, man loses his identity, while his life is deprived of value and meaningfulness."[309]

With his penchant for rapidly switching between vicious tirades and anomic laments, Linkola reminds of the heathen contingent of black metal bands, who largely take up "Pagan Right" positions and can be coaxed into admitting that some generalized love for organic life is behind their malice towards the human species. Linkola remains just one in a long parade of critically denounced "representatives of absolute evil" who, upon closer examination, is more wounded sentimentalist than brutal libertine. When historical accounts manage to rise above the most propagandistic levels of distortion and falsehood, they rarely - if ever - portray historical figures that have been able to live a public life while holding the public in total contempt.

This is not to say that some black metallers don't try their damndest to do so. Unlike major touring rock bands whose contempt of the public is reached partway through their careers, and comes about from being disillusioned with their audiences' inability to grasp their message, this deep dislike is stated from the very outset as part of these black metallers' campaigns. The Ukrainian duo Lucifugum is notable not only in this regard, but also for inadvertently shining light on another paradoxical tendency within the more misanthropic grottoes of "extreme" music: namely, the odd capitulation to political correctness that comes from "hating everyone equally" rather than focusing hatred on a particular ethnicity, social class etc. This is something seen with increasing regularity in the music subcultures that fetishize distortion and other electronically-aided excesses - "extreme" metal, power electronics, "scum" noise and so on - although it is largely absent from less sonically extreme forms that nonetheless are animated by extreme sentiments. 'Gangsta' hip hop, for example, deploys a varying set of rationales when called upon to explain its more misogynist or ethnocentric rhymes, but rarely falls back on the

---

[309] Pentti Linkola, *Can Life Prevail?*, trans. Eetu Rautio, p. 171. Integral Tradition, UK, 2009.

excuse of a generalized hatred for all humanity: if and when it does, it does so by invoking the "that's just the way things are" atmosphere of helplessness which the rhyming protagonists are caught up in, and stresses that they are only documenting this ambient condition of social mayhem rather than giving their stamp of approval to it.

Lucifugum, on the other hand, gleefully announce their commitment to a more 'homicidal' form of music, claiming *"we don't play...we attack by antihuman poisonous black metal!"* For good measure, the group also issues its recordings of asphyxiating, dissonant metal "poison" in editions of "999 nails" (rather than 999 "copies.") Of the Pagan Front, a rival metal network that irresponsibly binds paganism to National Socialist ideology, Lucifugum's Igor "Khlyst" Naumchuk says "any sheep which is able to bleat 'sieg heil'...can join this sheep fold. [...] In today's life-styled 'white' scene, demagogy continues to remain the main way of rinse of [sic] brains."[310] Naumchuk's former Ukrainian comrades in Nokturnal Mortum are members of the Pagan Front, a fact that has led to a cessation of communications between the two groups. Meanwhile, Mikko Aspa concurs with Naumchuk's statement by stating that "I'm not a socialist of any kind, and I don't think any black metal should be. Nationalists think that their country or people in it are somewhat special, but I tend to think most people are just meat. Useless flesh, often stupid and unimportant."[311]

However, one doesn't have to venture too far into the overgrown forest of black metal releases to find sectors where the ideal of "equally distributed" animosity is scorned, and where a clear hierarchy of hate exists. One hardly needs to look further than the band name of "Satanic skinheads" Der Stürmer (named after the anti-Semitic newspaper published in National Socialist Germany by Julius Streicher) to ascertain what their opinions on this subject might be. Just in case anyone is still uncertain, though, 'Hjarulv Henker' fires a Pagan Front-endorsed salvo back at those who take Naumchuk's side in this conflict:

---

[310] Igor Naumchuk quoted at http://www.propaganda666.com/666.htm. Retrieved August 8, 2010.

[311] Mikko Aspa quoted at http://www.chroniclesofchaos.com/Articles.aspx?id=1-335. Retrieved August 16, 2010.

> Whore-bands like Mayhem, Gorgoroth, Dimmu Borgir, Behemoth, etc., have nothing to do with black metal, they are simply "extreme rockers", harmless entertainers with an extreme outlook, a safe way for kids to feel "special" and shock their moms and their friends in the classroom and make the corporal [sic] labels richer. Many opportunists tried to jump on the NSBM [National Socialist Black metal] scene but when they faced the agents of ZOG ['Zionist Occupation Government'] in open battle, they saw that it was deadly serious and not something that they could have fun with- and disappeared or turned into the usual "we-hate-all-humans-equally" trend, because they know that no one is going to hurt them that way.[312]

Just a quick survey of both self-released and professional works shows that Christianity remains Public Enemy Number One for the scene; and that other major world faiths (e.g. Hinduism, Islam) receive only implicit scorn when black metal bands lambaste "religion" or "the masses." Oddly enough, Mikko Aspa adds to the confusion here, in spite of his comments above, by mocking bogus "egalitarian misanthropy". In this case, at least, he sees it a hastily erected defense by bands that are confronted with losing some of their fan base. This time around, Aspa seems to favor the 'particularist' model of confrontation, calling out the promoters of 'universalist' hatred as follows:

> What can be worse than the idea of totally non-political black metal? In that sense, we end up in a similar politically correct, safe 'Dungeons And Dragons' world. People feel it's ok to write lyrics of killing "people", burning "churches", raping "Christian cunts" or some other vague day dreams, but as soon as you insert a specific agenda (for example: kill niggers, burn synagogues, rape children) it turns out to be some horrible thing people feel a need to protest against. As an escapist entertainment, all

---

[312] http://www.thepaganfront.com/dersturmer/interviews/LEGEONES.html. Retrieved August 17, 2010.

the atrocities were accepted as a "kick ass"-thing, but the line is being drawn as soon as it is no longer "nice" and it represents true emotions of intolerance and focused hatred...which SHOULD be the key of black metal, instead of the pathetic "I hate all equally" hippie shit you hear today, in [constantly] increasing volume, when black metal moves further and further into possession of the common music consumers.[313]

Aspa claims that the aims of his personal black metal project, Clandestine Blaze, should not be interpreted as expressing National Socialist sentiments. Although, for those who may find that to be a relief, he also states that "these days I don't really care if this happens."[314] Aspa also has few qualms about hitching his wagon to more "out and proud" neo-fascists, by way of being represented by their labels. Conversely, he apparently doesn't mind acting as a proxy or middleman for admittedly racialist outfits, offering a good deal of their merchandise in his Northern Heritage distribution service. Northern Heritage customers can even, if so inclined, purchase an authentic triskelion flag (the emblem used in apartheid South Africa by the late Eugene Terre'Blanche's white separatist Afrikaner Weerstandsbeweging.)[315] To illustrate what the purchased flag will look like, Aspa usefully links browsers to the Anti Defamation League's gallery of "hate symbols"- suggesting that, if he does not outright endorse the message contained in the triskelion emblem, he is well aware of its ability to offend.

Aspa's puzzling vacillation between universal misanthropy and more 'preferential treatment' is not an isolated occurrence within the global and "unofficial" underground of black metal. Yet it is doubly strange for him when he associates with musicians that have always unrepentantly indulged in carefully targeted hatreds. Aspa's colorfully named Finnish colleague "Satanic Tyrant Werwolf" (with whom he shares a split LP), fronts the one-man outfit Satanic Warmaster and has never been

---

[313] http://diabolicalconquest.com/interviews/clandestine_blaze_interview_with_mikko.htm. Retrieved August 16, 2010.

[314] *Ibid.*

[315] See http://www.cfprod.com/nh/index4.php?nw=1&lst=zine#clothing. Retrieved August 16, 2010.

particularly ambivalent about his pet topics of literalist Satanism, National Socialism and self-mutilation as "meditation." S.T.W. has shown a mild bit of inconsistency on the topic of warfare (for a man who celebrates bloody strife in song after song, he still finds time to decry the "useless wars" of the "Jew.S.A.")[316], but otherwise, his belief template is firmly in place. Satanic Warmaster has toured with Der Stürmer[317] (whose lyric sheets are, bar none, some of the most incendiary in the underground) and German "Luciferian pagans" Absurd, whose personal history of murder and fascist agitation has been recounted at length elsewhere.[318] Werwolf's own lyrics, particularly from the diabolically lo-fi *Strength And Honor* LP, drip with venomous spite towards Christianity and Judaic tradition, as evidenced by some quatrains from "Der Schwarze Orden": "*In the forest of broken crosses / The Aryan wind has blown / The blazing torch of death's majesty / Reflected on the skull / Torching winds of war / The Semite creation in ashes / The remains blown away to the past / Of the new Hyperborean order.*" Other songs from the LP feature nearly identical wording and sentiments.

The point here is not to merely shame Aspa and company with a series of "guilt by association" revelations, but to show how these alliances reveal, in turn, an opportunistic gap between actions and official pronouncements. More specifically, the unapologetic connections to card-carrying anti-Semites cause Aspa's claim of blanket misanthropy to lose any 'reassuring' effect it was meant to have. And then, why should someone who forwards an aesthetic of terror, cruelty, and degradation *want* to reassure anyone? Is this, in the end, just about playing to both camps of 'universal intolerance' and 'focused hatred' (as well as to curious, casual music consumers who have no commitment to any sustained hatred) and hoping that no one will notice this duplicity? Or, put another way, is it a wholesale submission to the "kapitalist fuckers" so hated by Meyh'nach and company? If the answer to any of these questions is "yes,"

---

[316] See http://www.sunandmoonrecords.com/mirgilus/interviews/satanicwarmaster.html. Retrieved August 17 2010.

[317] 'Hjarulv Henker' salutes Satanic Warmaster as one of the few bands to have his "full support" because of a demonstrable fascist commitment : http://www.thepaganfront.com/dersturmer/interviews/LEGEONES.html. Retrieved on August 17, 2010.

[318] See Michael Moynihan & Didrik Søderlind, *Lords Of Chaos: The Bloody Rise Of The Satanic Metal Underground*, pp. 241-263. Feral House, Los Angeles, 1997.

this is just one more item in a laundry list of acts that bring the misanthropic extremist artist closer to the humanity he loathes. Some of the most misanthropic musicians engage in a very human altruism when they decide to share their works (if only on impossible-to-obtain, homemade cassettes), and not to merely opt for complete seclusion from public life. It is also a uniquely human act to believe one can "save" life on earth: this urge is not made any less human by suggesting that a massive depopulation, race war, or other negative means will produce the desired "salvation". Whatever ploy the misanthrope artist resorts to, it seems like the concept of a perfectly misanthropic artist - one who can simultaneously repel humanity with his or her aesthetic approach, and yet attract it with the promise of revealing humanity's ugliness to itself - becomes more and more of a conceit. Furthermore, the unyielding cynicism that informs the misanthropic attitude is less "underground" than any of us may like to believe.

Extreme And Mainstream: Separated At Birth?

The above discussion, though more concerned with larger social dilemmas than with the technicalities of unofficial releasing, is not irrelevant to our larger theme. If, for no other reason, because thousands of listeners become introduced to the unofficial culture via consumption of music's most extreme varities, and all the controversial attitudes that accompany them. Having touched upon these facts, though, it is unfair to single out the underground as the sole province of egregious offenses. One of the most taboo forms of "darkside p.r." - either legitimately harboring or pantomiming fascist sympathies - has hardly been confined to bands of home-taping miscreants still mourning the *Götterdammerung* of Hitler's Germany. Many in the upper echelons of rock stardom went beyond merely adopting crypto-fascist pantomimes for their bombastic live shows, and went on record expressing admiration for what they believed were the centerpieces of a fascist state (resolute will, willingness to 'wipe the slate clean' and so on.) It was the acclaimed David Bowie in his aristocratic 'Thin White Duke' incarnation, not some random bedroom-bound experimenter, whose ringing endorsements for a fascist Britain partially led to the formation of the 'Rock Against Racism' campaign in 1976.[319]

Looking over Bowie's *oeuvre* today, we can discern a pattern whereby he publicly portrays the same characters he acts out on stage, and later re-evaluates the attitudes of those characters when they have been discarded. As he put it to *Rolling Stone*'s Cameron Crowe, ""I have to carry through with my conviction that the artist is also the medium…the only way that I can be this abrasive as a person is to be this confoundedly arrogant and forthright with my point of view."[320] So, in other words, a refusal to publicly portray his fictions as such was a way to strengthen their impact on objective reality, and give audiences the most direct connection to whatever message they espoused. Bowie's fascistic remarks have, of course, also been dismissed as meaningless, coming as they did at a time of fleeting obsessions brought about by a near-lethal combination of sleep deprivation, malnutrition and cocaine binges. Bowie's period behavior was typical of the ever-tightening paranoia experienced by those who exchange nutrients and rest for intense stimulants: his televised warnings about 'black noise bombs,' to say nothing of his well-documented fear of witches and warlocks (likely inspired by a meeting with occult film magus Kenneth Anger,) all suggested a man whose ability to distinguish internalized phantasms from external reality occasionally faltered.[321]

Still, none of these caveats detract from the fact that Bowie, and a very select number of other mega-stars, could safely make "extreme" proclamations without being banished to the most far-flung peripheries of pop culture. Bowie's misinterpreted dalliance with theatrical fascism didn't prevent him from remaining in the spotlight for an almost unprecedented four decades of activity. Meanwhile, the swastika-laden fashions of his punk rock progeny have long since been shrugged off by music buffs as one minor detail of their "holding up a mirror to society"

---

[319] Eric Clapton's drunken 1976 rant against 'wogs' and 'coons,' in which he also offered support for anti-immigration minister Enoch Powell, provided the other major spark for the formation of Rock Against Racism.

[320] David Bowie quoted in "Ground Control to Davy Jones" by Cameron Crowe, *Rolling Stone*, Feb. 1976.

[321] Other interviews from Bowie's mid-'70s phase are, however, highly lucid in comparison with his fumbling appearances on *The Dick Cavett Show* and *Soul Train*, while still another famous interview (his 1975 satellite-linked conversation with Russell Harty) owes its awkwardness more to unfamiliarity with that interview format than to any apparent chemical excess.

campaign. Where these artists erred was in overestimating their audiences' ability to see certain public poses as sardonic commentary on extremism, rather than outright endorsement of it. When courting a millions-strong audience of pop music fans, efforts to police and mold all of their ideological inclinations will only be so successful, and artists should expect that quite a few will mistake the "mirror" as a very useful window onto a new world of wanton destruction without compunction.

There is something definitely paradoxical in the act of using inflammatory material to separate wheat from chaff, to galvanize a long-term fan base while showing poseurs and post-modern eclectics the door. The irony resides in the fact that material inspired by inverted religious mores, human disregard and social mayhem is *not* incommensurate with a degree of consumer popularity. In fact, recordings doused in socially irresponsible subject matter are, on average, considerably more popular than those which take more nuanced approaches and which rely on pure abstraction to offer a maximum number of 'readings' to a diverse body of listeners. And this, in itself, is just one embodiment of the increasing 'market share' held by purely titillating art. As Paul Virilio describes it in this comparison:

> It was noted in 1996 that the major Cézanne exhibition did not achieve the expected success (600,000 visitors) in spite of praiseworthy efforts of the organizers. Conversely, at the same time the public rushed to the Georges Pompidou Center to see the little exhibition 'Masculin / Feminin' with its rows of genital organs and pornographic graffiti, which were clearly more exciting than Cézanne's austere bathers.[322]

In the era of instantaneous communication that we inhabit, each kind of artistic approach is bound to find its target audience sooner rather than later, but the target audience for simplistic and sensationalist art remains larger than the audience seeking out art that, say, illustrates theoretical constructs. The broad masses tend to join together in "extreme" moments

---

[322] Paul Virilio, *The Information Bomb*, p. 47. Trans. Chris Turner. Verso, New York, 2000.

of negation, rejection or disgust (*a la* Beavis & Butthead's endless litany of things that "suck"), rather than in exploring 'affirmation-based' philosophies. Gustave Le Bon has written that "crowds are only cognizant of simple and extreme sentiments; the opinions, ideas, and beliefs suggested to them are accepted or rejected as a whole, and considered as absolute truths or as not less absolute errors...this is always the case with beliefs induced by a process of suggestion instead of engendered by reasoning."[323] The mass mind has, in effect, always been wired for obscene "extremes": if an extremist product manages *not* to sell, it may have more to do with the novel or experimental aspects of its aesthetic presentation (Le Bon also notes crowds' "unconscious horror of all novelty capable of changing the essential conditions of their existence")[324] than anything to do with the harshness of its message.

In fact, until it had left plenty of corpses in its wake (beginning with Mussolini's invasion of Ethiopia in 1935), the doctrine of classical fascism had attained a level of public acceptance that today seems unbelievable for such an extreme political orientation. One fine example of this comes from Hollywood, courtesy of a 1923 film -*The Eternal City* - where Benito Mussolini stars alongside Lionel Barrymore and is treated quite sympathetically. In 1928, the *Saturday Evening Post* was enraptured enough by Mussolini to allow him space for an 8-part autobiography to be serialized in the journal. *Il Duce* even returned to the silver screen in 1933 for a talkie, *Mussolini Speaks,* in which he "was portrayed as a heroic strongman and national savior [...] Columbia took out an ad in *Variety* proclaiming the film a hit in giant block letters because 'it appeals to all RED BLOODED AMERICANS and 'it might be the ANSWER TO AMERICA'S NEEDS.'"[325] Viewed in this light, David Bowie's instructive attempts at playing a fascist character seem downright penny-ante in comparison. The early Stateside popularity of classical fascism shows that Le Bon's skepticism of the thriving multitudes was not totally unjustified.

---

[323] Gustave LeBon, *The Crowd: A Study Of The Popular Mind,* p. 24. Dover Publications, Mineola NY, 2002.

[324] *Ibid.,* p. 26

[325] Jonah Goldberg, *Liberal Fascism: The Secret History Of The American Left, From Mussolini To The Politics Of Meaning,* p. 30. Doubleday, New York, 2007.

The rank and file of "extreme culture" can defend their program of total negation by saying that we see the truth about ourselves only in moments of penultimate intensity. People, especially in an age of complex technological mediation, seem to instinctively hunger after a purer and truer vision of themselves: if constant, violent engagement with self-inflicted or targeted suffering is the way to achieve this, then why not? Well, for starters, the truth does not always follow from punishing conditions: victims of institutional torture, when expected to disclose information to their captors, will tend to say anything they think their tormentors want to hear, rather than what they themselves perceive as being true in that situation. Constant engagement with extremism also means that this becomes the *normal* way of being, and thus no longer revelatory- if all one experiences is abjection, horror and sensory bombardment, then we can easily enough imagine a situation in which mundane or banal aspects of life provide the inspiration once provided by the former set of extremes. Moreover, if those banalities are just a falsehood concealing the perennially dark heart of mankind, then "the extreme" is also illusory, since it can't be measured against something that is non-existent.

And so, "anti-promotion" through the methods discussed earlier is a safety measure employed by underground artists to prevent losing the most unique aspects of their identity: as the self-releasing subculture expands, one can no longer claim uniqueness merely by involvement in it. And if the vaunted extremes of these artists were to become societal norms, their romanticized role as messengers of the new age would come to an abrupt end. Another likely result would be an awkward skin-shedding process, followed by the adoption of new tenets of extremity- although this would justifiably appear to the public like an insincere and desperate attempt at continued relevance. Even the implausible fantasies of global annihilation put forth by *Les Legiones Noires*, if they actually came to pass, would see their original standard-bearers become irrelevant.

Pentti Linkola has said that "perhaps mankind is more stupid than evil,"[326] and his assessment seems fair when applied to the more

---

[326] Pentti Linkola, *Can Life Prevail?*, trans. Eetu Rautio, p. 152. Integral Tradition, UK, 2009.

outrageous specimens on display here. The "extreme underground," when it manifests itself in forms that literally beg others to hate them, deserves a different response than that which it craves. That is to say, it deserves not to be hated, but to be pitied.

Release-a-holics Anonymous:
A Few Faces Of Output Addiction

Shakespeare and Byron possessed 80,000 words in all:
The future genius-poet shall in every minute
Possess 80,000,000 words, squared.

-Vladimir Mayakovsky

If you were to conduct a survey today of problems plaguing the most technically advanced nations on Earth, chances are that restlessness would not be one of them. While you'd almost certainly encounter large percentages of survey respondents who bemoan "the loss of traditional values", or who rail against everything from high-level corruption to lowered educational standards, the lack of meaningful reflective pauses in between materially productive activities would hardly register as a faint blip on the radar screen of pressing social dilemmas. Yet the mania for constant material progress, however unrealistic such a state may be, is clearly contributing to what William Dennett of Stanford University calls a "pandemic of fatigue," in which most citizens of industrialized nations spend each day with a cumulative sleep deficit of 25-30 hours.[327] Despite sleep's taking up (ideally) a third of human life, its conspicuous absence from the literature of the industrialized world underscores that world's counter-productive obsession with total vigilance and increased levels of output. This extends even to scientific literature, where author Paul Martin reminds us that "...the average amount of time devoted to sleep and sleep disorders in undergraduate teaching [is] five minutes, rising to a princely peak of 15 minutes in preclinical training. Your doctor is unlikely to be an expert on the subject."[328]

It should follow that the fine arts, often being in opposition to the motives of the hard sciences, would rush to fill this particular void: but a closer look shows that this isn't the case. Once there might have been great

---

[327] Paul Martin, *Counting Sheep*, p. 26. St. Martin's, New York, 2005.
[328] *Ibid.*, p. 6.

rifts between the puritanical workaholic and the lounging bohemian dandy, although nowadays it is harder to draw distinctions between workers and bohemians based on their relative level of activity. Even in those bohemian or "hipster" enclaves noted for their languor and stylized prevarication, a great deal of maintenance is required in order to project a nicely disaffected image, while good old post-industrial competitiveness oozes from the Facebook pages and micro-blog updates designed to these ends. A condition of proud relentlessness worms its way into the DIY realm of counter-cultural production as well, including the realm of self-released audio currently under investigation in this book. *I'll sleep when I'm dead* is a slogan that can be proclaimed with gusto by just about anyone who sees themselves as rising above the indecision and hesitancy of their peers, and an ethos of unflagging dedication certainly does have a little more sex appeal to it than meaningless slumming and carefully cultivated numbness. Still, 'unflagging dedication' in and of itself can often be seen as a virtue without the follow-up question "dedication to *what?*" ever being posed. And so, it would do us well to do at least a brief survey here of the explicit and implicit rationales for 'losing sleep over' one's art, via a program of unremitting self-releasing. Motivations run the gamut from the most base and predictable to the most intriguingly sublime, from ambitions towards personal betterment to campaigns aimed at bettering society.

As Frans de Waard stated earlier in his interview, many self-releasing artists may unleash a double-digit number of products in a year's time just to "keep their name out there." This admission says perhaps a little more about the audience for this material than it does for its creators: are their memories so poor, and does art make such a meager impression on them, that they need a weekly deluge of 'reminders' that their muses even exist? And could it also be the case that *they* are the ones addicted, that each new audio discovery provides a rush that needs to be quickly replicated? As a single-minded quest for the ultimate sound results in the diminishing returns typical of overconsumption, are the artists themselves just frantically striving to meet their insatiable supporters' demands? Such questions are likely to continue floating in the ether without being attached eventually to honest answers, since few people are likely to answer in the affirmative to any of them.

There is also, naturally, the cloud of desperation and anxiety that hang over many creators of currently challenging music: conditions brought on by the fact that, in an unpredictable, high-velocity cultural scene, just about any cultural product be snatched out of the hands of its creators and hammered into something less sincere or, worse still, totally contrary to what the original creators had intended. Csaba Toth describes this situation in relation to "noise", which

> ...operates in the shadow of recontainment by the very commodity structures it intends to challenge. But resistance to such commodification continues to occur, and what cultural critic Russel A. Potter says about hip-hop appears to be true also for Noise music: 'the recognition that everything is or will soon be commodified has ... served as a spur, an incitement to productivity.'[329] Let it be enough to mention here the hundreds of recordings by Merzbow, Francisco López, Muslimgauze, and, most recently, the endless stream of cassettes and CD-Rs released by Wolf Eyes.[330]

The fear of impending commodification is certainly one valid explanation for "output addiction," although it's doubtful that the artists cited by Toth need this as an incitement to productivity. Those who *do* have this as their sole justification for "mass-releasing" are, after all, tacitly admitting that they have already lost the game: they feel impotent in the face of a more powerful media machine, and all that remains is to crank out as much material as possible in a narrow time frame to prove that they have "gotten there first." Being seen as the originator of a sonic idea or entire aesthetic becomes more important than continuing to shape and develop it. Seen this way, Toth's essay is deeply critical of the capitalist culture industry, but the conditions of fear / anxiety and addiction to production, however interrelated they may really be, are clearly not exclusive to that economic system. For example, the State-owned

---

[329] Russell A. Potter, *Spectacular Vernaculars: Hip-Hop and the Politics of Postmodernism*, p. 8. State University of New York Press, Albany, 1995.

[330] Csaba Toth, "Noise Theory." *Noise And Capitalism*, p. 29. Arteleku, Madrid, 2009.

publishing industry in Honecker's East Germany awarded its authors on the basis of copies *produced* rather than on the basis of copies *sold,* the latter being the RIAA's principal means of determining artistic merit among American recording artists. Authors held in high esteem by the East German authorities would naturally be granted exorbitant print runs for their works, and from that we can easily deduce what the position of out-of-favor authors was. At any rate, wherever the propagation of an absolutist ideology is at stake, it seems there will be an excessive bombardment of look-alike and sound-alike cultural products.

However, our focus here is not on how and why 'systems' churn out excess amounts of product, but on how and why isolated individuals choose to do so. When mentioning unremitting self-releasing among these iconoclastic cells, one of the first names that comes to mind is the previously profiled Masami Akita, a.k.a. Merzbow.[331] As a musician who works in a field of qualitative excess (e.g. the aural qualities of volume and frequency), it seems only natural that Akita would connect this to a practice of quantitative excess. Akita has stated that his hyper-activity is an outgrowth of his interest in fetishism, which has in the past been inseparable from his art. Akita claimed earlier in his career "...it's more a question for sound texture itself [...] this is the prime mover of all our musical thoughts."[332] Though Akita's work as Merzbow would become heavily associated with the definition of fetishism as a type of paraphilia, his own statements on the subject hint that he is equally interested in the concept's pre-modern sense. Akita claims that "I'm deeply influenced by Japanese Buddhist philosophy, and verbally we can talk, say, of the belief that there's a living soul belonging to every object. This idea might be felt unconsciously in the music, but we have no conscious intentions as far as the Japanese cultural tradition is concerned."[333] Recognizing the "souledness" of incorporeal forms brings the concept of fetishism back to pagan roots, and in doing so, provides the artist with an acute sensitivity towards those materials that have been cast off by society at large: thus Akita's use of the name Merzbow, a reference to the *Merzbau* sculpture of

---

[331] Please refer to my previous book *Micro Bionic: Radical Electronic Music And Sound Art In The 21ˢᵗ Century* (Creation Books, 2009) for a more thorough profile of Merzbow.

[332] Masami Akita quoted in "Japan" by Fred Frith. *OP* issue "J" (March-April), Olympia WA., 1982.

[333] *Ibid.*

Dadaist Kurt Schwitters (and, by extension, Schwitters' habit of elevating the base materials 'excreted' by the urban landscape - discarded paper scraps, metals, etc. - to the status of revered art.) With such an attitude permeating Akita's work, it is no stretch to understand why he came to embrace the "lowly" home-dubbed and self-released cassette as a major vehicle for his works (both as an 'instrument' and a sound storage medium) throughout the 1980s.

Akita's hyper-releasing seems to be as much a 'cultural critique' as a means of keeping his name in steady circulation (and this releasing tendency now spans almost every conceivable audio format, 'unofficial' or no.) As such, it is tempting to look for more regional cultural influences on Akita's working method. Akita would not be the first among his countrymen to be cited as a quintessentially Japanese artist, and in fact many selections from his oeuvre go beyond passive disinterest in cultural tradition and betray a distinctly anti-nationalist cynicism[334], especially as regards Japan's more ecologically unsustainable pursuits (Akita is a committed vegan who casts a harsh eye upon Japan's ongoing separation from nature, and has also staged protests against the local infiltration of multinational food chains like KFC.) Like the Genet-obsessed Japanese counter-culture of the 1960s, Akita draws upon the work of a trans-national group of intellectual outcasts like Georges Bataille (and the latter-day musical emissaries of their philosophies, such as Whitehouse[335]) to provide the theoretical mortar for his house of *Merz*.

The caveat here is that, by the time Akita's operations began, such foreign influences were deeply ingrained in Japanese counter-culture, and said counter-culture's means of interpreting and projecting these influences gradually caused their foreign character to be subsumed by the local scene. Merzbow owes at least a small stylistic debt to this fusion of

---

[334] Merzbow's release *Music For True Romance Vol. I*, for instance, features endlessly looped snatches of what sounds like Japanese *gunka* or military music, arranged alongside blasting cacophony in a less-than-adulatory way. A title like "Injured Imperial Soldier's Marching Song," from the same release, also commits a breach of national optimism by merely *acknowledging* Japan's imperial period. There is scant precedent for this in any contemporary Japanese pop music.

[335] Incidentally, Whitehouse have followed a more conventional releasing schedule than Merzbow, but only as regards studio recordings: the entirety of Whitehouse's live career has been archived on cassette and now DVD-R.

avant-cultural imports and local atmosphere, with at least one precedent for Merzbow's work visible in Toshio Matsumoto's film *Funeral Parade Of Roses:* in an intense, brief 'film within the film', the amusingly named bohemian character 'Guevara' screens for his friends a film of himself battling the camera's zoom lens, while in the center of a whirlwind of ephemeral strobing images and radically noisy audio.

Akita is only one member of a fairly cohesive Japanese underground movement that adopted releasing habits similar to his (if not quite to the same degree of intensity.) Although it may be a little perverse, it's tempting to view the intensely prolific releasing of Japanese artists (along with their ability to supplement their audio output with equally prolific forays into other creative media) as an offshoot of the prevalent attitudes in the country's business sector. Japan's post-war economic productivity, particular in the boom period of the 70s and 80s, was largely driven by the general trading companies or *sougou shosha:* ambitious corporations offering a diverse array of products and services, whose only common feature was often the company logo. For example, the same Sony Corporation that provided recording media and playback equipment to the artists profiled herein also made gains in the insurance and securities fields. Japan's private railway companies are also prime examples of *sougou shosha,* which

> [...] epitomize the all-things-to-all-customers company, offering a broad array of services for people who live along the railway line. Typically, their businesses include a department store at the urban terminal as well as hotels, supermarkets, housing developments, driving schools, museums, restaurants, travel agents, athletic facilities, real estate agents, and amusement parks.[336]

We can even add professional baseball teams to the above list: the Hanshin Electric Railway Company is the occasionally proud sponsor of the long-suffering Hanshin Tigers baseball team. The ownership of private rail lines, in particular, is a genius stroke that sees masses of daily commuters

---

[336] Michael E. Porter, Hirotaka Takeuchi and Mariko Sakakibara, *Can Japan Compete?*, p.172. Perseus Pubishing, New York, 200

not only paying for tickets on these lines, but also purchasing their daily needs from the supermarkets strategically located outside of the ticket gates. Also highly significant is the role that the *sougou shosha* play as investment banks.

What's also interesting is that, within these organizations themselves, the phenomenon of 'wearing many hats' is not so common as the phenomenon of the highly specialized worker. On a 'molecular' level, the *sougou shosha* employ people whose roles may be very clearly defined and allow for little deviation, and whose interaction with other company departments is negligible. The actions of the so-called *noizu-kei* (the "noise circle" centering around first-wave Japanese noise acts like Merzbow, Hijokaidan and KK Null) invert this scenario by seizing for themselves the functional diversity that would likely only occur at the higher organizational levels within the *sougou shosha*. This is, of course, a salient feature of DIY artwork in general, which takes on a new life when placed in the context of corporatist Japan. Both Akita and other *noizu-kei* contemporaries like Nakahara Masaya (of Violent Onsen Geisha) also busy themselves with writing a healthy number of books, which tend to explain the subject matter outlining their noisy sonic abstractions in greater detail. Akita remains active in many different areas of the plastic arts, and - perhaps unsurprisingly - was a mail art enthusiast with strong links to the Italian scene formed around networkers like Nicola Frangione and Vittore Baroni. Although the assumption of numerous creative functions by a lone individual seems commonplace in the 21st century, the principle can still be radical within Japan's national boundaries (even though the technology to become an inter-disciplinary creator is as widely available, if not more so, than in other post-industrial nations.)

Whether it is associated with the *sougou shosha* or no, the Japan-wide standard of workmanship is so high that one popular insult is *ii kagen,* or "good degree": by doing something to a "good" degree rather than to the highest possible standard, one might as well just do an honestly shoddy job. The tendency towards perfectionism has spilled over into leisure time, and so our recurring concept of "serious play" finds one clear precedent within Japanese culture. Roland Barthes, in his book-length essay on the Japanese experience, was surprised at the intensity with which people played the popular *pachinko* game, and how the sense of any casual involvement was absent from the gameplay in *pachinko* parlors:

> The imperious meaning of the scene is that of a deliberate, absorbing labor; never an idle or casual or playful attitude, none of that theatrical unconcern of our Western players lounging in leisurely groups around a pinball machine and quite conscious of producing for the other patrons of the café the image of an expert and disillusioned god.[337]

Curiously, the overwhelming noise of the *pachinko* parlor - caused by the simultaneous movement of thousands of ball bearings through the machines - has an analog to the noise music of Merzbow, which cascades down upon the listener much like so many determined *pachinko* balls. In live performance, Akita also strikes a figure very similar to that of Barthes' *pachinko* players; his unfazed and non-emotive countenance like that of a surgeon, his wire-rimmed glasses reflecting the insistent screen glow of the laptop computers that process his torrential sound.

There is more than just a hint of agonistic character present when Akita says, in a 1999 issue of *Wire,* that he wants to release 1,000 albums in order to eclipse the total output of jazz titan Sun Ra (estimated by Akita to be about 250 albums.) Yet Akita's past activities suggest that this contest is not being fought for the purposes of increasing Merzbow's esteem and satiating his ego (or, indeed, for "beating" the late Sun Ra, since Akita is an avid fan of psychedelic, celestial music of all kinds and has no need to prove his musical form as superior.) Akita's mid-'90s book on the history of noise refers only once to Merzbow in the entire volume, hardly the product placement expected of a rank egotist. Meanwhile, beginning with the international compilation tapes assembled for his ZSF Produkt label, Akita has served as much as a "switchboard operator" for the underground as a stand-alone artist, setting up connections between a number of different points on the grid. His manic self-releasing, followed by equally manic releasing on official formats, is often seen as an effort to "crowd out" other artists in the scene, although this criticism would have more heft to it if he

---

[337] Roland Barthes, *Empire of Signs,* p. 28. Trans. Richard Howard. Hill & Wang, New York, 1982.

did not perform these ancillary tasks of "scene" promotion.

Akita is also cognizant of his own unpopularity within his native Japan, having been much better received in Europe and the U.S.- a pure egotist would develop all kinds of complex rationales for why this was the case, whereas Akita merely admits this fact and moves on from there. If we imagine popular acceptance to be a kind of sustenance, then Akita can be mischievously likened to an amoeba which "deprived of food, becomes for a time *more* active...its energy expenditure is an inverse function of energy input."[338] While this tendency is becoming increasingly associated with "noise", select representatives of other musical genres share this defiance of the "psychic energy" boost conferred by popularity.

"I Wish I Could Sing For You"

Going back briefly to those musicians who "mass release" in order to "keep their name out there," the case of R. Stevie Moore is a particularly interesting one. Unlike much of the post-industrial cassette underground, teeming as it was with proud confrontationists, Moore's wittily crafted form of pop music could have been played on commercial radio stations. To pick just one Moore release out of many, 1984's *What's The Point* fused then-current New Wave methods of syncopation and deliberate stiffness with a style of fun and accessible (though not bowdlerized) lyricizing that transcends that particular era. His music was not even, despite being tagged as such, appreciably "lo-fi": for home recordings, many of his works eschew the sonic murk that is often associated with that label, and all the instruments played are recognizable as being distinct components within the mix. Often, it is only the jarring up-front presence of the vocals, or the incongruous precision of his drum machines, that mark Moore's productions as being done without 'professional' recording studio. Even then, these technical details don't tarnish the singular, tragic-comic aura that makes Moore's songs decidedly more addictive than most 'pop' music. What Merzbow is to violent post-industrial rapture, R. Stevie Moore is to the American 'warped humor' ballad. Music writer Alfred Boland wrote in

---

[338] Gregory Bateson, *Steps To An Ecology Of Mind*, p. xxix. University Of Chicago Press, Chicago / London, 2000.

a 2000 edition of *Perfect Sound Forever* that "R. Stevie Moore was still around, and his cassette club was still operational, and had a whopping 247 items for sale."[339]

Though Moore's staggering eclecticism may have ultimately worked against him (in a music industry that had been genre-oriented since at least the days of disco), his critical acclaim remained at a fairly high level throughout his one-man recordings career. Providing one example to back up both of these claims, the *Trouser Press Record Guide* gushes over Moore's "wonderful world" while lamenting that "the American record industry's failure to recognize and promote the unique gift of this giant talent is a case of criminal neglect."[340] To see Moore merely as a thwarted dreamer would be inaccurate, though: the mutual embrace shared by Moore and the cassette underground suggested a magnetism to music that did not have to go hand-in-hand with public magnetism towards him. Among other things, Moore was a participant in Rod Summers' VEC Audio Exchange series (despite the curator's disdain for the series becoming more "music"-oriented.) His R. Stevie Moore Cassette Club (succeeded by a CD-R club, although Moore still offers titles on a choice of CD-R or cassette) still stands as a fine example of what can be done within the limitations of that format. Like many artists who recorded on self-released cassettes (Moore also released a sizable number of pro-duplicated LPs), he was famously reluctant to perform live gigs,[341] something frowned upon by record companies that thrive on offering "ancillary products" (i.e. taking a cut of merchandising and concert tickets sold.)

Much of Moore's innate knack for song craft is attributed to his genes: father Bob Moore's vocation - Nashville 'session bassist – may seem ignominious to those not identifying as music buffs, but Moore's membership in the "Nashville 'A' Team" saw him backing some of the

---

[339] Alfred Boland, "Do It Yourself 'Til You Bleed." Available online at http://www.furious.com/perfect/rsteviemoore.html. Retrieved March 10, 2011.

[340] *The Trouser Press Record Guide (4th Edition)*, p. 441. Ed. Ira Robbins. Collier Books, New York, 1991.

[341] Moore's trip to France for a promo tour, during his mid-'80s heyday, is a prominent exception: his *Everything You Wanted To Know About R. Stevie Moore But Were Afraid To Ask* 2LP compilation, on the French New Rose label, cemented an 'international cult hero' status for the artist.

most recognizable names among casual music fans: Elvis Presley, Roy Orbison, Bob Dylan and Jerry Lee Lewis, among many others. If this was not enough to boast of, *Life* magazine crowned Moore Sr. as the #1 country bassist of all time in 1994. The younger Moore's sibling Linda starred in the 'all-girl' country pop band Calamity Jane (and, if her musical career was not as storied as her father's, she did take home both the beauty pageant titles of Miss Tennessee and top 10 Miss America contender.) Of course, Moore Sr. certainly did not discourage young Stevie's forays into music, since he provided his son an opportunity to record a duet with future Country Music Hall of Fame inductee Jim Reeves at age 7: the results of this pairing were, on one hand, a great boost in Moore's passion for recording, but also an association with a local "musical lineage" that he would have to work hard at separating himself from. This latter fact would also mean that the huge discography Moore later amassed was, from time to time, viewed as a pure product of overcompensation. Critic Irwin Chusid offers one speculation as to the impact of growing up within the 'musical family':

> If Nashville is an uncertified, non-degree-granting university of higher musical knowledge, and Bob Moore could be considered one of the more distinguished professors, then R. Stevie Moore had all the benefits of that education – then said 'fuck it' and dropped out. [342]

By way of illustration, Chusid points to what he calls Moore's "Angloholic" style, or the attempt to form a "Nashville-London" linkup with a vocabulary of sleek electronic FX and crisp enunciations replacing the expected twangs and "high lonesome" atmosphere of the American South's music studio capital. In truth, Moore's oeuvre does contain some un-subtle affirmations of what Chusid suggests, especially in some of the goofy skits that pad his cassette releases (most of these feature Moore interviewing himself or altering his voice in order to play different characters.) The skit "Mr. Nashville" features an interview between Moore and a frustrated Nashvillean expressing his frustration at being typecast as a country musician (the latter has his voice comically pitch-shifted downwards to the point where he is almost incomprehensible.) Moore

---

[342] Irwin Chusid, "R. Stevie Moore". *Op* issue "M." Oympia, WA, 1982.

seems to have had an innate drive to become a musical omnivore (his official website claims his goal is to "preach the gospel of stylistic variety"), and he answers the stock interview question about his favorite music with "...man, I've been a slave to 'all' music since 1955. A better question would be: 'tell us the music you hate.' (Don't ask.)"[343] His ecumenical approach to music, influenced somewhat by being an attentive radio listener in the age before stations limited themselves to a single musical genre, saw him drifting steadily towards the margins of music:

> I was more interested in absorbing the sounds of the past, obscurities that didn't really mean much to any scene. Heck, I wasn't recording on my own back in 1973 to start a trend or a goddamn movement. I guess, like Dadaists, I was reacting to what was around me and putting myself forth into the world.[344]

As Moore's output steadily built, though, album and track titles began to betray - if only temporarily - a hint of compulsion behind his activities rather than just a pure joy of creating. Whether it was a compulsion to shed the stereotypical "Nashville musician" identity, a compulsion to meet or exceed family standards of craftsmanship, or some unstated combination of other anxieties, Moore's work occasionally gave off the whiff of being a Sisyphan battle with no end. An album entitled *Unpopular Singer* (now a series of similarly titled albums), included a track entitled "Why Do You Hate Me So Much?" This provided some evidence of Moore's frustrations, as did the liner notes to the *Contact Risk* sampler of work. "If you don't like this, I quit," the liner notes threatened, hinting that Moore's enterprise was becoming more of a burden of proving himself to himself, and less of an exercise in serious playfulness. A wholesome kind of self-deprecation was always at work in Moore's quasi-hits (e.g. his "I Wish I Could Sing For You," containing couplets such as *Listen to Sinatra and see/ God didn't give that to me/ I escaped the draft by my ear / I told them I couldn't hear.*) It is difficult to tell whether any of Moore's regular self-deprecations are sincere "cries for help" (especially when he lists his

---

[343] Quoted at http://www.furious.com/perfect/rsteviemoore.html. Retrieved March 10, 2011.
[344] *Ibid.*

"outside occupations" in one interview as being "poverty" and "zero earning power")[345] or plain eulogies not intended to elicit any transformative social reaction.

That Moore could be so self-deprecating while also being so breathtakingly productive is noteworthy, since the question of "prolific artist as egotist" is so central to this investigation. Like Masami Akita, R. Stevie Moore is another "amoeba" whose output steadily increases despite a deficit of "psychic energy," which would ideally come from a positive reinforcement that compensates for the energy expenditure. One can, of course, "fake it", maintaining a public image of humility while privately seething with jealousy of others' apparent success. Yet nearly everyone, it would seem, submits to an immutable urge to excel and to succeed at their craft: when Moore makes the battle for success the dramatic theme of his songs, it matters little whether Moore is singing "in character" or not, since the adventures of this "lovable loser" archetype can be understood and followed regardless of its closeness to actuality. Indeed, Moore's obstinacy in the face of the music industry's ignorance of him is just a pop music update of mythological struggles in which the gods bravely resist even with the complete foreknowledge that Asgard will crumble and fall at the end of time. The pleasure, then, is in the act of struggle itself, something that comes through clearly in the way Moore's hundreds of songs reconcile defeatist attitudes with exuberant melodies and rhythms.

Not everyone, though, has followed Moore's example as a prolific artist who also goes to great pains to deny his greatness. It seems unlikely that the act of "mass releasing" would not be used, on at least some occasions, as a brazen public image booster. Having detoured to Nashville, we return once again to Japan to examine one personality that fully embodies that tendency.

Don't Talk To Strangers: Kenji Siratori's Prolific Parasitism

In the latter half of the "noughties," another Japanese player emerged

---

[345] Available at http://www.babysue.com/rsteviemoore.html. Retrieved April 11, 2011.

who raised new questions about the necessity and legitimacy of "releasing addiction." Hailing not from the culture industry epicenter of Tokyo, like Masami Akita, but from the northern island of Hokkaido, the elusive cyber-poet and musician Kenji Siratori has conducted the vast majority of his creative enterprise with self-released media (particularly CD-Recordables and net-releases, as well as an e-book or two.) Despite a titanic output, little biographical information on Siratori has been disclosed- great efforts have been made by him to appear somehow other-than-human, or perhaps overtaken and "possessed" by his work, to the point where the man called Kenji Siratori is merely the current host for a parasitic "word virus" that is living only for its own propagation. One point of speculation surrounding the unlimited nature of Siratori's activity is that it is a work of science fiction carried out in real time: the conflict with, and eventual submission to the viral entity gives Siratori's recorded vocalizations their vertiginous quality and gives his writing its unedited, violent flow. Unlike *R.U.R.*, Karel Čapek's classic sci-fi play of robot takeover, Siratori's story does not end with the parasitic techno-entity 'discovering' human qualities like love, but continues to interminably accelerate into a void of raw data. Siratori's work, like much tech-oriented art to have appeared since the 1990s, borrows many of its code words and images from the neo-Gnosticism of that era, which saw technological advancement and occult wisdom as proceeding synchronously.

To some, Siratori is either the digital-age avatar of Antonin Artaud, or the harbinger of an age where communication will be vacuumed of emotive content and come to more closely resemble the simple "command line interface" of computer text terminals (or, maybe both.) However, whereas command line interfaces have traditionally favored communication using the imperative form of verbs, Siratori's writings are strange modular assemblages of noun phrases with little indication of what action may be taking place when and where. These random bursts of vulgarity, religious terminology and technical jargon zip past the listener / reader with a furious speed and with the impersonality of texts sent by telegram. Trying to figure out *why* Siratori is motivated to do this emboldens the reader / listener, if only briefly, to fight on and see if the individual atoms of madness eventually coalesce into some revelatory final statement. So, at the least, Siratori's campaign of mass releasing cannot be charged with dullness. However, when seeing Siratori self-advertise as a *"brilliant superhip writer of great intellectual hypermodern fiction,"* it becomes irresistible to pick up this gauntlet he has thrown down and slap him in the face with it. A little modesty might have saved him from a critique that sees his work as an unfortunate excrescence of the free-for-all digital media age, but modesty is as alien a concept to Siratori as his writing is to the vast majority of readers.

Despite the insane velocity at which his writing and recording career has progressed, Siratori still advertises himself as a cyberpunk author: his 2002 novel *Blood Electric,* which is rarely brought up for consideration without its being "acclaimed by David Bowie"[346] as a selling point, is certainly one of the more curious entries in this literary genre. While the post-modern[347] novelty of the book merits it at least a passing mention in the history of 'experimental' fiction (it's written partly in HTML markup language, and partly in a maddening, nonsensical English translated by machine), it utterly lacks the depth of historical and anthropological knowledge, the skewed humor, and the uncanny serendipitous power of the Burroughsian style that it claims to be inheriting. If nothing else, Siratori's writing seems to display that the cut-up method, although it relies heavily on chance operation, still 'works' better in some hands than in others (much in the same way that different readings of the same *I-Ching* hexagram could produce a host of effects from disastrous to triumphant.) The riotous 'Interzone' of Burroughs' novels (*Naked Lunch, Cities Of The Red Night, etc.*) still seems very much with us, populated as it is by characters whose archetypal qualities manage to remain relevant despite their being dressed in the swashbuckling, pistol-packing finery of old-fashioned boys' adventure stories. The tortured "futurist" neo-logisms of Siratori's noun-dominated prose, acting as stand-ins for characters, already feel like relics from the brief, giddy interregnum between the Cold War and the Global War On Terror- in which anything prefixed with 'cyber' was enthusiastically and uncritically received.

To experience Siratori's writing, then, is to witness an autoerotic

---

[346] No verifiable source for the Bowie endorsement can be found, although it regularly appears in Siratori's promotional literature.

[347] "post-coherence" cyberpunk is actually a more appropriate tag for Siratori's writing than "post-modern." The phrase is coined by reviewer Matthew Flaming, retrieved from http://www.wordriot.org/template.php?ID=414 on April 14, 2010.

asphyxiation being drawn out, through the aid of video editing technology, to some interminable length. However, like a significant number of other artists operating in the 21st century, Kenji doesn't limit himself to a single expressive medium: he is also a recording artist with a triple-digit number of releases already on the market since 2006. Beginning in that year, Siratori began a campaign of e-mailing practically every music producer within the post-industrial underground, with a future collaboration as the ultimate goal. One of these missives was directed at me personally, and my music was described within as something that can

> ...turn on ill-treatment to the paradise apparatus of the human body pill cruel emulator that compressed the brain universe of the hybrid corpse mechanism gene-dub of a chemical anthropoid acidHUMANIX infectious disease of the soul/gram made of retro-ADAM.

While it would be flattering if someone had really thought my humble work capable of such apocalyptic effects, the 'catch' here is that exact facsimiles of the above review (or very slightly modified variations thereof) were often sent out with only the recipient's name changed from one mailing to the next. When not exact duplicates, Kenji's breathless reviews still remain very much interchangeable- those that have appeared in public forums, rather than just functioning as personal e-mails meant to temporarily ensnare other artists in Siratori's cyber-obsessive void, bristle with much of the same verbiage on display above. Countless references are made to phenomena like the "cruel emulator," "the human body pill", "fuckNAMload," "spiral world" and so on *ad nauseum*. Meanwhile, the visual works adorning his album and book covers are, like his recycled catchphrases, permutations on a theme of biomechanical dystopia occasionally populated by soiled, decaying, wan humanoid figures or by predatory insectoid creatures. The oxidized metallic environments of his photo-realistic artwork are compellingly bleak, but the generalized sense of doom they evoke is already a step closer to banality than the riotous, polyphonic collages of the *noizu-kei*.

Siratori's over-zealous proliferation of work has impressed a good number of people with 'alternative' or 'underground' credentials, but, in this author's opinion, the bumper crop of Siratori releases never matches the urgency, iconoclasm, and occasional otherworldliness provided by the previous generation of Japanese home-tapers. It's possible that his supporters, respecting this previous generation, see Siratori as an extension of it. More generously, he might be seen as a new standard-bearer of a simultaneously ecstatic and tormented Japanese artistic tradition formerly advanced by agents like Yukio Mishima and Tatsumi Hijikata. While Siratori's work does evince some similarities in attitude with those artists (the standard Siratori press kit is likely to mention Artaud along with the alleged David Bowie quote), the "ultrahip cyberpunk" no longer lives in a world where, according to Japanologist William Klein, "[Japanese artists] know every picture published or filmed, and these they translate into their own particular genius."[348] This was a fact that held true for many of the post-WWII avant-gardes up until the age of digital mass communications, even though it seems hard to believe at present: access to a complete canon of works was not impossible in a time when fewer facilities for arts production existed.

Siratori is, on the other hand, a product of the "pro-sumer" age, and would probably not have survived the scrutiny that came along with being a radical artist in a time when each new 'radical' artwork - be it sound recording, film, or performance action - was met with a 'make-or-break' chorus of critiques from a body of respected peers. With artists like Siratori, we can see, in broad daylight, the trade-off that was made during the transition from the 'old' mid-20th century avant-garde to that of the 21st century: that older avant-garde was indeed closely 'guarded' since it was not seen as being capable of an abundant output, while the output of 21st century experimentalists expands too quickly to elicit a single critical consensus acknowledged as authoritative. In most cases, that is a good thing, and there is no point in turning back now on this book's proposal that a parallel art world outside of "official" recognition is still necessary. Yet newer artists like Siratori find themselves in an interesting situation: the digital proliferation of new audio works also coincides with a digital resurrection of never-before-experienced artifacts and "lost treasures" from the former avant-garde; with an impassioned rescue mission attempting to load all these recorded works onto the Ark ahead of a Flood of magnetic

---

[348] William Klein quoted in Stephen Barber, *Hijikata: Revolt Of The Body*, p. 50. Solar Books, London, 2010.

media decay (and other disasters.) Writers such as Stephen Barber remind us that "for every vital image that reaches the eye in the contemporary world, an infinity of others have evanesced or been expunged,"[349] tacitly endorsing the ongoing project to port the 20th century's gleaming obscurities onto DVD and onto online servers. In an age where the invisible canon of yesteryear has been rehabilitated for all to experience anew, does Siratori's mild technological tweaking of time-tested 'avant' attitudes have any great relevance? He perhaps realizes the challenge he is up against, and his solution has been to carry on the late 20th century avant-garde's obsession with transgression: not by merely adding to the lexicon of erotic horror or techno-primitivism, but by engaging in different kind of creative criminality: identity theft.

Indeed, where things really get interesting, is when Siratori's transgressions against networked art go beyond the realm of aesthetic sensibility and into the realm of outright fraudulence and misrepresentation. If the allegations against him are true, a number of artists working within the esoteric / post-industrial music realm (Content Nullity, Contagious Orgasm, Bonemachine, Andrew Liles, Roto Visage, Nordvargr, etc.) have had "collaborations" released with Siratori that credit the aforementioned artists as participants but, in reality, feature no actual musical contributions from them. The 'dark ambient' producer Henrik "Nordvargr" Bjorkk, for example, first learned about his being 'bootlegged' by Siratori when a fan innocently asked about a collaborative release that Bjorkk was unaware of (I was like... "*what* release?" Then I emailed [Siratori]...guess what...no response."[350]) While this would have been reason enough to sound the alarm, the one legitimate collaboration involving the two parties was also suspected by Bjorkk of foul play: "I am actually not even sure if the spoken word samples he sent me actually was him talking - the Japanese stuff, sure, but there are some parts in English that do not sound like his voice at all... but he took credit for it all. Maybe some other artist he lied to and then violated?"[351] Bjorkk's negative opinion of his collaborator is riveted into place with the following:

---

[349] Stephen Barber, *Hijikata: Revolt Of The Body*, p. 69. Solar Books, London, 2010

[350] Henrik 'Nordvargr' Bjorkk, email correspondence with the author, April 19 2010.

[351] *Ibid.*

He did email me a few times asking to do another collab, but by then his intentions were obvious. He only did this to "get famous" or get noticed as much as possible. There is no artistic motivation, no quality control, no deeper meaning about what he is doing. He is just bullshitting his way into trusting him at first, only to use you as a way to be seen.[352]

Nordvargr's angered response toward Siratori's actions seem to indicate that, although the "underground" has long been tolerant of sampling copyrighted materials without official permission, it does not look favorably on this new development in the history of creative plundering. That is to say, receiving permission from artists to sample and re-build their audio materials, only to have those materials re-assigned to final products attributed to different artists, and to have the sampled artists' names appear on products that they had nothing to do with. Much has been made in the networked art communities of the "multiple-user name," with its ability to short-circuit artistic cults of personality and to de-"commodify" creativity: fictional characters like the "Monty Cantsin" proposed by mail artist David Zack were "connected to radical theories of play...the idea is to create an 'open situation' for which no one person is responsible."[353] However, the breach of trust and outright falsification involved in Siratori's "collaborative" methods is a completely different animal: though networked art and self-released art has encouraged some distance from self-promotion, it is ultimately a culture where basic rules of consent still must precede involvement in projects. Nobody really wishes to have their name appropriated for work that contradicts their ideals or falls below their personal aesthetic standards, and certainly no one involved in an anti-egotistical project wants to be seen as complying with the work of a man whose own work is on trial for rampant egotism.

"The question remains: Who is Kenji Siratori? Where did he come from? Has anyone actually met him in real life?[354]": these questions resound through at

---

[352] Henrik 'Nordvargr' Bjorkk, email correspondence with the author, April 19 2010.

[353] Stewart Home, "Plagiarism: Art As A Commodity And Strategies For Its Negation." *Force Mental* #15, p. 551. Club Moral, Antwerp, 1987.

[354] Available online at http://www.someplaceelse.net/site/2010/03/18/kenji-siratori-revealed/. Retrieved August 18, 2010.

least some parts of the musically-inclined blog-o-sphere. It has become tempting, in light of Siratori's prolific activity, to assume that he is some sort of data mining tool designed by State authorities to collect sensitive information from the musical underground, in which some real dissidents could indeed be lurking. The conspiracy theory has turned out to be false though, as Siratori has begun making more and more public appearances, sometimes at prestigious events like the March 13, 2009 edition of the 'Présences électroniques' showcase hosted by the French GRM [Groupe de Recherches Musicales.] As of this writing, he remains active in just about any sector of underground audio that features overloaded electronics and a tincture of dystopian attitude: his quivery vocals appear on albums of harsh, paranoiac 'breakcore' outfits such as Scrap.edx, on recordings of sardonically smirking, dark electro, and on more much besides. Having thoroughly mined these "darker" territories of music for recognition, though, perhaps some other enterprising artist would do well to follow his lead and appropriate the Siratori "brand" for their own ends: an album of lachrymose country-western ballads, lively *merengue* or lite R & B attributed to "Kenji Siratori" would be more radical at this point than any further attempts at cyberpunk ultra-hipness.

Hyper-Graffiti

Interestingly enough, a scan of the labels releasing Siratori's work opens a window onto a whole new world of wanton releasing, much of which will prompt listeners to throw up their arms in dismay and repeat the self-effacing catchphrase of R. Stevie Moore: *"what's the point?."* Newer net-labels such as Industrial Noise and Non Quality Audio, manned and populated by faceless electro-shockers such as To-Bo and RedSK, hang suspended in some strange limbo between alienating the greatest number of people possible (through the morbid subject matter) and welcoming as many people as possible (through the policy of free net-releases.) This generates some confusion as to the motives of the releasing parties, especially since interviews and public statements by them are kept at a minimum. Of course, this book has maintained that creative products without a 'point' can still be deeply meaningful, but then there are always disingenuous cases of popularity-seekers feigning pointlessness so as to cover up their social desperation with an air of cool detachment. We have seen this earlier with the "promotion via anti-promotion" of *Les Legiones Noires,* and we see it again with one of Siratori's parent labels, Smell The Stench of Australia: when celebrating their 500th (!) net-release, the label proclaimed *"we have found a solution that will motivate you to get the job done...to kill yourself! 43 tracks, over 4 hours in length...enough time for you to make that important decision...you're not worth it."[355]* With such exhortations, it is puzzling why the authors of such promotional materials do not volunteer themselves for the grand mass-suicidal experiment. More puzzling still is the fact that, scrolling further down the web page where this statement is made, the label is again seeking approval from those that it previously encouraged to remove themselves from the land of the living: *"if you enjoy a release, please contact the artist and let them know your opinions, thanks."[356]*

Surely, the era of broadband Internet, begun in the early 21st century, has yielded a fascinating crop of micro-cultures that seem to thrive on pointlessness: 'rate-a-kitten' websites, tearful YouTube confessionals whose anguish is disproportionate to the subject at hand[357], and countless digital altars to the otherwise forgotten cultural detritus of the Anglo-American landscape. Information transfer now occurs at such a merciless speed, that some can rightfully take pride in stumbling across such 'viral' data or 'Internet memes' before they evaporate from public consciousness. They can then attempt to carve out some sort of celebrity status as a presenter of these ephemeral materials. This leads to a sub-cultural industry based almost entirely on self-reference, on the acknowledgement that multiple people have seen or heard the same obscure video, song etc. It should be no surprise that a violent backlash would occur, but the violent attitudes of fringe labels like Smell The Stench end up being just as banal as the banal cuteness that they aim to turn on its head: neither mode, in spite of continual repetition of key information, manages to effect change beyond a closed circuit of fans already inclined towards it. The quirky YouTube novelty and the net-released porno-horror album are united in the short-

---

[355] http://www.smellthestench.net/net.htm. Retrieved March 10, 2011.

[356] *Ibid.*

[357] The perennial example of this is Chris Crocker's "leave Britney alone" viral video of 2007.

term limits of their appeal.

So, ultimately, it isn't merely the lack of inventiveness endemic to mp3s by Industrial Noise, Smell the Stench and company that qualifies them as bad art. Neither is it their would-be offensive subject matter, which we've already seen deployed in emotionally potent and thought-provoking ways elsewhere. It is the fact that, following Clement Greenberg's aesthetic observations "...quality in art appears to be directly proportionate to the density or weight of decision that's gone into its making [...] A good part of that density is generated under the pressure of resistance offered by the medium of communication."[358] Greenberg insists that this constraining pressure can "evoke and inspire" just as easily as it offers up resistance to the creative act, stating that rhythmic patterns in music, dance, and drama have all "empowered creation at the same time as they have constrained it...and because they have constrained it."[359] What the examples cited above lack is evidence that any deep decision-making process has been involved in their creation, but this alone is still not ground for immediate disqualification. That comes about when we realize that, latching onto Greenberg again, "...the essence of decision lies in the fact that it involves a risk...there are no surprises - surprising satisfactions - without risk."[360] All of these examples listed above seem to have involved one initial act of deciding, after which pure automatism took command, and as such they all committed themselves to a situation where their 'best' work (if any of it was really 'good' to begin with) was already behind them. All these examples of sonic extremity may do a good job at terrifying pop music fans, but risks also need to be taken *within* the creative milieu that one inhabits. Communications professor Brian Massumi, quoted elsewhere in this volume, muses further on risk's essentiality to creativity, and how temporary relinquishing of intentionality can be enough to facilitate this state of risk:

If you know where you will end up when you begin,

---

[358] Clement Greenberg, *Homemade Esthetics*, p. 48. Oxford University Press, New York, 1999.
[359] *Ibid.*
[360] *Ibid.*, p. 132.

> nothing has happened in the meantime. You have to be
> willing to surprise yourself writing things you didn't think
> you thought. Letting examples burgeon requires
> inattention as a writing tool [...] you have to be prepared
> for failure. For with inattention comes risk: of silliness or
> even outbreaks of stupidity. But perhaps in order to write
> experimentally, you have to be willing to 'affirm' your
> own stupidity.[361]

Having noted this, Messrs. Massumi and Greenberg would likely throw their hands up in exasperation if confronted with the output of 'Non Quality Audio,' one of the final exhibits in our release-a-holic Rogues' Gallery. The material streaming forth from this net-label and its many tributaries (e.g. 'Far From Showbiz, 'Trash Fuck Net') shows what can result when a certain variety of social malcontent insulates themselves from all forms of restraint and risk. Make no mistake, the superficial *image* of risk-taking is there in spades, exhibited by the label's manifestly anti-p.c. humor: the representatives of the label (actually a handful of individuals inflating their numbers through multiple pseudonyms) plead for the public to be offended by their mean-spirited attitudes towards ethnic minorities, gays, the mentally disabled, *ad nauseum* with equal disrespect. In this regard, predictably vulgar project names like "Niggerchrist", "Kids Shooting Kittens" and "Endometrium Cuntplow" provide good examples of the label's intentions. Yet even their hostile attitudes towards the prevailing climate of political correctness do not steer them towards the realm of risk- when confronted with accusations of abuse directed at any one particular group, they can do as the previously discussed black metal acts have done, and invoke this "nihilistic egalitarianism" as a defense, or basically insist on some generalized feeling of discontent. In an American society that still largely champions egalitarianism, this scattershot approach is infinitely safer for N.Q.A. than honing in on any specific groups as objects of contempt.

Now, the reader can probably see that, by framing this discussion in terms of "art", and calling upon the grand old men of aesthetic assessment

---

[361] Brian Massumi, *Parables For The Virtual*, p. 18. Duke University Press, Durham / London, 2002.

like Clement Greenberg, we are already misrepresenting a small clique that is based more on agitated communication / expression than aesthetic development. N.Q.A. has attempted, through their own label name and declarations of intent, to cut critics off at the pass by insisting that making objectively understood "art" was never the intent. To which we can ask the question, ok, what *is* the intent? From this distance, it seems as though N.Q.A.'s net-releases serve the same function as graffiti (of the most banal hit-and-run variety), especially considering more thought has gone into fashioning the track and album titles as punchlines than worrying about the audio content (e.g., the preponderance of 7-second 'albums' on the label, or pieces that have no discernable 'compositional' quality to them.) Sometimes it seems that audio content is merely an excuse to infiltrate the distribution networks of music, in order to have a good laugh at the expense of those who take themselves too seriously and who may be cloaking egotistical exercises in the guise of altruistic projects. Yet mocking laughter and defacement of 'respectable' institutions, while providing a fleeting feeling of mastery over them, don't necessarily confer that mastery itself, and can easily enough expose the emotional fragility of the defacer. Bruno Latour once wrote of grafitti artists as disenchanted ex-dreamers, noting the following:

> The guy who spray-paints his innermost feelings on the white walls of the Pigalle metro station may be rebelling against the drab reality of the stations, the cars, the tracks, and the surveillance cameras. His dreams seem to him to be infinitely remote from the harsh truth of the stations, and that's why he signs his name in rage on the white ceramic tiles.[362]

Couldn't the same be said of the people who, disillusioned with the unrealized utopian potential of the Internet, abuse its various "walls" by vomiting up an endless number of crass dismissals and insults? Could it be that many of those who were promised the world on a string (or fiber optic cable), only to see it reinforcing the exclusivity of certain in-groups and the homogeneous nature of consumerism, want to cry out in genuine dismay?

---

[362] Bruno Latour, *Aramis: Or, The Love Of Technology*, p. 28. Trans. Catherine Porter. Harvard University Press, Cambridge, 1996.

These artists' relation to the Internet remains a "love-hate" one, however disgusted and confused their cries may be. The particular releasing addiction associated with N.Q.A. could have only happened concurrently with an Internet addiction: their output paints a picture of what can happen when with a disproportionate amount of life is spent using the Internet as an escape from organic activity, rather than as a adjunct to it (people who do so have been aptly referred to as *otaku* or 'my home' in Japanese.) Paul Virilio, himself following writer Withold Gombrowicz, summarized the situation by claiming "...immaturity is one of the most effective terms to describe our contemporaries...an immature state which *a culture that has become inorganic* creates and releases within us."[363]

Addiction As The Cure?

In Jacques Barzun's essay "A Surfeit Of Fine Art," a controversial proposition is made: namely, that government subsidies should be provided in order to prevent artists from contributing to the over-abundance of fine art, much in the same way that such subsidies presently keep farmers from growing certain crops. Barzun wonders why the overabundance of publicly accessible artwork is not considered detrimental at a time when other surplus conditions (overpopulation, overeating etc.) remain crises central to humanity's further development. In doing so, he traces the genesis of this dilemma to the late 19th century's advancement of the artist as a new 'heroic' social type, something that had taken since at least the Renaissance period to accomplish (this was the first time, in Barzun's reckoning, that artists were even known by name or known to have their personal dramas made public.) As his logic goes, the cultural transformation of the last 150-odd years resulted in a state where the artist as social type "...knew and proclaimed the ultimate truths that condemned the materialism of everyday life...he denounced the world, flouted its rules of behavior, and also foretold the march of culture, because he was leading it- hence the term *avant garde*."[364] With the arrival

---

[363] Paul Virilio, *The Information Bomb*, p. 42. Trans. Chris Turner. Verso, New York, 2000.

of this new social type came a natural enemy in the form of materialist and utilitarian forces: the finance-oriented majority whose eventual designation as *bourgeois* had its roots in the new culture of artist-as-visionary.

If applied to the voluminous output of the sonic arts underground, though, such a scheme would probably be a failure, for the sole reason that many of the artists in this community view their output as more of an automatic or instinctual response to their environmental conditions than as a work of "fine" art, i.e. art that is a commodity first and a means of personal life enrichment second. If nothing else, those that use these artistic strategies as a means of patting themselves on the back, *a la* Kenji Siratori and his claims to "super-hip" status, are the exception rather than the rule. It has also remained unstated, to this point, that the "addictive" outpouring of small-run releases can be as much of a therapy for some as it is an affliction for others. Hal McGee, editor of *Electronic Cottage* and curator of the HalTapes label, confesses to the following:

> I have battled mild schizophrenia all my life, and just in the last few years I have really learned how to manage it to my advantage. When I take on a project, I focus all of my concentration and mental energies into that project. I bore holes with my laser beam mind. I sponge up and totally absorb anything that I take an interest in. I actually experientially live inside ideas and concepts. When I take on big projects like the Dictaphonia Microcassette Project, I live it totally. When that project is finished, I will be ready to do other things. Now I set goals for myself - instead of feeling trapped inside projects my enthusiasm for which has waned before they are completed - I set boundaries and limits on how far they will go.[365]

From statements like these, it would seem that McGee's work is intended as a healing, equilibrium-restoring technique before the social

---

[364] Jacques Barzun, *The Culture We Deserve,* p. 31. Wesleyan University Press, Middletown, 1989.

[365] Hal McGee in conversation with Don Campau, forwarded via email to the author on October 21, 2009.

phenomenon of 'recognition' even enters into the picture. Still, more importantly than the present McGee wrestles with, his work also provides a buffer against a future inevitability- one that should already be familiar to those who have absorbed the "art is inseperable from life" message. McGee clarifies this as follows:

> What keeps me motivated to keep on making music and not slacken the pace is simply this: my mortality. I might be dead tomorrow. I feel the necessity to fill the world with as much of my sounds as I can. I don't want to die with the thought in my mind that I could have done more, that I could have made more Halsounds, more Halnoise, could have cluttered up the world with more of my sounds, could have audio trash-heaped and junk-piled. I look at the entirety of my recorded output as one mass ... layer upon layer, like geological strata, with oozing rotten rusted broken twisted forms. My audio art output is my self-portrait - it's a map of my experience and of my brain activity on this planet, in this time. I am a total egotistical bastard, a first-born child, the center of the universe, and delusional as hell! Hahahahaha. But I love what I am doing and it's the reason I am alive - there is no other reason.[366]

So, in the final reckoning, it is difficult, and more than a little imperious, to bombard "release-a-holics" with condemnation if and when they are receiving therapeutic, life-affirming value from their actions. We don't need to be wary of artists who are hyperactive for these reasons alone, yet we should look with suspicion upon those who make quantity the *defining* feature of their artistic program. There is a difference between McGee's "doing as much 'x' as possible" because 'x' is so validating, and "doing as much 'x' as possible" because the "much" is so important: in the later case, a gratification based on statistics take place of pride above a gratification that takes both the physical and the spiritual into account. Both the positive and negative messages of a quantity-for-its-own-sake

---

[366] Hal McGee in conversation with Don Campau, forwarded via email to the author on October 21, 2009.

creative endeavor seem to have passed their "sell-by date" long ago, and can no longer be counted on even as propagandistic messages (to quote Alain Touraine, "the multiplication of spectacles does not transform the spectator into an actor.")[367] Yes, the "future genius poet" may indeed possess "80,000,000 words squared" as Mayakovsky foretold, but should their possession become the theme of all poems to follow, then poetry is in deep trouble.

---

[367] Alain Touraine, *The Post-Industrial Society*, p. 199. Trans. Leonard F.X. Mayhew. Random House, New York, 1971.

Sleeper Cells And Turning Worms:
A 21st Century "Tape Revival?"

At this point, a confession needs to be made: the author of this book also has gotten his hands dirty by releasing a number of audio products on cassette format. However, these were not released during the previously discussed heyday of "Cassette Culture," but during the same period as the composition of this book. For most 21st century audio consumers, committing audio to this format is evidence of sheer insanity or, at the very least, evidence of the kind of contrarian perversity that only allows for unpopular cultural products to be given the time of day. As it happens, a musical colleague of mine[368] has also been offered a spot on the roster of one cassette label to which I'm contributing, but he is refusing on the grounds that cassettes are a "cheap" format only embraced by "noise" enthusiasts. My label boss retorts by insisting that the retail sales of the compact disc, despite its stubborn persistence as the home audio format of choice, are in the tank. It follows that niche markets, such as the one for cassettes, are the ones to be courted- their numbers may be smaller and unlikely to expand dramatically, but their belief that a certain audio format represents a certain ideal is a salient marketing point not as applicable to buyers of CDs or digital downloads. Furthermore, she insists that cassettes are *not*, in fact, cheap to professionally duplicate: a planned 3-tape compilation will cost as much, for a 250 copy run, as 1,000 CDs in 'deluxe' digipaks or even 1,000 DVDs, the format that my aforementioned anti-tape colleague now prefers. Yet, in this unpredictable world of transient desires and sudden inversions of popular taste, it is the cassettes which she believes will actually generate a return on the initial investment, whether they are indeed embraced only by an aesthetically stagnating audience of "noise" fans or by a much more eclectic set of listeners.

The label I'm offering my services to is far from the only one to be dealing exclusively in cassettes here in the second decade of the 21st century. The "cassette revival" is a phenomenon that, although it is most deeply entrenched in the marginal musical scenes, has also been

---

[368] He prefers to remain unnamed, owing to a general dislike of music criticism.

championed by makers of more conventional 'indie' pop, and by artists for whom commenting upon technological progress is not the end goal of awakening the "little boxes" from their digital-age slumber. Whenever an eclectic constituency is involved, then an eclectic variety of motivations can also be inferred, and so this "revival" owes itself just as much to the practical concerns outlined above (e.g. a greater possibility of 'breaking even' and funding further projects) as it does to matters of aesthetic taste and, yes, occasional flashes of contrarian perversity. Some among the new breed of "tape-heads" follow the anti-promotional strategies of *Les Legiones Noires* and other black metal merchants of misanthropy, attempting to regain 'aura' in the age of mechanical reproduction by making the reproduced object difficult for many to obtain, or even to play back. Others, like myself, can claim no motivation more noble than just liking the way the format engages with the senses.

Plastic-Shelled Invertebrates

Philip Marshall, the project manager and spokesperson for the Tapeworm label, is among those who takes his work with tapes seriously, and claims that it is not the side dish to some main course of yet more "serious" artistic involvement. The Tapeworm roster, drawing largely on the artist pool that comprises the English Touch label, is notable for getting such icons of "digital" music (Christian Fennesz, People Like Us, Pita, et. Al.) to make their respective debuts on cassette. The incongruity of hearing such typically '21st century' manifestations of digitally-processed, computer software-aided sound coming from a cassette adds a satisfyingly unique feeling of displacement to the listening experience; a welcome short-circuiting of expectations. Getting others to appreciate the label's efforts has not always been easy, though: due to these same associations with the more established "parent" label, and its venerable back catalog of singular sound experiments, Marshall admits that he "...spent ages fighting a sub-label tag, or being viewed as something of a Touch boutique label."[369] He contends that, like myself, his attraction to cassettes comes mainly from a fusion of emotional and kinetic responses related to the

---

[369] Personal correspondence with the author, June 10 2010.

'thing-in-itself':

> [Cassettes are] personal in the same sense vinyl is
> personal. As with vinyl, it requires you to interact. Fast-
> forward, rewind, spool on. It's mechanical, it hisses. It's
> present, warm and audibly "there". I would maintain that
> the heightened degree of effort required to enjoy the music
> on a tape, as opposed to digital or, to a lesser degree, CD,
> makes the experience more focused and involved.[370]

Elaborating on this concept of involvement, Marshall states that "part of what we want to do is to make things awkward again, in the sense that, it strikes us, in this iPop era, everything you ever wanted is running hot and cold, a mouse click away, [and] that something gets lost."[371] Marshall's particular dislike of iPod culture is informed not just by its favoring of playlist-powered convenience over "deep listening," but also by the tendency of the iPod "playlist" to encourage personal cherry-picking of highlights from a multitude of artists' catalogs rather than immersing in the sequential, programmatic listening suggested by the releasing artists themselves. The audiocassette, since it contains comparatively "work intensive" mechanisms for skipping over individual tracks or sound passages, remains the ideal vehicle for Marshall's positive awkwardness. For Tapeworm, the challenge to the listener does not begin with the playback of the cassette, though. Rather, it starts with the denial of easy access to samples of the music, and with it a tacit disapproval of music browsers who may feel that they "know what they're getting into" on the basis of auditioning brief samples at an online shop. Marshall claims that

> ...it's fascinating to remove perceived digital era
> pressures, to discourage immediacy, to *not* allow shops to
> feature mp3 samples of a 30 second snippet. The musician,
> hopefully, is freed from pressures of digital formats, the
> audience is freed from the tyranny of expectation - they
> buy blind, they buy into the process.[372]

---

[370] Personal correspondence with the author, June 10 2010.

[371] *Ibid.*

[372] *Ibid,*

As this quote reveals, the expectation of work on the behalf of the listener is not paralleled by a desire by the artists to do extra work in seeking out a potential audience. Nor is the label particularly interested in suffering to make music available. Regarding experiences in releasing on other recorded formats, Marshall recalls that

> ...we found ourselves constantly frustrated by the mundane draining of pleasure from a release process. We asked some artist friends, and they agreed- these days there can [only] be so much work for so little reward. So, we thought out loud: what if we eliminated the painful parts of the process? What if we set up a self-sufficient micro-label where no one profits but no one loses, where an object needs sell just enough, or a minute amount, to break even? What if we do not need to 'pimp' our product? What if, in this self-sufficiency, press and PR makes no difference?[373]

The common answer to all the above questions seems to be "you would have become a label that is more satisfied with the creative process than with its results." If that is the honest intention of Tapeworm, then it could truly be said that its existence is not based wholly on nostalgia. However, it can't be assumed that all such labels think in this manner.

Cassette Conservation And The Nature Of Nostalgia

The curiously ironic effects of the 21st century boom in instantaneous communication have been manifold. One of these effects has been the way in which this omnipresent global technology has encouraged an intense re-examination of the different manifestations of 'low tech': hand-crafted clothing and housewares, "slow food," and highly targeted face-to-face "meet-up" groups (as opposed to, but not always separable from, online

---

[373] Personal correspondence with the author, June 10 2010.

equivalents of the same) have all experienced spikes in popularity as the age of hyper-information has progressed. Attributing the resurgence in these movements to a single cause (e.g., an anxiety over a quickening mono-cultural obliteration of local traditions) is, as always, a little wrongheaded, but there are a few definite concerns which overlap or intersect within these practices. The frantic need to 'ease up' on the mortally wounded ecology, the desire to re-assert a vibrant singular identity in an age oriented towards stripped-down pragmatism, the altruistic urge to alleviate exploitative labor practices by personally controlling as much of the production process as possible: all of these are frequently cited as motives for engaging in these activities. The resurgent interest in "Cassette Culture" should not, then, be seen as an isolated fad: it is symptomatic of a larger cultural trend towards conservation and reassessment of archaic, yet still usable, objects and ideals. Of course, conservation on an ecological level would involve not making more products which use non-biodegradable plastics, but the salvage of the natural environment is just one of the conservationist impulses that occasionally come into conflict with each other- for some, like Philip Marshall and others who are defiantly starting or re-starting tape labels, the preservation of a culture's unique means of interaction and presentation seem to take precedence. For the moment, it will not be argued which mode of preservation - preserving either material or spiritual resources - is superior, but it should be noted that they *can* be compatible with some effort. One question needs to be borne in mind as we proceed, though: is the call for saving spiritual resources a means of bringing about a more ethical, sustainable future, or is it a nostalgic retreat into an idealized past disguised as the former?

Like many things which seem completely novel to those who have experienced only the digital age, these movements have been well under way for a while now, and are only intensifying or refining approaches that have been developed since the age of mass production began in earnest. Even the history of late 20th-century counter-culture shows marked tendencies towards an ethos of 'reduced convenience, increased individuation.' The several different strains of Gothic rock culture were (and, in many cases, still are) a prime example of this: they challenged the one-size-fits-all utilitarianism of urban / suburban modernity with their aristocratic affectations, their acumen for salvaging and hand-crafting ornate articles of clothing, and their skill for linking together successive periods of historical decadence (e.g., Weimar-era Berlin) into an aesthetic continuum. Of course, the attempt at complete severance from a corrupt and decaying modern world provided more challenges than just arranging a new wardrobe and choreographing new dances: the characteristic Goth refusal to compromise on matters of public image often meant severely limiting the options for employment, with I.T. or computer programming positions ironically becoming one of the best routes.[374] As such, participation in a 'Goth' lifestyle has always come with a built-in nostalgia for times in which no such compromises were necessary. Following on Bruno Latour's critique of modernism, it's also plausible that Goths' being situated in digital cultures of convenience produced the need to become walking exhibitions of long-lost ideals:

> As Nietzsche observed long ago, the moderns suffer from the illness of historicism. They want to keep everything, date everything, because they think they have definitively broken with their past [...] maniacal destruction is counterbalanced by an equally maniacal conservation.[375]

When dealing with a syncretic subculture like Goth, the concept of nostalgia is deeply interwoven into their stylistic rebellion- yet this is a term whose resonance has altered throughout the ages, or has at least had its meaning broadened during the reign of modernity. Coming from the Greek terms *nostos* [home] and *algos* [suffering, pain], nostalgia originally denoted a state of literal homesickness: the profound sense of loss felt by soldiers deployed to the front, for example. As late as the early 20th century, the term still retained a kind of geographical gloss to it, when it was used to refer to those uprooted peoples moving from villages to urban centers. Goth culture, on the other hand, seems opposed to any kind of domesticity and indeed celebrates the fact that aristocratic spirit and inflamed passion have previously taken root in numerous eras and nation-states. Goth iconography, though purposely limited in its black-dominated

---

[374] The Goth habit of patronizing 24-hour Denny's restaurants, hardly an isolated phenomenon, was another comical concession to modern conveniences and less-than-aristocratic standards of living.

[375] Bruno Latour, *We Have Never Been Modern*, p. 69. Trans. Catherine Porter. Harvard University Press, Cambridge MA, 1993.

color scheme, takes in everything from Egyptian hieroglyphs to *geisha* cosmetics to 18th century corsetry, with this baroque symbolism strongly suggesting a longing for an idealized *spiritual* homeland rather than any *terra firma* defined by physical borders.[376] When 'nostalgia' is used in this more generalized sense of longing for a climate more suitable to spiritual development, then Goth is the nostalgic music subculture *par excellence*.

Art critic Therese Lichtenstein describes this particular nostalgia as "longing for the past, [that] can be converted into a fantasy of a fulfilled past that never existed. As pain turns into pleasure, past deprivations are repressed under a screen memory of fulfillment."[377] Lichtenstein's simultaneous invocation of pain and pleasure here reminds us that nostalgia-tinted subcultures can also feature masochism as an aesthetic device, an evolutionary mechanism, or both. Goth adherents are especially fond of the iconography of martyrdom, as evidenced by the number of crucifix pendants worn by atheistic members of the tribe, or by the stylized dancefloor poses that are intended to pantomime a state of intense exhaustion. There is also Lichtenstein's suggestion, following Gilles Deleuze, that "disavowal, suspense, waiting, fetishism, and fantasy make up the constellation of responses to masochism,"[378] and again these characteristics are practically synonymous with the dramatic games played out on Gothic club nights or in private rituals. Erotic, sado-masochistic games played with tight restraints and flagellation are only the most obvious of these rituals, which also include daily dressing in the most impractical and uncomfortable outfits imaginable- heat-trapping fabrics like velvet and PVC are a staple of Goth costumes, as are brutally high heels, weighty necklaces and other masochistic "accessories" like the omnipresent cigarette (the Javanese *kretek*, coming wrapped in black paper and with an "exotic" aroma of clove, owes a significant amount of its sales to its popularity as a Goth accoutrement.)

---

[376] The definition of nostalgia based on a physical space, that takes the homesickness of male soldiers into consideration, is also inappropriate given the relative feminization of Goth culture: the historical icons and spiritual leaders adopted by the culture are female to a greater degree than in most other "post-punk" subcultures (to say nothing of the highly androgynous cosmetic presentation of males in the scene.)

[377] Therese Lichtenstein, *Behind Closed Doors: The Art of Hans Bellmer*, p. 145. University of California Press, Berkeley, 2001.

[378] *Ibid.*, p. 85.

Fans of the revived cassette scene also partake in some of these masochistic characteristics (as Marshall's earlier comments make clear), and for similar purposes of anti-passivity and general enlightenment through "taking the path less traveled". However, these same fans would likely wince at being lumped in with another subculture that is as flagrantly nostalgic as Goth, for the reasons of its perceived kitschy sentimentality and its limited appeal to non-Westerners (exceptions abound, as always, to either of these critiques.) This begs the question-what are the essential differences between nostalgia for a pre-industrial or pre-managerial age, and "tech-nostalgia" which romanticizes previous points on the timeline of the post-industrial age? What is the real degree of difference between their notions of authenticity?

Interrogating Tech-Nostalgia (An Exchange With Alexei Monroe)

Nostalgia for a certain point on the brief timeline of the machine age is a relatively new phenomenon; or at least it is a condition that is being more explicitly integrated into audio artists' public statements than before. Past music subcultures with a nostalgic component to them have hewn as closely as possible to an organic presentation (although the suspicion of insincerity is rightly aroused when 'folksy' and 'organic' acts insist on ultra-modern promotional machinery to aid them in their projection of such an image.) This is less evident in revivals of the kind abetted by labels like Tapeworm, where there is no hint that mechanization is an automatic disqualification for a work's being considered "authentic." As mentioned earlier, cassette stalwart Hal McGee has even referred to the post-industrial music released during the prior Cassette Culture as a kind of "folk" music in and of itself: in both cases, the locus of authenticity shifts away from the implementation tools and towards the overall attitudes of the artists towards both creative process and end result. The need to further the expressive life of a small tribe of individuals, and the precedence this takes over commercial concerns, is a common feature of folk music and of self-released electronic music. In fact, with the history of electronic music being much more open to examination now than in any previous era, it seems more and more naïve to believe this music has been made entirely in the service of futurism. For example, the enveloping two-note synth drones and primal vocal whoops on the first album by the *ur*-electropunk duo, Suicide, had much more to say about the time in which they were composed than about any future utopia or dystopia.[379] Also, much has already been written about electronic music's attempts at providing a shamanic 'trans-temporal' continuity not excluding the present, as in the trance states encouraged by all-night raves.

Certainly, the attachment of utopian hope to machinery and circuitry is far from dead, although it must compete more strongly than ever against the critique of constant technological novelty. For every *Wired* reviewer who lauds the "liberating" potential of the latest generation of iPods and their ability to serve a number of functions with no movable parts, there is a skeptic like Marshall who denounces the widening rift in the producer-consumer relationship that these devices create.

Over the past several years, cultural theorist Alexei Monroe has been one of the more reliable commentators on the phenomenon of "tech-nostalgia," and it seems logical to turn to him at this point in the discussion. When discussing this phenomenon, Monroe uses the metaphor of the "sleeper agent" for a cultural flashpoint that "will activate at some point in the future when they themselves are re-discovered and/or re-invented, destabilizing their own time and potentially releasing a further set of unintended consequences in another two to three decades."[380] It is a colorful analogy, and one that probably springs from Monroe's own interest in Cold War Europe and the history of espionage and subterfuge that accompanied that era. Currently recording electro artists like Franz Falckenhaus also romanticize the period's heightened suspense in the design schemes and track titles of their albums (Falckenhaus' *Stories From My Cold War* features tracks such as "Surveillance In The Hotel Lobby," "Escape From KGB Agents In The Old Town," and "A Tupolev Disappears In The Darkness.")

---

[379] This is to say nothing of the lyrical content on the record, which deals with very of-its-time (mid-1970s) issues: "Ghost Rider" invokes a post-Vietnam War national fatigue, while "Frankie Teardrop" is a dirge memorializing the suicide of the titular character (who can be seen as a symbol of urban claustrophobia and American financial collapse.)

[380] Alexei Monroe, "The False Scent Of Asparagus." Previously unpublished.

Yet, despite the potentially ominous overtones of the term "sleeper agent," Monroe contends that their creating an explosion of unintended consequences is a positive scenario where "tech-nostalgia" is concerned. He also proposes a negative scenario involving the exploitation of consumers who seek out authenticity and inspiration in re-discovered "sleeper cell" artifacts, which could certainly include rarities from the early days of the underground cassette network. Considering how that culture relied so heavily on minimal recording and reproductive techniques, it is easy for a savvy rip-off artist to emulate their model with today's powerful microprocessors: "pre-stressed" graphic design and simulated "lo-fi" audio can very easily be confused for legitimate period pieces, especially when prospective buyers have convinced themselves that there was far more clandestine audio activity from the previous generation than has already been documented. When such items are being sold through the digital marketplace rather than in physical retail shops, the con is that much easier to pull off on hopeful "tech-nostalgics" before they realize the extent to which they've been duped. Monroe likens this process of falsification to the production of bogus relics by the pre-Reformation Catholic Church, one aspect of the "barter in spiritual things" which became known as the crime of simony:

> As in the present, this was partly based on people's genuine and continued need to possess what they believed to be lost relics, that might reduce the time spent in purgatory or show their devotion to the community (as the fan demonstrates their devotion by possessing a rare artifact such as a "lost" album.)[381]

While Monroe casts a wary eye on modern-day producers of fake cultural relics, he also suggests that there will always be a portion of the listening audience that enjoys these fakes and the spiritual rewards that they may confer in spite of their dubious origins- even if they are fakes, they may still comfort the "tech-nostalgic" listenership by reassuring them that yesteryear's ideals of truth and beauty can survive in the present. With

---

[381] Alexei Monroe, "The False Scent Of Asparagus." Previously unpublished.

this in mind, he also warns against "zealots" that may narrow the range of "acceptable" listening to certifiable originals, despite the fact that the carefully constructed fakes may have some redeeming value.

Monroe's insights in the following conversation, though informed by his personal tastes, are applicable to the broad spectrum of "tech-nostalgic" thinking.

++++++++

One thing I was thinking of the other day- some of the quirky 'retro-futurist' trends we see now, such as people selling hand-crafted fashion items made to resemble vintage synthesizers, seem unique to me- I think this is because most 'traditionally' nostalgic cultural manifestations have tended to champion pre-industrial, 'organic' modes of living as being the most 'authentic' ones. Do you feel the pop culture from, say, the 90s to the present is really the first to have such a penchant for 'tech-nostalgia,' or for seeing previous eras of as electronic development as being more sincere?

From a historical perspective, it seems unlikely that any pattern is totally unprecedented, and as I began to write this I was struck by the most obvious 1970s example of tech-nostalgia, which in some ways has structured the sonic and visual manifestations of all tech-nostalgia in electronic music. Kraftwerk - *Radioactivity*. In particular the way they used the romantic aura surrounding the early days of radio. Firstly there's the image of the *Volksempfänger* (Third Reich-era radio set) on the cover. They could have chosen a contemporary shortwave set of the type which now has a nostalgic aura around it, but they chose a 1930s set (and were criticised for using this icon of Nazi technological modernism.) "Radioland" is the best example of their technostalgia, but also "Airwaves" and "Radio Stars". There's a pervasive technostalgic romanticism at work in the album, even if it's also ambivalent and ironic.

In the aftermath of Punk, there was a kind of *Denkverbot* (mental/conceptual prohibition) against anything associated with the 70s and this included (for instance) Moog synthesisers and analogue generally. Cubase, the Atari, and sequencing were making it possible to create electronic music without using expensive units that were tainted by association with the hippie and prog eras. If we look at pop culture from the 90s, then one of the dominant forces from about '92 to maybe 2000 was techno, and techno carries the influence of Kraftwerk's retro-futurism in its DNA (even if it's not always apparent on the surface). It's interesting that almost simultaneously with the vanguard era of techno, you also had producers like Sven Vath straying into '70s- influenced synthesiser motifs and starting to discuss the devices of the period. My (sketchy) theory is that the techno and rave movements met with repression just as the previous *Denkverbot* wore off. Techno either went underground (into specialist forms like minimal techno or gabber - both of which fetishise vinyl as a technology) or went closer to the mainstream. In both cases, this is maybe symptomatic of a loss of faith in explicit futurism, and/or a belief that past futurism was more powerful and authentic.

I think another reason for this loss of faith was that just as music became more explicitly post-human and futuristic, music technologies became ever blander and utilitarian as objects. This led people back to boxes with wires, and to the unpredictability of analogue technology. It's as if when the (aesthetic) future finally arrived, it was so anti-climactic and instantly quotidian that people needed to search for it in the past. Other factors might be the general rehabilitation of the 70s that began in the mid-90s, first as irony and then as unapologetic fetishism (I have another theory about how 70s revivalism was a symptom of increasing populism and reactionary politics in Britain.) This was very much a market-driven process as is much of technostalgia (for instance limited edition reproduction synths and mixing desks with walnut veneers etc). This is not to say that analogue technology doesn't have some real sonic virtues, which are hard to replicate with contemporary gear, but this kind of technostalgia can't be considered in isolation from market and cultural trends (in my own project we're moving away from laptops to physical devices, although nothing older than a [Roland] TB-303). In summary, you could say that digital is banal and omnipresent, and this only adds to the lost futuristic aura surrounding analogue (which of course is very important to the (re)-production of 80s electronic and industrial sounds). Perhaps there's even something culturally positive in this rejection of perfection in favour of rawer and less stable technologies.

Do you feel that, as you've mentioned here with people's love of analogue technology, these period-specific references are being used because they provide a convenient metaphor for the geopolitical anxiety and utopian hope we now deal with (and perhaps are intended to offer us a bit of comfort as well, by hinting that the early 21st century is not the only age to have experienced its 'unique' shocks?) Or do you feel this re-appropriation is being done on a more naïve level- that is to say, cultural flashpoints as diverse as the DeLorean DMC-12 or Soviet MiG fighters just look and sound "cool"?

The Cold War is a very rich and evocative period, particularly the period of 'New Cold War' from 1980-1985, which I remember clearly. I think that the general cultural awareness of the proximity to mass annihilation did directly influence the aesthetics of the period, and even that there is a type of 'Cold War poetics'. Perceived mortality and ongoing crisis tend to generate deep and even sublime cultural responses. A track like Test Dept's "Comrade Enver Hoxha" transports you back to that time instantly (and helps those to young to remember it experience it vicariously). I would even say this period is so intense (and far from fully processed) that there is as much legitimacy in contemporary producers addressing as there was at the time. The only question is whether those with no lived experience of the period can do more than replicate the style or aura of the period. One comparison might the be the explosion (literally) of interest in World War Two, and all the films made on it during the sixties and seventies. Certainly it was a cultural obsession for my generation (born 1969). By this cyclical logic, a fascination with the New Cold War seems unsurprising. It may also be a way of relativising the current real and imaginary threats the West faces as these (currently) do not include mass global annihilation.

I can partly relate to the fascination among with the period among younger people because although I remember the news and general atmosphere of the period, I was about 5 years too young to be directly involved in the industrial culture of the early 80s. However, I like to think I can re-imagine myself in the culture of that time better than someone 5, 10 or 15 years younger.

Regarding the DeLorean example, that can be seen in directly political terms as part of what I term the kleptocratisation of culture that's been ongoing since the mid-1970s and accelerated massively in the 90s. What we have now is an unashamed klepto-culture and it's entirely natural and absolutely functional for those in line with the klepto-culture to celebrate the icons of the first 'Greed is Good' era. Even after the sub-prime crisis and the recession, I think there are many who would fight or even kill to preserve the klepto-culture and the economic relations it celebrates and fetishises. This has penetrated so deep into the social and cultural subconscious that many producers are not even aware of the extremity of the ideological statements they are making in this way. Of course some present these references as irony, but that serves the status quo just as well as those that unashamedly celebrate these references.

Given what you've said here, do you feel the current wave of retro-futurism would be possible (or, at least, as enthusiastic as it is now) without the fact that many of its original progenitors are still alive (and, in many cases, artistically active?) After all, I seem to remember a lot of the more acclaimed retrospectives of the second World War –like the 1973-1974 'World At War' TV series- got their credibility from the participation, as interview subjects, of people who had been frontline combatants. A feat that obviously can't be replicated now, 35 odd years later. So, in short, how valuable is the present-day input of 'elder statesmen' for the culture we've been discussing, especially since access to records of their work is fairly simple for anyone with an Internet connection and a will to parse a good deal of information?

Yes, I think this presence is important, perhaps especially as a 'corrosive comparator' - with veteran performers still active/present (assuming they're still artistically effective) then it's much harder (though not impossible) for younger producers to pass off sub-standard replicas. It's also important that the old guard are present in the clubs, passing on knowledge and (sometimes) adding authenticity. That said, my experience of the Reeperbahn club night was that I was the oldest person there (at 39). The average age was mid to late twenties but they were playing records I bought or danced to between '89 and '92. It was also clear that for 99% of the audience it was simply a style statement, they had no awareness of, or interest in, the social or political contexts that generated these sounds. On the other hand, there are many veteran 80s artists now touring, re-releasing and issuing new material almost exclusively because of the neo-80s trend that began around 2000.

One thing I find interesting about the revival of home-taping, which is happening to a significant degree in the various Industrial or esoteric underground sectors, is that it is often being done for the opposite reason that people once again pick up analogue synths- while the latter confer 'authenticity' along with a sound that people argue is superior to digital emulation, the former is seen as 'authentic' because of its inferior qualities- e.g., the cassette's surface noise is more audible and adds somewhat to the intimate drama of listening. So this makes me wonder, is the 'scene' really as paradoxical as it seems here, or can these different takes on the concept of authenticity be logically reconciled somehow?

I think the confusion here is that authenticity and superior sound are not always the same thing (or not perceived to be.) Vintage Russian synthesisers are much in demand now, not because they sound better but because they sound 'other' and (arguably) 'worse' compared to Western models. I don't think the cassette revival is purely due to what we can call inverted sonic snobbery. More significant is that it's an attempt to connect with the eighties tape underground which is enjoying an afterlife, both through official re-releases (on Vinyl on Demand etc.) and through the ever-growing number of blogs dedicated to obscure Cassette Culture (there's even one on Yugoslav experimental music now.) As ever we can't wholly ignore the market factor - when buyers make purchases now they want something collectible - a standard CD digipak is insufficient. These cassettes are instant collector's items and symbolically connect the producers with their predecessors. Currently they also confer an 'underground' aura that isn't necessarily plausible - Touch Records are releasing a series called Tapeworm, but it's many years since they were an underground tape label, and for me doesn't quite ring true. That said, I will buy new tape releases if they're unavailable otherwise. It's also worth mentioning my favourite cassette album (Laibach's *Kapital*) contains different and better versions than those on the CD and vinyl (which also differ from each other)...

++++++++

It is interesting to note Monroe's criticism of Tapeworm in the foregoing conversation, especially because his criticism is not based on any "tech-nostalgic" aspirations of the label, but rather because of the label's "implausible underground aura." What, exactly, makes it implausible? Perhaps it bears mentioning, since it has gone unmentioned up until this point, that the cassettes released on Tapeworm are professionally reproduced items, unlike most of the cassettes that were part and parcel of the 1980s cassette networks. Unsurprisingly, Marshall himself takes inspiration from the more successful European indie labels to have released pro-duplicated records over that same time span,[382] but denies that taking cues from them (as opposed to contemporary tape label equivalents like Sound Of Pig) makes his work any less viable: "The Tapeworm sits somewhat strangely in 'tape culture,' I think, but what we do is heartfelt."[383]

To this point, the exact coordinates of the term "revival" may have been a little too insufficiently mapped out. In order to make their revivalist work seem that much more fantastic, some proselytizers of revivalism use this term as a stand-in for "resurrection," that is to say, suggesting that they have brought back to life something that had vanished entirely from the earth. For obvious reasons, the "big tent" revivals of the Christian evangelical movement have used the two concepts interchangeably: the marquee events at these gatherings have been the granting of vision or ambulatory ability to those who have been handicapped for life, or the return of some long-forgotten "spirit tongue" through mass demonstrations of glossolalia. Speaking on the early 21st-century revival of synthesizer-based pop known as electroclash, Monroe again suggests a kind of "sleeper cell" situation rather than the return of a fully dead and discredited art form:

> In Europe, particularly, these tendencies have been
> continuously present. Their un-fashionability in most of
> the 90s gave them an ersatz 'underground' status, but a
> similar mix of original artists, imitators and updaters has
> always been present, if less visible.[384]

---

[382] "I always loved labels with strong identities, such as Les Disques du Crépuscule, Factory, Basic Channel, ZTT and of course Touch." (personal conversation with the author, June 6 2010.)
[383] *Ibid.*

To a lesser degree, this can be said of the enthusiasm for cassettes: even in the format's "darkest hour" in the mid-1990s, there were those who embraced these objects for precisely the reason Marshall gives for founding Tapeworm- i.e., that the *jouissance* of recording and packaging an audio release was more important than promoting it. Like the 78rpm, 10" shellac records of the blues that still command a cult following, the cassette never "died", despite the rising quantity of tapes in landfills and the declining numbers in retail outlets. Thusly, tapes never required a resurrection so much as rehabilitation.

Akifumi Nakajima's G.R.O.S.S. label, which began operations in the early 90s, was one venture whose serious consideration of package design could have only been possible, at that time, with self-released cassettes and with a lack of promotional middlemen. One of Nakajima's most rightfully acclaimed visual works, the design for the *Three Temples* triple cassette set, is a hexagonal piece of black, corrugated plastic onto which the cassettes held are fastened by black linen rope, and its professionalism comes paradoxically from Nakajima's refusal to outsource the design to a 3rd-party design house (Nakajima's background in industrial design does give him something of an advanced knowledge of such processes, though.) Nakajima was not completely alone during this period, either. In his native Japan, a number of other micro-labels also "carried the torch" for cassette fans throughout this period[385], even though the labels' catalogs partially justified my unnamed colleague's complaint that only "noise" fanatics would purchase a cassette release. Nevertheless, these objects fulfilled their destiny as "sleeper agents" and have been rewarded with a retroactive importance by the compilers of 'out-of-print music' weblogs and by archivists in general.

Having already discussed the "tech-nostalgia" that runs through the

---

[384] Alexei Monroe, "Deca-Disco: Electro Disco Revival As A Political Symptom." Available online at http://pluralmachine.blogspot.com/2009/05/deca-disco-electro-disco-revivalism-as.html. Retrieved September 4, 2010.

[385] Japan's vast 2nd-hand bazaars for previous generations of consumer electronics, such as "Den Den Town" in Osaka, deserve some credit here for giving locals access to playback and recording equipment that will accommodate unpopular formats.

resurgent cassette scene and other forms of "retro-futurist" music, some thought should also be given to the utopian yearning once associated with mechanized living in general. Among Marxist poets and intellectuals, the societal leveling caused by mechanization would result in a widespread dissolution of conflicts. Despite varying degrees of adherence to classical Marxism (which did, after all, scoff at 'unscientific' utopianism), successive movements on the Left would take up this theme of total freedom through total automation: in the case of the Situationists, an optimism persisted that physical labor would eventually be phased out entirely. One textual example, from as late as 1987, will suffice as an illustration of such attitudes. From the Yugoslav artist Mangelos:

The world is not only changing
It has changed.
We are in the second century
Of the second civilization. The machine one
The social use of the machine
Has put an end to the civilization of manual work
And to all the social phenomena
Rooted in manual work

By changing the character of work
The world changes its way of thinking.
The revolution of thinking has the character
Of a long-term evolution.
In the course of this process
The previous artistic or naïve thought
Has integrated itself in the process of application
With another one based on
The principles of mechanical work.[386]

This is precisely the type of bold proclamation that raised the ire of anti-political artists like Gerhard Richter, who once growled "no religion

---

[386] Mangelos, "Manifesto Of Manifesto." *Impossible Histories: Historical Avant-Gardes, Neo Avant-Gardes, and Post Avant-Gardes in Yugoslavia, 1918-1991,* ed. Dubravka Duric and Misko Sukakovic. MIT Press, Cambridge, 2003.

has ever promised Paradise on Earth. Only the Communists have ever been stupid enough to do that [...] anyone who believes that he can change the whole world is bound to regard any small improvement of the status quo as sabotage."[387] Of course, the viewpoint contradicting Mangelos' manifesto (that technological advancement allows for enough convenience and free time to permit endless, colorful individualities that deviate from "the norm") is no less utopian, and can even play a significant role in the "kleptocratic" manipulations that Monroe mentions above. Anyway, Richter would likely reject this form of utopianism as well: indeed, he claims "progressive ideas are largely independent of economic systems."[388]

The problem with both these capitalist and socialist projections of techno-utopia is the same as the many forms of tech-nostalgia: the present is scorned to such a degree that examinations of the past and future rarely rise above the level of a homesick retreat. If the current "cassette revival" is to have any staying power, those who truly love these objects would be wise to not call this newfound interest a "revival" at all: such loaded terms just admit that the currently existing products are inferior to those coming from *l'âge d'or*, spending too much time comparing the different generations of product to maximize impact in the here and now. Meanwhile, the noble attempt to promote some sort of sustainability by "recycling" unloved formats places too much emphasis on end result to effect any "small improvement of the status quo": by immersing itself completely in the processes of creation and interaction, without fearing the unintended consequences of these processes, the original cassette network arguably gained its greatest successes. That is to say, it accomplished its goal of international, heterogeneous communication (Andrej Tisma's "human sculpture") without entirely and explicitly orienting itself in that direction. Had it trumpeted this as its goal in advance, rather than letting this state of affairs arise spontaneously, I submit that the overall effect of the original tape underground would be attenuated: as Gregory Bateson notes, the expectation that one "act as a pure, uncorrected consciousness," with no allowances made for non-intentionality, breeds "a dehumanized creature."[389] As such, the "revival" of a mere audio format seems like a

---

[387] Gerhard Richter, *The Daily Practice of Painting: Writings 1962-1993*, p. 244. Ed. Hans-Ulrich Obrist, trans. David Britt. MIT Press, Cambridge MA, 1995.

[388] *Ibid.*, p. 96.

foolish exchange to make for such a dehumanization.

---

389 Gregory Bateson, *Steps To An Ecology Of Mind*, p. 452. University of Chicago Press, 2000.

Conclusion: What Is To Be Taped?

While this book has mainly attempted to deal with the phenomenon of unofficial *audio* rather than unofficial *music*, let's mischievously put that distinction aside at this very late stage in the game. It has to be admitted that the vast majority of recorded material, "official" or "unofficial," remains in the realm of the musical, or at least hopes to set up residence there while we argue over the very subjective definitions of what music is. As far as these subjective definitions go, disputes over their fixity are as intense as religious quarrels, and possess an above-average ability to bring the debaters to blows (although sports-related arguments should get an honorable mention in this regard.) *"No music, no life"* was the slogan once printed on the red-and-yellow plastic shopping bags handed out by cashiers at the Tower Records chain, and this has become a salient fact accepted and embraced by millions upon millions of people. That it can remain as such, despite the most lab-assembled forms of inanity being the most heavily promoted forms of music, is a testament to its obduracy, but also to what an integral life function it serves. Its ability to simultaneously mirror life and provide windows onto new life is done with a universality no language has ever matched.

At the very least, music remains the centerpiece of arts and culture in the post-industrial society. When we speak of a city that has a strong "scene," that "scene" will irrevocably be built around an infrastructure for presenting live music events. Film festivals, theatrical events, gallery walks: all of these are fine and good, but without the key ingredient of a thriving musical community, there is no "local scene." The degree to which live music performances are now integrated into the above events, to provide more of a "draw" for the promoters, is a testament to this fact, as is the increasing number of art shows that claim to be inspired by modern music (e.g. exhibitions which specialize in "the art of the album cover", "rock 'n roll photographs" and so on.) It would seem that anyone wanting to rally new troops to their cultural cause would be wise to learn at least something about music's psycho-spiritual effects: virtually all of history's great propagandists have already done so.

So, the question has to be asked- did music's intense marketability arise from its rapturous or ineffable qualities, or were these qualities themselves a projection of careful marketing? Given the historical evidence, which easily precedes the post-industrial, commercial applications of music, I would place my bets on the former. Arthur Schopenhauer had already heralded music's supremacy in the realm of the arts in the early 19th century, when he stated "music is by no means [...] the copy of the Ideas, but the *copy of the will itself,* whose objectivity the Ideas are."[390] For a 20th century echo of his theory (with a sufficiently '21st century' gloss of scientific erudition), we can turn to the late composer Iannis Xenakis, always a reliable source for explaining the atomic structure of sound and its ability to sculpt new cultural forms:

> When you compose or listen to music, you manipulate more abstract notions than that of the visual world [...] the dimensions of what we hear - pitch, frequency, intensity - are closer to us in their structures. There are no photons, only *phonons* - phonons can be perceived, touched...photons only leave a global imprint. So, maybe when you manipulate sound, you reach something closer to Man, and therefore much more perceptible, where the function (the discovery of ideas) is also closer, more accessible.[391]

Xenakis, though no home taper or self-releaser by any means (his sponsors have included everyone from the Philips Corporation to the Shah of Iran), is inarguably perceptive here. When he adds elsewhere that "music, by its very abstract nature, is the first of the arts to have attempted the conciliation of artistic creation with scientific thought,"[392] he also implies that the mutual arising of technological advances and sonic advances will likely always be with us, and that the former will never be able to domesticate or extinguish the latter. More beneficially, though, successful attempts at this mutual arising will lead to what Xenakis calls a

---

[390] Arthur Schopenhauer, *The World As Will And Idea,* p. 164. Trans. Jill Berman. Orion Books, London / North Clarendon, VT, 1995.

[391] Iannis Xenakis quoted in *Owl: What Is Music?,* dir. Chris Marker, 1989

[392] Iannis Xenakis, *Formalized Music: Thought And Mathematics In Composition,* p. 133. Trans. Christopher A. Butchers. Indiana University Press, Bloomington IN / London, 2001.

"total exaltation in which the individual mingles, losing his consciousness in a truth rare, enormous, and perfect [...] this tremendous truth is not made of objects, emotions, or sensations; it is beyond these, as Beethoven's Seventh Symphony is beyond music."[393]

Given how the passion for music has been maintained since the age in which Schopenhauer first declared it to be the sovereign art form, there is good reason to hope for its future survival, even as the economic conditions modulating musical production violently fluctuate. In an early 80s column for *Op* magazine, "There Will Always Be Music," Irwin Chusid gets to the meat of the matter with a quintessentially American analogy:

> In 1981 pandemonium broke out when professional baseball went on strike. There was much anxious talk about the impending demise of the game. What most people forgot was that "baseball" was not on strike. The "business of professional baseball" was. I played in quite a number of challenging softball matches that summer, and it never occurred to me that "baseball" was at all jeopardized. If the player reps and owners had never reached an agreement and the strike persisted to this day, there would still be baseball [...] I predict, despite MTV and exorbitant record prices, despite home taping and bootlegging, despite one-dimensional radio formats, and despite Stanley Gortikov- there will always be music.[394]

The baseball analogy is apt, because, despite all the "democratic" revolutions in recordable music formats, home studio equipment, and self-promotional apparatus, there are many who still have their reservations about music-making being a thing of the "people": that is to say, if one gets involved with it at all, it should be for the ultimate purpose of forging a career. While teaching classes of university-age students in Japan, many expressed astonishment at the fact that I was playing music "on the side", as if this entailed living a dual life as a mild-mannered teacher who nightly

---

[393] Iannis Xenakis, *Formalized Music: Thought And Mathematics In Composition*, p. 1. Trans. Christopher A. Butchers. Indiana University Press, Bloomington IN / London, 2001.

[394] Irwin Chusid, "There Will Always Be Music." *OP* (issue number / publication date unknown)

shed his suit and tie for black leathers and thrilled audiences in the thousands. The truth was, of course, that I was happily playing in tiny "live houses" for which a sellout crowd would be in the very low triple digits. Yet for those who weren't familiar with the presence of an independent music circuit (again, a surprising number,) my public appearances were imagined to be more lavish affairs. Music as a means of piecemeal social engineering, or even as a *pro bono* activity aiming for Xenakis' "total exaltation", was largely taken for granted: those who identified "musician" as their vocation were taken more seriously than any other musically involved individual, even if their demonstrable skill was no better than that of the many street buskers who peppered the urban Japanese landscape. This illustrates the degree to which "official music" has become, like pro baseball, the only variation that is taken seriously (and this itself points towards some deeply instinctual trust of authority, although this is a subject for another day.)

When Chusid compares the state of music to that of baseball, he also inadvertently reminds us how much music has become a competitive enterprise. Just as fans thrill to see their favorite team climbing in the league standings, they thrill to watch their favorite artist battle their way to a respectable Billboard chart position- and in both cases they value the success as their own, since their participation in consuming these entities charged them with the immaterial qualities of stamina and confidence needed to attain stardom. It's worth speculating that the absence of a "chart system" for rewarding audience participation contributes to the visual and plastic arts' lagging so far behind music and film in terms of popularity: what effect might a "top 40 paintings" or "sculptural standings" have on increasing public enthusiasm for these artifacts? It can even be said that another system of rankings played a major part in making video games one of the major competitors to music:[395] had the early coin-operated arcade games not complemented their brutally repetitive gameplay and minimal interfaces with a player ranking system, much of the appeal may have been lost.

---

[395] Video games were seen as enough of a 'competitive' industry that they prompted Warner Communications to purchase Atari Inc. in 1976. Nevertheless, video games (both home consoles and coin-op games) remained a fashionable scapegoat for the music industry's failings in the 1980s.

If we see the individual musicians' or music genres' battles for public recognition as contests between the opposing "teams" in a league of ideas, then the battle between mass music and self-determined music is the World Series, the pinnacle of inter-league play, a match with the highest of stakes: no less than the ability to shape the future of music itself. Each "side" has their own strengths and weaknesses. Team Official, representing mass music, can claim a much larger number of listeners, yet cannot decisively prove that this huge constituency enjoys their product without some kind of coercion or some aggressive denial of living space to musical alternatives. These negative features also betray a certain lack of confidence in the staying power of its own musical players, otherwise it would not have a history clouded over by "payola" schemes and other such attempts to rig the results of the game (even thorough background information on musical 'hit parade' standings, like Nielsen TV ratings, is not accessible by the general public.) Team Unofficial, while righteously authentic and unencumbered by the need to turn a profit or the need to prove value with sales volume, nonetheless has its weaknesses too: it can suffer from crippling nostalgia for times that never existed, can generate its own kinds of false scarcity, and often pushes would-be shocking extremes to the point where they become a 'hell of the same'. But wait: aren't these weaknesses of Team Unofficial also shared by the mass music culture? Don't they, too, put forth a number of products that project the counterproductive traits of unchecked extremity, sighing nostalgia and phony scarcity? If this is the case, hasn't Team Unofficial already won this game, since only it can make claims to authenticity and indifference to profit?

Unfortunately, it is still too early to say. Baseball games are won and lost by external or "intangible" factors as much as by what happens on the field, and the same can be expected of the competitive game of distributing music. One external intrusion that we've seen, with the PMRC / RIAA alliance outlined earlier, showed that industry and government can collude with each other in ways that attempt to make independent music-making an unaffordable enterprise. Regulatory and censoring bodies such as these still have plenty of tricks up their sleeve: the spread of self-released music making to computer technology has accelerated its rate of diffusion, but has also given these bodies that many more "choke points" to stop its growth when it becomes too troublesome to their interests. So, at this point, it's tempting to drop the belabored baseball analogy entirely, yet the world of professional sports provides one more comparison to be made. Pro sports teams, despite their superior spectacle-generating power, often become far too costly too maintain once players' salary demands strain the team "salary cap," and also when the upkeep of facilities (stadia, training grounds etc.) become too expensive if a sudden downturn in team fortunes negatively influences the audience's attendance habits. The world of "pro music" is also prone to a collapse after over-extending itself in the name of short-term gains. As Fredric Dannen describes it:

> By the late 70s, the majors found they needed more market share. This was only natural. Once you have set up sales branches, warehouses, and shipping depots across the map, you need tremendous volume to keep them running at capacity. A huge 'pipeline' must be filled all the time or else it does not pay for itself.[396]

The reliance of the music business upon this complex organizational model was, as Dannen tacitly implies here, a weak point that cannot be highlighted boldly enough. Preserving this physical infrastructure required generating an unnatural level of demand for the major labels' product, a demand that seemed to have a definite ceiling on it even as the world population continued to expand. "Unofficial" music was never, and still is not, under any obligation to build this complex supply chain: since the advent of recorded sounds being exchanged via direct correspondence, few physical sites have been required that fulfilled an extra-musical function. The chore of maintaining and staffing these myriad facilities is a surprisingly untold chapter in the story of the "record industry crisis," which is so often attributed to file-sharing networks alone. Meanwhile, the simplification of distribution has rehabilitated the focus on music and sound itself, for all those who choose to take that route.

Future makers of self-released audio should brace themselves for the inevitable: you will, once being realized as "amateurs," get written off by

---

[396] Fredric Dannen, *Hit Men: Power Brokers And Fast Money Inside The Music Business*, p. 112. Random House, New York, 1990.

significant portions of society in the same way that Jacques Barzun noted earlier (e.g. being denounced as "bunglers and triflers".) These critics will not appreciate the personal risks you take in trying to further and refine your chosen form of expression (ironically, these critics will mostly be "amateurs" themselves, in the sense that they will not be receiving compensation for their attacks- but this is besides the point.) It's worth remembering that these critics are a subset of a population that has grown up with a dominant communications medium - television - that itself never passed through an "amateur" phase, or came into being with any protracted debate over, say, the role advertising should play in programming, or what type of content should be available. And, yes, for many of these critics, an open medium like the Internet will still be seen as a mere assistant in consumption or as a surrogate television: protests that we are living in a hitherto unprecedented age of "open media" will be lost on them. All in all, the sharp division between "official" and "unofficial" modes of creative production will remain, and though the former will be able to disguise itself as the latter, it will not be able to totally appropriate all things "unofficial." To do so, it would have to scrap its entire business model and emulate a culture that often works without any type of business model whatsoever. Speaking the language of "authenticity" and hiring design teams to crank out a faultless approximation of DIY graphics is one thing, embracing a culture of gift-giving, one-to-one communication, and collaborative, non-"goal oriented" games is quite another thing altogether.

It is my belief that unofficial audio will continue to mutate and survive in the face of all the challenges presented to it by economic forces, by authoritarian governments, and by the vicissitudes of public opinion. Consequently, it is also my belief that if it "dies," it will have done so by successive acts of self-destruction: while this practice has proven that it can survive the aforementioned external challenges, it will not be able to survive a lack of further interest from its own creators and promoters. We have seen that, so far, that this crucial resiliency has not been lacking in this culture: it has tolerated and even encouraged an astounding number of different attitudes, from quirky explorations of paraphilia to deep philosophical reflection. The occasional clashes between artistic or anti-artistic motives have been mostly allowed, because their agonistic character has been seen as a necessity for making individual artworks more durable, and for making the "network" itself a more compelling work of living art.

    This networked artwork can only remain relevant, though, if its contributors continue to value practice above results. To achieve this, the idea that sound storage media can confer meaning by themselves has to be done away with. Sartre once said of humans that "their existence precedes their essence," and this book has cautioned against believing that sonic objects, be they self-released or released "officially," can invert this formula. The transposition of networked and self-released audio practices onto immaterial formats has only intensified the fetishization of older storage media, and the tendency to employ the format itself as a "statement" has taken some tragicomic turns: the extreme / underground groups who force fans to go on "treasure hunts" for their deliberately limited releases, the gigantic discographies built around already exhausted concepts, and the attempts at forming a speculator market around false "lost relics". Too many repeated attempts to tease exoticism out of these objects will just lead to another purely object-oriented industry, not much different in character from what we have now. The objects of the self-released audio world are the bonding cement for myriad forms of social interaction and reaction: ironically, by treating them as useful intermediaries rather than as idols, we confer upon them their greatest power.

END

Index

M

Maciunas, Georges, 88

Maggi, Ruggero, 189

Mago, Il, 199

Mangelos, 281, 372-373

Manifesto Of Surrealism, 271

Manson, Charles, 134, 151, 292

Marclay, Christian, 118

Margolis, Al, 12, 89, 222-225, 305

Marinetti, Filippo Tommaso, 46, 63, 162

Marroquin, Raul, 64, 69

Marsalis, Branford, 289

Marshall, Philip, 356-359, 363-364, 371-372

Martin, Paul, 327

Marx, Karl, 79

Massumi, Brian, 105, 128, 131, 348-349

Matkovic, Slavko, 52

Matsumoto, Toshio, 332

Matsushita, 251-252

Mauthausen Orchestra, 310

Mayakovsky, Vladimir, 135, 327, 354

Mayfield, Curtis, 282

Mayhem (band), 312, 318

MCA, 94

MCA Records, 91

McGee, Hal, 76, 97-98, 101, 153-154, 169, 171, 230, 352-353, 362

McKay, Windsor, 201

McLuhan, Marshall, 76, 313

Mediala, 47

Meelkop, Roel, 219

Megaupload, 124

Melodiya, 169

Menche, Daniel, 290, 302

Merzbow, 194, 219-220, 229, 238-239, 249, 329-334

Metal Hurlant, 201

Metallic KO, 134

Metallica, 118

Meyer, Peter R., 36, 195, 237

Micić, Ljubomir, 46

Microbit Records, 121-123

Miles, Barry, 175

Milli Vanilli, 249

Milligan, Spike, 70

Milstein, Phil, 266-267

Mimica, Svetlana, 48

Minarelli, Enzo, 70, 74

Mind Invaders, The, 190, 199, 283

Mingering Mike, 13, 282-283

MiniDisc (album), 249

Minoy, 195

Miro, Joan, 70

Mishima, Yukio, 298, 343

Mistafide, 286

Mobro 4000, 81

Moebius, Dieter, 160

Moevot, 310

Monroe, Alexei, 362-365, 369-371

Montgomery, 'Gen' Ken, 28, 40, 83, 86, 160, 171, 179, 233

Moog, Robert, 73

Moore, Barbara, 231

Moore, Bob, 337

Moore, Linda, 337

Moore, R. Stevie, 86, 231, 249, 335-340, 346

Moore, Thurston, 233

Morita, Akio, 78, 245, 250-252

Morozov, Evgeny, 180-183, 185

Morphogenesis, 99

Morrison, Reg, 235-236

ABOUT THE AUTHOR

Working with a number of different communications media, Thomas Bey William Bailey's body of work interrogates notions of utopia, anthropocentrism, and "the extreme," while refusing to reject any unpopular cultural manifestation as invalid until its parameters have been fully mapped out and its more nuanced aspects brought to light. His writings have been published in numerous languages and in newsstand magazines (*The Wire, HiS Voice, A2 Cultural Weekly, Plot*) as well as the weblogs and online presences of arts and culture institutions (*Rhizome.org, Vague Terrain, Perfect Sound Forever.*) His first book *Micro Bionic* was released in 2009 on Creation Books (defunct.) He has released numerous audio recordings under his name, and his lived and worked in Japan, Central Europe, Spain, and the United States. He is currently at work on a new title dealing with the cultural history of synesthesia. See **www.tbwb.net** for regular updates.

Printed in Great Britain
by Amazon